LINCOLN'S SWORD

LINCOLN'S SWORD

The Presidency and the Power of Words

Douglas L. Wilson

Alfred A. Knopf   New York   2007

THIS IS A BORZOI BOOK
PUBLISHED BY ALFRED A. KNOPF

www.aaknopf.com

Illustrations and documents appear courtesy of the following:
Abraham Lincoln Presidential Library and Museum, Springfield,
Illinois; John Hay Library, Brown University, Providence, Rhode
Island; Library of Congress, Washington, D.C.; New York
State Library, Albany, New York; Special Collections Research
Center, Morris Library, Southern Illinois University, Carbondale,
Illinois; Wadsworth Atheneum Museum of Art, Gift of
Miss Elizabeth Dixon, Hartford, Connecticut.

Library of Congress Cataloging-in-Publication Data
Wilson, Douglas L.
Lincoln's sword: the presidency and the power of words /
Douglas L. Wilson.—1st ed.
p. cm.
Includes bibliographical references and index.
ISBN 1-4000-4039-6
1. Lincoln, Abraham, 1809–1865—Literary art.
2. Presidents—United States—Biography. 3. English
language—19th century—Style. I. Title.
E457.2.W74 2006
973.7092—dc22 2006045259
[B]

Manufactured in the United States of America
Published November 17, 2006
Second Printing, January 2007

To Sharon

Contents

LINCOLN'S SWORD

Prologue

I N   T H E   F O U R   Y E A R S that Abraham Lincoln would be president, the American public would gradually discover, much to its collective astonishment, that this unprepossessing Illinois politician had remarkable abilities as a writer. In that brief period, and in the midst of a relentless siege of crises and distractions, he would produce not one or two examples of provocative writing (which would itself be more than most presidents could manage) but a whole series of unmistakably impressive documents. Even though confined to such unpromising formats as ceremonial speeches, messages to Congress, proclamations, and public letters in newspapers, Lincoln's presidential writing proved to be timely, engaging, consistently lucid, compelling in argument, and most important of all, invested with memorable and even inspiring language. Eventually it began to be recognized that Lincoln's unsuspected literary talent was having a decisive effect in shaping public attitudes and was a telling factor in the success of his policies. Only with his death, however, did it begin to dawn on his contemporaries that Abraham Lincoln's words were destined to find a permanent place in the American imagination.

All of this came to the American public, and particularly to members of the American intelligentsia, as a revelation. His nomination for the presidency over more familiar and established candidates had been a disappointment to the literati, to say the least. The verdict of Charles Francis Adams, son and grandson of presidents and a leading Republican, was typical: "Good natured, kindly, honest, but frivolous and uncertain." The last thing the intellectual establishment looked for from this folksy, self-educated prairie politician was literary ability.

"Perhaps no point in the career of Abraham Lincoln has excited more surprise or comment," wrote John G. Nicolay, "than his remarkable power of literary expression." As Lincoln's private secretary and later biographer, Nicolay had witnessed the unfolding of this surprising phenomenon at first hand, a phenomenon that continued to mystify the learned long after Lincoln's death. "It is a constant puzzle to many men of letters how a person growing up without the advantage of schools and books could have acquired the art which enabled him to write the Gettysburg address and the second inaugural." They could accept that such a man might be an exceptional storyteller or stump speaker, but writing—especially writing of a high order—was some-how different. For Nicolay, this was not so much a mystery as a fact. "The remarkable thing," he wrote, "was that while nature and oppor-tunity gave him talent and great success at story-telling and extempo-raneous talking, he learned to write—learned to appreciate the value of the pen as an instrument to formulate and record his thought, and the more clearly, forcibly, and elegantly to express it."

Nicolay's verdict, or something like it, would eventually be ac-cepted by the American public, and even by the world at large. Lincoln has thus become one of the most admired of all American writers. "Alone among American presidents," Edmund Wilson has written, "it is possible to imagine Lincoln, grown up in a different milieu, becom-ing a distinguished writer of a not merely political kind." If one were to judge the importance of a writer by the familiarity of his words and the depth of meaning and feeling they evoke, few if any American writers would compare with him. But for all this implicit recognition of his lit-erary abilities, Lincoln's standing as a great national hero—war presi-dent, savior of the Union, emancipator, man of the people—is such that he is still not widely or well understood as a writer.

His background in writing, for example, began in his childhood and was far more extensive than is usually recognized. For much of his adult life, contributions to newspapers were habitual, encompassing a considerable body of lively political writing, much of which, having been printed anonymously or pseudonymously, will probably never be recovered. Famous in the 1850s for his speeches and his ability on the platform, as in his debates with Stephen A. Douglas, Lincoln was always carefully prepared, with many of his arguments and positions written out and polished in advance. He lives in legend as a trial lawyer who was successful before juries, but his skills as an appeals lawyer, whose arguments were submitted in writing to a panel of judges, though less recognized, may have been more impressive. His surviving personal papers attest that he was, from the time he began to preserve them in the 1840s, a careful and conscientious draftsman, who knew the value of revision. And yet, well as we think we know the essential character of this most written about of all Americans, his habits and practice as a lifelong writer have scarcely been explored.

Writing is admittedly a solitary activity. While artists have made it possible to summon up a picture of Lincoln reading by firelight, swinging an axe, or speaking from a platform, depictions of him working at his writing desk are rare. An exception is provided by the president's son Robert Todd Lincoln, who late in life sent a correspondent this word picture of his father at work.

> He was a very deliberate writer, anything but rapid. I cannot remember any peculiarity about his posture; he wrote sitting at a table and, as I remember, in an ordinary posture. As to dictation, I never saw him dictate to anyone, and it certainly was not his practice to do so. He seemed to think nothing of the labor of writing personally and was accustomed to make many scraps of notes and memoranda. In writing a careful letter, he first wrote it himself, then corrected it, and then rewrote the corrected version himself.

Though not a familiar pose, this is nonetheless a revealing picture. Perhaps most striking is Robert's identification of a distinctive characteristic that is very little recognized—that even though a slow and "very deliberate" writer, Lincoln was not in the least put off by what most people consider the onerous labor of writing. For anyone interested in Abraham Lincoln's presidential writing, this is an important point to keep in mind.

Lincoln's presidency, as is well-known, was extraordinarily crisis-ridden and hectic. In spite of his surface calm and good-natured demeanor, his performance in office was totally engaged. While never well organized or systematic, he was in fact an energetic, hands-on, detail-oriented administrator. If any president's performance in office deserved the overused epithet "indefatigable," it was his. His willingness to make time for ordinary members of the public and hear personal requests is well-known. He kept extremely close tabs on military developments, spending a substantial amount of time in the telegraph office of the War Department. Though the demands of the patronage system drove him almost to distraction, he insisted on involving himself personally in the contentious process of sorting out the competing claims of hundreds of applicants for government posts.

One has only to peruse his personal papers (most of which are on view on the Library of Congress Web site) to get some idea of the amazing number of details that received his personal attention. The testimony of those who saw him regularly is replete with confirming evidence of Lincoln's exertions. As is often pointed out, the physical toll that these efforts exacted is visible in the photographs taken over the course of his four years in office. He kept longer hours and in almost every way outworked his subordinates, which prompted an old friend and frequent visitor, Joshua Speed, to inquire about it. "I remember asking him on one occasion, when he slept—his answer was—'just when every body else is tired out.'"

In the midst of all this exertion, Lincoln found an astonishing amount of time to write. In fact, no small part of that overall effort was given over to writing. Published items from his hand as president in the *Collected Works* run into the thousands, and recent searches in the National Archives indicate that there are many more that have gone unrecorded. As these discoveries show, Lincoln not only sent a constant stream of small notes and endorsements to various government offices and officials, but he sometimes drafted complicated documents that were issued over the signature of subordinates. He wrote frequently to his generals, as a way of keeping in touch and of offering advice. It is indicative that his reaction to his first taste of military defeat (the disastrous first battle of Bull Run) was to take up his pen, staying up all night to set down on paper what needed to be done to redeem the situation. In short, he responded to almost every important development during his presidency, and to many that were not so important, with some act of writing. Except for ceremonial proclamations, he seems to have delegated relatively little official writing and rarely dictated the documents that went out over his signature. By almost any means of gauging his presidential activity, it becomes apparent that writing—both the activity and its products—was indispensible to Lincoln's way of performing his office.

But writing, especially the drafting of a consequential text, usually requires time, quiet, and an absence of interruptions, the very things that Lincoln most often lacked. How did he manage this? Another recollection of Joshua Speed's helps to explain how so much writing was possible. "He had a wonderful faculty in that way," Speed recalled. "He might be writing an important document, be interrupted in the midst of a sentence, turn his attention to other matters entirely foreign to the subject on which he was engaged, and take up his pen and begin where he left off without reading the previous part of the sentence." But the record also reveals that Lincoln frequently sought sanctuary—in the telegraph room, at the Soldiers' Home, and even behind the usually open doors of his own office—to immerse himself in his writing. Indeed, there is more than a little to suggest that writing was often a form of refuge for Lincoln, a place of intellectual retreat from the chaos and confusion of office where he could sort through conflicting options and order his thoughts with words.

IN A MASTERLY ESSAY, "The Words of Lincoln," the late Don E. Fehrenbacher suggested that in addition to their meanings "within a definite historical context, some of Lincoln's words have acquired *transcendent* meaning as contributions to the permanent literary treasure of the nation." Fehrenbacher is here pointing to the fact that Americans have for a long time turned to Lincoln's words not only for inspiration but to understand their own history. To ask the question "What are American values and ideals?" is inevitably to invite an appeal to some of Lincoln's most illustrious words. But those words, as Fehrenbacher reminds us, came out of concrete historical circumstances, having been devised in response to specific situations.

As president, Lincoln was not a national hero. For most of his presidency, he was beset by critics on all sides. He found himself operating in a perpetual cross fire from congressmen, governors, generals, office seekers, ordinary citizens—all dissatisfied, and many sincerely convinced that he was incompetent and leading the nation down the path of destruction. His writings were an important part of his effort to respond to this pressure. His achievement is all the more remarkable when we consider that many of the presidential writings for which Lincoln is best known—the Emancipation Proclamation, the Gettysburg Address, the Second Inaugural—were formulations of ideas and positions that were not immediately popular. That they eventually came to be widely admired and even venerated is a tribute to Lincoln's rare combination of leadership and literary ability.

"When we put ourselves back into the period," Edmund Wilson

wrote in *Patriotic Gore*, "we realize that it was not at all inevitable to think of it as Lincoln thought, and we come to see that Lincoln's conception of the course and meaning of the Civil War was indeed an interpretation that he partly took over from others but that he partly made others accept, and in the teeth of a good deal of resistance on the part of the North itself." Wilson was no worshiper of Lincoln, but he knew forceful and effective writing when he saw it. He was satisfied that Lincoln had succeeded in molding American opinion and that this "was a matter of style and imagination as well as of moral authority, of cogent argument and obstinate will." One of the aims of this book is to shed light on the way, and the extent to which, Lincoln's writing contributed to the process that Wilson described.

To approach Lincoln's presidency from the aspect of his writing is to come to grips with the degree to which his pen, to alter the proverb, became his sword, arguably his most powerful presidential weapon. This is a book about some of the products of that pen. It was first prompted by a three-year encounter with the Lincoln manuscripts in the Library of Congress, as part of a project to transcribe and annotate Lincoln's personal papers for posting on the Library's Web site. As anyone with Web access can readily discover, the documents in Lincoln's hand in this collection are numerous and diverse. But while enormously interesting in their own right, most are not the kind of Lincoln document with which the public is familiar. Many are letters, but not the finished copies that were sent to recipients. Rather, these are the handwritten drafts that Robert described his father as typically producing, showing the changes and revisions made in the process of composition. In most cases, Lincoln later copied the finished text with his own hand, sending the fair copies to the recipients and retaining the drafts for his files. For some of his most important speeches and messages, the Library of Congress collection has multiple versions, showing the successive stages of revision that the document went through. Lincoln's papers, some of which are in other collections, tell us a great deal about his way of working, about his skill as a writer, and about the role that writing played in his presidency. In the pages that follow, the focus is often on these manuscripts.

A few caveats are in order. The first is that the treatment of notable writings presented here is not intended as an exhaustive survey, but rather is highly selective. Another has to do with the scope of treatment. For any given presidential document, especially an important one, there are a great many aspects worthy of attention, such as its historical context, its content, its rhetorical strategy, its style, its intended and its actual effect. Whole books could be and have been written to address all these aspects of a single important Lincoln document. While all of these things are touched on to a greater or lesser extent in the discussions that follow, they are usually subordinated to the principal enterprise of exploring the circumstances associated with the creation of certain documents and illuminating, wherever possible, the role such writing played in Lincoln's presidency.

To explore Lincoln's presidential writing is to create, in effect, a window on his presidency and a key to his accomplishments. One of the dramas that this perspective brings into focus has already been referred to, the gradual realization by the public that its unprepossessing president was actually an accomplished writer. A parallel drama had to do with how the power of Lincoln's words gradually began to assert itself during the course of his presidency and how he sought to take more and more advantage of it. While blessed with considerable self-confidence, Lincoln did not think of himself as a great writer. His secretaries declared emphatically, "Nothing would have more amazed him while he lived than to hear himself called a man of letters." Nonetheless, as a result of favorable reactions to things he had written, Lincoln eventually came to realize how effective he could be before the public in a literary medium. And as his writing became an increasingly useful means to achieve his presidential ends, it seems certain that he began to see how it might play a larger role. By the time he came to write the Gettysburg Address, for example, he was attempting to help put the horrific carnage of the Civil War in a positive light, and at the same time to do it in a way that would have constructive implications for the future. By the time he came to write the Second Inaugural Address fifteen months later, he was quite consciously in the business of interpreting the war and its deeper meaning, not just for his contemporaries but for what he elsewhere called the "vast future" as well. From that time forward, Lincoln's most memorable writings have been at the heart of whatever positive interpretation Americans have been able to put on the Civil War. In fact, it is by now hard to imagine how we could engage the question of what that terrible war was about without Lincoln's words.

CHAPTER ONE

Springfield Farewell

ON THE DAY BEFORE his fifty-second birthday, February 11, 1861, President-elect Abraham Lincoln boarded a train in Springfield, Illinois, and set off for Washington. Before leaving his hometown, he had said a series of good-byes. Ten days earlier he had paid an emotional visit to his aged stepmother and visited the grave of his father. He had hosted a public reception, personally greeting the hundreds of well-wishers who streamed into and out of his house at Eighth and Jackson. The day before, he had made a final, nostalgic visit to his law office and his law partner of sixteen years, William H. Herndon. Inside the Great Western Railway station, just prior to his train's departure, he gravely shook hands with the loyal contingent of close friends who had braved an early morning hour and drizzling rain to see him off. Ordinarily a man of remarkable self-control, Lincoln was unable to disguise his feelings. As he shook hands with his friends, according to a reporter on the scene, "his face was pale and quivered with emotion so deep as to render him almost unable to utter a single word."

Lincoln's rare display of emotion must have been evident to the larger crowd of well-wishers waiting outside the station. They had gathered in the street, between the station and the "stub," or sidetrack, into which the special train was backed for boarding, and Lincoln and his party had to pass through them to reach the train. "As Mr. Lincoln mounted the platform of the car," observed another reporter, many in the crowd seemed "deeply affected, and he himself scarcely able to check the emotions of the hour." The night before, he had told the reporters traveling with him that he would make no remarks at the station, but once inside the car, he changed his mind. He returned to the platform at the rear of the car and removed his hat. The crowd grew silent, and the men in the crowd responded by removing theirs. An old friend who was present, James C. Conkling, wrote the next day to his son: "It was quite affecting. Many eyes were filled to overflowing as Mr. Lincoln uttered those few and simple words which you will see in the papers. His own breast heaved with emotion and he could scarcely command his feelings sufficiently to commence."

Different versions of Lincoln's "few and simple words" were reported in newspapers, but in 1887, his former secretaries, John G. Nicolay and John Hay, published an authoritative text of the speech, which they transcribed from a manuscript in Lincoln's own hand (see Fig. 1-1):

> My friends—No one, not in my situation, can appreciate my feeling of sadness at this parting. To this place, and the kindness of these people, I owe every thing. Here I have lived a quarter of a century, and have passed from a young to an old man. Here my children have been born, and one is buried. I now leave, not knowing when, or whether ever, I may return, with a task before me greater than that which rested upon Washington. Without the assistance of that Divine Being, who ever attended him, I cannot succeed. With that assistance I cannot fail. Trusting in Him, who can go with me, and remain with you and be every where for good, let us confidently hope that all will yet be well. To His care commending you, as I hope in your prayers you will commend me, I bid you an affectionate farewell

This handwritten text confirmed the judgment of the original Springfield audience that his farewell had been a very poignant and affecting speech. As many commentators have pointed out, these nine sentences admirably display Lincoln's talent for conciseness, for weaving together appropriate words and rhythms, and for saying ordinary things in an extraordinary and memorable way. This text is duly reported in all modern biographies and has been inscribed in stone at the Illinois State Capitol. But these words are not the ones he uttered at the railway station in 1861.

❧

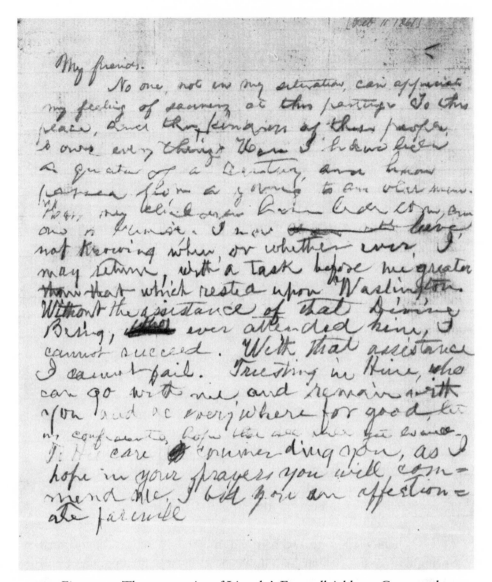

Figure 1-1. The manuscript of Lincoln's Farewell Address. Composed on the train, it is in the handwriting of both Lincoln and his secretary, John G. Nicolay. Library of Congress.

WHAT LINCOLN ACTUALLY SAID on that occasion is difficult to determine with any degree of precision, for the contemporary accounts vary. What is clear from abundant testimony, and from the evidence of the manuscript itself, is that he wrote out this text not before the speech, but afterward, on the train. That his manuscript text is not an exact replication of the words he had spoken on the platform can be shown by a close comparison of the various accounts, but it is also evident from the many eyewitness reports of the dramatic climax of the occasion. The *New York Herald* reporter Henry Villard, who had been in Springfield covering the president-elect closely for six weeks, wrote in his report: "Towards the conclusion of his remarks himself and audience were moved to tears. His exhortation to pray elicited choked exclamations of 'We will do it; we will do it.' " The dispatch that was most widely printed and whose text is probably the closest to what Lincoln said also noted the visible emotion in the audience and recorded a similar response: "Loud applause and cries of 'We will pray for you.' " This spontaneous emotional exchange between Lincoln and the crowd seems to have escaped the notice of most of his biographers, but it is, in fact, clearly evident in all the on-the-scene accounts.

According to Lincoln's hometown paper, this touching moment was marked by his appealing to the crowd "with the earnestness of a sudden inspiration of feeling." The report that would seem to be the nearest approximation of Lincoln's spoken words renders the passage this way:

> He [Washington] never would have succeeded except for the aid of Divine Providence, upon which he at all times relied. I feel that I cannot succeed without the same Divine aid which sustained him, and on the same Almighty Being I place my reliance for support, and I hope you, my friends, will all pray that I may receive that Divine assistance . . .

It was doubtless at this point that the crowd, responding to his emotional plea, began to erupt with cries of "We will pray for you" or "We will do it," even before the conclusion of the sentence:

> . . . without which I cannot succeed, but with which success is certain.

In his manuscript text, this earnest appeal for the prayers of his audience is present but deliberately muted and unobtrusively folded into the final sentence: "To His care commending you, as I hope in your prayers you will commend me, I bid you an affectionate farewell." This raises an obvious question: why did Lincoln, in writing out a revised version of his speech, play down its most electrifying moment so that it virtually disappeared from view? One possibility is that he had second thoughts about how it would look to have his first public utterance as president-elect be a plea for prayers. Indeed, J. G. Holland recalled in his 1866 biography that there had been just such public comment at the time. But why Lincoln effectively suppressed what had been the most affecting part of his speech when he came to write it out is surely best understood not in terms of message but of medium.

Lincoln knew from long experience that addressing a live audience is very different from addressing readers on the page. A speaker before an audience has special tools at his command—body language, gestures, facial expressions, volume and tone of voice, pace, and so on. Because he has direct contact with his audience, a speaker can gauge its mood and receptiveness and can take immediate advantage of its reactions. The writer must rely on other devices, and a seasoned practitioner of both forms of expression like Lincoln could be expected to adapt his text accordingly. In speaking to the crowd at the train station, for example, he could sense the emotion of the audience rising to meet his own and spontaneously put in an appeal for their prayers. But in an address for the consumption of silent and invisible readers, who were not in the grips of an emotional leave-taking, the situation would be very different. The appeal therefore had to take a different form.

What is of interest here is that Lincoln's manuscript text is not a reiteration of his speech, but a revision. Asked by Villard to write out his remarks after the speech, Lincoln knew instinctively that what he had said extemporaneously would have to be reshaped and reconstituted to work as well for readers as it had for those present at the send-off. And because he was a seasoned practitioner in the art of revision, this was a clear opportunity to improve upon what he had said. Looking at some of the differences between the spoken and the written versions affords an opportunity to see the results of this process. Take, for example, the sentence from the spoken version "To this people I owe all that I am." In its revised form, this became "To this place, and the kindness of these people, I owe everything." One of the most discerning admirers of Lincoln's writing, the historian Jacques Barzun, has called attention to this sentence in making the case that the key to "Lincoln's extraordinary power" as a writer was his ability "to make his spirit felt." Lincoln's writing, Barzun argues, tends to reflect a complicated sense of himself in relation to his audience. In his typical self-deprecating way, he often managed to create an "emotional distance" between himself and his audience that he used to advantage in his speeches and writings. Nowhere is this clearer, according to Barzun, than in the second sentence of the Farewell Address. "If we stop to think, we ask: 'This place'?—yes. But why '*these* people'? Why not 'you people,' whom he was addressing from the train platform, or 'this place and the kindness of *its* people'? . . . 'These' is a stroke of genius," Barzun says, because it has "Lincoln talking to himself about the place and the people whom he was leaving, foreboding the possibility of his never returning." The linchpin of Barzun's observation—the word "these"—was not, of course, in the reports of the spoken address but appears only in Lincoln's written revision.

Another good example is the passage considered earlier, which the likeliest report of the speech as actually spoken renders like this:

I feel that I cannot succeed without the same Divine aid which sustained him, and on the same Almighty Being I place my reliance for support, and I hope you, my friends, will all pray that I may receive that Divine assistance without which I cannot succeed, but with which success is certain.

With the plea for prayer removed, this becomes in revision

Without the assistance of that Divine Being, who ever attended him, I cannot succeed. With that assistance I cannot fail.

Here Lincoln has seized the necessity for recasting his plea for the prayers of his audience to refine and bring out the latent rhetorical antithesis in the passage. In fact, as we shall see, a special talent for antithesis, the balanced opposition of words or phrases, would stamp nearly all of Lincoln's greatest writings as president.

Another example of how Lincoln improved his text in revising his speech for general readers, as opposed to local listeners, is a subtle change to the treatment of his life in Springfield. The report that seems closest to what he actually said on the platform has one notable omission, an element that appears in all other accounts. This is the reference to growing from a young to an old man. For purposes of comparing the spoken with the written versions, this element has been inserted in brackets.

Here I have lived more than a quarter of a century [and have passed from a young to an old man]; here my children were born, and here one of them lies buried.

This is an effective passage whose appeal depends on a parallelism of clauses and the cadenced repetition of the word "here." But in the revision, the modification, though not great, results in a significantly different feel.

Here I have been a quarter of a century, and have passed from a young to an old man. Here my children have been born, and one is buried.

There are a number of changes in this passage that are worthy of comment, but here it will suffice to point out but one, the change from "Here I have *lived*" to "Here I have *been*." Because Lincoln's train-shaken handwriting was so difficult to decipher (see Fig. 1-2), his secretaries failed to note this change, which does not seem to have been detected until recently.

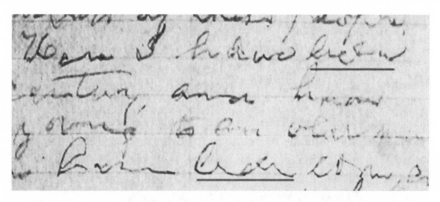

Figure 1-2. A magnified portion of the manuscript of Lincoln's Farewell Address showing two occurences of the word "been," which have been underlined here for identification. Library of Congress.

Nonetheless, it is confirmed by the text printed the next day in the *New York Herald,* which Villard says came from a copy Lincoln gave him. The speaker on the platform who spoke the word "lived" almost certainly did not know that he would shortly use the words "born" and "buried," much less that, taken together, they would poignantly sum up a full range of life experiences. But the writer on the train did know it. The word he substituted, "been," clearly anticipates the words "born" and "buried" and forms an alliterative bond with them, but it also gives a different sense of the speaker. It conveys a certain rooted-ness and has a subtle resonance of its own.

The comparison with George Washington, the most revered figure in American history, as a way of calling attention to the difficulty he faced, was bold to the point of presumption. In the largest chamber of the Illinois State Capitol, which was regularly used for public events and where Lincoln had frequently appeared, the speaker stood directly under a large, looming portrait of the first president, an image that was probably summoned to mind by his Springfield listeners at the railway station. In calling attention to his mission of somehow preserving what Washington had established, Lincoln managed to conjure up, without having to name them, a cluster of deep-rooted patriotic meanings, such as loyalty, service, dedication, and sacrifice.

As originally uttered, the comparison with Washington was effectively introduced:

> I know not how soon I shall see you again. A duty devolves upon me which is, perhaps, greater than that which has devolved upon any other man since the days of Washington.

Spoken by a fellow townsman taking his leave, the first sentence must have been quite affecting, but given the slightly stilted and self-conscious character of its expression, its appeal on the page to strangers would likely be much less. Better to begin on a stronger note and meld the messages of the two sentences (thirty-three words) into one (twenty-four).

> I now leave, not knowing when, or whether ever, I may return, with a task before me greater than that which rested upon Washington.

Less, with Lincoln, was often more, as in this case, but as serious writers know only too well, this is much easier said than done. The revised lead-in to the comparison of himself with Washington is a good demonstration that Lincoln knew how it was done.

❧

ESPECIALLY SEEN IN THE light of its revision, the text that became known as Lincoln's Farewell Address is an impressive literary performance. The speech as delivered had been a great success, but it owed as much to the inherent dynamics of the occasion—the somberness of Lincoln's demeanor, the emotional timbre of his voice, the mood of the crowd, the gloomy weather, the enveloping national anxiety about the fate of the Union—as it did to the choice and ordering of the spoken words. What should be emphasized here is that the most accurate text of his impromptu remarks could never produce on readers the emotional effect that was felt by the listeners at the station. It is a measure of Lincoln's ability as a writer that he was able to take the same thoughts and reweave them into a more artful literary fabric, creating a new ending and a new context for a much subdued appeal for prayers. In short, Lincoln refashioned his spontaneous live performance, preserving its appeal by giving it a different but more durable form. It goes without saying that this remarkable feat was possible only because the writer, who was about to assume the office of president, possessed a rare facility with the spoken and written word that amounted to a formidable literary talent. This talent we now tend to take for granted, but on February 11, 1861, as Lincoln began his journey to Washington, it was almost entirely unknown.

CHAPTER TWO

A Long Foreground

NOT EVEN EMERSON SAW him coming.

When Abraham Lincoln was elected president, the leading man of letters in America, Ralph Waldo Emerson, was something of a literary prophet. A poet and essayist whose philosophical writings attracted the most discriminating readers, Emerson enjoyed an immense popularity on the lecture circuit that made him a household name. But it was largely his dissatisfaction with much of American writing that made him a prophet. The American experience, he held, was Adamic, a new beginning, and as such it required a new language and new literary forms to give it expression. American writing, he believed, should honestly reflect the vitality and uniqueness of its culture, rather than merely imitate British and European models. "As long as our people quote English standards they dwarf their own proportions."

Emerson was thus open to new ideas and new possibilities, and as such was receptive to the notion of remarkable things coming from an unexpected quarter. A famous instance of this occurred in 1855 when he received an unsolicited book of truly original poetry in the mail. Refusing to be put off by its unconventional versification, its lack of recognizable poetic form, or even by its scandalous subject matter, he had impulsively written the unknown author: "I greet you at the beginning of a great career." The unknown poet, of course, was Walt Whitman, and the book, which would eventually help to revolutionize American literature, was *Leaves of Grass*.

Emerson's lecture tour in 1853 had taken him to Springfield, Illinois, where Abraham Lincoln had gone to hear him. Eight years later, in 1861, Lincoln began, as president, to perform for Emerson, but the literary prophet would be slow to respond. Like most of his anxious countrymen, Emerson was too engrossed in the drama of a disintegrating Union and the sudden eruption of civil war to take note of the special qualities of the president's writing. Not until the time of Lincoln's death would Emerson, in a moving eulogy, make good his prophetic role and predict (accurately) that "the weight and penetration of many passages in his letters, messages, and speeches, hidden now by the very closeness of their application to the moment, are destined hereafter to wide fame." But initially, there had been no shock of recognition. In the case of Whitman, Emerson had sensed immediately that his racy and eccentric book was a literary bombshell. And since Whitman had appeared out of nowhere, the prophet's first reaction was that his career as a writer "must yet have had a long foreground somewhere for such a start." He was right, of course, and the same consideration applied in Lincoln's case, for his surprising and unsuspected skills did not proceed from a vacuum, but rather had emerged through a long process of development.

ONE OF LINCOLN'S first biographers, John L. Scripps, complained that Lincoln had been reluctant to discuss with him the details of his early life, but the campaign biographer did manage to elicit a few facts about the candidate's early years not already on record. Lincoln had told, in his own autobiographical sketches, of attending school as a small boy in Kentucky, but in his personal interview with Scripps he apparently added a detail that the biographer seized upon as significant. "In his seventh year," Scripps wrote, "Abraham was sent for short periods to two of these [Kentucky] schools, and while attending them progressed so far as to learn to write. For this acquirement he manifested a great fondness." Scripps might have left it there, but he underscored his point with a vivid image of the six- or seven-year-old future president. "It was his custom to form letters, to write words and sentences wherever he found suitable material. He scrawled them with charcoal, he scored them in the dust, in the sand, in the snow—anywhere and everywhere that lines could be drawn, there he improved his capacity for writing."

Scripps was a key editor for the leading Republican newspaper in Illinois, the *Chicago Press and Tribune*, and he was intimately familiar with Lincoln's prose, having helped to put an ample portion of it into print. In addition to his description of Lincoln's boyhood habit of scrawling words "anywhere and everywhere," Scripps took note of the young Lincoln's role, after moving from Kentucky to Indiana at age seven, as the family and neighborhood secretary. Like the boy's own mother and father, many of their Indiana neighbors could not write and thus needed help in corresponding with the friends and family they left behind. "In this emergency Abraham's skill was put into requisition," Scripps wrote, presumably repeating something told him by his subject. What he added, however, may have been speculation based on his familiarity with Lincoln's verbal gifts, namely, that the boy was chosen not just because he could write and was obliging, but for "his ability to express the wishes and feelings of those for whom he wrote in clear and forcible language."

Scripps's attention to Lincoln's early fondness and propensity for writing would be less provocative were it not for the abundance of related testimony that was later offered by people who had known him during his boyhood years in Indiana. Interviewing many of these after Lincoln's death in 1865, his law partner and biographer, William H. Herndon, was told a good deal about his subject's youthful literary inclinations and habits, beginning with the testimony of Sarah Bush Lincoln, the stepmother who became a member of the family when the boy was ten years old. She described the young Lincoln as a serious student who, contrary to the opinions of some, was not lazy: "he didn't like physical labor—was diligent for Knowledge—wished to Know & if pains & Labor would get it he was sure to get it." In this industrious pursuit of knowledge, according to Mrs. Lincoln, writing played an important part. "Abe read all the books he could lay his hands on—and when he came across a passage that Struck him he would write it down on boards if he had no paper & keep it there till he did get paper—then he would re-write it—look at it repeat it—He had a copy book—a kind of scrap book in which he put down all things and this preserved them."

The young man depicted in the testimony of his stepmother and of other Indiana informants was conspicuously verbal, a precocious boy obsessed with words. She described the way he struggled with the meanings of words and references he didn't understand, questioning and brooding over them until he found a solution. Achieving clarity, it seemed, was a large part of his obsession. "Sometimes he seemed pestered to give Expression to his ideas and got mad almost at one who couldn't Explain plainly what he wanted to convey." Sarah Lincoln was an elderly woman when interviewed by Herndon, and she was recalling things that happened roughly forty years earlier, but her memories of these matters are uncannily confirmed in Lincoln's own recollections, as reported by the Reverend John P. Gulliver. In an accidental meeting on a train in 1860, Gulliver had told Lincoln that he regarded "the clarity of your statements" as the most remarkable aspect of the speech he had heard Lincoln deliver, and Lincoln responded with a description of his childhood passion to understand unfamiliar words and ideas, and his particular need for clarity. He told Gulliver that "among my earliest recollections I remember how, when a mere child, I used to get irritated when any body talked to me in a way I could not understand." When he had at last come to a clear understanding of the matter at hand, he related, he was not satisfied "until I had put it in language plain enough, as I thought, for any boy I knew to comprehend." Lincoln's passionate concern to find the right words with which to frame his own thoughts and those of others marked him, even in boyhood, as a writer.

His early interest in writing is well attested by those who knew him in southwestern Indiana, where he lived from age seven to twenty-one. Herndon discovered in his interviews that Lincoln was still well remembered there for some verses he had written called "The Chronicles of Reuben," a satiric send-up of a pretentious wedding reception that people in the neighborhood never forgot. There is more than a suggestion that this mock-biblical account was written in retaliation for some real or imagined slight. That a young man would use literary means to punish his adversaries impressed Lincoln's neighbors and earned him a measure of local distinction. "This called the attention of the People to Abe intellectually," Joseph C. Richardson remembered. "It showed the boy" was the way another neighbor, William Wood, expressed it, and Wood further remembered that Lincoln had shown him two essays that he had composed, one on the superiority of the American form of government and the other on temperance. According to Wood, the teenager's temperance essay so impressed a local minister that he arranged to have it published in a temperance newspaper in Ohio. If Wood remembered this correctly, it would have been the first of Lincoln's writings to see print.

❧

Abraham Lincoln's earliest literary interest was poetry. His Indiana neighbors remembered well his talents as a comic versifier, and the surviving pages of a notebook he kept in his teens contain samples of a sort.

> Abraham Lincoln
> his hand and pen
> he will be good but
> god knows When
>
> Abraham Lincoln is my nam[e]
> And with my pen I wrote the same
> I wrote it in both hast[e] and speed
> and left it here for fools to read

The remembered samples of his more original verses at this time are too dubious to afford more than a sense of their subjects, but the budding poet's success as a satirist, at least as judged by his mainly illiterate neighbors, was roundly acknowledged.

After he left Indiana, Lincoln probably continued writing verses, but he seems to have kept them largely to himself. His New Salem friend William Greene claims to have been shown some products of the poet's pen in the 1830s, but little other evidence of such poetic activity has come to light. By 1845, Lincoln was a well-established Springfield lawyer and a politician about to be elected to Congress. A young man named Gibson Harris, who began a two-year stint clerking in the Lincoln-Herndon law office that year, reported finding in the office a cache of manuscripts in Lincoln's handwriting. Harris later remembered that "on turning the leaves I saw they were covered with stanzaed effusions in Mr. Lincoln's neat running-hand, all evidently original. As I remember, they were all, or nearly all, iambics and pensive in tone." Lincoln declined to discuss them, but Herndon told Harris, "Yes, he has sometimes scribbled verses, I believe, but he seems unwilling to have it known."

So far as can be determined, this form of writing remained a kind of underground activity, and Lincoln never published an original poem under his own name. Only recently has it come to light that a Byronic poem of his about suicide had been published anonymously in the *Sangamo Journal* in 1838, which may be an indication that others had preceded and followed it. In April 1846, Lincoln confessed to a fellow lawyer and literary friend in Quincy, Illinois, that he had written some verses inspired by a visit to his former neighborhood in Indiana. "The piece of poetry of my own which I alluded to, I was led to write under the following circumstances. In the fall of 1844, thinking I might aid some to carry the State of Indiana for Mr. Clay, I went into the neighborhood in that State in which I was raised, where my mother and only sister were buried, and from which I had been absent about fifteen years. That part of the country is, within itself, as unpoetical as any spot of the earth; but still, seeing it and its objects and inhabitants aroused feelings in me which were certainly poetry; though whether my expression of those feelings is poetry is quite another question." Eventually, Lincoln sent his Quincy friend, Andrew Johnston, three of these Indiana poems, or "cantos," which he represented as three parts of a projected poem in four cantos. The first canto begins:

> My childhood's home I see again,
>   And sadden with the view;
> And still, as memory crowds my brain,
>   There's pleasure in it too.
>
> O Memory! thou midway world
>   'Twixt earth and paradise,
> Where things decayed and loved ones lost
>   In dreamy shadows rise,
>
> And, freed from all that's earthly vile,
>   Seem hallowed, pure, and bright,
> Like scenes in some enchanted isle
>   All bathed in liquid light.

While the versification is somewhat mechanical and the diction has long since lost its appeal, the ideas are rather interesting and complex—the simultaneous but inseparable mixture of sadness and pleasure that the scene evokes, for example, and the complicated characterization of memory and its appealing distortions.

Except for the recently discovered fugitive poem on suicide, the

Indiana poems are the only specimens of Lincoln's serious efforts at poetry to survive. They are by no means great works of art, but neither are they mere doggerel, as some of his critics have claimed. In the judgment of Roy P. Basler, "it is safe to say that Lincoln's poems are superior to the average run of verse published in America before 1850, and that the first and best of them reveals a quality which wears better than Lincoln's biographers have supposed."

That Lincoln seems to have abandoned his efforts to write serious poetry at about this time may have been a fortunate development, for becoming a poet seems to have been an early aspiration for many writers who went on to produce great writing in prose. Certainly Lincoln's strong sense of cadence and sophisticated ear for rhythmic patterns, so evident in his early speeches and so prominent an element in the greatest works of his maturity, suggest why he was drawn to verse and why, as an ambitious young man, he may have aspired to master it. But with poetry, the allure is common, while the gift itself is rare. The great American novelist William Faulkner more than once suggested that, in his own case and that of many others, distinction as a writer of prose owed something to being a "failed poet."

IT WAS POLITICS, NOT poetry, that would eventually engage Lincoln's deepest intellectual interests and resources, and it would be distinguished political writing for which he would eventually become known. When he made his debut in Illinois politics a few years after leaving Indiana, Lincoln's first impulse was to put himself before the public in writing. In March 1832, at the age of twenty-three, he published a letter in the local newspaper announcing his candidacy for a seat in the state legislature. Somewhat stiff and formal in its manner, certainly not the work of a self-assured writer, the letter was nonetheless an obvious product of much care and deliberation, and one for which he seems to have solicited help from friends in New Salem, the village in which he settled after leaving home in 1831: "FELLOW-CITIZENS: Having become a candidate for the honorable office of one of your representatives in the next General Assembly of this state, in accordance with an established custom, and the principles of true republicanism, it becomes my duty to make known to you—the people whom I propose to represent—my sentiments with regard to local affairs." Unsuccessful in his first attempt, Lincoln ran for office two years later, in 1834, without a written campaign statement, and won. When he declared himself for reelection in 1836, he did so with a jaunty letter to the editor, in which the earnest and self-conscious manner of his earlier letter had been transformed: "In your paper of last Saturday, I see a communication over the signature of 'Many Voters,' in which the candidates who are announced in the Journal, are called upon to 'show their hands.' Agreed. Here's Mine!"

The New Salem years, a period much celebrated in the Lincoln legend, were a time of intensive reading and study for Lincoln, with his literary output being confined largely to anonymous and pseudonymous political writing for partisan newspapers. Its luster is much deserved, for this was a clear case of a poor and poorly educated boy taking himself in hand and mastering hard subjects, like English grammar and mathematics, to say nothing of reading his way through Blackstone's formidable treatise *Commentaries on the Laws of England*. The schoolbooks he is supposed to have studied so assiduously, such as *Scott's Lessons* and *Kirkham's Grammar*, had much to say about speaking and writing effectively. "Grammar," said the latter, "instructs us how to express our thoughts correctly; Rhetorick teaches us to express them with force and elegance." Lincoln applied himself to both.

But the legend knows little or nothing of Lincoln's partisan newspaper writing, which meant active participation in an inelegant war of words, a war in which invective and vituperation were the norms, and civility took a backseat. Until very recently, no specimen of Lincoln's pseudonymous newspaper writing was known prior to 1838, but an example from an obscure Beardstown newspaper dating from 1834 has been recovered that can be traced directly to him. Another letter to the editor, it is an attack on a political enemy, the Reverend Peter Cartwright, the most famous circuit rider in frontier Illinois, and it was published over the signature of Lincoln's employer, New Salem storekeeper Samuel Hill, who was carrying on a personal feud with Cartwright.

By an ingenious reading of Cartwright's own letter and close scrutiny of his language, Lincoln purports to trip up the hypocritical "Uncle Peter," and then proceeds to roast him for his preacherly sins. But this is mere pretext; the true object of the letter, as every reader was aware, was to discredit a political adversary. This is not, of course, the work of the forbearing man who, as president, cultivated his adversaries, appointed his opponents to responsible positions, and refused to engage in or take offense at personal abuse. The Beardstown letter reflects the attitudes and behavior of a much earlier and rougher version of that man, but it is illustrative of how he got ahead as a frontier politician and gained the admiration of his peers—by making use of his abilities as a writer.

❧

ONCE HE HAD ESTABLISHED himself as a politician a few years later, Lincoln stepped out onto the public stage in his own persona and began authoring and delivering a series of carefully written public speeches, each of which he arranged to have published in the Springfield newspaper to which he was contributing, the *Sangamo Journal*. "The Perpetuation of Our Political Institutions" was the title of a memorable speech given before the Young Men's Lyceum in Springfield in January 1838, incorporating some of the themes that were said to have characterized the Indiana essay described by William Wood. The Lyceum speech was his first public lecture and seems to have been designed in part to show that he was capable of the florid style of oratory then in vogue. A passage on the nation's founders, for example, reaches for the tried and true rhetorical effects of the day:

> Their's was the task (and nobly they performed it) to possess themselves, and through themselves, us, of this goodly land; and to uprear upon its hills and its valleys, a political edifice of liberty and equal rights; 'tis ours only, to transmit these, the former, unprofaned by the foot of an invader; the latter, undecayed by the lapse of time, and untorn by usurpation—to the latest generation that fate shall permit the world to know.

The language and mannerisms were conventional, for it was important that the gawky country boy demonstrate that he was capable of performing in the approved manner. But as this ambitious young lawyer and politician gradually began to acquire stature, the conventional language and mannerisms would begin to fade and eventually cease to characterize his public utterances. It comes as no surprise, for example, to learn that most of the self-conscious *u*-words in the sentence just quoted—"uprear," "unprofaned," "undecayed," "untorn"—do not reappear in Lincoln's published writings. Even the twenty-five-cent word "usurpation" would disappear after 1848.

Nearly two years after the Lyceum address, a partisan political speech (for which, atypically, a complete text exists) takes a very different oratorical tack. Tightly focused, methodical, and closely reasoned, his 1839 speech in a public forum on the Federal Sub-Treasury (then a timely political topic) was considered so effective that, in addition to being published in the *Sangamo Journal*, it was later printed for distribution as a campaign document in the hard-fought campaign of 1840. The speech largely avoids flights of rhetoric and confines itself to a strictly rational appeal in unadorned language.

> By the Sub-Treasury, the revenue is to be collected, and kept in iron boxes until the government wants it for disbursement; thus robbing the people of the use of it, while the government does not itself need it, and while the money is performing no nobler office than that of rusting in iron boxes. The natural effect of this change of policy, every one will see, is to *reduce* the quantity of money in circulation.

Those familiar with the celebrated writings of Lincoln's presidential years may be forgiven for not recognizing the mannered style of the Lyceum address, but in the Sub-Treasury speech one begins to hear, in the tone and choice of language, a harbinger of the distinctive voice of the writer to come. The Lyceum and Sub-Treasury addresses have long been recognized by students of Lincoln as valuable early indicators of the future president's basic ideas and political inclinations. The Lyceum speech, for all its conventionality, displays a deep commitment to the rule of law and a reverence for the example of the founders of the American government, ideas that would inform Lincoln's political outlook throughout his career. The Sub-Treasury speech exhibits a remarkable ability to vivify a dry-as-dust political issue and make it the subject of an engaging and logical argument. Two years later, in February 1842, Lincoln delivered and had published a third public speech that shows evidence of careful literary construction, the Temperance address. Like the Lyceum and Sub-Treasury speeches, this one affords glimpses of more than Lincoln's evolving literary ability and technique. Here, for example, he expounds a theory of persuasion that has implications for his future political efforts: "It is an old and true maxim, that a 'drop of honey catches more flies than a gallon of gall.' So with men. If you would win a man to your cause, *first* convince him that you are his sincere friend. Therein is a drop of honey that catches his heart, which, say what he will, is the great high road to his reason."

The Temperance address reflects ideas and concerns that are traceable to Lincoln's Indiana boyhood and his first serious attempts at writing, but its specific arguments are directed toward issues then current. Lincoln was speaking before the Washingtonians, a group of reformed drunkards that was gaining public visibility by reason of its conspicuous success in helping fellow sufferers, and he took the occasion to contrast the humane and supportive approach of the Washingtonians with the traditional scourging of drunkards by the clergy as sinful and wicked men. Thus, his theory of persuasion. But rhetoric, as he well knew, is itself a matter of finding literary means of being persuasive, and the evidence is clear that the author of the Temperance address took great pains in fashioning his remarks. Consider the care with which the cadence and the rhythmic patterns have been molded in this passage on the manufacture and merchandizing of liquor:

> The making of it was regarded as an honorable livelihood; and he who could make most, was the most enterprising and respectable. Large and small manufactories of it were every where erected, in which all the earthly goods of their owners were invested. Wagons drew it from town to town—boats bore it from clime to clime, and the winds wafted it from nation to nation; and merchants bought and sold it, by wholesale and by retail, with precisely the same feelings, on the part of the seller, buyer, and bystander, as are felt at the selling and buying of flour, beef, bacon, or any other of the real necessaries of life. Universal public opinion not only tolerated, but recognized and adopted its use.

Many of the rhetorical effects for which Lincoln's writings would be famous in his presidential years are in evidence here in an incipient and less polished form.

In a letter to Joshua Speed, who had just moved back to Kentucky, Lincoln called attention to the appearance of his Temperance address in the *Sangamo Journal* and directed "that Fanny [Speed's bride] and you shall read [it] as an act of charity to me; for I can not learn that any body else has read it, or is likely to. Fortunately, it is not very long and I shall deem it a sufficient compliance with my request, if one of you listens while the other reads it."

This plea by the underappreciated author reminds us that while the Temperance address was indeed written, and by a self-conscious craftsman, it was written to be heard. With the writings of Abraham Lincoln, sound always matters. He had learned to read in "blab" schools, where the students recited their lessons aloud (and usually at the same time), and he continued into maturity to do most of his reading aloud, much to the annoyance of his law partner. Lincoln explained to a long-suffering Herndon that it enabled him to "catch the idea by 2 senses," by hearing and sight. It also served to give him a feel for the sounds and combinations of sounds that tend to gratify listeners and favorably dispose them toward the author's or speaker's ideas. This kind of aural awareness helps to explain how Lincoln was able eventually to become a master of language and to excel at what Robert V. Bruce has called "the shaping of words to ideas, of sounds to sense."

One feature of conventional antebellum oratory that could not be dispensed with was the peroration—the rousing conclusion that was an expected and necessary part of any self-respecting public speech. The three early speeches of Lincoln mentioned here all contain perorations that significantly raise the emotional pitch and try valiantly for a slam-bang finish. The Sub-Treasury speech, being a strictly partisan political effort, rolls to a rollicking conclusion on the theme of loyalty, wherein the avowed loyalty of the speaker to his country is somehow indistinguishable from his loyalty to the Whig Party, and while an electoral triumph by the incumbent Democrats is pictured as a national calamity.

> I know that the great volcano at Washington, aroused and directed by the evil spirit that reigns there, is belching forth the lava of political corruption, in a current broad and deep, which is sweeping with frightful velocity over the whole length and breadth of the land, bidding fair to leave unscathed no green spot or living thing, while on its bosom are riding like demons on the waves of Hell, the imps of that evil spirit, and fiendishly taunting all those who dare resist its destroying course, with the hopelessness of their effort; and knowing this, I cannot deny that all may be swept away.

This peroration's rhetorical excesses have been duly noted by commentators, but Roy P. Basler wisely balanced his evaluation with a practical consideration: "The fact that his audience loved such rhetoric perhaps made the performance expedient, for certainly the speech as a whole, though a tight bit of reasoning, could hardly have been inspirational and needed some political fireworks as a tailpiece."

The perorations of the Lyceum speech and the Temperance address, though four years apart, are in some way remarkably similar. In spite of their elevated and often overheated language, both make pointed appeals to Reason—"all conquering mind," in the language of the latter—as the ultimate means of resolving human conflict and preserving free institutions. And both invoke, as a means of ending on the highest possible note and appealing to the greatest possible number, the name that was undisputedly first in the hearts of his countrymen, George Washington. In the Lyceum speech, the first president is unexpectedly summoned up at literally the last minute, somewhat in the manner of a surprise witness. But in the Temperance address, which was delivered on Washington's birthday before a society named for him, the concluding note was more predictable: "In solemn awe pronounce the name, and in its naked deathless splendor, leave it shining on."

⁓

SPEED, WHO ROOMED WITH Lincoln from 1837 to 1841, was perhaps the closest friend Lincoln would ever have. Many years later, at the prompting of Herndon, Speed related something of Lincoln's interests as a writer during the period of these early speeches:

> So far as I now remember of his study for composition it was to make short sentences & a compact style—Illustrative of this— he was a great admirer of the style of John C Calhoun—I remember reading to him one of Mr Calhouns speeches in reply to Mr Clay in the Senate—in which Mr. Clay had quoted precedent—(I quote from memory.) Mr. Calhoun replied "that to legislate upon precedent is but to make the error of yesterday the law of today" Lincoln thought that was a great truth greatly uttered

"Short sentences" and a "compact style" must, of course, be understood in a comparative sense, meaning "shorter" and "more compact" than was typical in the notoriously verbose and effusive oratory of that day. Students of Calhoun's speeches might be surprised to hear his style characterized along these lines, but the passage that Speed says Lincoln admired holds clues to what may have attracted him. Calhoun had said:

> But it is attempted to vindicate the conduct of the Secretary on the ground of precedent. I will not stop to notice whether the cases cited are in point; nor will I avail myself of the great and striking advantage that I might have on the question of precedent: this case stands alone and distinct from all others. There is none similar to it in magnitude and importance. I waive all that; I place myself on higher grounds—I stand on the immovable principle that, on a question of law and Constitution, in a deliberative assembly, there is no room—no place for precedents. To admit them would be to make the *violation of to-day the law and Constitution of to-morrow; and to substitute in the place of the written and sacred will of the people and the legislature, the infraction of those charged with the execution of the laws.*

When this was read to him by Speed, what Lincoln heard was, in fact, a succession of seven relatively short sentences (end-stopped independent clauses), averaging eleven words each, and forming a continuous path leading up to the main argument. We can be sure that the strategy employed in this sequence of conceding point after point appealed to the young listener, for his colleagues at the bar would later affirm that this was a technique that he himself cultivated and eventually perfected. "I waive all that" is thus strategic prelude.

The felicitous nineteenth-century sound bite about the "violation of to-day" becoming "the law and Constitution of to-morrow" is, of course, a choice example of antithesis. It attracts our attention by linking opposites—in this case "violation" and "law"—and its function is to make the orator's point elegantly memorable. Speed's anecdote, told thirty years after the fact, is compelling testimony that it works. This recollection should also alert us to the fact that his roommate, who would become a master of antithesis, was already an ardent student of style, with an ear not only for eloquence but for the means by which it was created.

❧

A BACKCOUNTRY HOOSIER BY his dress and manners, with the indelible stamp of rural dialect in his pronunciation and diction, the Lincoln of these years was nonetheless recognized as a "rising man" by his more educated and socially polished contemporaries, who knew something of his abilities as a writer. They knew, for example, that in the ongoing political battles that were fought weekly in the fiercely partisan local newspapers, Abraham Lincoln was one of the stalwarts of the Whig position, verbally lambasting the opposition and making light of their arguments. We can be sure that Lincoln's pen was often employed in this form of combat during these years, but because they appeared either anonymously or under political pseudonyms, relatively few pieces can be identified with certainty as his. One of the few that can, a letter to the editor from an imaginary farmwife, written by Lincoln in 1842, shows a marked talent for comic dialogue and a well-developed sense of how to ridicule an opponent in print.

Working with a well-established model—a letter from the boondocks that innocently exposes the skullduggery of politicians—Lincoln provides deft touches of dialogue and situation. His object is to bring out the political perfidy of the Democratic state officers, but the fictional farmwife, named Rebecca, is shrewdly given a role other than accuser or critic. Rather, she is made to depict her angry neighbor, Jeff, and to teasingly draw out his reactions to a proclamation that makes the state banknotes he has been saving worthless for paying his taxes.

"There now," says he, "did you ever see such a piece of impudence and imposition as that?" I saw Jeff was in a good tune for saying some ill-natured things, and so I tho't I would just argue a little on the contrary side, and make him rant a spell if I could.

"Why," says I, looking as dignified and thoughtful as I could, "it seems pretty tough to be sure, to have to raise silver where there's none to be raised; but then you see *'there will be danger of loss'* if it aint done."

"Loss, damnation!" says he, "I defy Daniel Webster, I defy King Solomon, I defy the world,—I defy—I defy—yes, I defy even you, aunt Becca, to show how the people can lose any thing by paying their taxes in State paper." "Well," says I, "you see what the *officers of State* say about it, and they are a desarnin set of men." . . .

"Damn officers of State," says he, "that's what you whigs are always hurraing for." "Now don't swear so Jeff," says I, "you know I belong to the meetin, and swearin hurts my feelins." "Beg pardon, aunt Becca," says he, "but I do say its enough to make Dr. Goddard swear, to have tax to pay in silver, for nothing only that [Governor] Ford may get his two thousand a year, and [State Auditor] Shields his twenty four hundred a year, and [State Treasurer] Carpenter his sixteen hundred a year, and all without 'danger of loss' by taking it in State paper." "Yes, yes, it's plain enough now what these *officers of State* mean by 'danger of loss.' Wash [an embezzler], I 'spose, actually lost fifteen hundred dollars out of the three thousand that two of these 'officers of State' let him steal from the Treasury, by being compelled to take it in State paper. Wonder if we don't have a proclamation before long, commanding us to make up this loss to Wash in silver."

A measure of the effectiveness of Lincoln's satire is that it nearly got him killed. The main object of his wit, State Auditor James Shields, was so offended by the personal character of the letter's insults that he demanded the name of the writer and promptly challenged Lincoln to a duel. Only the intervention of respected leaders from both parties, together with a frank admission by Lincoln that he had written "wholly for political effect" and "had no intention of injuring [Shields's] personal or private character or standing as a man or a gentleman," enabled the writer to avoid the lethal consequences of his literary effort.

Lincoln was deeply mortified by his entanglement in this unfortunate episode and was averse to any reference to it in later life. To be dragged into a duel, which was illegal in Illinois, was bad enough, but an important aspect of his embarrassment was surely the public exposure of this unflattering, if disastrously effective, use of his literary talents.

❧

THE YOUNG ABRAHAM LINCOLN probably wrote hundreds of newspaper articles, most of them narrowly political and intensely partisan, but we know of at least one nonpolitical piece that he offered (anonymously) as artful exposition. His subject was a strange sequence of events involving the mysterious disappearance of a visitor to Springfield named Fisher. Fisher's hosts in Springfield had been three brothers named Trailor, and when one of them accused the other two of murdering Fisher and disposing of his body in nearby Spring Creek, the effect on the town was electric. For several days in June 1841 the citizens of Springfield were in a state of intense excitement over this case, assisting en masse in a widespread search of the area that included tearing down a mill dam. But at a hearing convened to investigate the matter, in which Lincoln appeared as a defense attorney for one of the accused Trailors, a physician from the distant county where Fisher lived arrived to testify that the missing man had not been murdered at all but was very much alive, having recently returned home in a dazed condition, unsure of where he had been or what had happened to him. The Trailors were discharged and the mystery never explained.

Lincoln's essay, in an obvious attempt to render the details in a strictly objective manner, steers clear of anything that might be taken as interpretation. Unfortunately, this has the effect of inhibiting the use of evocative language and depriving the narrative of its inherent color and human interest. What makes his failure so obvious is that Lincoln wrote a vivid account of the same incident, as it was unfolding, in a letter to his friend Speed. In his essay, which was printed in the *Quincy Whig* in 1846, Lincoln described the effect on the aroused citizenry of the unexpected news that Fisher was alive in a single sentence: "At this the multitude for a time, were utterly confounded." But in his letter to Speed five years earlier, Lincoln had brilliantly dramatized this point and given it a sharp satiric edge:

> When the doctor's story was first made public, it was amusing to scan and contemplate the countenances, and hear the remarks of those who had been actively engaged in the search for the dead body. Some looked quizical, some melancholly, and some furiously angry. Porter, who had been very active, swore he always knew the man was not dead, and that *he* had not stirred an inch to hunt for him; Langford, who had taken the lead in cutting down Hickoxes mill dam, and wanted to hang Hickox for objecting, looked most awfully wo-begone; . . . and Hart, the little drayman that hauled Molly home once, said it was too *damned* bad, have so much trouble, and no hanging after all.

Because we have his lively letter to Speed, we can be sure that the lackluster quality of his essay in the *Quincy Whig* is not due to a lack of ability. It seems rather a consequence of his conception of the style of writing that was appropriate for a serious literary undertaking of this sort. His fascination with the Trailor case in the *Quincy Whig* essay was firmly centered on the nature of its intellectual challenge, its apparent defiance of rational solution. In this respect, it bears a recognizable resemblance to something one might have read at the time in Edgar Allan Poe, Lincoln's exact contemporary and, according to one report, his favorite American writer. In fact, Poe's typically wordy and stilted mode of expression may be in part responsible for similar qualities in Lincoln's essay: "In the latter part of May in the year mentioned, William formed the purpose of visiting his brothers at Clary's Grove, and Springfield; and Fisher, at the time having his temporary residence at his house, resolved to accompany him."

While Lincoln's letter to Speed shows that he had been keenly aware of the situation's potential for satire and the comic exposure of human foibles, his reason for writing the Quincy essay was clearly something else. The essay was published at about the same time that Lincoln was trying to complete his sequence of Indiana poems, and its anonymous publication in the *Quincy Whig* was undoubtedly arranged by the same literary friend, Andrew Johnston, who later arranged the publication of the poems in the same place. Lincoln's sharing both the essay and the poems with Johnston, and Johnston's efforts in having them published, are evidence perhaps of a cautious literary debut, in which the author was offering his wares in the hope of praise and approval, but was protected by the shield of anonymity in the case of failure or indifference. Especially in the wake of his exposure as the author of the slanderous "Rebecca" letter four years earlier, Lincoln was probably concerned to gain, if he could, some measure of recognition for legitimate literary merit in the established forms of poetry and the essay. But in this he was to be disappointed, for his literary efforts seem to have attracted no attention whatever, and his energies were soon almost completely absorbed by partisan politics and his service as a member of Congress.

⤙

"Upon his return from Congress," Lincoln wrote of himself in a third-person autobiographical sketch, "he went to the practice of the law with greater earnestness than ever before." He had been, up to this time, strictly a party politician, whose speeches were mostly attacks on Democratic policies and politicians and followed a party line. "Always a whig in politics, and generally on the whig electoral tickets, making active canvasses," he admitted in an autobiographical statement, "I was losing interest in politics, when the repeal of the Missouri Compromise aroused me again." Indignation at the repeal of the Missouri Compromise, part of the legislation associated with the Kansas-Nebraska Act, was not a strictly partisan response. Because of its implications for the spread of slavery into the territories, it alarmed large numbers of politically oriented citizens, Whigs and Democrats alike, so that when Lincoln began speaking on this issue in 1854, at least two things were different. The first was his own motivation, which was no longer solely partisan, but reflected deeper human concerns. The evil of slavery was not dying out but was being actively expanded. The second was that the tremendous response he got from his audience, because it was so emotional and so broadly based, far exceeded anything he had experienced on the political platform before. The repeal of the Missouri Compromise may have aroused him, but it was a rousing speech he gave in Peoria on October 16, the culminating presentation of a heated campaign, that propelled him into the forefront of a momentous political movement.

The speech at Peoria was the keystone of Lincoln's political career. A carefully detailed attack on the Kansas-Nebraska Act, it was three hours long and was brilliantly delivered without notes. It is unlikely that it was completely written out until after its delivery, for William H. Herndon told one of Lincoln's first biographers: "Mr Lincoln was here [in Springfield] writing out his Speech some week or more after the Peoria debate. This I know, because I assisted him to gather facts."

The Peoria speech was probably the longest Lincoln ever gave, nearly seventeen thousand words when written out. The first of seven daily installments appeared in the local newspaper just five days later. He had given versions of the speech previously, and while much of it was undoubtedly plotted out in advance and memorized, the implication of Herndon's remark is that Lincoln still had research to do after the speech had been given and that he struggled under the pressure of his newspaper deadlines to get it into its final written form. Its spoken delivery had been a stunning performance. Horace White, a journalist who heard the speech, described it many years later: "Sometimes his manner was very impassioned, and he seemed transfigured with his subject. . . . I have heard celebrated orators who could start thunders of applause without changing any man's opinion. Mr. Lincoln's elo-quence . . . produced conviction in others because of the conviction of the speaker himself. His listeners felt that he believed every word he said, and that, like Martin Luther, he would go to the stake rather than abate one jot or tittle of it."

As with his Farewell Address, Lincoln was well aware that what generated authenticity on the platform at Peoria and what produced conviction on the page were not the same thing. While we have no notes or drafts from which to judge, many passages bear the marks of careful revision and the process of transforming spoken discourse into readable prose. Consider this paragraph on the moral neutrality of the Kansas-Nebraska Act, which would reduce slavery in the territories to a local option:

> This *declared* indifference, but as I must think, covert *real* zeal for the spread of slavery, I can not but hate. I hate it because of the monstrous injustice of slavery itself. I hate it because it deprives our republican example of its just influence in the world—enables the enemies of free institutions, with plausibil-ity, to taunt us as hypocrites—causes the real friends of freedom to doubt our sincerity, and especially because it forces so many really good men amongst ourselves into an open war with the very fundamental principles of civil liberty—criticising the Dec-laration of Independence, and insisting that there is no right principle of action but *self-interest.*

Six reasons to fault the act's supposedly neutral stand on slavery are here tightly woven into a compact paragraph of only three sentences. The hard word "hate" is used three times, but with a notable lack of vindictiveness. The hate is directed not toward Democrats or slave-holders but ultimately toward the inhumanity of the law and its shame-ful effect on the nation's reputation, and on people—not wicked people, but good people. Treating slavery as merely a property issue, as the Kansas-Nebraska Act did, was hateful because of its corrupt-ing effects on the republic. In 1837, Lincoln and a colleague in the Illinois state legislature had gone on record as believing that "the insti-tution of slavery is founded on both injustice and bad policy." Here in the Peoria speech, the wrongness of the law and its effects is based not on personal belief or a religious code but on its incompatibility with something cherished by all—"free institutions."

If there is passion in this appeal, there is also a balancing restraint. The element of passion introduced is given a patriotic cast, and it is kept in bounds by sadness and regret. The rhythm and organization of the paragraph reflect its emotion, with Lincoln's personal animus expressed strongly in the first two sentences, and the long final sentence giving it context and focus. This ingeniously structured sentence works as a verbal power pump, with the recurring verbs forcibly injecting energy into the argument.

The artfulness of the writing is not, to be sure, the most notable thing about the Peoria speech. What is most significant is that almost inadvertently, because of his having been "aroused" by the abolition of the Missouri Compromise, a distinctly new note was introduced into Lincoln's political discourse. Only two years earlier, he had given a speech to a Whig group during the presidential campaign of 1852 that was narrowly partisan, incessantly negative, and, if not mean-spirited, certainly undignified and unedifying. A sample sentence from the conclusion reads: "Why Pierce's only chance for presidency, is to be born into it, as a cross between New York old hunkerism, and, free soilism, the latter predominating in the offspring." It must have been gratifyingly clear to Lincoln from the enthusiastic response he received wherever he spoke in 1854 that he had turned a corner, and that he at last had found his voice and a theme worthy of his ambition. As we can see in the Peoria speech, he had hold of an authentic message that appealed to his audience on something more ennobling than a partisan basis. It was rooted in concern for the meaning of free institutions and the corrosive inhumanity of slavery, which would be his theme on the hustings until he was elected president in 1860, and throughout his presidency.

❧

ABRAHAM LINCOLN LIVED AT a time when the public lecture was a major source of education and entertainment. Nonpartisan and nondenominational, its subject could be almost anything of general interest. The popularity of public lectures in antebellum America prompted citizens in very modest-sized towns and even villages to construct "opera" houses and to create local lyceum groups—the former to accommodate the crowds attracted by famous traveling lecturers, such as Emerson, and the latter to provide a venue for aspiring local speakers. As a young man, Lincoln took advantage of such opportunities for public speaking, as we have seen, but in later years, as an established lawyer and politician, he tended to confine his speeches to patriotic occasions and electoral politics.

It was perhaps inevitable that a man with Lincoln's growing reputation would eventually be drawn into the public lecture arena. In 1860, just one month before he would become the Republican candidate for the presidency of the United States, and fresh from a triumphantly successful political speech at New York City's Cooper Union Institute, Lincoln was contacted by a literary agency that hoped to represent the budding national celebrity on the lecture circuit. With remarkable candor, he replied: "I regret to say I can not make such arrangement. I am not a professional lecturer—have never got up but one lecture; and that, I think, a rather poor one." If the prospective presidential candidate was not afraid to admit that his one and only public lecture was below par, apparently most of his listeners agreed. Even his admiring partner remembered Lincoln's lecturing as "a failure—utter failure."

The problem seems to have been that Lincoln's heart really wasn't in his lecture, which he called "Discoveries and Inventions" and which, in the surviving (and incomplete) manuscript, exhibits little coherence and no consistent theme. But there is one notable idea, especially in the context of Lincoln's view of the importance of verbal expression and its role in human affairs. The key to human progress, according to Lincoln's lecture, is a strictly human invention—writing. "When writing was invented, any important observation, likely to lead to a discovery, had at least a chance of being written down, and consequently, a better chance of never being forgotten; and of being seen, and reflected upon, by a much greater number of persons. . . . By this means the observation of a single individual might lead to an important invention, years, and even centuries after he was dead." In the printed oration that may well have been Lincoln's source of inspiration, the famous historian and orator George Bancroft had singled out printing for special emphasis as "the controlling agency in renovating civilisation." We know from Lincoln's manuscript (see Fig. 2-1) that he considered making printing the equal of writing in his estimate of what was most important for human progress, for he first wrote: "*Writing*

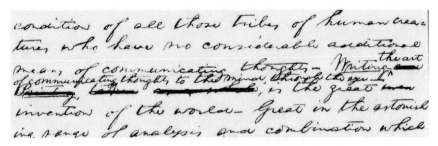

Figure 2-1. Passage from Lincoln's lecture "Discoveries and Inventions." Southern Illinois University Library.

and *Printing*, taken as a whole, is the great inven . . ." But here he stopped and reconsidered. Then the man who had discovered his special affinity for the written word at the age of seven amended the sentence to read: "*Writing*—the art of communicating thoughts to the mind, through the eye—is the great invention of the world_"

CHAPTER THREE

A Custom as Old as the Government

I N SPITE OF BEING pitted against candidates who were much better known and far more experienced in national politics, Abraham Lincoln won the presidential nomination at the 1860 Republican convention in Chicago, and then, largely because of the splintering of the Democratic Party, he prevailed in the presidential race itself over the premier politician of the day, Stephen A. Douglas. As a result, he would come to Washington to assume the presidency not so much as a known quantity but rather as something of a question mark. Even many of those who belonged to his party, or were sympathetic to its political positions, were dubious about Lincoln's ability to measure up to the task of being president in such extraordinary times. It was hardly enough to be able to dispense patronage and preside at cabinet meetings and ceremonies. The nation was in deep crisis, was in fact in imminent danger of dissolution, and had never been in greater need of a proven statesman at the helm. That a folksy politician from Illinois was capable of filling this large order was, for many informed Americans, too much to hope for. These anxieties were perfectly expressed in the blunt question posed by a skeptical newspaper editor, who asked, "Who will write this ignorant man's state papers?"

Such widely shared skepticism about Lincoln's abilities was, of course, more than a little shortsighted. This was, after all, the man who had taken on the formidable Douglas in the senatorial campaign of 1858 and held his own in an extended debate that was reported in newspapers across the country. And he had proved himself more than

just an able stump speaker when, on February 27, 1860, only a few
months before the nominating convention, he delivered an address at
New York's Cooper Union Institute in which he presented impressive
original research and compelling arguments to show that the Republican position on slavery was not, as Douglas and the Democrats had
been insisting, a departure from that of the nation's founders. The
speech had been a great success in the hall and was fulsomely praised in
the New York newspapers. Horace Greeley's *New York Tribune* led the
way, calling it "one of the happiest and most convincing political arguments ever made in this city." Even papers cool to the Republicans
acknowledged that Lincoln had delivered an effective speech to an
enthusiastic audience, and an editorial comment in William Cullen
Bryant's *New York Post* suggests that Lincoln's qualities as a writer, if
not expressly recognized or praised, were distinctly felt: "All this may
not be new, but it is most logically and convincingly stated in the
speech—and it is wonderful how much a truth gains by a certain mastery of clear and impressive statement."

If Lincoln's acknowledged mastery as a political platform speaker
served to mask his considerable ability as a writer, it was nonetheless
implicit in a letter he wrote soon after his nomination to Charles C.
Nott, one of the members of the Young Men's Central Republican
Union, which had issued him the invitation to speak. In view of the
strong reception of Lincoln's speech and its potential for shaping public opinion, Nott and his colleagues proposed to reprint the text of the
Cooper Union address in a pamphlet for use in the forthcoming campaign. Nott wrote to Lincoln on May 23, 1860, explaining the project
and enclosing an already edited text for Lincoln's approval. "Most of
the emendations are trivial & do not affect the substance," Nott
wrote, adding that "all are merely suggested for your judgment." Lincoln's reply tells much about his sensitivity to even minor details in his
text:

> So far as it is intended merely to improve in grammar, and ele-
> gance of composition, I am quite agreed; but I do not wish the
> sense changed, or modified, to a hair's breadth. And you, not
> having studied the particular points so closely as I have, can not
> be quite sure that you do not change the sense when you do
> not intend it. For instance, in a note at bottom of first page, you
> proposed to substitute "Democrats" for "Douglas." But what

> I am saying there is *true* of Douglas, and is not true of "Demo-
> crats" generally; so that the proposed substitution would be a
> very considerable blunder.

Having established his criteria and diplomatically laid the basis for
accepting or rejecting Nott's proposed changes, Lincoln briskly passed
judgment on five of them.

> Your proposed insertion of "residences" though it would do lit-
> tle or no harm, is not at all necessary to the sense I was trying to
> convey. On page 5 your proposed grammatical change would
> certainly do no harm. The *"impudently absurd"* I stick to. The
> striking out *"he"* and inserting *"we"* turns the sense exactly
> wrong. The striking out *"upon it"* leaves the sense too general
> and incomplete. The sense is "act as they acted *upon that ques-
> tion"*—not as they acted generally.

Lincoln's letter to Nott, which goes on in this vein, is valuable for
demonstrating his anything but casual attitude toward the use of
words, as well as for showing his keen sense of the perils of editorial
emendation and, as Harold Holzer has pointed out, "his attention to
the nuances of his own writing."

ONCE NOMINATED, LINCOLN RESOLUTELY refused to make any
additional speeches or offer any new explanations of his positions, rely-
ing instead on the existing public record to represent his views. But
after the election, as state after Southern state seceded, Lincoln's
continued silence contributed to the growing anxiety about how this
inexperienced and ill-connected politician would deal with so unprecedented and overwhelming an issue as the imminent dissolution of the
Union. Lincoln suffered greatly in this situation, as he confided to his
old friend Joseph Gillespie, but mostly he suffered in silence. His inaugural address was to be his answer, and he did not want to blunt the
edge of his message by premature disclosure.

Even in the absence of tangible evidence, we can safely assume that
Lincoln began taking notes for his inaugural address considerably in
advance, for his habit in such matters is well attested. Many of his closest associates describe independently the process whereby Lincoln

habitually made notes on scraps of paper of ideas that occurred to him, especially in preparation for a major speech. His son Robert, as we have seen, remembered that his father "was accustomed to make many scraps of notes and memoranda." William H. Herndon recalled the way his partner's famous "House Divided" speech was composed: "he wrote that fine effort—an argumentative one, in slips—put those slips in his hat, numbering them, and when he was done with the ideas, he gathered up the scraps—put them in the right order, and wrote out his speech."

John G. Nicolay, the personal secretary to the president-elect, was not sure when his employer had begun work on his inaugural address, but he had little doubt as to how he went about it. "While it is probable that he did not set himself seriously at this task until after the result of the November election had been ascertained beyond doubt, it is quite possible that not only had the subject been considered with great deliberation during the summer, but that sentences or propositions, and perhaps paragraphs of it had been put in writing."

If Lincoln's law partner remembered correctly, the drafting for the inaugural address was not begun in earnest until about two weeks before Lincoln's departure for Washington. "Late in January Mr. Lincoln informed me that he was ready to begin the preparation of his inaugural address," wrote Herndon, who recalled this circumstance because he was asked to provide some books from his library for the purpose. "I looked for a long list, but when he went over it I was greatly surprised. He asked me to furnish him with Henry Clay's great speech delivered in 1850; Andrew Jackson's proclamation against Nullification; and a copy of the Constitution." The late date and the short list of books both suggest that Lincoln, a careful worker and no procrastinator, was probably well along in his preparations.

Except for a single scrap pertaining to the opening sentence, none of the handwritten drafts of Lincoln's First Inaugural seem to have survived. Because he thought it important to keep his remarks secret, he took extraordinary precautions. "He locked himself up in a room upstairs over a store across the street from the State House," according to Herndon, where he could work "cut off from all communication and intrusion." Nicolay, in an unpublished essay found recently in his papers at the Library of Congress, offers more details on this secretive process. "His brother-in-law had a large store on the public square in Springfield, in the second story of which a small counting room had been partitioned off, which at the time was not in use. There he could hide himself, and the way to it easily foiled inquiring pursuit, and there the Inaugural was written and copied, and nearly every surplus fragment of manuscript destroyed."

Almost nothing is known about the first stages of composition, when Lincoln was drafting by hand. Ben: Perley Poore, a veteran Washington reporter, claimed that the president, in telling him the story of the inaugural's composition, had specified that "a number of sentences had been reconstructed several times before they were entirely satisfactory." This may have been Lincoln's way of admitting that he reworked his initial text very heavily, which is certainly true of his first sentence (see Fig. 3-4 below). When the handwritten draft was completed, it was entrusted to the publisher of the *Illinois State Journal*, William H. Bailhache, who locked himself and a loyal compositor into the newspaper office "and remained there until the document was set up, and the necessary proofs taken, and the form secure in the office safe until Mr. Lincoln could correct and revise the proofs." A pristine copy of what is presumably the first setting of type from the manuscript is preserved in Lincoln's papers, on which its proud author has written "First edition" (Fig. 3-1).

Figure 3-1. Lincoln's designation "First edition" written on a pristine copy of the first printed draft of his First Inaugural, printed at the newspaper office in Springfield. Library of Congress.

❧

THE TEXT OF THIS first printing was thus the product of an unknown number of previous drafts, and while the speech itself would be subjected to extensive changes before delivery, this "First edition" makes extremely interesting reading. From the point of view of the writing, what stands out conspicuously in this version is Lincoln's careful attention to tone. Created by a calculated choice of words, tone is what indicates the writer's *attitude*, over and above his literal meaning. Its most familiar manifestation is in spoken discourse, where tone of voice refers to the modulation of sounds that enables a speaker to say he loves something in a way that indicates he loathes it. By manipulating the tone of his work, the author can thus appear either apologetic or petulant, despairing or disparaging, haughty or humble. The tone of Lincoln's first draft of his First Inaugural is unmistakable—firm and forceful.

The basic message is aimed at the dissatisfied South and may be paraphrased as follows: I and my party have done nothing more provocative than win an election; it is your unwillingness to accept the results of a fair election that is causing the crisis. The forthcoming Republican administration is pledged to maintain things as they are and is willing to accept new laws and even constitutional amendments to address your concerns. I will keep the oath I am now taking to defend the Constitution and see that the laws are executed in all the states. It is for you to decide whether you want constitutional government or war.

Without being unduly harsh or insulting, the language is direct, its meanings clear and relatively unequivocal. There is very little that could be called conciliatory. The tone of the address as a whole, of course, accrues gradually and by stages. In the opening paragraphs the emphasis is upon reasonableness. Having been elected upon a "declared platform of principles," he is "not at liberty to shift his position." Lincoln says he is "bound by duty" to follow these principles, and "by no other course" could he meet the country's "reasonable expectations." There are apprehensions in the South, but "there has never been any reasonable cause for such apprehensions." He affirms that he is taking the oath with "no purpose to construe the Constitution or laws, by any hypercritical rules."

In introducing the subject about which all are waiting to hear—the secession of the Southern states—Lincoln is vaguely ironical but circumspect: "A disruption of the Federal Union is menaced, and, so far as can be on paper, is already effected." To this development he responds directly and in the first person:

> I hold, that in contemplation of universal law, and of the Constitution, the Union of these States is perpetual.

[It follows from this view] that no State, upon its own mere motion, can lawfully get out of the Union,—that *resolves* and *ordinances* to that effect are legally nothing; and that acts of violence, within any State or States, are insurrectionary or treasonable, according to circumstances.

Hard words have now been used, albeit with some qualification. The ordinances of secession passed by seven states of the deep South are characterized as "legally nothing," and any acts of violence that might follow would either be acts of treason or of insurrection. Lincoln then applies his own logic:

I therefore consider that the Union is unbroken; and, to the extent of my ability, I shall take care that the laws of the Union be faithfully executed in all the States.

There is no disguising the fact that this means war. Knowing this, Lincoln adds in mitigation:

I trust this will not be regarded as a menace, but only as the declared purpose of the Union that it will have its own, and defend itself.

The Union's insistence on having its own—that is, possession of the federal forts, armories, and other property that had been appropriated by the seceding states—would, as was already apparent, become the crux of the war's inception. If there were any issue about which the president-elect might wish to appear flexible or to be slightly ambiguous, what to do about these already appropriated federal properties would have been that issue. But Lincoln is uncompromising:

All the power at my disposal will be used to reclaim the public property and places which have fallen; to hold, occupy and possess these, and all other property and places belonging to the government, and to collect the duties on imports; but beyond what may be necessary for these, there will be no invasion of any State.

At this point, with the pressure having been applied fairly relentlessly, Lincoln takes a different tack. He pauses to address those "who really love the Union," and to consider the question of whether any constitutional rights have been violated and, thus, whether any solid basis for secession exists. As a matter of organization, this is an issue that might well have been raised earlier, prior to and in justification of his declared intention to defy the secessionists. What this shows is that Lincoln structured his speech so as to foreground and thus amplify his firmness and determination.

> Is it true, then, that any right, plainly written in the Constitution, has been denied? I think not. Happily the human mind is so constructed, that no party can reach to the audacity of doing this.

Paying attention to the tone of this draft helps us to see that this last sentence is not, in fact, part of the argument per se, but is rather the author's way of saying such a claim was counterfactual and unreasonable. Given the context and the earnestness with which Southerners were speaking of their "rights," this may be the nearest thing in the draft to being confrontational. Why Lincoln should risk insulting the very people he is trying to persuade is a question to be pursued in due course.

Consider not only the tough, no-nonsense tone and the logical rigor but the breathtaking economy of this four-sentence argument, which begins by stating its conclusion:

> Plainly, the central idea of secession, is the essence of anarchy. A constitutional majority is the only true sovereign of a free people. Whoever rejects it, does, of necessity, fly to anarchy or to despotism. Unanimity is impossible; the rule of a minority, as a permanent arrangement, is wholly inadmissable; so that, rejecting the majority principle, anarchy or despotism is all that is left.

There is no theoretical wiggle room here. This is uncompromising language, backed up by the earlier forceful insistence that no plainly written constitutional right had been denied. From the point of view of tone, this is perhaps the high-water mark of the "First edition," that is, at least until the conclusion.

In the balance of the address, the arguments are more measured and the points addressed less confrontational. But the spirit of defiance returns in the conclusion of this first printed version, which, with its strong pattern of emphasized words, seems to be as firm and as clear as Lincoln can make it:

> In *your* hands, my dissatisfied fellow countrymen, and not in *mine*, is the momentous issue of civil war. The government will not assail *you*, unless you *first* assail *it*. You can have no conflict, without being yourselves the aggressors. *You* have no oath registered in Heaven to destroy the government, while *I* shall have the most solemn one to "preserve, protect, and defend" it. *You* can forbear the *assault* upon it; *I* can *not* shrink from the *defense* of it With *you*, and not with *me*, is the solemn question of "Shall it be peace, or a sword?"

Firm in tone this surely is, but we should note that there is a measure of Lincolnian indirection here. A Southerner's first reaction might be that this conclusion constituted a direct challenge: He asks us whether it is to be peace or a *sword*! But such an interpretation could not be sustained by a reference back to the text. In fact, the firmness and force of Lincoln's text proves to be invested in *not* offering a challenge. "With *you*, and not with *me*" is Lincoln's way of reminding his audience that any challenge will have to come from the secessionists. This is defiance with a twist, but defiance nonetheless.

THERE WERE GOOD REASONS for Lincoln's deliberately forceful tone. After the election, he had only to read the newspapers to know that he was widely perceived as not being up to the job. The reporter sent by the *New York Herald* to cover the president-elect in Springfield, Henry Villard, wrote candidly on November 19 what many were thinking: "The present aspect of the country, I think, augurs one of the most difficult terms which any President has yet been called to weather; and I doubt Mr. Lincoln's capacity for the task of bringing light and peace out of the chaos that will surround him. A man of good heart and good intention, he is not firm. The times demand a Jackson."

This was a symbolism that everyone could understand and explains why Lincoln, once in the White House, hung a portrait of Old Hickory in his office. If the times demanded a stern taskmaster like Andrew Jackson, what they had instead, prior to Lincoln's inauguration, was

James Buchanan. Although he was an experienced politician and diplomat, Buchanan seemed completely at a loss to know what to do about the secession of the Southern states. The *London Times*'s ridicule of Buchanan's rationalizations and political paralysis was not far off the mark:

> He frequently examines the Constitution, and the more he looks at it the less he finds in it. When the secession was first threatened he made the discovery that this remarkable instrument conveyed no power either to the President or to Congress to prevent the States from appropriating to themselves those powers which had solemnly been bestowed upon the Federal Government. . . . It was very wrong, very unconstitutional, very distressing, but he could not help it, and now he finds himself equally unable to promise a suspension of hostilities. The war which he could not make he now finds that he has no power to prevent.

Lincoln's draft of his inaugural address was designed to show that he saw the presidential responsibilities in a very different light, and that once in office, he was determined to chart an entirely different course.

Still, the version of the inaugural that emerged from the first printing needed more work. It was presumably viewed by its author as too unrelenting, for in his next pass he proceeded to tone it down. He removed a slighting remark about South Carolina picking a quarrel with Kentucky, as well as a defensive section on the Republican Party's position on slavery. He also dropped three paragraphs in which he had argued that a candidate who yields to the demands of his critics before taking office "betrays those who elected him, by breaking his pledges, and surrendering to those who tried and failed to defeat him at the polls." Omitting this three-paragraph appeal to honor was not for the purpose of backing away from his position, but rather to incorporate it into a speech that he hoped to deliver to Kentuckians but that was never given.

A further change that had a somewhat conciliatory effect dealt with the issue of sending federal office holders into the South, where resistance to them might be expected to be intense (see Fig. 3-2). This passage was inserted immediately after his stated intention to "reclaim" the public property appropriated by the secessionists and shows a flash

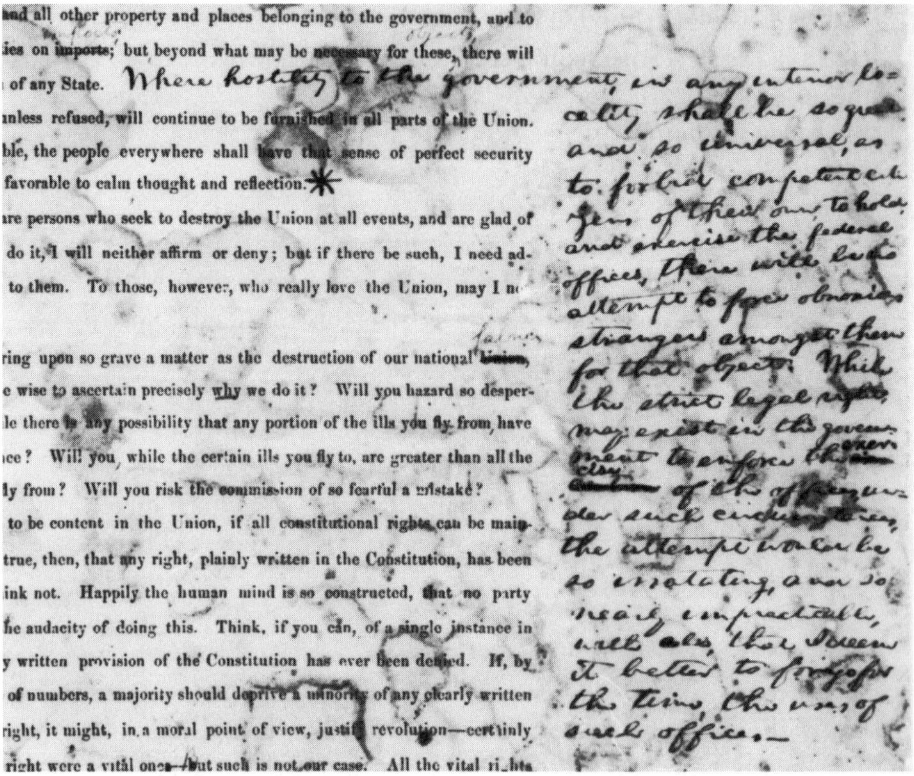
and all other property and places belonging to the government, and to
ies on imports; but beyond what may be necessary for these, there will
of any State. Where hostility to the government, in any interior lo-
unless refused, will continue to be furnished in all parts of the Union.
ble, the people everywhere shall have that sense of perfect security
favorable to calm thought and reflection.*
are persons who seek to destroy the Union at all events, and are glad of
do it, I will neither affirm or deny; but if there be such, I need ad-
to them. To those, however, who really love the Union, may I n
ring upon so grave a matter as the destruction of our national Union,
e wise to ascertain precisely why we do it? Will you hazard so desper-
le there is any possibility that any portion of the ills you fly from, have
ice? Will you, while the certain ills you fly to, are greater than all the
ly from? Will you risk the commission of so fearful a mistake?
to be content in the Union, if all constitutional rights can be main-
true, then, that any right, plainly written in the Constitution, has been
ink not. Happily the human mind is so constructed, that no party
he audacity of doing this. Think, if you can, of a single instance in
y written provision of the Constitution has ever been denied. If, by
of numbers, a majority should deprive a minority of any clearly written
right, it might, in a moral point of view, justify revolution—certainly
right were a vital one—but such is not our case. All the vital rights

cality shall be so great and so universal, as to forbid competent citizens of their own, to hold, and exercise the federal offices, there will be no attempt to force obnoxious strangers amongst them for that object. While the strict legal right, may exist in the government to enforce the exercise of the offices, under such circumstances, the attempt would be so irratating, and so nearly impracticable, with all, that I deem it better to forego for the time, the uses of such offices.—

Figure 3-2. Addition in Lincoln's hand to the first printed draft of his First Inaugural Address. Library of Congress.

of the pragmatic style that would characterize his presidential dealings in the years ahead.

> Where hostility to the government, in any interior locality shall be so great and so universal, as to forbid competent citizens of their own, to hold, and exercise the federal offices, there will be no attempt to force obnoxious strangers amongst them for that object. While the strict legal right, may exist in the government to enforce the ~~execution~~ exercise of the offices, under such circumstances, the attempt would be so irratating, and so nearly impracticable, with all, that I deem it better to forego for the time, the uses of such offices.

Making a distinction between the "strict legal right" and "irratating" and therefore "impracticable" implementation is a small but

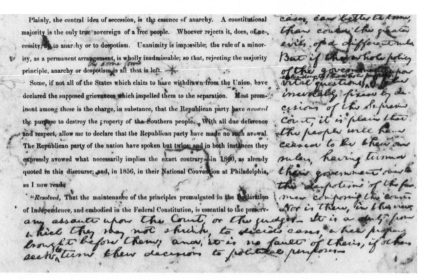

Figure 3-3. Part of a long addition on the Supreme Court that Lincoln made to the first printed draft of his First Inaugural. Library of Congress.

unmistakable signal of a willingness to compromise that looks at first glance like an olive branch, but that actually cuts both ways. It offers to placate the feelings of the seceders on what would have seemed to them the relatively trivial issue of having to put up with Republican postmasters and revenue collectors. On the other hand, it could also be seen as a reminder that, for so momentous a matter as dissolving the federal Union, the operative political issues really were trivial.

The longest addition to this "First edition" text was a section on the Supreme Court that filled both the right-hand and bottom margins of the printed page (see Fig. 3-3).

He also, in revising this printed copy, thought of a good objection to secession, which he duly inserted: "The supposed purpose, then, of one section to destroy the property of the other, has no real existence; and to break up the government for that imaginary cause, would be a most melancholy mistake." But why, then, does this insertion not appear in the so-called second printing? Nicolay's account of the composition process speaks of "a second and a third revision . . . after which an edition of about a dozen copies was printed, and the type distributed." This would mean that there were *four* successive printings in all—of which only the first and fourth survive—and would explain why some of the changes made by Lincoln to the "First edition" (such as the one above) do not appear in the final printing, having been discarded in one of the intervening drafts. It would explain as well why parts of the text of the final printing are not found in Lincoln's revisions of the first printing: they had been introduced in one of the subsequent drafts. Lincoln also rearranged some paragraphs by literally cutting them out and pasting them in a new location. All in all, the evidence of the surviving drafts indicates a painstaking process that resulted in a very thorough and deliberate crafting of the text contained in the final printing.

❧

A MAJOR POINT OF strategy for any work involves the question of audience—who is to be addressed? The speech that Lincoln carried with him from Springfield was obviously focused on the South and its grievances, and its forceful conclusion would suggest that its reasoning and arguments were directed mainly at the Southern people. But there are good reasons for thinking that this is more apparent than real, and that the speech was actually aimed primarily at the citizens of the loyal states and those on the fence. While it is true that Lincoln at this time probably underestimated the extent of disaffection among ordinary Southerners and overestimated the extent of Southern loyalty to the Union, he was under no illusion that he could change the minds of those politicians leading the charge toward secession. A year earlier, in his speech at Cooper Union in New York City, he had acknowledged, after laying out an inspired defense of Republican principles, that there was little hope of convincing Southern politicians that they were wrong. "What will convince them? This, and this only: cease to call slavery *wrong*, and join them in calling it *right*. And this must be done thoroughly—done in *acts* as well as in *words*." Since then, the situation had only gotten worse, and the confederacy of seceded states was being formalized even as Lincoln was composing his speech in his hideaway in Springfield. The audience that Lincoln most needed to convince was largely composed of the very people who had elected him and other loyalists.

Speaking to one audience as a way of getting through to another is, by definition, an artful enterprise. If it is not done well, the result will appear hypocritical and alienate everybody. Lincoln would prove himself up to the challenge, but there are some indications of his dual intentions in the drafting itself, particularly in the revisions. As we saw, both the message and the tone of the address were unremitting in their rejection of Southern claims. We also saw that there were passages that might be very much resented by Southerners, most of which he subsequently struck out. Even his softening of the message can be understood in terms of the need not to overreach or to overpersonalize his defiance of the Southern arguments and actions.

Another reason for thinking that Lincoln did not regard the South as the most important audience for his speech is that he simply declined to respond to the secessionists' most important arguments. That he knew what they were and knew how and why he disagreed with them can hardly be doubted, but in his inaugural address he largely ignored them and concentrated attention on expounding his own views. After the war began, Lincoln would send a long message to Congress that included a detailed and aggressive examination of the secessionist arguments, which is a clear indication of what he withheld from his inaugural address.

The strongest reason for thinking that the speech was aimed primarily at the loyal public is, of course, the situation Lincoln found himself in. As one who was little known and whose abilities were very much in doubt, his most important task was to convince the Unionists, many of whom were skeptical Democrats, that he was a capable leader. In a confusing situation, with the Union dissolving and no emerging sense of what legislative or constitutional remedies were called for, he had somehow to present a credible image of himself and a reasoned but firm response to secession.

THE MORE ONE EXAMINES the First Inaugural in all its phases, the more one becomes aware of how thoughtfully it was composed. What is apparently the only surviving manuscript scrap relating to this speech shows Lincoln grappling with what would become the opening sentence of the address (see Fig. 3-4):

> In compliance with a custom as old as the government, I appear before you to address you briefly, and, in your presence, to take the oath prescribed by the Constitution and laws to be taken by whomever ~~enters upon~~ assumes ~~to~~ perform the ~~discharge~~ duties of our national chief magistrate_

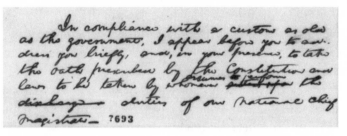

Figure 3-4. The only surviving manuscript remnant of Lincoln's hand-written draft of the First Inaugural. Library of Congress.

This tells us that the opening phrases of the speech probably originated as one of those ideas that he noted down on a scrap of paper and used in drafting. It also calls attention to the way these words and phrases reverberate thematically throughout the finished work. This is, after all, a speech about *compliance*, about adhering to the *forms* of a long-established government. It is a speech about the *Constitution* and what constitutional government means and requires. The manuscript scrap also serves as a reminder that *oath taking* is not simply the prime activity of the occasion but would become, in the course of the speech, an important motif, or theme. This artful use of the oath is yet another evidence of how skillfully the fabric of the speech was woven together. It appears several times, and these references anticipate and prepare for the powerful double antithesis at the end that turns on the swearing of that presidential oath. After the initial Springfield printing, its author even sought to sharpen the bite of the second antithesis by making the opposing statements end on the contrasting words "assault" and "defense" (Fig. 3-5):

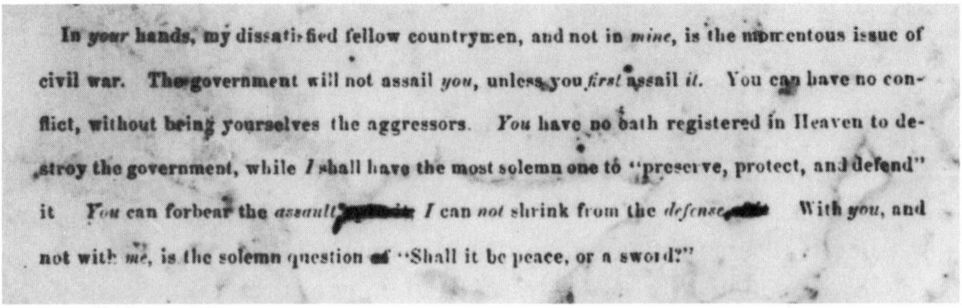

In your hands, my dissatisfied fellow countrymen, and not in *mine*, is the momentous issue of civil war. The government will not assail *you*, unless *you first* assail *it*. You can have no conflict, without being yourselves the aggressors. *You* have no oath registered in Heaven to destroy the government, while *I* shall have the most solemn one to "preserve, protect, and defend" it *You* can forbear the *assault* I can *not* shrink from the *defense* With *you*, and not with *me*, is the solemn question *Shall it be peace, or a sword?"

Figure 3-5. The original conclusion to the first printed draft of Lincoln's First Inaugural, with handwritten modifications. Library of Congress.

You have no oath registered in Heaven to destroy the government, while *I* shall have the most solemn one to "preserve, protect, and defend" it. *You* can forbear the *assault* ~~upon it~~; *I* can *not* shrink from the *defense* ~~of it~~.

It was to be a moment of high drama, acted out on the inaugural platform erected on the east portico of the Capitol. It would dramatize his determination to do no more—and no less—than was called for in the presidential oath he was about to swear.

WHEN LINCOLN BOARDED THE train for Washington on February 11, he carried with him "about a dozen" printed copies of his inaugural address. The product, as we have seen, of considerable drafting and revision, this was the last of four printings and the one that Lincoln would share with a few chosen advisers in the days ahead. According to Nicolay, he locked these copies in a "small, old-fashioned black oil-cloth carpetbag," and without telling him what was in it, he entrusted the bag to the care of his seventeen-year-old son, Robert.

Upon arrival at the hotel in Indianapolis, Lincoln inquired about the carpetbag, only to be told by Robert that he had checked it with the hotel clerk along with the party's other bags. Nicolay's firsthand description of what followed speaks for itself.

A look of stupefaction passed over the countenance of Mr. Lincoln, and visions of that Inaugural in all the next morning's newspapers floated through his imagination. Without a word he opened the door of his room, forced his way through the crowded corridor down to the office, where, with a single stride of his long legs, he swung himself across the clerk's counter, behind which a small mountain of carpetbags of all colors had accumulated. Then drawing a little key out of his pocket he began delving for the black ones, and opened one by one those that the key would unlock, to the great surprise and amusement of the clerk and bystanders, as their miscellaneous contents came to light. Fortune favored the President-elect, for after the first half dozen trials, he found his treasures.

Other than Judge David Davis, his closest Illinois adviser, and the newspaper publisher who supervised the setting of the type, Lincoln had apparently shown his address to no one until he read it aloud, the day before his departure, for an effective German-born campaigner, Carl Schurz. He was secretive by nature, and he went to extraordinary lengths to prevent the premature disclosure of the contents of his first presidential performance. In Indianapolis, another trusted adviser who had accompanied Lincoln on the train, Orville H. Browning, decided to leave the party and return to Illinois, prompting Lincoln to ask him, before leaving, to read and give his reaction to the inaugural address. Browning found nothing to object to, but he carried it with him and wrote the president-elect a letter several days later, in which he recommended "omitting the declaration of the purpose of reclamation [of federal properties], which will be construed into a threat, or menace, and will be irritating even in the border states."

Browning's second thoughts may very well have been prompted by the sharp reaction in the press to a rhetorical question Lincoln had posed in Indianapolis about "coercion." Would it be "coercion," he asked in a prepared speech, if the government "simply insists upon holding its own forts, or retaking those forts which belong to it?" Almost certainly meant as a trial balloon, Lincoln's question at Indianapolis had been widely interpreted in the press for what it was—an indication of what he thought was the appropriate presidential response to the confiscation of government property. American newspapers were quick to seize upon this part of Lincoln's Indianapolis remarks, and even the faraway *London Times* immediately noted the implication: "In speaking of his policy a few days since we said that he would, no doubt, hold those arsenals and dockyards which remained to the Federal Government, and collect the revenues at the Southern ports. But Mr. Lincoln is more explicit, and tells us that he means to do much more than this." Not until Lincoln's speech in Indianapolis did it dawn on Eastern editors that the glimpse of his views that they had been so eagerly awaiting had actually been put forward the previous week in the Springfield newspaper the *Illinois State Journal*, where, doubtless with Lincoln's permission and perhaps even at his direction, two editorials had appeared entitled "Compromise Not to Be Thought Of" and "The Forts Must Be Retaken—The Revolution Must Be Checked."

Browning's letter makes interesting reading in light of what happened two months later. "On principle the passage is right as it now stands," he wrote to the president-elect. "The fallen places ought to be reclaimed. But cannot that be accomplished as well, or even better, without announcing the purpose in your inaugural?" He had a specific application in mind: "The first attempt that is made to furnish supplies or reinforcements to Sumter will induce aggression by South Carolina, and then the government will stand justified, before the entire country, in repelling that aggression, and retaking the forts. And so it will be everywhere, and all the places now occupied by traitors can be recaptured without affording them additional material with which to inflame the public mind by representing your inaugural as containing an irritating threat."

BROWNING WAS NOT THE only adviser to suggest dropping the reference to retaking the captured forts. The man designated to be Lincoln's secretary of state, William H. Seward, had fully expected to be the Republican nominee for president, in which case he, and not Abraham Lincoln, would have reaped the benefit of the acrimonious split in the opposing party and been elected the first Republican president. After considerable urging, he had agreed to serve in the cabinet of his rival, with the expectation that, as an established political leader with long experience in national affairs, he would play an active managerial role in the administration. Soon after arriving in Washington, Lincoln asked Seward to go over the text of his address and make suggestions.

Seward took the request seriously. As he made clear in the covering letter that he included with his long list of recommended changes, Seward wanted the president to be acutely aware of his own superior standing and experience in national politics generally, and he emphasized that he was acting on what he had learned in his recent conversations with influential Southerners. "I, my dear sir, have devoted myself singly to the study of the case here—with advantages of access and free communication with all parties of all sections." Republican loyalists may counsel "tenacity" but they "know nothing of the real peril of the crisis. It has not been their duty to study it, as it has been mine. Only the soothing words which I have spoken have saved us and carried us along thus far. Every loyal man, and indeed every disloyal man, in the South, will tell you this."

Lincoln appreciated Seward's political and diplomatic assets and intended to make full use of them in the trials ahead, and his asking Seward to read and comment on his carefully guarded address was at least partly an acknowledgment of the special value he placed on his opinion. But Seward's letter may also have appeared to a wary Lincoln as the opening wedge in a plan to dominate policy making in the forth-coming administration. Well aware that he needed to use Seward and not be used by him, Lincoln would have to gauge, in reading Seward's recommendations, the motive as well as the message.

The message was conciliation. Lincoln's address was sound in its constitutional arguments, Seward advised, but deficient in diplomacy. His letter opened: "I have suggested many changes of little importance severally, but in their general effect tending to soothe the public mind." And he concluded with a flattering comparison of Lincoln's sit-uation with that of Thomas Jefferson. "He brought the first Republi-can party into power against and over a party ready to resist and dismember the Government. Partisan as he was, he sank the partisan in the patriot in his inaugural address, and propitiated his adversaries by declaring: 'We are all Federalists, all Republicans.' I could wish that you would think it wise to follow this example in this crisis." Lincoln was shrewd enough to know without reading further that the carefully constructed tone of his address was under fire.

The enclosure that accompanied Seward's letter showed that he had not taken his assignment lightly. Sitting down with a copy of the final Springfield printing, he first numbered each of the lines on all of its seven pages. Then, using the page and line numbers to identify the pas-sages he wished to refer to, he drew up a detailed list of recommended changes. As he admitted, many of the changes were slight, but most were intended to make the address more palatable to what he called "the defeated, irritated, angered, frenzied party." Here, for example, are his recommended changes for page three of Lincoln's seven-page draft:

Line   1   Strike out "now"

       4   Strike out "on the whole," and write "generally"

   7, 8   After the word "Union" strike out the rest of the sentence, and insert, "heretofore only menaced is now formidably attempted."

    31   Strike out the whole line.

    33   For "nothing" write "void"

    35   For treasonable write "revolutionary"

The first two changes are hardly substantive, and seem to reflect only minor stylistic preferences. But the third one goes well beyond that. Where Lincoln had written:

A disruption of the Federal Union is menaced, and, so far as can be on paper, is already effected.

Seward proposed to make it read:

A disruption of the Federal Union heretofore only menaced is now formidably attempted.

Lincoln's sentence was intended sardonically. It implicitly denied the force of what the secessionists had set down in their declarations by suggesting that they constituted a paper rebellion. Seward saw this as needlessly antagonistic and consequently suggested that Lincoln emphasize instead that the disruption of the Union was not just being threatened but was being "formidably attempted."

The other suggested alterations on page three are of the same character. The line (31) that Seward thinks should be stricken features a strong word—"absurd"—that would doubtless be resented. Calling the Southern states' resolutions and ordinances of secession "legally *void*" would doubtless be less offensive than calling them, as Lincoln had proposed, "legally *nothing*." And to substitute "revolutionary" for the inflammatory word "treasonable" would be to exchange an objectionable term for one that Southerners might even embrace.

Seward's suggested modifications in the text of the address number about fifty, and their general tenor is to take much of the sting out of Lincoln's words and the sharper edges off his arguments. While Seward had pleaded in his letter that his aim was "to soothe the public mind," the effect of most of his proposed changes was to placate the South and to play down the seriousness of the crisis. Lincoln's papers at the Library of Congress contain two sets of the Springfield printing in which Lincoln has incorporated into his text handwritten changes suggested by Seward. One clearly supersedes the other, being the final version of the address and embodying the actual text that Lincoln read at the March 4 inauguration. The earlier copy shows Lincoln acceding to many of Seward's suggestions, but resisting the full force of some, and ignoring others. In an appendage to his letter labeled "General Remarks," Seward had granted that Lincoln's argument was "strong and conclusive, and ought not to be in any way abridged or modified." This was somewhat disingenuous, but the target of most of his suggested changes was the tone.

What happened to change Lincoln's mind is not entirely clear, but when he came to work out the final version of the address, presumably not long before its delivery on March 4, he decided to yield to most of Seward's suggestions. Michael Burlingame has found contemporary evidence that he also consulted about its contents with his advisers in the cabinet and the Congress during the week before delivery. This is reflected in a letter from William H. Bailhache, who had supervised the printing of the Springfield drafts and who, having followed Lincoln to Washington, wrote to his wife back in Springfield on March 3 that the "original draft has been modified every day to suit the views of the different members of the Cabinet. The amendments are principally verbal & consist of softening some of the words & elaborating more at length some of the ideas contained in the original draft." This may well explain the origins of some of the handful of changes Lincoln made to his text that were not suggested by Seward (see Fig. 3-6).

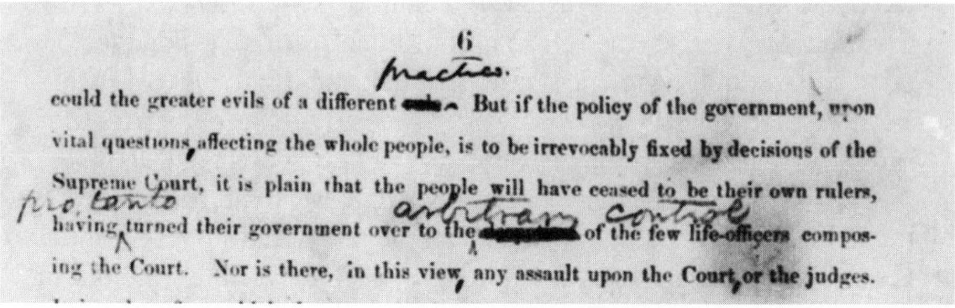

could the greater evils of a different ~~rule~~ ∧ But if the policy of the government, upon vital questions affecting the whole people, is to be irrevocably fixed by decisions of the Supreme Court, it is plain that the people will have ceased to be their own rulers, having turned their government over to the ~~~~ of the few life-officers composing the Court. Nor is there, in this view, any assault upon the Court, or the judges.

Figure 3-6. Changes, in Lincoln's hand, to the "second" printed draft of Lincoln's First Inaugural, showing contemplated changes not suggested by William H. Seward. Library of Congress.

Fast-moving events may have altered his view of the situation since the time he had finished his draft in Springfield, nor would it be surprising if things looked different in Washington, where, as president-elect, he had listened to the opinions of dozens of observers, advisers, and adversaries. For whatever reasons, Lincoln ultimately decided to follow Seward's lead, a decision that substantially altered the tone and thus the character of his address.

In their monumental biography of Lincoln, John G. Nicolay and John Hay were sure that Seward had "only suggested two important changes." The first was "to omit the reference to the Chicago platform," and the second was to drop the declared intention to "reclaim" the captured federal property and "to speak ambiguously about the exercise of power, and to hint rather at forbearance." The other modifications, they believed, "were simple changes of phraseology—affecting only the style, and changing no argument or proposition of policy." But many of those changes in phraseology had, and were calculated to have, a decisive effect on the tone, which constituted a crucial part of the message that Lincoln had originally intended to send. As David Herbert Donald has written, "The draft that he completed before leaving Springfield was a no-nonsense document." The address that emerged under Seward's tutelage was, by contrast, almost a model of conciliation.

In his preliminary attempt to integrate Seward's suggestions into his text, Lincoln had resisted the wordy evasions, such as one on the Supreme Court. Lincoln had written:

> But if the policy of the government, upon vital questions, affecting the whole people, is to be irrevocably fixed by decisions of the Supreme Court, it is plain that the people will have ceased to be their own rulers, having turned their government over to the despotism of the few life-officers composing the Court.

Seward's recommendation amounted to substituting this:

> At the same time the candid citizen must confess that if the policy of the government, upon vital questions, affecting the whole people, is to be irrevocably fixed by decisions of the Supreme Court, made in the ordinary course of litigation between parties in personal actions, the people will have ceased to be their own rulers, having practically resigned their government into the hands of that eminent tribunal.

In his preliminary grappling with Seward's suggestions, Lincoln had resisted this change and had seen fit only to replace the harsh word "despotism" with "arbitrary control" and make one other minor qualification (see Fig. 3-6 above), changes that, in fact, may have been suggested by others. But in the final version of the address, he adopted the whole of Seward's murky and obsequious wording. Lincoln's point, Nicolay and Hay might argue, was still intact: that the Supreme Court deciding all the important political questions contravenes true democracy. But the sense of firmness and determination that emerges from each passage is quite different. In one can be heard overtones of "Don't tread on me"; in the other, an almost wistful note of regret.

∾

IF THE CHANGES PROPOSED by Seward had the overall effect of significantly toning down the First Inaugural, there is no denying that Lincoln was a willing, if initially reluctant, partner in the enterprise. In finally adopting either the letter or the spirit of upward of thirty of Seward's suggestions, Lincoln knowingly accepted not just a few cosmetic alterations, but rather a significant moderation of the tone of his address. Nor is there any reason to think that he regretted the changes he made in his Springfield draft, then or later. That he entered fully into the spirit of conciliation is evident in the most famous part of the address, its ending. From its earliest known state, and through several revisions, the address had consistently ended on an emphatic note that, as we have seen, deftly managed to be defiant without being hostile or unduly confrontational. It found expression in Lincoln's elegant double antithesis on his oath, and it concluded with the forceful insistence that it was the secessionists, not he, who must decide the question of whether there would be war or peace.

But William H. Seward, a canny and experienced politician, held that this was not what the situation called for. In the "General remarks" he appended to his covering letter, he insisted that the address as Lincoln had written it, though sound in argument, was still somehow lacking. "But something besides or in addition to argument is needful—to meet and remove prejudice and passion in the South, and despondency and fear in the East." What was needed, he added, was "some words of affection—some of calm and cheerful confidence."

A document in the hand of Seward's son Frederick, who acted as his father's personal secretary, may well represent an early attempt by the new secretary of state to help the new president strike the proper note. Labeled "Suggestions for a closing paragraph," it begins with an over-ambitious sentence of some 139 words, whose meandering and lack of direction undermine its message. But possibly from this abortive effort came the germ of what Seward famously wrote on the back of one of the sheets containing his page-by-page list of suggested changes—the prototype for what would become one of the most celebrated passages in Lincoln's writings. Writing under the influence of Lincoln's prose, and seizing on his own image of the *strained ties of brotherhood*, Seward sketched out a new conclusion that would answer his call for "some words of affection—some of calm and cheerful confidence," and would, at the same time, be the culmination of all the other conciliatory changes he had suggested (Fig. 3-7):

> I close. We are not we must not be aliens or enemies but ~~countrym~~ fellow countrymen and brethren. Although passion has strained our bonds of affection too hardly they must not ~~be broken—they will not~~, I am sure they will not be broken. The mystic chords which proceeding from ~~every ba~~ so many battle fields and so many patriot graves ~~bind~~ pass through all the hearts and ~~hearths~~ all the hearths in this broad continent of ours will yet ~~harmon~~ again harmonize in their ancient music when ~~touched as they surely~~ breathed upon ~~again~~ by the ~~better angel~~ guardian angel of the nation.

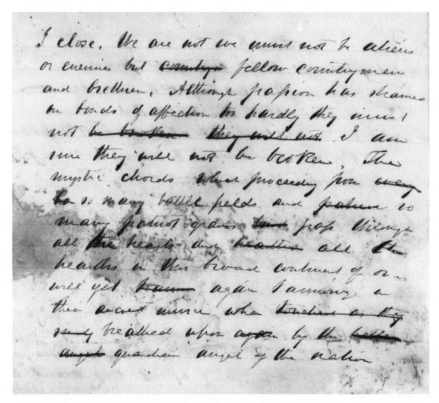

Figure 3-7. William H. Seward's suggested conciliatory ending for Lincoln's First Inaugural. Library of Congress.

There is evidence that Lincoln's first interest in this haunting image may have been as a brief addition to his address, probably to be placed somewhere near the end. On the back of the letter sent by Orville H. Browning (Fig. 3-8), which Lincoln likely reviewed as he pondered Seward's suggestions, Lincoln wrote: "Americans, all, we are not enemies, but friends_ We have sacred ties of affection which, though strained by passions, let us hope can never be broken."

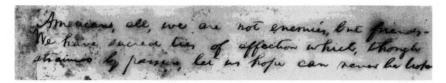

Figure 3-8. Lincoln's draft of a sentence based on suggestions for his First Inaugural offered by Seward, written on the back of a letter from Orville H. Browning. Library of Congress.

With his usual knack for economy, Lincoln here managed to combine the essence of both Seward's suggested closing and Jefferson's "We are all Federalists, all Republicans." Such a sentence could readily have been worked into the Springfield draft without displacing the original ending. But to adopt Seward's conciliatory strategy and his "soft" closing would necessitate modifying the tone he had so carefully constructed and abandoning the dramatic note of defiance that marked his ending. Could Lincoln afford to make such a concession, especially on the advice of a man who was maneuvering to install himself as the guiding spirit of the new administration—the very man who, as Lincoln told his private secretary, must not be allowed to "take the first trick"? It was a fateful decision.

Don E. Fehrenbacher had many illuminating things to say about Lincoln's abilities as a writer, one of which was that "Lincoln's literary skill is most readily observable in those instances when he took someone else's prose and molded it to his own use." Fehrenbacher gave a number of examples of this but believed that the best was the conclusion of the First Inaugural, which he calls "the moving appeal that was the first oratorical summit of his presidency." Where Seward had written "I close," Lincoln, reversing roles with the usually more prolix Seward, expanded this to "I am loth to close." Fehrenbacher helps us to see why. "The improvement in cadence is obvious enough, but the addition of three words also makes the sentence throb with connotative meanings and emotive force. It expresses an almost elegiac reluctance to break off discussion of the crisis—a sense of remnant opportunities slipping away, of a cherished world about to be lost."

Taking our cue from Fehrenbacher, we might observe that what Lincoln's three extra words did for Seward's first sentence holds true for the entire passage. The manuscript of Seward's prototype (see Fig. 3-7 above) shows that it is still very much a rough draft. Not only are its phrases yet to be melded smoothly together and its cadence firmly established, but its ideas are still largely amorphous and unrealized. The central image of the mystic chords haltingly conveys the notion that all Americans are connected by their geography and history. But Seward's sketch does no more with these metaphorical chords than to promise or predict that they will again "harmonize in their ancient music when breathed upon by the guardian angel of the nation," a concept that has only a very hazy meaning and little magic.

After trying out a compact and straightforward statement of Seward's idea on the back of Browning's letter, Lincoln apparently saw an arresting possibility in Seward's raw material. What is perhaps most remarkable about Lincoln's version of Seward's close is the way he capitalized on Seward's discarded language. Seward's first impulse, as the manuscript shows, was to have the mystic chords be "touched" by the "better angel of the nation." He then decided to drop "better" for the more conventional "guardian" angel. It is a measure of Lincoln's superior powers as a writer that he saw the literary potential in some of Seward's abandoned words and recycled them. Seward may have regarded "touched" as less poetic than "breathed upon," just as he probably drew back from "better angel" as too derivative of an image made familiar by Dickens. But Lincoln was one of the few Americans of his day and standing who didn't read Dickens, and it may be said that he outdid Dickens in immortalizing this phrase found on Seward's cutting-room floor. The final result is one of the most memorable passages in American English (Fig. 3-9).

> I am loth to close. We are not enemies, but friends_ We must not be enemies. Though passion may have strained, it must not break our bonds of affection. The mystic chords of memory, streching from every battlefield, and patriot grave, to every living heart and hearthstone, all over this broad land, will yet swell the chorus of the Union, when again touched, as surely they will be, by the better angels of our nature.

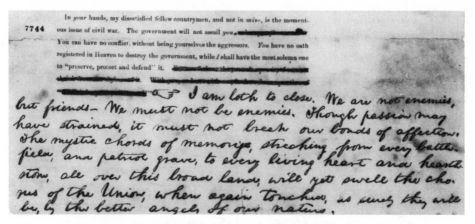

Figure 3-9. Lincoln's revised conclusion to his First Inaugural, based on a paragraph suggested by Seward (see Fig. 3-7). Library of Congress.

There is scarcely a better way to bring out the richness of Lincoln's poetic conclusion than to compare it with Seward's prototype and note how ingeniously Lincoln reshaped the contours of Seward's imagery. Take, for example, what Lincoln does with Seward's image of the "mystic chords." Both play on the musical dimension of the older spelling of the word "cord," but Lincoln manages to make more of it. In Seward's admittedly still-evolving conception, the "chords" are a continuation of the "bonds" of affection, the familiar ties that bind, and these, he says, will produce the harmony enjoyed in former times (the "ancient music") when breathed upon by the nation's guardian angel, presumably the Divinity. Not only is Lincoln's phrasing more apt and more engaging, but he adds a whole new dimension to the imagery—memory. In Seward's prototype the "mystic chords" are simply connectors, but Lincoln infuses these with the quality of memory, which gives them, in Fehrenbacher's words, "connotative meanings and emotive force." Where Seward had the chords *proceeding from* and *passing through*, Lincoln invigorates the image by having the mystic chords *stretching* between every conceivable American person, place, and event, forming an almost visual network. Thus stretched, the "mystic chords of memory" become something like a musical instrument, capable of producing a harmonious music that will return us to our commonality. This can occur, according to Lincoln's version, when our common memories are invoked, not by an outside force, but by the "better angels" of our own nature. The effect of this calculated refinement, as Lucas E. Morel has pointed out, is to shift the emphasis from divine intervention to the "agency" of our own best impulses.

Ultimately, what a close scrutiny of the writing of the First Inaugural tells us is that Lincoln's ability was such that he could go in different directions, and do so effectively. In other words, as a writer he could do conciliation as convincingly as he could do confrontation. The Springfield draft was a more crisp, a more incisive, and in some ways a more severely elegant address. The penultimate draft, which incorporated some of Seward's changes, shows that Lincoln had managed to maintain the character of his Springfield text, to preserve its resolute tone and dramatic ending, and at the same time partially accommodate Seward. When he decided finally to reverse himself and go with Seward and conciliation, he admitted into his speech a good many passages more wordy and less clear than he would have liked, and he had to sacrifice some things that had been important to his original conception, such as the second half of his double antithesis at the end. But his talents as a writer were such that he could successfully cover his retreat, principally by means of a truly memorable conclusion whose warmth and conciliatory tone left a lasting impression.

∾

In New York City, the well-connected Wall Street lawyer George Templeton Strong recorded his reaction to the address in his diary. Strong was keenly intelligent, relatively independent in political matters, and had a decidedly skeptical temperament. He was originally quite skeptical, for example, of Abraham Lincoln's abilities and doubted that he was up to the difficult challenges of the presidency. Strong had voted for him, but only because, after much soul searching, he considered the other choices worse. In his diary, Strong's reaction to the inaugural address comes by way of a report of a discussion of the speech by a group of New York businessmen: "Southronizers approved and applauded it as pacific and likely to prevent collision. Maybe so, but I think there's a clank of metal in it."

"Southronizers" was Strong's term for those sympathetic to the South—a large segment of New York City—for business or political reasons, or for both. Strong himself was not particularly antislavery, but he had decided, after a brief flirtation with disunionism (that is, simply letting the South go its own way), that secession was at bottom a treasonous attempt to destroy the government and, with it, all the blessings thereof. "I hold secession unlawful and most calamitous," he had written after the election in November, "but the South is likely to do this wrong and folly and mischief if it find the North acquiescent and good-natured." This concern, presumably, is part of what disposed him to hear "the clank of metal"—the quality of firmness and determination—in Lincoln's speech. The "Southronizers," in New York and elsewhere, were legion, and Seward's conciliatory theme was aimed primarily at people like them. In Lincoln's capable hands it struck home, as Strong attests, but Strong himself detected the resoluteness that had originally been a principal element in the speech. And Strong heard something else in the speech, something that caused him to see the new president in a fresh light. His diary entry continues:

> It is unlike any message or state paper of any class that has appeared in my time, to my knowledge. It is characterized by strong individuality and the absence of conventionalism of thought or diction. It doesn't run in the ruts of Public Documents, but seems to introduce one to *a man* and to dispose one to like him.

CHAPTER FOUR

The Message of
July 4, 1861

H ORACE GREELEY WAS THE most famous and widely read Republican journalist of his day. Independent and often eccentric in his views, the editor of the *New York Tribune* would prove a frequent critic of Abraham Lincoln, but he was, from the outset, a great admirer of the president's First Inaugural Address. At the time of Lincoln's Second Inaugural, which would eventually eclipse the first in the public imagination, Greeley characteristically made a point of preferring the first, which he went so far as to reprint in his newspaper. In a lecture delivered a few years after Lincoln's death, Greeley praised the First Inaugural as "a masterly effort at persuasion and conciliation by one whose command of logic was as perfect as his reliance on it was unqualified."

The trouble was that not everyone shared this view. Careful and deliberate as the new president had been to spell out his disposition toward the rebellious states and their "supposed" acts of secession, he was chagrined on taking office to discover that Southerners still professed to be in doubt as to how he proposed to deal with these developments. For example, the Virginia convention that was being held to determine whether that state should remain in the Union passed a resolution on April 8, fully a month after the inaugural, prompted by "the uncertainty which prevails in the public mind as to the policy which the Federal Executive intends to pursue toward the seceded States." When presented with this resolution by three delegated representatives of the convention, Lincoln replied in dismay: "In answer I have to say, that having, at the beginning of my official term, expressed my intended policy, as plainly as I was able, it is with deep regret, and some mortification, I now learn, that there is great, and injurious uncertainty, in the public mind, as to what that policy is, and what course I intend to pursue." He then urged "a careful consideration" of his inaugural address, a key passage of which he quoted: "The power confided to me will be used to hold, occupy, and possess, the property, and places belonging to the Government, and to collect the duties, and imposts; but, beyond what is necessary for these objects, there will be no invasion—no using of force against, or among the people anywhere."

The attempt to draw the new president out could not have come as a surprise, but what he must have found even more mortifying was that his own secretary of state claimed to entertain similar doubts. In a letter written on April 1, in the ill-disguised hope of being given authority over government policy, Seward had protested that the administration was "at the end of a month's administration, and yet without a policy, either domestic or foreign." In exasperation, Lincoln wrote back, duly quoting the same key passage from the inaugural address. There is reason to think that the president may not have sent this letter, opting instead to deal with the situation in a personal interview, which serves only to underscore the role that writing played in helping to crystallize his thinking. In any event, having this passage quoted back to him would have had for Seward a dual meaning, for, as both men well knew, the expression "the power confided to me" had been suggested by Seward himself.

By the time Lincoln had drafted his response to the Virginia convention, what he called "an unprovoked assault" had been made upon Fort Sumter, "in pursuit of a purpose to drive the United States authority from [such] places." This meant, in effect, that the government restraint so carefully articulated in the inaugural address was off, and the war was on.

❧

THE WEEKS LEADING UP to the firing on Fort Sumter on April 12, 1861, were nothing less than a horrific nightmare for the neophyte president, with difficulties coming so thick and fast that his capacity to function was threatened. The machinery of the new administration was not yet in place, and could not be until hundreds of patronage claims had been adjudicated, a process that, despite its rancorous character, Lincoln insisted on presiding over himself. Only after these sometimes bitterly contentious matters had been settled could the appointments to government offices be made. The nation's military resources were being daily reduced by massive defections from its officer corps and the wholesale confiscation of its Southern forts and armories. The new administration's decision making proved so lacking in coordination as to constantly trip over itself and cause its officials to act at cross-purposes. With all this, and the constant threat of the capital being invaded, the White House was a center of chaos and confusion. Lincoln reportedly told Orville H. Browning a few months later "that all the troubles and anxieties of his life had not equalled those which intervened between this time and the fall of Sumter." His secretary remembered his saying in the same conversation that his troubles "were so great that could I have anticipated them, I would not have believed it possible to survive them."

Survive them he did, but his trials were merely beginning. It wasn't enough for the president to try to cope with the rebellion from day to day on an ad hoc basis. To fully engage the resources of the government, Congress had to be called back into special session. The date was fixed, with obvious symbolism, for the Fourth of July, at which time the president would provide a suitable account of what had happened and would spell out what was needed to meet the emergency. Given the extraordinary demands on his time and attention, the chief executive in such a situation might have been expected to delegate the drafting of a straightforward, factual report for this purpose, to be accompanied by estimates of what was needed by each of the governmental departments. But as his associates were soon to learn, Lincoln was no ordinary administrator, and he decided early on that he was going to prepare his own message to Congress and that it would be something much more ambitious than a utilitarian document. Accordingly, during the months of May and June, some of the most hectic in American history, even as he exerted himself on scores of other fronts, Lincoln worked assiduously on what his secretaries referred to as his "Message."

Many of those who would become aware that the new president insisted on doing his own writing were not favorably impressed. This was only another example of how an inexperienced executive wasted his time doing what might better be delegated. Ralph Waldo Emerson would later remark disapprovingly in his journal that the president "writes his own message instead of borrowing the largest understanding as he so easily might." Far from being a waste of time, Lincoln clearly regarded the writing of his Message to Congress as a prime presidential opportunity. How the nation would respond to the crisis would largely depend on what was perceived to be at stake. Not everyone was sure it was worth the horrors of civil war just to force the slaveholding states back into the Union. Whether, and in what spirit, loyal citizens would fight to preserve the Union would depend on what they believed they were fighting for—or against. Lincoln clearly saw the presidential Message to Congress as a public platform from which to seize the intellectual initiative and define the issues.

A FEW WEEKS AFTER the firing on Fort Sumter, and two months before Congress was to convene in special session on July 4, Abraham Lincoln was already thinking hard about fundamental considerations. What, when he spoke for the nation, was to be the bedrock issue? On May 7, he tried out his ideas on his secretaries, John G. Nicolay and John Hay, both of whom made a contemporary record of it. Nicolay's memorandum reads:

> The conversation turning on the subject of the existing contest he [Lincoln] remarked that the real question involved in it, (as he had about made up his mind, though he should think further about it, while writing his message) was whether a free and representative government had the right and power to protect and maintain itself. Admit the right of a minority to secede at will, and the occasion for such secession would almost as likely be any other as the slavery question.

Writing in his diary on the same day, Hay quoted the president as saying: "I consider the central idea pervading this struggle is the necessity that is upon us, of proving that popular government is not an absurdity. We must settle this question now, whether in a free government the minority have the right to break up the government if they choose."

These two contemporaneous memoranda capture Lincoln engaged in what would be a characteristic mode of presidential reflection and deliberation. While he had long been known to his close associates in Illinois as a deeply contemplative man who kept his thoughts to himself, he also liked to try out his conclusions aloud, to hear them, and he typically reasoned in logical steps, as he did on this occasion. Slavery is not the key issue, he seems to be saying, because it is just an excuse for secession, which might be justified for any reason. This is, in fact, what President Andrew Jackson had concluded thirty years earlier (see page 90). But secession is not the key issue either, because there is something even more fundamental: "whether a free and representative government had the right and power to protect and maintain itself." What was most at stake was the viability of popular government. But having reasoned his way to this conclusion, Lincoln was not yet ready to commit himself. He had "about made up his mind," Nicolay noted, "though he should think further about it, while writing his message." Writing was thus an opportunity to think, to consider and reconsider. Hay's diary entry concluded: "He is engaged in constant thought upon his Message: It will be an exhaustive review of the questions of the hour & of the future."

THE SURVIVAL AND PRESERVATION of several drafts of the July 4, 1861, Message to Congress in Lincoln's papers at the Library of Congress testify to the diligent effort that went into it, as well as the importance its writer placed on it. The earliest surviving draft is a handwritten manuscript of forty pages. The pagination indicates that this draft had started off as a twenty-three-page document, which was then expanded. Following the practice established with the First Inaugural, Lincoln eventually had the revised handwritten draft set in type. The resulting printed copy was then itself revised, and this draft was, in turn, sent to the printer to be reset. Additional changes in Lincoln's hand appear on the second printing, and another copy of this printing in the Lincoln papers contains changes suggested by Seward, many of which Lincoln adopted in the final version. All of this draft material permits us to identify stages in the writing of Lincoln's Message to Congress:

1. Making notes (one example?)
2. Preliminary drafts (likely, but none extant)
3. First extant handwritten draft (23 pages, 3,300 words)

4. Expanded handwritten draft (40 pages, 5,500 words)
5. First printed copy, with revisions
6. Second printed copy, with revisions
7. Final version sent to Congress, containing additional changes (6,400 words)

We don't know how many preliminary drafts were made, if any, but we do know that stages three through seven each resulted in a new version of the text, making a total of five known versions of the Message. The existence of these successive drafts, the fullest and most complete such set in the Lincoln papers, offers a rare opportunity to look over the writer's shoulder and observe the process of composition.

Lincoln probably began working on his Message as he usually did, by making notes on scraps or slips of paper. At least one such note has survived (see Fig. 4-1), and the way he has labeled it suggests that it was part of a series of notes that were written down before the speech was actually organized. It reads in part:

> Random 6.
> I recommend that you give the legal means for making this contest a short, and a decisive one—that you authorize to be applied to the work, at least three hundred thousand men, and three hundred millions of dollars_ . . . A right result will be worth more to the world than ten times the men, and ten times the money_ The evidence reaching us from the people leaves no doubt that the material for the work is abundant; and that it needs only the hand of legislation to give it legal sanction, and the hand of the Executive to give it practical shape and efficiency_ The departments here have had more trouble to avoid receiving troops faster than they could provide them than from any other cause_ In a word, the people will save their government, if the government itself will allow them_ ·

From the position of this passage in the earliest (twenty-three-page) version of the manuscript, the material in "Random 6" was originally intended for the final part of the Message. One indication of how the magnitude of the work expanded in the course of its composition is that the text of "Random 6" would eventually appear nearer the middle. While the two other documents that were possibly notes writ-

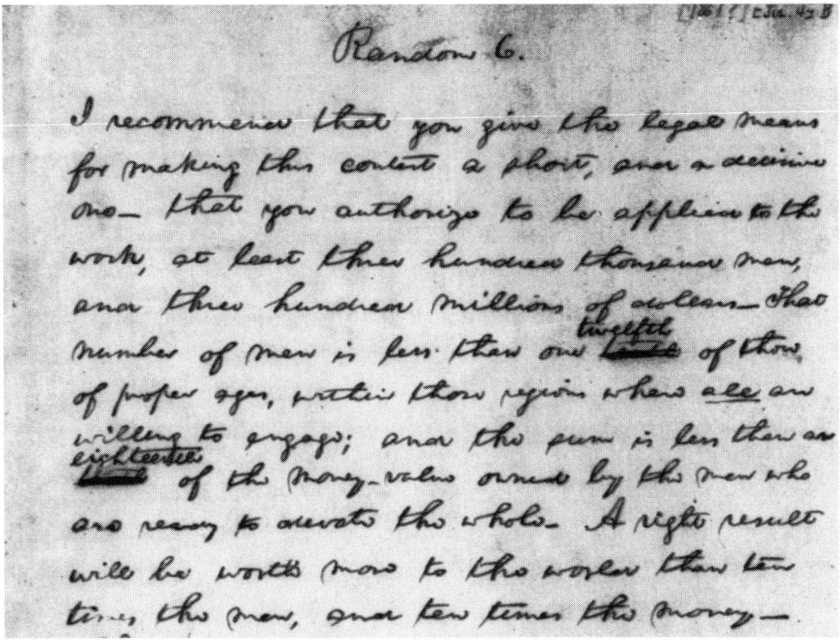

Figure 4-1. One of the few surviving notes that Lincoln was known to have made for his speeches and other writings, "Random 6" contains text that eventually appeared in his Message to Congress of July 4, 1861. Library of Congress.

ten out in advance for the Message bear no label, it seems likely that at the earliest stage of preparation, there were probably other notes labeled "Random 5" and "Random 4" and so forth, and that each of these incorporated one or more points that Lincoln intended to include in his Message. In fact, numbering randomly generated notes seems to have been a part of the incremental mode of composition he had practiced a few years earlier and that Herndon remembered being used in drafting his "House Divided" speech in 1858.

It seems likely in retrospect that one such note would have dealt with an idea touched on in "Random 6" that became seminal to Lincoln's Message: that the outcome of the contest was of great importance to the entire world. As he indicated to his secretaries, Lincoln was inclined toward the position that much more was at stake in the rebellion of the Southern states than purely national questions. As a lawyer, he had been noted for his ability to sort through the complex issues of a case and sift out the "nub," the point on which the case would finally turn. In the earliest stages of preparing the Message, Lin-

coln seems to have been concerned to identify the single most important issue that the rebellion presented. In the handwritten draft, this is
brought to the fore just as soon as the events leading up to the outbreak of civil war have been described. The firing on Fort Sumter, the
president wrote, has "forced upon the country the distinct issue
'Immediate dissolution, or blood.' "

> And this issue embraces more than the fate of these United
> States. It presents to the whole family of man, the question
> whether a democracy—a government of the people, by the same
> people—can, or can not, maintain it's territorial integrity,
> against it's own domestic foes_ It presents the question, whether
> discontented individuals, too few in numbers to control admin-
> istration, according to organic law, in any case, can always, upon
> the pretences made in this case, or on any other pretences, or
> arbitrarily, without any pretence, break up their Government,
> and thus practicaly put an end to free government upon the
> earth.

The evidence of the manuscript shows his questions about the fate
of free government originally ended this part of Lincoln's Message,
which then moved on to other matters. But Lincoln subsequently
extended this section on a new page with two more penetrating questions:

> It forces us to ask: "Is there, in all republics, this inherent, and
> fatal weakness?" "Must a government, of necessity, be too *strong*
> for the liberties of it's own people, or too *weak* to maintain it's
> own existence?"

This passage presents in forceful terms a theme that would return
in various forms and reverberate throughout Lincoln's presidential
writings. It is doubly useful here, for it spotlights a characteristic of his
best writing, his remarkable gift for the interrogatory mode of exposition, exploring complex issues by asking pointed questions. At the
same time, the passage presents a central theme of Lincoln's presidency. Its core, as Reinhold Niebuhr observed, was "a Jeffersonian
belief in the mission of the new nation to initiate, extend and preserve
democratic self-government. Thus for him not only national survival

but the survival of democracy itself was involved in the fortunes of the Civil War." Not just the integrity of the federal Union but the fate of democracy—its very soundness and viability—was being tested.

THE EARLIEST DRAFT OF the Message is surprisingly autobiographical. In his public persona, Lincoln usually seemed quite open and candid, but his friends knew that he was a man not given to private revelations or self-disclosure. Personal questions could easily elicit a colorful story purporting to come from his past, but rarely direct answers or confidential information. Those who knew him best all agreed that he was a deeply private man. Judge David Davis, who presided over the Eighth Circuit, where Lincoln practiced, and who managed his presidential nomination, allowed that "he was the most reticent—Secretive man I Ever Saw—or Expect to See." When he began to command national attention in 1858 as the opponent of Senator Stephen A. Douglas, he resisted all requests by his advisers and publicists for biographical information. Even though they had made it clear that his career had a rags-to-riches character that could be politically advantageous, he was unwilling to cooperate. When, the following year, his situation as a potential presidential candidate forced his hand, he responded with a very brief sketch, of which he said: "There is not much of it, for the reason, I suppose, that there is not much of me."

But presumably because the crisis he was called upon to describe in the Message to Congress had been so recent and, as he had confided to Browning, so personally harrowing, Lincoln at first had trouble writing about it other than subjectively. His handwritten draft shows that he began by carefully referring to himself as "the present incumbent" and "the executive," but when he came to describe the difficult situation he found himself in as he prepared to make his first major decision as commander in chief, he lapsed into the first person. In reporting that all his military advisers, after due consideration, believed that Fort Sumter must be evacuated, he undertook to explain why he opposed it.

In a purely military point of view, this reduced the duty of the administration, in the case, to the mere matter of getting the garrison safely out of the Fort. In fact, General Scott advised that this should be done at once.

I believed, however, that to do so, would be utterly ruinous—that the *necessity* under which it was to be done, would not be fully understood—that, by many, it would be construed as a part of a *voluntary* policy—that, at home, it would discourage the friends of the Union, embolden it's foes, and insure to the latter a recognition of independence abroad—that, in fact, it would be our national destruction consummated. I hesitated—

This passage, rendered as it was originally written, offers a prime example of what can be learned from the scrutiny of Lincoln's manuscripts, for no published edition has presented the text in sufficient detail to reveal what had happened at this early stage of the president's message. For anyone interested in Lincoln's personal ordeal, this part of his manuscript is immensely revealing. It contrasts the narrow, tactical view of his advisers with Lincoln's broader, more strategic view of the situation. It further brings out the unwitting "decisiveness" of the military advisers, who feel no hesitation to proceed, as opposed to the warier, and ultimately wiser, reluctance of the president. This wariness is based, revealingly, on a finely tuned sense of public perception and the all-importance of public opinion, even in what seems a strictly military question. Perhaps most revealing of all is the degree of self-possession and strength of character on display when, in making a critical first decision, the neophyte president resisted the clear recommendation of his much more experienced advisers.

Two-word sentences are rare in any kind of writing, but considering the context, where the fate of the nation is likely hanging in the balance, it would be hard to find one more resonant, or more revealing, than Lincoln's naked admission—"I hesitated." Ostensibly offered to minimize the disagreement with his advisers and the need to reflect, this admission inadvertently has the effect of calling attention to his coolness in the face of his dilemma, and thereby magnifies the moment. It shows him in the act of calling an unpopular halt, risking his standing and stature with his new subordinates, while he considered alternatives and made mental calculations. And of course, for these and other substantive reasons, the paragraph could not stand as written.

It did not take the writer long to see that, however acutely this passage might represent his own baptism by fire as a presidential decision maker, hesitation and a divided administration were not things he could afford to draw attention to, let alone emphasize. His first revision reflected the realization that he should not underscore the personal aspect of the situation. He had not been acting as a private citizen but as duly elected chief magistrate of the nation, so the anguished "I" at the beginning of the passage became "the executive," while at the end of the passage it became "the administration" that hesitated (see Fig. 4-2).

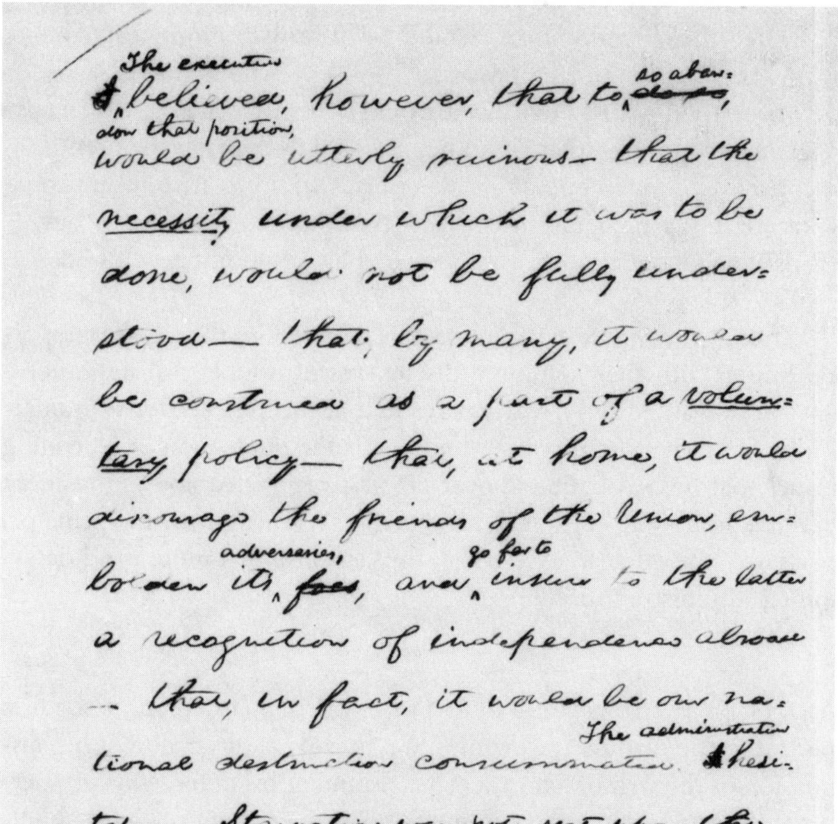

Figure 4-2. A portion of the handwritten draft of Lincoln's Message to Congress of July 4, 1861, showing changes to a particularly autobiographical passage. Library of Congress.

But even this, apparently, put too much emphasis on the differing views of individuals, so the reference to General Scott and his advice was stricken, and the prevailing view (the president's) was rendered in the passive voice: "It was believed . . ." All traces of hesitation were finally expunged when the two-word admission was replaced by another brief sentence: "This could not be allowed." In its final form, this passage would thus read:

> In a purely military point of view, this reduced the duty of the administration, in the case, to the mere matter of getting the garrison safely out of the Fort.
>
> It was believed, however, that to so abandon that position, under the circumstances, would be utterly ruinous; that the *necessity* under which it was to be done, would not be fully understood—that, by many, it would be construed as a part of a *voluntary* policy—that, at home, it would discourage the friends of the Union, embolden its adversaries, and go far to insure to the latter, a recognition abroad—that, in fact, it would be our national destruction consummated. This could not be allowed.

After at least three separate rounds of revision, the autobiographical traces, with their damning disclosures of doubts and hesitations, have been washed away, with the result that the final version is dramatically different from the first. The one is the confession of a fledging leader that he had hesitated over his first major decision as president because he found himself in strong disagreement with his principal advisers. The other is a report on the response of a united and determined administration.

❧

ANOTHER INDICATIVE EXAMPLE OF the unguarded use of the first person in the earliest draft comes in a four-page discussion of his suspension of the writ of habeas corpus. Framing his defense in very personal terms was no doubt prompted by the president's being publicly taken to task by the chief justice of the United States, Roger Taney, in a decision known as *Ex Parte Merryman*. John Merryman had been arrested on May 25 for drilling troops in Maryland to aid the rebellion, and the chief justice, sitting as a circuit judge, had promptly issued a writ of habeas corpus to have the prisoner brought before him, which was deliberately disobeyed by the military. On May 30, Taney issued a harsh opinion, in which, in the words of constitutional scholar Daniel Farber, "he went out of his way to undermine any claim of emergency power of any kind." Not only this, says Farber, "he failed to give the government a genuine opportunity to be heard, mocked Lincoln for failing to observe his oath of office, and widely publicized his opinion in order to undermine the administration."

The four-page section of the Message on this issue was written and inserted after the handwritten draft was already well along, which almost certainly tells us that the president had begun his drafting before the opinion was issued. "I felt it my duty," Lincoln begins by saying, to authorize the arrest and detention of such persons as the Commanding General might "deem dangerous to the public safety," which was done "very sparingly."

> Nevertheless, the legality and propriety of what has been done under it, are questioned; and I have been reminded from a high quarter that one who is sworn to "take care that the laws be faithfully executed" should not himself be one to violate them_ So I think.

Here Lincoln, the experienced lawyer and debater, takes command. He knows exactly how to turn the words of an opponent to his own advantage by quoting them and expressing agreement. Choosing his words carefully, and referring again to his oath of office, he responds: "The whole of the laws which I was sworn to see faithfully executed were being resisted, and failing of execution, in nearly one third of the states." He then puts a skewering question (Figs. 4-3 and 4-4): "Must I have allowed them to finally fail of execution, even had it been perfectly clear that by the use of the means necessary to their execution, some provision of one law, made in such extreme tenderness of the citizens liberty, that more rogues than honest men find shelter under it, should, to a very limited extent, be violated?"

Lincoln's defense of his suspension of the writ of habeas corpus was first drafted in these very personal terms for the understandable reason that he had been accused not just of a mistake but, by implication, of malfeasance in office. His first impulse was to compose a written defense. To the charge that he had broken his oath to "take care that the laws be faithfully executed," he responded:

> I should consider my official oath broken if I should allow the government to be overthrown, when I might think the disregarding the single law would tend to preserve it_ But, in this

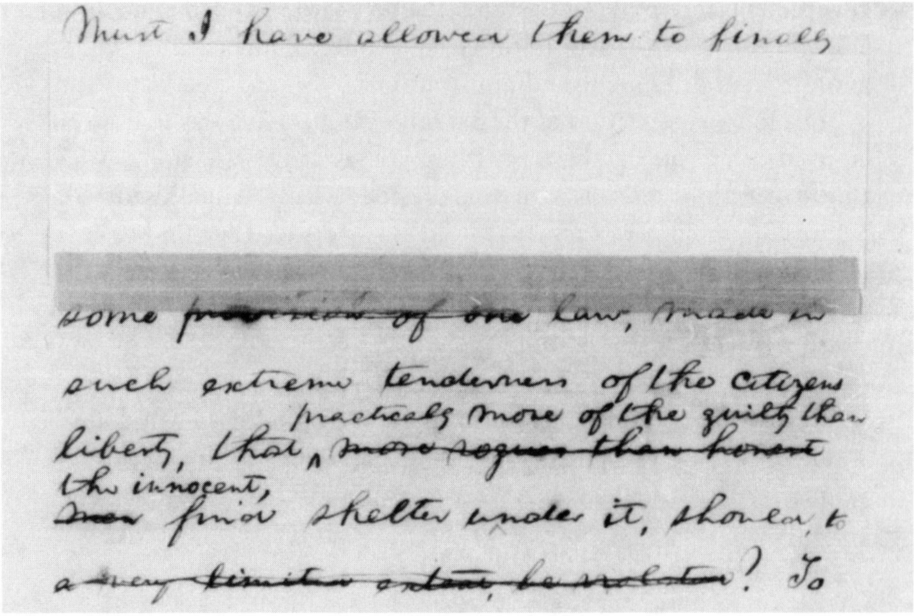

Figures 4-3 and 4-4. Depicted here is a passage from Lincoln's hand-written manuscript that shows the original text in two stages of revision. The first stage is seen in the strikeouts and interlineations of the original text; Lincoln's revision was written on the tab (folded back in Fig. 4-3) that was then pasted over the earlier writing. Library of Congress.

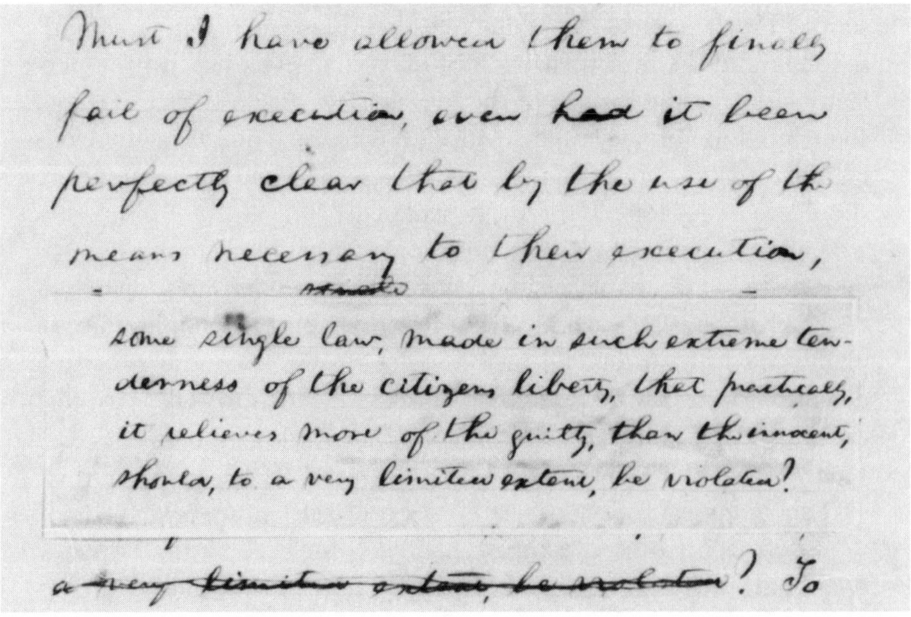

case I was not, in my own judgment, driven to this ground‐ In my opinion I violated no law‐

As with the passages discussed earlier, Lincoln would eventually see fit to revise his discussion of the habeas corpus matter so as to make it less personal. And as with earlier examples, by the final draft he found it expedient to resort to the passive voice. "Must I have allowed" becomes "Must he [the executive] have allowed," which was later revised to "Must they [the laws] be allowed to finally fail of execution . . . ?" The sentence quoted above avoids the first person by yet another method, by shifting to the interrogatory mode:

> Even in such a case, would not the official oath be broken, if the government should be overthrown, when it was believed that disregarding the single law, would tend to preserve it? But it was not believed that this question was presented. It was not believed that any law was violated.

In both of these cases, Lincoln's revisions are a guide to his way of thinking about and dealing with difficult issues as president. Being human, he experienced both crises and criticism as personal experiences, but in writing them out, and by allowing due time for rethinking and revision, his own reactions could be reworked and transformed. His differences with his advisers, his reluctance to follow their advice, his feelings about his oath of office, his natural defensiveness at being accused of malfeasance by the chief justice—all of these are confronted as personal matters in the earliest drafts of his Message, but appear in decidedly different form by the final version.

As he revised his text, Lincoln played down his own role at least partly in order to play up the rationale for his suspension of habeas corpus, a rationale which he managed to encapsulate in an arresting question that legal scholars and civil libertarians still find difficult to answer. The groundwork for this historic question is laid by one that precedes it, which is as convoluted as its successor is direct. In the final version, the initial question takes this form: "Must they [all the laws] be allowed to finally fail of execution, even had it been perfectly clear, that by the use of the means necessary to their execution, some single law, made in such extreme tenderness of the citizen's liberty, that practically, it relieves more of the guilty, than of the innocent, should, to a very limited extent, be violated?" As Mark E. Neely Jr. has rightly observed, the syntax here is "unusually labored," but there would appear to be a reason that Lincoln let it stand. Not only does the construction allow him to work in, however awkwardly, a telling point about the habeas corpus law, but its knotty complexity provides an appealing contrast to the simplicity and directness of the question that follows: "are all the laws, *but one*, to go unexecuted, and the government itself go to pieces, lest that one be violated?" Interestingly enough, the manuscripts reveal that, while the syntactically convoluted sentence went through several revisions (for the earliest, see Figs. 4-3 and 4-4 above), the clincher—the question that lives on in the history of constitutional law—remained intact throughout the extended drafting process. This suggests that Lincoln may well have written the first with the second in mind, and that allowing the syntactical briars and brambles of the first question to remain somewhat tangled was perhaps part of an artful preparation for the second. This is certainly the effect, and it is never safe to underestimate Lincoln.

As he had done in drafting the First Inaugural, Lincoln had the handwritten text of his Message set up in print, which is why a series of names—Ketcham, Scrives, Davis, Allen, Flemming, H. Rodgers, Mac-Murray, etc.—appear on the manuscript (see Fig. 4-5). These are the names of the printers assigned to set type for parts of the manuscript. The person who oversaw the printing was a Republican politician and newspaper editor from Indianapolis, John D. Defrees, whom Lincoln had appointed superintendent of public printing. In handling the manuscripts of Lincoln's state papers and seeing them through the press, Defrees became, in effect, the president's editor, and the Message to Congress of July 4 was probably the first document they worked on together. While Defrees seems to have admired Lincoln's writing, his background as a newspaper editor gave him a more critical view of the president's unconventional punctuation. "He knew nothing of the rules of punctuation," Defrees told the biographer J. G. Holland, "yet the manuscripts of very few of our public men are as well punctuated as his uniformly were, though his use of commas was excessive." "I had frequently to labor with him to reduce the number."

Because both Lincoln's handwritten draft and the printed copy that Defrees edited have both survived in Lincoln's papers, it is possible to

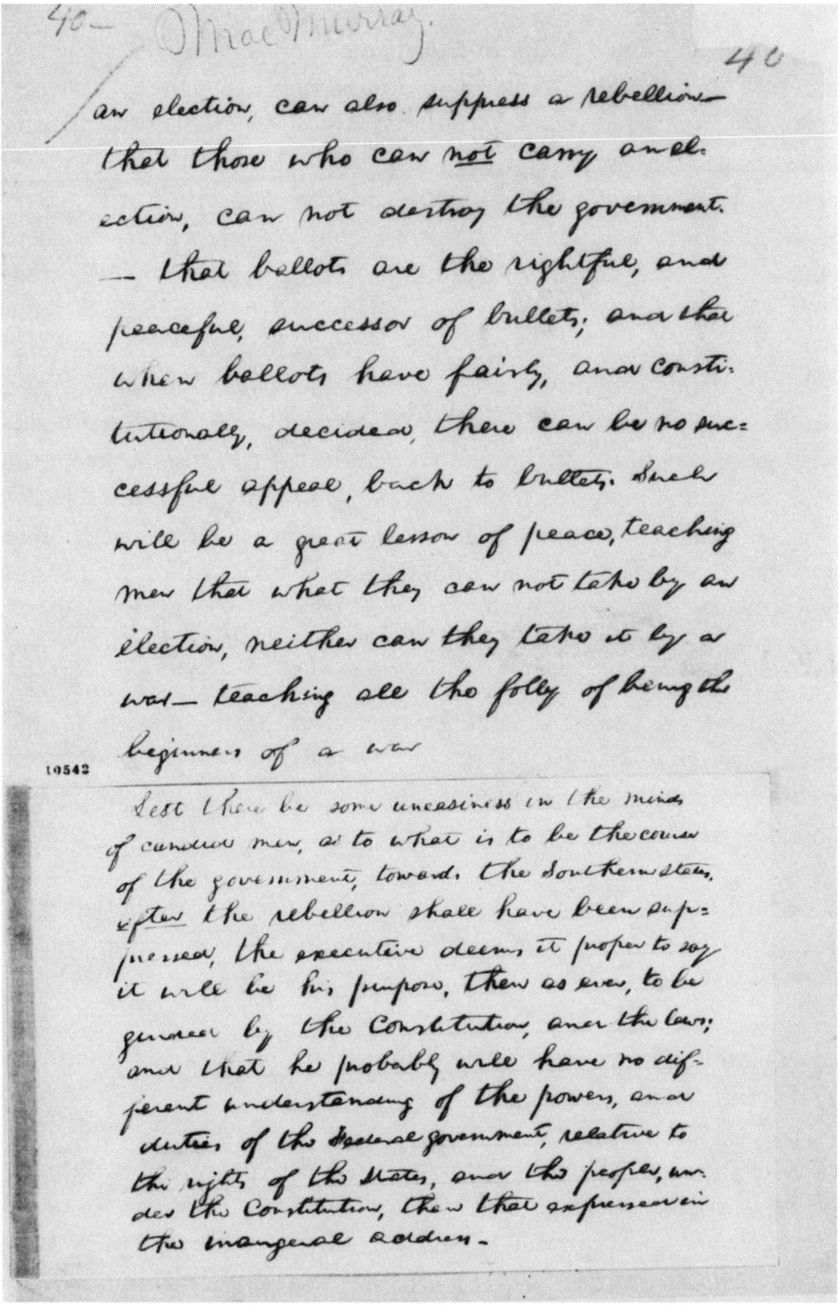

an election, can also suppress a rebellion—
that those who can not carry an election, can not destroy the government.
— that ballots are the rightful, and
peaceful, successor of bullets; and that
when ballots have fairly, and constitutionally, decided, there can be no successful appeal, back to bullets. Such
will be a great lesson of peace, teaching
men that what they can not take by an
election, neither can they take it by a
war— teaching all the folly of being the
beginners of a war

10542

lest there be some uneasiness in the minds
of candid men, as to what is to be the course
of the government, towards the southern states,
after the rebellion shall have been suppressed, the executive deems it proper to say
it will be his purpose, then as ever, to be
guided by the Constitution, and the laws;
and that he probably will have no different understanding of the powers, and
duties of the federal government, relative to
the rights of the states, and the people, under the Constitution, then that expressed in
the inaugeral address.

Figure 4-5. "MacMurray" here indicates that a typesetter by that name has been assigned to set the final page of Lincoln's handwritten manuscript of his Message. Note that the final paragraph of this draft is written on a slip that has been pasted onto the page. Library of Congress.

observe the disagreements over punctuation between the president and his editor. In fact, the battle of the commas with Defrees provides an unexpected window on Lincoln's distinctive practice. Comparing the handwritten with the printed copy produced from it makes it evident that Defrees regularly removed a large proportion of Lincoln's freely bestowed commas and that Lincoln accepted many of these changes, just as he accepted Defrees's careful corrections of his errant spelling and haphazard capitalization. But not infrequently, Lincoln put back into the printed text some of the commas that Defrees had removed from the manuscript version. On page four of the first printed draft, for example, one can tell by comparison with the handwritten manuscript that Defrees had removed seven commas from the text, and Lincoln put back only two. But doubtless much to Defrees's chagrin, Lincoln also introduced two *new* commas. This disposition to add commas the second time around, in fact, proves to be part of Lincoln's regular practice. On the very next page, he put back two more of the commas Defrees had removed and inserted five new ones (see Fig. 4-6).

One can get a sense of Lincoln's unconventional punctuation, and at the same time understand why an editor like Defrees might protest it, by considering some examples from this flurry of newly introduced commas on page five (shown here in brackets):

> This last would be a clear indication of *policy*, and would better enable the country to accept the evacuation of Fort Sumter[,] as a military *necessity*.

> . . . landing of the troops from the steamship Brooklyn[,] into Fort Pickens.

> The news itself was[,] that the officer commanding the Sabine . . .

> To now re-enforce Fort Pickens[,] before a crisis would be reached at Fort Sumter . . .

None of these commas is strictly necessary, and a responsible editor, who was only trying to bring the president's prose into conformity with recognized conventions, would hardly welcome any of them. But done would not be fully understood; that by many, it would be construed as a part of a *voluntary* policy; that at home, it would discourage the friends of the Union, embolden its adversaries, and go far to insure to the latter, a recognition of independence abroad; that, in fact, it would be our national destruction consummated. *This could not be allowed.* Starvation was not yet upon the garrison; and ere it would be reached, Fort Pickens might be re-enforced. This last would be a clear indication of *policy*, and would better enable the country to accept the evacuation of Fort Sumter, as a military *necessity*. An order was at once directed to be sent for the landing of the troops from the steamship Brooklyn, into Fort Pickens. This order could not go by land, but must take the longer and slower route by sea. The first return news from the order was received just one week before the fall of Fort Sumter. The news itself was, that the officer commanding the Sabine, to which vessel the troops had been transferred from the Brooklyn, acting upon some *quasi* armistice of the late administration, (and of the existence of which the present administration, up to the time the order was despatched, had only too vague and uncertain rumors to fix attention,) had refused to land the troops. To now re-enforce Fort Pickens, before a crisis would be reached at Fort

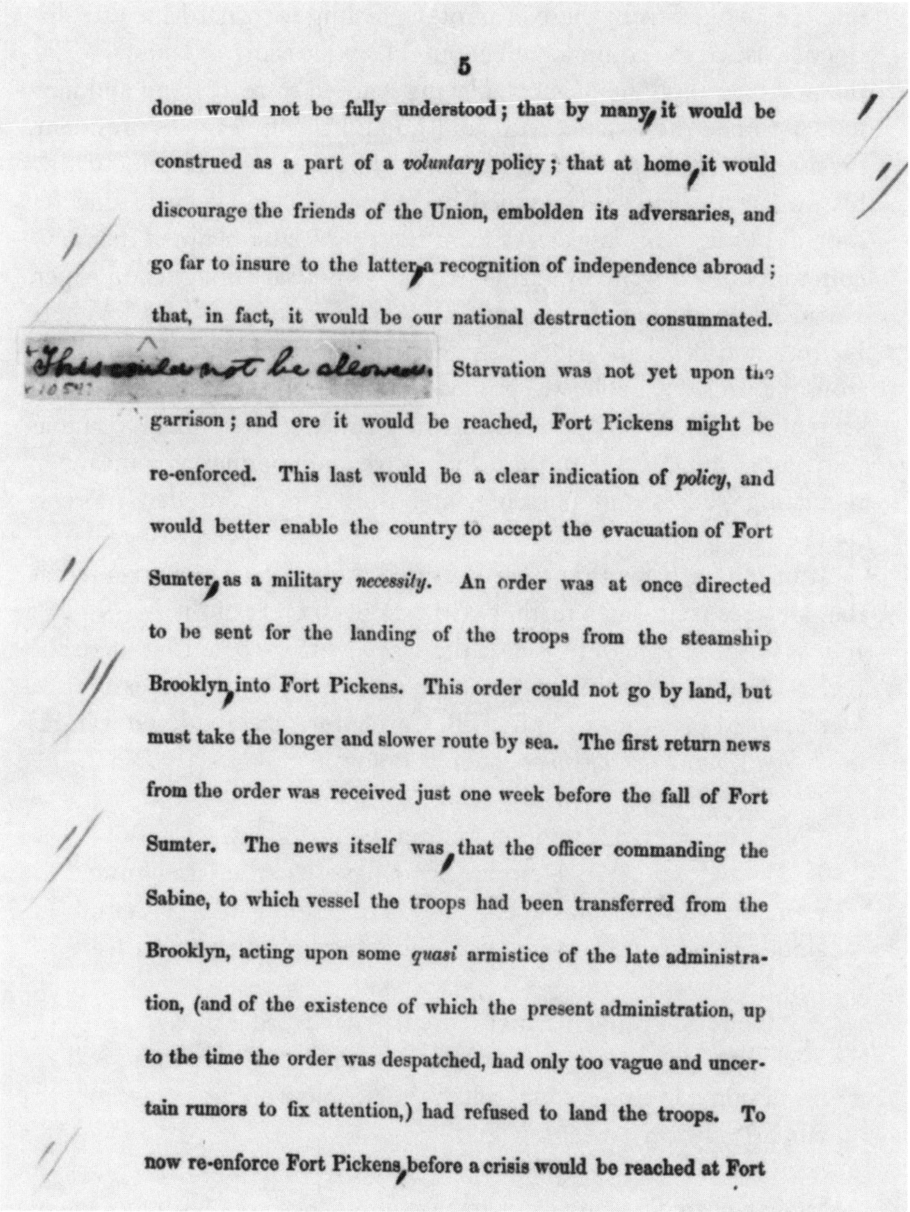

Figure 4-6. From the first printed draft of the Message. The marks in the margins indicate the location of commas Lincoln wants added to the text. The tab with the handwritten text ("This could not be allowed.") has been pasted over the previous text ("The administration hesitated.") as a revision. Library of Congress.

one can also get from these examples a feeling for what Lincoln's distinctive use of the comma is all about. His basic sense of language, like the poet's, is aural; he hears it. Having learned to read aloud and having continued the practice into adulthood, Lincoln, even as president, persisted in reading aloud to his friends. Such a man, in punctuating his own prose, is clearly guided by his ear and his keen feeling for cadence. One of his law clerks from the 1840s later claimed that Lincoln told him, "I write by ear. When I have got my thoughts on paper, I read it aloud, and if it sounds all right I just let it pass." Where Defrees consulted the rules of punctuation, which ultimately derive from the sense, Lincoln was guided by sound, the sound of the living sentence. His editor operated on the principle that where commas were concerned, less is more; Lincoln treated commas as a means of regulating pauses and phrasing, and thus considered that more is more.

It may have been after they had aired their differences on commas that Defrees ventured a further criticism of the text of the Message of July 4, namely, Lincoln's use of the word "sugar-coated" to describe the insidious way rebellion had been promoted by the secessionists. Defrees told the story to Francis B. Carpenter, who rendered it in his book *Six Months at the White House* as follows:

> "What is the matter now?" inquired the President.
>
> "Why," said Mr. Defrees, "you have used an undignified expression in the message;" and then, reading the paragraph aloud, he added, "I would alter the structure of that, if I were you."
>
> "Defrees," replied Mr. Lincoln, "that word expresses precisely my idea, and I am not going to change it. The time will never come in this country when the people won't know exactly what *sugar-coated* means!"

"Sugar-coated" is, in fact, a key word in Lincoln's Message. One of the things that makes the Message still interesting reading today is its author's incisive analysis of what secession was and what was threatened by it. Secession by a state from the Union was not a new idea, nor was the idea of a new confederation formed exclusively of slaveholding states. Nearly thirty years earlier, a slaveholding president, Andrew Jackson, in dealing with the attempt by Southern states to "nullify" federal tariff laws, had concluded knowingly that "the tariff was only the pretext and disunion or a Southern confederacy the real object—the next pretext will be the negro, or slavery question." The question was, what to do when states actually secede and declare themselves part of a new entity? Lincoln's predecessor, James Buchanan, viewed secession as unconstitutional and highly regrettable but claimed to possess no constitutional power to oppose it. If this could be described as the "hand-wringing" position, many others, including many of Lincoln's fellow Republicans, took the same view, but without the regret. This might be called the "good riddance" position. Lincoln, as we have seen, had an altogether different view of how the government should respond. It should resist, but it should choose its measures carefully, lest it be perceived either as provoking the seceders, on the one hand, or voluntarily yielding to their aggressive actions, on the other. Walking this line had proved excruciating for Lincoln, but a federal fort had at last been blatantly attacked, and the argument about whether there should be fighting was at an end.

But the next argument was crucial, for this would be about why the two sides were fighting, and what they were fighting for. Believing from the beginning that the stakes here were very high, Lincoln had said in his inaugural address that the whole idea of majority rule was at stake; whether the minority, by threatening to secede, could dictate to those who had been fairly elected. Here in his Message, he had insisted, as we have seen, that "more than the fate of these United States" was involved, and the fate of self-government was on the line. But it was one thing to make such grand claims and clearly another to offer arguments to back them up. In the final version, almost half of the Message is given over to Lincoln's analysis of these matters.

Characteristically, he begins with the meanings of words. Lincoln's intense interest in meanings was part of his early attraction for language, and it was an interest he had successfully pursued to great advantage in politics and at the bar. It is thus no accident that his discussion of secession begins as it does: "It might seem, at first thought, to be little difference whether the present movement at the South be called 'secession' or 'rebellion.' The movers, however, well understand the difference." What to call the activities, the leaders, and the institutions of secession was itself a delicate problem, for as Lincoln the lawyer knew, yielding to the other side's own terminology was to take a step in the direction of yielding to their premises. In the early part of his first draft he referred to "this supposed Federal government, under the name and style of 'The Confederate States of America,' " but this was eventually changed to "this illegal organization in the character of confederate States." Their actions he characterized a few lines later as an "attempt to destroy the Federal Union." Here at the opening of his analysis, he carefully refers to "the present movement at the South," whose promulgators he calls "the movers." More neutral and unyielding terms would be hard to imagine.

As with any argument or debate, Lincoln knew that much would depend on how the terms were defined. Of course, it mattered immensely whether what the Southern states had done constituted the exercise of a peaceful legal right—*secession*—or the perpetration of a violent unlawful act, *rebellion*. Lincoln's strategy was to begin by showing how rebellion had been sold by the "movers" to a law-abiding public as secession.

> At the beginning they knew they could never raise their treason to any respectable magnitude, by any name which implies *violation* of law. They knew their people possessed as much of moral sense, as much of devotion to law and order, and as much pride in, and reverence for, the history and government, of their common country, as any other civilized, and patriotic people. They knew they could make no advancement directly in the teeth of these strong, and noble sentiments.

This is designed, of course, to take the people themselves off the hook, and while Lincoln may have been maximizing the degree of deception being practiced for the sake of his argument, he sincerely believed at this time (albeit mistakenly) that a large proportion of Southerners were still basically loyal to the Union.

But how could such a class of people be persuaded to support "an attempt to destroy the Federal Union"? By being hoodwinked, of course.

> Accordingly they [the movers] commenced by an insidious debauching of the public morals. They invented a single ingenious sophism which, if conceded, was followed by perfectly logical steps through all the incidents to the complete destruction of the Union_ The sophism itself was and is, that any State

of the Union may, consistently with the national constitution, and therefore lawfully and peacefully, withdraw from the Union, without the consent of the Union, or of any other state.

What was for the Southerners an all-important principle—the natural right of revolution cited in the Declaration of Independence—is given short shrift: "The little disguise that the supposed right is to be exercised only for just cause, themselves to be sole judge of it's justice, is too thin to merit any notice_"

This is where the importance of "sugar-coated" comes in. Lincoln was certainly aware that his argument, while it would wear well in the North, would never convince any large number of Southerners. In the South, where the secession principle had been enunciated by Jefferson and Madison in the founding generation, it had been kept alive by the threats of the New England states during the hated Federal Embargo, and for most of the intervening years by the speeches and writings of John C. Calhoun. But Lincoln was not trying to persuade true secessionists, who, as he well knew, had already made up their minds. He was attempting to show Northern and border state loyalists how decent, law-abiding Southern citizens could be persuaded, in overwhelming numbers, to take up arms and threaten to aid in the destruction of their own government. It was, he said, because they had not realized what they were swallowing.

> With rebellion thus sugar-coated, they [the movers] have been drugging the public mind of their section for more than thirty years; and, until at length, they have brought many good men to a willingness to take up arms against the Government the day *after* some assemblage of men have enacted the farcical pretence of taking their state out of the Union, who could have been brought to no such thing the day *before*.

Defrees thought "sugar-coated" undignified, but Lincoln realized instinctively not only that it could be readily understood, but that it was more forceful than the obvious alternatives, such as "disguised" or "concealed." By using "sugar-coated," he conveys figuratively the idea of unwittingly internalizing something harmful, of being surreptitiously "drugged." This is how law-abiding people could be made to support rebellion. In fact, Lincoln could not readily substitute another word for "sugar-coated" without either changing or mixing his metaphor of *drugging the public mind.*

❧

DEFREES MAY HAVE LOST this particular appeal, but he told biographer Holland that his protests about Lincoln's excessive punctuation eventually bore fruit: "At other times he would tell me that he would furnish the words—and I might put the periods to suit." But zealous as he was about protecting the language of his text, Lincoln didn't furnish all the words of the Message of July 4. As he had done with the First Inaugural, he sought the advice of his secretary of state. Though there was a certain amount of awkwardness about Seward's serving in the cabinet of a man he considered less qualified and less deserving of the presidency than himself, Lincoln genuinely respected Seward and worked at gaining his confidence and approval. Eventually successful in this effort, Lincoln did not find it easy at first, as the exchange about whether the administration had a policy illustrates. Nonetheless, he persisted. Even as Seward was trying, on the day of the inauguration, to back out of his cabinet at the last minute and embarrass him, Lincoln followed Seward's advice about altering the tone of his First Inaugural. Two months later, Lincoln returned the favor by skillfully toning down an intemperate and potentially disastrous letter Seward had written instructing the U.S. minister to Great Britain, Charles Francis Adams. Now, having weathered various differences and embarrassments over the handling of Fort Sumter and the initiation of hostilities, the president again approached the secretary of state for advice on his all-important Message to Congress.

The copy of the second printed draft of the Message that contains Seward's suggested changes is in the Lincoln papers, enabling us to see what he proposed and what Lincoln accepted. As with the First Inaugural, most of Seward's suggestions were aimed at softening the expression and eliminating potential problems. A good example of the latter is his recommending that mention of the blockade of Southern ports—deemed a necessity by the administration but thoroughly at odds with international law—be dropped. Lincoln agreed. Perhaps the best example of a Seward recommendation for toning down the language comes in Lincoln's discussion of a proposal that the slaveholding border states should observe a policy of "armed neutrality." Lincoln had attacked this idea as "disunion consummated" and added: "and while they may not all be traitors who have favored it, the thing is, in fact, treason in disguise."

"Treason" and "traitors" were strong words, especially when applied to citizens in states that were still loyal. Seward didn't disagree with the description, but he suggested a more tactful way to put it: "and while very many who have favored it are loyal citizens it is nevertheless treason in effect." Lincoln accepted this change, though he added one word, "doubtless," and five commas. In the final version printed in the *Congressional Globe Appendix*, Defrees succeeded in eliminating two of these commas, and the passage was subsequently softened even further: "and while very many who have favored it are doubtless loyal citizens, it is, nevertheless, very injurious in effect."

While Seward's role in drafting the Message to Congress of July 4, 1861, was much the same as it had been with the First Inaugural, and while his suggestions were mostly followed, they did not have nearly as much effect on the overall character of the document. Seward's admonitions about the tone of the First Inaugural had chastened Lincoln and caused him to reconsider. His decision to modify his defiant ending and follow instead the conciliatory path pointed out by Seward had a major impact on his address and the way it was received. With the Message, the secretary had less to criticize and more to approve.

⁓

The Message of July 4, 1861, when finished and delivered to Congress, was a substantial and wide-ranging document that not only reported on events and developments relating to the immediate crisis but delved deeply into constitutional and historical questions, examined the claims of proponents of secession, and offered, as with the suspension of habeas corpus, justifications of the government's actions. Such a comprehensive message may have been Lincoln's intention all along, but it is possible that his original plan was for a more compact, businesslike treatment, which simply expanded as he worked on it. The evidence of the manuscripts and printed drafts is not conclusive either way, but traces of the gradual evolution of the document throw light on an important aspect of the writer's task that figures in every composition, namely, the search for a suitable ending.

Every written work—whether it be a letter, a story, a poem, an essay, a brief, a proclamation, or a presidential message—is, as a practical matter, an effort to arrive at a point of completion. If the beginning is crucial to success, the note upon which the writer takes leave of the reader is at least as important, if not more. One of the things Lincoln's many drafts shed light on is his quest for the most appropriate ending.

It is possible that he first contemplated concluding the Message at the end of the twenty-three-page draft, which rounds off the critical exposé of the effort by Southern extremists to stealthily drug their constituents with their "sugar-coated" sophism.

> These politicians are suttle and profound on the rights of minorities, ever elevating them above the rights of majorities_ The dread of their existence is that power which made the constitution, and speaks from the preamble, calling itself "We, the People."

But the manuscript shows that, having reached this point, he still had much that he wanted to impart, and a very substantial addition ensues. One of the things shown by the contents of the Message, as mentioned in the previous chapter, is that the First Inaugural had deliberately avoided responding to the arguments and line of reasoning with which secession was then being justified. Presumably Lincoln passed up this opportunity in the belief that it was better, at that point, not to argue but rather to emphasize how he saw his duty as president and what his oath required. Now the situation was otherwise. A forbearing government, for its pains, had been violently attacked, and the time was now propitious for showing why what had been promoted as lawful "secession" was nothing less than treasonous "rebellion."

Lincoln's treatment of the legal, constitutional, and historical issues is forceful and energetic. The advocates of secession, he says, have argued "that any State of the Union may, consistently with the national constitution, and therefore lawfully and peacefully, withdraw from the Union, without the consent of the Union, or of any other state." This he vigorously disputes on several grounds.

Historically, he insists, this is spurious. "The Union is older than any of the states; and, in fact, it created them, as states." Contrary to the rule that nothing in law should lead "to unjust, or absurd consequences," secession would permit states on whom the government has spent millions of dollars to walk away free and clear. Again, the principle on which secession works, which would allow further secessions for "unjust object[s]," "is one of disintegration, and upon which no government can possibly endure." Lincoln questions the extent of "popular sentiment" that actively supports secession. He argues that the "free institutions we enjoy, have developed the powers, and improved the condition of our whole people," and that the government that made all this possible is the one being "broken up" by secession. The secession faction has adopted a Declaration of Independence and a constitution that deviate from the venerated documents created by the founders. "Why?" asks Lincoln. "Why this deliberate pressing out of view, the rights of men, and the authority of the people?"

This is the cue for one of the most memorable passages in the Message, and one that, from its similarity to what Lincoln's secretaries reported hearing, may well have been drafted in advance (Fig. 4-7):

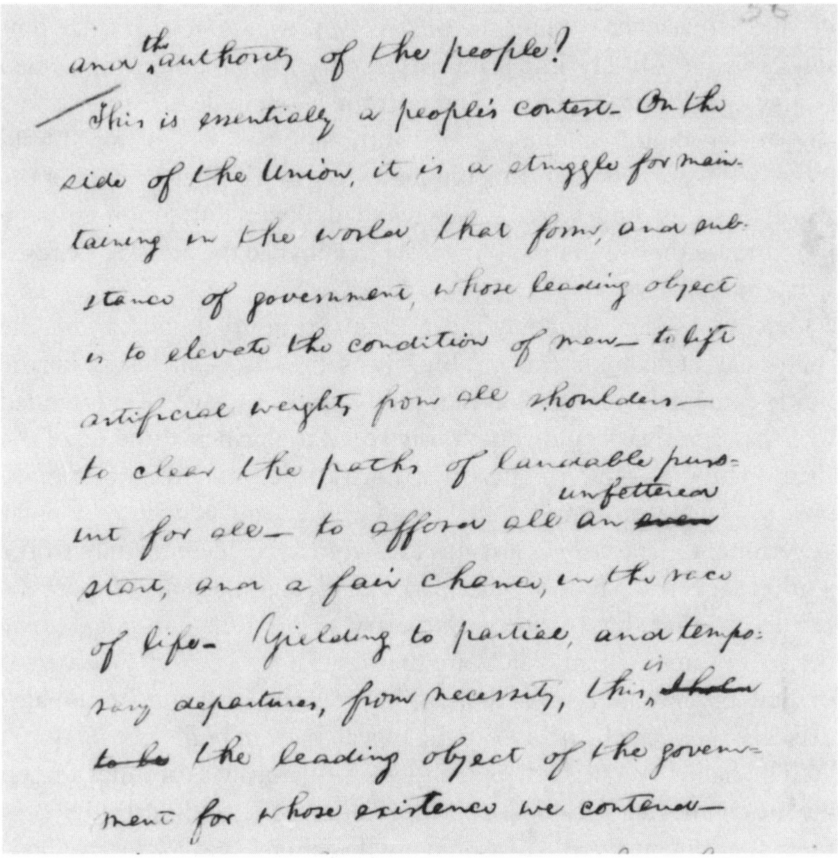

Figure 4-7. Handwritten draft of a famous passage in the Message showing Lincoln's revisions. Library of Congress.

> This is essentially a people's contest— On the side of the Union, it is a struggle for maintaining in the world, that form, and substance of government, whose leading object is to elevate the condition of men—to lift artificial weights from all shoulders—to clear the paths of laudable pursuit for all—to afford all an even start, and a fair chance, in the race of life— Yielding to partial, and temporary departures, from necessity, this I hold to be the leading object of the government for whose existence we contend—

This passage was surely designed to enlist the sympathies and loyalties of ordinary citizens by underscoring the benevolent and progressive character of popular government, which was under attack and whose existence was at risk. In a document that, by design, will make no direct reference to the issue of slavery, this passage also fairly pulsates with antislavery implications: *elevating* the condition of human beings and lifting *artificial* weights from *all* shoulders. Except for a slight rewording to eliminate a use of the first person ("is" for "I hold to be"), the only revision Lincoln made to this passage—changing the word "even" to "unfettered"—suggests a deliberate intention not only to reinforce the alliteration but subtly to enhance the antislavery resonance as well.

Such a passage, in sounding a thematic flourish and raising the rhetorical pitch, could conceivably have served as a conclusion for the newly extended Message, but that honor seems to have been intended for a passage that would consciously recall the principal theme of the First Inaugural—the sanctity of majority rule—and restate it more vividly. Having proven that they could *establish* and *administer* popular government, Americans must now, Lincoln says, "demonstrate to the world that those who can fairly carry an election, can also suppress a rebellion—that those who can *not* carry an election, can not destroy the government,—that ballots are the rightful, and peaceful, successor of bullets; and that when ballots have fairly, and constitutionally, decided, there can be no successful appeal, back to bullets."

The ballots-versus-bullets antithesis is obviously a carefully chosen mnemonic device designed to capture attention and imprint itself in the reader's memory, and he would use it again two years later in a public letter. In retrospect, we can readily see that Lincoln had an eye and an ear for dramatic images to help carry his message. He had succeeded to perfection in his "House Divided" speech in 1858, where he used a well-known biblical verse—"A house divided against itself cannot stand"—to create an image for the divisive effect of slavery on American society. In fact, many of his closest associates thought the image had been *too* successful and, having been turned into a rallying cry for the opposition, was responsible for the Republican defeat. Again, the biblical phrase with which he had long planned to end his First Inaugural—"Shall it be peace or a sword?"—would have indicated his readiness to meet the Southern challenge decisively, but he had been persuaded to abandon it at the last minute in favor of more conciliatory imagery.

Even though "ballots" seems an apt symbol for the democratic process and "bullets" for rebellion, the image proved hard to frame in a few words, and Lincoln's formulation lacks the compact symmetry of a really memorable antithesis. If it had been originally intended as the concluding note for the Message, it did not long remain so. Before sending his handwritten manuscript off to the printer, he pasted a slip containing an additional paragraph onto the last sheet (see Fig. 4-5 above). That it was written on a separate slip and not on the sheet itself (where there was still ample room) suggests that this paragraph, like "Random 6," may have been a note made in advance of composition. In tone and in vividness, this paragraph is a decided comedown from the ballots-versus-bullets passage and, in fact, sounds something like an afterthought. This makes one ask why Lincoln would have considered deploying it in so strategic a location. The answer may well be that he felt the need to soften the tone somewhat, and he wanted to end, as this paragraph does, by referring his readers directly back to the First Inaugural.

> Lest there be some uneasiness in the minds of candid men, as to what is to be the course of the government, towards the Southern states, *after* the rebellion shall have been suppressed, the executive deems it proper to say it will be his purpose, then as ever, to be guided by the Constitution, and the laws; and that he probably will have no different understanding of the powers, and duties of the Federal government, relative to the rights of the states, and the people, under the Constitution, than that expressed in the inaugeral address_

This is the form the conclusion took when Lincoln sent his handwritten manuscript off to be set in type, but he was still not satisfied with his ending. As with the First Inaugural, the issue most on his mind in the long paragraph he added in the next draft was conciliation. He wanted to stress that in resisting secession he was trying to "preserve the government," to furnish loyal citizens the government they were entitled to and that he had "no right to withhold." In so doing, there wasn't "any coercion, any conquest, or any subjugation, which any honest man should regret." Employing the "war-power, in defence of the government," was a duty, done with regret. Interestingly, the personal element, which is always lurking in such protestations, comes frankly into the foreground. Referring to himself, Lincoln writes: "As a private citizen, he [the executive] could not have consented that these institutions shall perish; much less could he, in betrayal of so vast, and so sacred a trust, as these free people had confided to him." He has done his duty, and Congress and the country must now do theirs.

The revised Message receives, at the end of this handwritten addition to the first printed draft, a one-sentence concluding paragraph, an ending which thereafter would not change (Fig. 4-8):

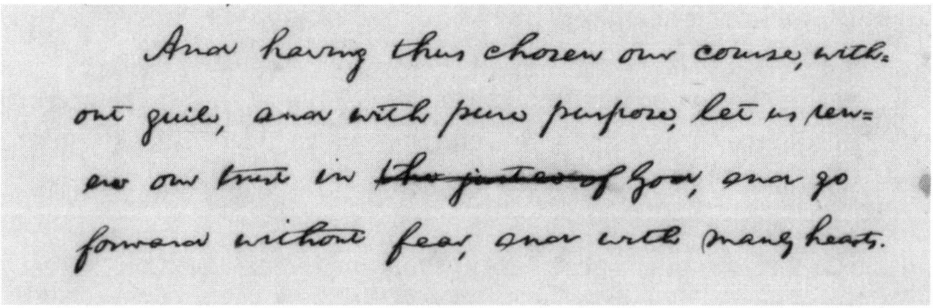

And having thus chosen our course, without guile, and with pure purpose, let us renew our trust in ~~the justice of~~ God, and go forward without fear, and with manly hearts.

Figure 4-8. Handwritten text of the final paragraph of Lincoln's message. Library of Congress.

Coming, as it does, at the end of a long process of earnest, and even anguished, drafting, this brief conclusion could easily be considered as little more than a perfunctory flourish, with its obligatory references to noble motives and to God. Certainly its elements are conventional, but its remarkable brevity is not, and there are several indications that the ending, though brief, is thoughtfully set down. For one thing, being privy to Lincoln's striking out the part about the "justice" of God gives us perhaps the first glimmering of what would become an obsessive attempt by Lincoln to fathom the part that Providence was to play in the war. His apparent reluctance here to claim the justice of God for his cause, which he emphatically believes is just, is a telling discrimination. It may reflect a judgment that such a claim is simply unseemly, but it may also prefigure the sense that he would try to enunciate four years later—that divine justice proceeds independently of our hopes and expectations.

The new conclusion acknowledges very clearly that the nation's courage is to be tested. Courage is something that can't be faked and is sustained by sincere belief—"without guile, and with pure purpose." Taking the same form, Lincoln's expression for the way to meet that test—"without fear, and with manly hearts"—would not pass muster in our gender-conscious era, but in his own time it would have had a strong appeal. Manliness invoked the age-old role and responsibility of men to fight when their community was threatened, and Lincoln's phrase further invoked the comradely spirit in which that responsibility was properly met—readily and willingly. Death and sacrifice are not mentioned specifically, but they hover in the background and are silently acknowledged in the references to fear and manliness. "Without fear, and with manly hearts" is thus a kind of abbreviated antithesis that means something like: Let us have the courage to master our fear of death and rise to our responsibilities.

That this was not a typical nineteenth-century rousing exhortation is noticeable now and would have been even more obvious then, but precisely in not being such, Lincoln's conclusion makes a telling statement. This was to be no ordinary war, and giving voice to the conventional national bravado was somehow inappropriate. The adversary to be confronted was not a foreign invader but the nation's own errant citizens, in some cases one's own brothers. At such a time, what was needed was courage, confidence, and determination.

❧

ON JULY 3, the day before the Congress reconvened and the Message would be read aloud to the legislators, the president's chief aide, John G. Nicolay, wrote to his fiancée in Illinois, "Since my return from Illinois [on June 18], the President has been engaged almost constantly in writing his message, and has refused to receive any calls whatever, either of friendship or business, except from members of the Cabinet, or high officials." Clearly, Lincoln had determined that, at a time when the country was in danger of coming apart and the very survival of the government was at stake, the most important thing he could do was to retreat into seclusion and write—to draft and revise and so refine his Message that the actions and proposals of the government would be on the soundest possible footing and would be embraced by the Congress and by the country at large. Less than two weeks before it was due to be submitted, the president read his still unfinished draft to the diplomat John Lothrop Motley, who wrote to his wife that it impressed him "very favourably." With the exception of a few expressions, it was not only highly commendable in spirit, but written with considerable untaught grace and power." On the night before it was submitted to Congress, Lincoln read the finished product aloud to Orville H. Browning, who happened to be in the White House at the time. Browning wrote in his diary that it was "an able state paper and will fully meet the expectations of the Country."

Lincoln's Message was, in fact, generally well received. For a majority of loyalists, who deplored the attack on American forces and supported armed federal resistance, the substance of the Message as reported in the newspapers was politically acceptable and probably reassuring. It may be doubted that a large proportion of the reading public went so far as to peruse the entire Message, some sixty-four hundred words, though many newspapers would have printed either the whole or long excepts from it, and many in that day would have routinely read any presidential message.

One who did read it through, and with keen satisfaction, was the discriminating Philadelphia lawyer and diarist Sidney George Fisher. His assessment is notable in its favorable judgments of things Lincoln most wanted to accomplish and communicate:

> It is wholly free from egotism or desire to produce an effect, but is earnest & candid. It shows, moreover, remarkable power of thought & argument. The reflections are eminently just and the right of secession is treated in a manner at once clear, comprehensive and original. It contains the following happy definition of a sovereign state, 'a political community without a political superior,' which is so terse & complete, that it deserves a place in the science of politics.

Some of the editorial commentary was very encouraging. The reaction of the nationally distributed *Harper's Weekly* could hardly have been more gratifying to a writer:

> While many Presidents of many parties would have endeavored to save the Government by force of arms, not all Presidents would so clearly comprehend or so simply state what the Government was that they were saving. This Government was founded upon the rights of man; and for the first time in long years the President recognizes that fact. Presidents' messages for many years have been labored defenses of an oligarchical and aristocratic administration of the Government. At length there is a people's President, in no mean sense; and the Government of the United States is restored to its original principles. It is not a matter of party, but of patriotic congratulation.

While the Message was generally well received, its silence on the subject of slavery did not go unnoticed. The black abolitionist Frederick Douglass printed a long section from it in his paper *Douglass' Monthly*, but he did not disguise his disappointment.

> In the late Message of our honest President, which purports to give an honest history of our present difficulties, no mention is, at all, made of slavery. Any one reading that document, with no previous knowledge of the United States, would never dream from any thing there written that we have a slaveholding war waged upon the Government, determined to overthrow it, or so to reconstruct it as to make it the instrument of extending the slave system and enlarging its powers. . . . The proclamation goes forth at the head of all our armies, assuring the slaveholding rebels that slavery shall receive no detriment from our arms.

But as Douglass himself would later realize, this was precisely the reaction Lincoln was looking for. Abolitionist discontent with this aspect of his Message was proof, of a sort, that Lincoln's purpose and measures were sharply focused on preserving the Union and constitutional democracy. This singleness of purpose would reassure the wavering border states and the many loyal but suspicious Democrats, who wanted no part of a Republican war to destroy slavery.

While not one of the most famous or most familiar of Lincoln's presidential writings, the July 4 Message to Congress was nonetheless one of his most important in establishing his stature as a stand-up leader and a man to be reckoned with. As we have seen, producing this document required a massive expenditure of time and energy, exemplifying Lincoln's confidence in his own ability to accomplish important ends through his writing. This is reflected in the judgment of one of the notable twentieth-century Lincoln scholars, James G. Randall, who wrote: "The message which Lincoln presented to the called session of Congress stands as one of his most elaborate and carefully prepared papers. It comprised a history of events, a report of stewardship, a constitutional argument, and an exalted commentary on fundamentals." Such a judgment would require the perspective of history, but for some of the most discriminating contemporary readers, there was, at least, a realization that this Message was the product of an able mind. George William Curtis, the editor of *Harper's Weekly* and almost certainly the writer of the editorial quoted above, confessed to a friend that, as a result of the Message, he saw the president in a new light: "I can forgive the jokes and the big hands, and the inability to make bows. Some of us who doubted were wrong."

CHAPTER FIVE

Proclaiming Emancipation

NOTHING THAT ABRAHAM LINCOLN would write as president would be more celebrated or considered more important by his contemporaries than the Emancipation Proclamation of January 1, 1863. Even Frederick Douglass, the black abolitionist, who up to that time had been one of the president's harshest critics, greeted the proclamation as "the greatest event of our nation's history." Lincoln himself almost certainly considered it his most consequential effort, for in the final year of his presidency he reportedly described it as *"the central act of my administration."* Nor would this prove overly optimistic. Since his assassination in 1865, Lincoln's worldwide reputation as the Great Emancipator has been the cornerstone of a pervasive legend. Granted that legends are only shorthand versions of history that emphasize symbolism and simplicity at the expense of complexity and fact, Lincoln's central role in the momentous ending of slavery in the United States is nonetheless impossible to ignore. A judicious historian has declared the Emancipation Proclamation "perhaps the greatest document of social reform in American history."

And yet the text of the Emancipation Proclamation is entirely unlike Lincoln's other famous writings. Without eloquence, almost entirely devoid of rhetorical ornament, and lacking even the usual qualities of Lincoln's prose, its legalistic language is conspicuously unquotable, being utterly utilitarian both in its terminology and its mode of address. The culminating sentence is all too representative:

And by virtue of the power, and for the purpose aforesaid, I do order and declare that all persons held as slaves within said designated States, and parts of States, are, and henceforward shall be free; and that the Executive government of the United States, including the military and naval authorities thereof, will recognize and maintain the freedom of said persons.

If emancipating slaves was a noble undertaking, it is scarcely evident in the language of this brief proclamation. Writing in 1948, the historian Richard Hofstadter famously observed that Lincoln's celebrated proclamation "had all the moral grandeur of a bill of lading."

The mundane character of the Emancipation Proclamation has contributed to a steadily more skeptical view of both the practical effects of the document itself and the motivation of its author. It has become commonplace, if not obligatory, for historians to point out that Lincoln's proclamation did not immediately unshackle a single slave, while it purposely withheld emancipation from tens of thousands still in bondage. These were the slaves held in states that remained loyal, the border states, and in certain pacified parts of rebellious states, which areas, in the language of the proclamation, "are, for the present, left precisely as if this proclamation were not issued." What, skeptics might well ask, does such selective liberation and soulless prose say about the humanitarian purposes of the Great Emancipator?

These doubts about Lincoln's language and intentions are in accord with a more general questioning in our own time of his antislavery credentials. It is certainly true that Lincoln was not an abolitionist, though the legend that features the Great Emancipator often manages to convey the impression that he was. While he stoutly insisted in his famous debates with Stephen A. Douglas in the 1850s that slavery was wrong and that the Negro, being human, was indeed included in Jefferson's declaration that "all men are created equal," he openly acknowledged in the same speeches that he was not in favor of making either voters or jurors of the free blacks of Illinois. Because slavery where it already existed was protected by the Constitution, he never advocated its abolition, and as we have already seen, he had been at pains to say two years earlier in his inaugural address that he had "no purpose, directly or indirectly, to interfere with the institution of slavery in the States where it exists. I believe I have no right to do so, and I have no inclination to do so."

Especially from the perspective of the second half of the twentieth century, which witnessed the stunning breakthrough of the civil rights movement, and more especially to black Americans, Lincoln's positions and declarations on slavery and race have appeared less and less compelling. "Blacks have no reason to feel grateful to Abraham Lincoln," wrote Julius Lester in 1968. "How come it took him two whole years to free the slaves? His pen was sitting on his desk the whole time. All he had to do was get up one morning and say, 'Doggonit? I think I'm gon' free the slaves today.'" A fair question, to which Don E. Fehrenbacher knowingly replied, "But *which* morning? That turned out to be the real question."

❧

THE STORY OF THE Emancipation Proclamation is many-faceted and anything but straightforward. Fortunately, the complex weave of interrelated factors and events that led up to the signing of the document on January 1, 1863, has been comprehensively presented and analyzed in a recent book by Allen C. Guelzo, *Lincoln's Emancipation Proclamation,* by far the most thorough and illuminating study of its kind. The reader who wishes to pursue this story in all its complexity will find no better guide. Here, where our primary concern is with Lincoln's writing and the role it played in his presidency, the focus is much narrower, but it seems necessary nonetheless to review certain basic issues involving Lincoln, race, and slavery.

What, to begin with, were Lincoln's attitudes toward slavery and what had he proposed, as a politician, should be done about it? Though the historical record has always been reasonably clear, the Great Emancipator legend has had a decidedly distorting effect. It is therefore useful, in considering the circumstances behind the writing of the Emancipation Proclamation, to begin by distinguishing Lincoln from the abolitionists, those who openly advocated the abolition of slavery. First, Lincoln was always keenly aware that slavery, though morally wrong in his eyes, was sanctioned by law, and he had frequently acknowledged that the rights of slave owners, both to retain their slaves and to have runaways returned, were guaranteed in the Constitution. Before the outbreak of civil war, he advocated nothing that would directly challenge those rights. This position sharply distinguished him from the abolitionists, many of whom were actively involved in supporting fugitive slaves, and all of whom viewed returning them as unconscionable, whatever the Constitution or the Compromise of 1850 might dictate. Lincoln, by contrast, never put his antipathy for slavery ahead of his allegiance to the Constitution. He admitted privately that he hated to see slaves "hunted down, and caught, and carried back to their stripes," but he classed himself in 1855 with "the great body of the Northern people [who] do crucify their feelings, in order to maintain their loyalty to the constitution and the Union." His public support of the Fugitive Slave Law moved the implacable abolitionist Wendell Phillips to label him "the Slave Hound of Illinois."

Perhaps in even starker contrast to most abolitionists, Lincoln did not believe that slaveholders were inherently evil. He argued, rather, that they were, like their Northern counterparts, merely products of their environment. "I have no prejudice against the Southern people," he declared in 1854. "They are just what we would be in their situation. If slavery did not now exist amongst them, they would not introduce it. If it did now exist amongst us, we should not instantly give it up." In fact, Lincoln was willing to go even further: "I surely will not blame them for not doing what I should not know how to do myself. If all earthly power were given me, I should not know what to do, as to the existing institution."

These candid protestations and admissions preceded the Emancipation Proclamation by nearly ten years, but they are evidence of a view of human behavior that was on display even earlier. In the Temperance speech of 1842, which was glimpsed in an earlier chapter, Lincoln weighed in against heavy-handed reformers in a way that has clear implications for slavery and its reform. The speech took, for its time, a startlingly sympathetic view of drunkards, picturing them mainly as unfortunates, whose addiction had deprived them of the ability to govern their own behavior. He praised the efforts of the Washingtonians, the society of reformed drunkards whose members were actively helping fellow sufferers, and he came down hard on the those he called the "old reformers" for their lack of charity and their blindness to what makes people willing and able to change.

> Another error, as it seems to me, into which the old reformers fell, was the position that all habitual drunkards were utterly incorrigible, and therefore, must be turned adrift, and damned without remedy, in order that the grace of temperance might abound to the temperate *then*, and to all mankind some hundred

years *thereafter.* There is in this something so repugnant to humanity, so uncharitable, so cold-blooded and feelingless, that it never did, nor ever can enlist the enthusiasm of a popular cause.

By an obvious analogy, the abolitionist approach to the problem of slavery was like that of the "old reformers," calculated to turn slave owners adrift and damn them without remedy. For Lincoln, such a self-righteous and uncharitable approach not only was inhumane, but it had, for a politician in a democratic society, a fatal flaw: it could never earn widespread popular support. This last point says much, for enlisting popular support for a cause was the guiding star of Lincoln's political philosophy.

All of this helps to explain why his first efforts as president were directed toward conciliation, which meant preserving the Union, slavery and all. This put him at odds with his abolitionist allies, some of whom, like Horace Greeley, were content to let the South secede, and others, such as Senator Charles Sumner, who urged the earliest possible resort to a general emancipation. Once the fighting began, Lincoln worked assiduously to keep the four border states, where slavery was alive and well, from joining the Confederacy. This meant giving assurances that the property rights of slaveholders in Delaware, Maryland, Kentucky, and Missouri would be respected. When his military commander in Missouri, General John C. Frémont, declared the emancipation of slaves owned by those in resistance to the federal government, Lincoln moved quickly to countermand this order and thus quiet the fears of loyal (or neutral) slaveholders in Kentucky, where the reaction was immediate. "I think to lose Kentucky is nearly the same as to lose the whole game," he wrote to his friend Orville H. Browning. "Kentucky gone, we can not hold Missouri, nor, as I think, Maryland. These all against us, and the job on our hands is too large for us. We would as well consent to separation at once, including the surrender of this capitol." Such a conciliatory strategy was, of course, anathema to abolitionists and to others who favored a more vigorous prosecution of the war.

The border states figured prominently in another aspect of the president's strategy for dealing with slavery—compensation. In the second year of the war, when it was clear that a quick conclusion to the conflict was not forthcoming, Lincoln began to argue that, as an

alternative to waging war, it would be cheaper for the government simply to buy the slaves from their masters. Moreover, he was convinced
that if the border states agreed to gradual and compensated emancipation, the South would see the futility of its rebellion and capitulate.
Much to Lincoln's chagrin, this pilot program kindled little interest in
the border states. Meanwhile, the idea of compensating slave owners
infuriated the abolitionists. When Lincoln went so far as to propose, in
his annual message of December 1862, an amendment to the Constitution that would authorize a federal buyout of slavery, the exasperated
editors of the abolitionist journal the *Liberator* called the proposal
"something more deplorable than lack of common sense; it closely
borders upon hopeless lunacy."

But if abolitionists deplored Lincoln's conciliatory treatment of
slaveholding and slaveholders, they had equal contempt for his efforts
to colonize free blacks outside the country. During the first two years
of his presidency, Lincoln explored several schemes to promote the
voluntary emigration of blacks, for which Congress duly appropriated
funds. Believing that a biracial society was inherently discriminatory,
Lincoln argued that blacks would be better off in a place where they
constituted a majority and could live on terms of equality. To a group
of black leaders he had invited to the White House in August 1862, he
reportedly said:

> Your race are suffering, in my judgment, the greatest wrong
> inflicted on any people. But even when you cease to be slaves,
> you are yet far removed from being placed on an equality with
> the white race. You are cut off from many of the advantages
> which the other race enjoy. The aspiration of men is to enjoy
> equality with the best when free, but on this broad continent,
> not a single man of your race is made the equal of a single man
> of ours.

This, he urged, was simply "a fact with which we have to deal," and
he pleaded for their endorsement of an experimental plan to colonize
at government expense a small group of free blacks in a location in
Central America. But free blacks, by and large, were no more interested in colonization than the border states were in compensation, and
Lincoln's considerable exertions in both of these areas went for
naught. Or did they?

❧

ONE INTERPRETATION OF LINCOLN'S hapless ventures with conciliation, compensation, and colonization is that he was simply floun-
dering, that these were, at bottom, unworkable ideas that had almost no
popular backing and, as he should have known, were bound to fail. This
interpretation is reinforced by Lincoln's previous history of public support for colonization and his obviously sincere belief that loyal, law-
abiding citizens should not be deprived of their property, much less
their livelihood, without compensation. There is little doubt that this
was the way Lincoln's efforts appeared at the time to an influential portion of the Northern public, particularly to the critics in his own party
who saw this ineffective grappling as being of a piece with his inept
handling of military affairs. Not only firebrand Radicals like Ohio
senator Benjamin Wade and Pennsylvania congressman Thaddeus
Stevens, but relatively sympathetic Republicans like Senators Charles
Sumner and Lyman Trumbull would go to their graves thinking that
Lincoln's presidential maneuverings, though ultimately successful,
were inept and put the country through a torturous and more lengthy
ordeal than was necessary. Emancipation was clearly the right way to
defeat the rebels, according to this view, but the president wasted too
many mornings before deciding to pick up his pen and proclaim it.

But such a position assumes that Lincoln's critics had a better grasp
of the overall situation, something that the passage of time and the
perspective of hindsight have not convincingly borne out. On the contrary, the view that has emerged and to a large degree prevailed in subsequent historiography is that Lincoln's feel for public opinion—what
it would and would not support, and how it might be brought to accept
unpopular measures such as emancipation and the use of black soldiers—was extraordinarily acute and that it successfully guided the
timing of his most crucial decisions as president. "There had been
enough Republicans to win the presidential election," wrote Fehrenbacher, "but there were not enough to win the war. They needed help
from Northern Democrats and border-state loyalists, who were willing to fight for the Union, but not for abolition. A premature effort at
emancipation might alienate enough support to make victory impossible." Thus, trying out alternative schemes served to demonstrate that
he was trying to avoid outright and uncompensated emancipation if
possible, while providing the time and opportunity to monitor the

public's mood. In pursuing this course, Lincoln had time to think hard and long about emancipation and to calculate when and how to use it most effectively.

❧

THE EARLIEST TEXT WE have of the Emancipation Proclamation is a manuscript that bears the endorsement in Lincoln's hand, "Emancipation Proclamation as first sketched and shown to the Cabinet in July 1862" (Fig. 5-1).

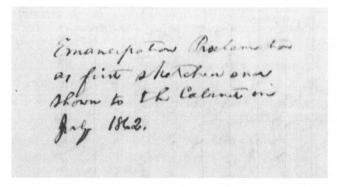

Figure 5-1. Lincoln's retrospective endorsement on a document containing a text of the preliminary verson of a proclamation of emancipation proposed to his cabinet on July 22, 1862. Library of Congress.

A number of stories have emerged about the writing of this historic document, but most of them are effectively contradicted by a fact often overlooked—that the first paragraph of its text (see Fig. 5-2) explicitly cites the date of passage for the second Confiscation Act, July 17, 1862, thus providing an ironclad terminus a quo, or the earliest date on which the document could have been written.

This means that this document could not have been the one supposed to have been read to Vice President Hannibal Hamlin or Congressman Owen Lovejoy in June, could not have been the one read to Senator Orville H. Browning on July 1 or to James Speed soon after, could not have been the one composed over a period of several days in early July in the War Department's telegraph office, or the one the president worked on during his boat trip back from visiting General McClellan at Harrison's Landing on July 9 and 10. Nonetheless, it would be a mistake to lose sight of the fact that all these stories are

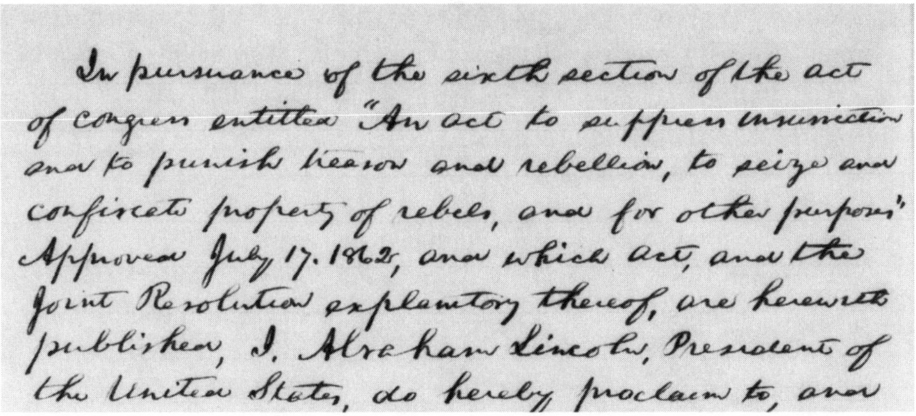
In pursuance of the sixth section of the act
of congress entitled "An act to suppress insurrection
and to punish treason and rebellion, to seize and
confiscate property of rebels, and for other purposes"
Approved July 17. 1862, and which act, and the
Joint Resolution explanatory thereof, are herewith
published, I, Abraham Lincoln, President of
the United States, do hereby proclaim to, and

Figure 5-2. Part of the first paragraph of the document presented to the cabinet on July 22, 1862, referring to the Confiscation Act signed five days earlier. Library of Congress.

indications that the president, at this very trying period, was actively engaged with his pen, and that he was, true to form, trying out his text, or texts, on friendly ears. Nor does it diminish the significance of the fact that all these witnesses were sure that the subject of these presidential writings was emancipation.

It probably was. Lincoln had been brooding about the issue for months, and it would have been not only in character but virtually inevitable that he would have been putting his thoughts down in writing. His White House servant William Slade told his family about the president's "peculiar manner of doing things. Often while reading or sitting alone, he would tear off a little piece of paper and write something on it and put it away in his desk, or in his vest or pants pockets, and continue his reading." Realizing the importance of these scraps, Slade said he often found them and saved them for the president. In the case of the president's writings on emancipation, Slade's daughter testified that "Lincoln frequently would talk with her father [a black man] about slavery and his emancipation plans, and that long before anyone else knew about the Emancipation Proclamation, her father had destroyed many old pieces of paper with notes upon them." This may well tell us why none of the various versions of his proposed proclamation that Lincoln tried out on so many people in June and July 1862 have survived.

Private and preliminary as such jottings may have been, Lincoln

knew how to prepare the public for what might be on the horizon. He
went out of his way on May 19, for example, in canceling General
David Hunter's order freeing the slaves under his military jurisdiction,
to say publicly more about the issue than he really needed to. His draft
proclamation (see Fig. 5-3) reads in part:

> I further make known that whether it be competent for me, as
> Commander-in-Chief of the Army and Navy, to declare the
> Slaves of any state or states, free, and whether at any time, in any
> case, it shall have become a necessity indispensable to the main-
> tainance of the government, to exercise such supposed power,
> are questions which, under my responsibility, I reserve to
> myself, and which I ~~will permit to be decided for me by neither
> any, nor all of my military subordinates.~~ can not feel justified in
> leaving to the decision of Commanders in the field.

This was clearly to make more of a public display of the presidential
prerogative than the situation required, and having his manuscript
draft enables us to see even more. It is reasonably clear in retrospect
that the pains Lincoln took in revising the language of the final part of
this sentence were not merely stylistic but had more to do with self-
presentation (from "I will not permit" to "I can not feel justified") and
with leaving a subtle but more forceful impression that a presidential
decision on emancipation was under active consideration.

While the story of his working on the proclamation in the telegraph office of the War Department probably pertains to a wider range
of activity than the creation of the document he read to his cabinet, it
does include a rare description of the presidential author at work. This
comes from a military officer who knew Lincoln well, the manager of
the War Department's telegraph office, Major Thomas Eckert:

> Upon his arrival early one morning in June [presumably a mis-
> take for July], 1862, shortly after McClellan's "Seven Days'
> Fight" [June 26–July 2], he asked me for some paper, as he
> wanted to write something special. . . . He would look out of the
> window a while and then put his pen to paper, but he did not
> write much at once. He would study between times and when he
> made up his mind he would put down a line or two, and then sit
> quiet for a few minutes. After a time he would resume his writ-
> ing, only to stop again at intervals to make some remark to me

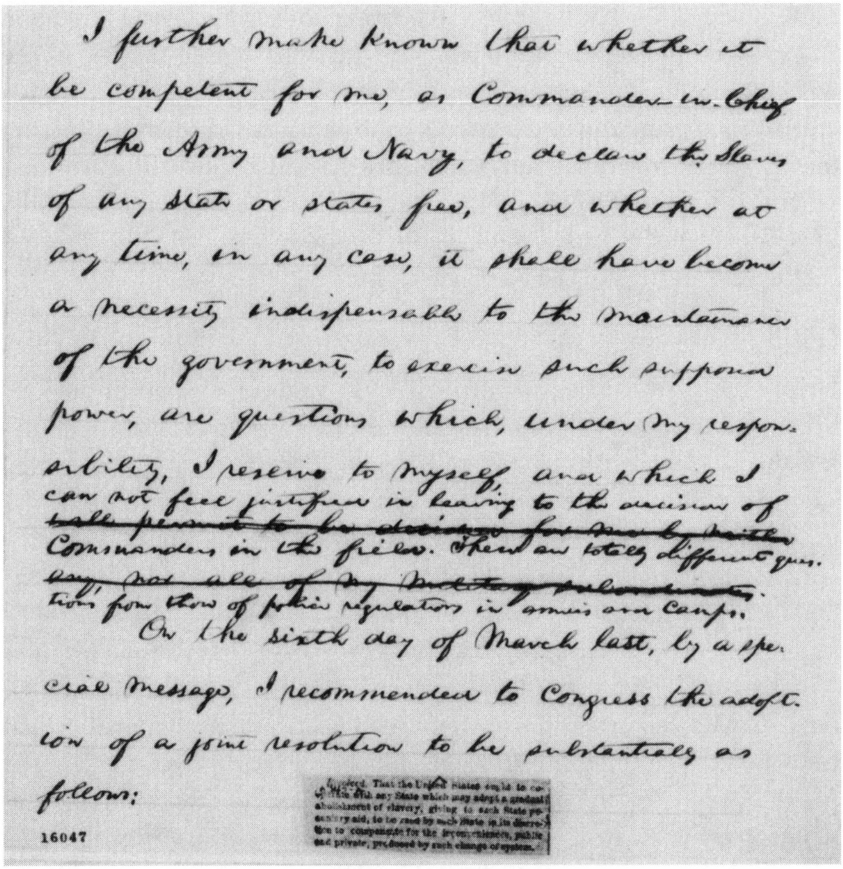

Figure 5-3. Passage from Lincoln's proclamation revoking General David Hunter's General Order No. 11 on military emancipation of slaves. Note that Lincoln has formed part of his text with a pasted clipping. Library of Congress.

or to one of the cipher-operators as a fresh despatch from the front was handed to him.

Eckert says that Lincoln left this manuscript in his care and called for it "nearly every day for several weeks." "Sometimes he would not write more than a line or two, and once I observed that he had put question-marks on the margin of what he had written. He would read over each day all the matter he had previously written and revise it, studying carefully each sentence." Though no document has survived that matches this description, there is little reason to doubt the authenticity of Eckert's account of Lincoln at work or that the president told him substantially that what he was writing concerned giving "freedom to the slaves in the South, for the purpose of hastening the end of the war." While it does seem doubtful that the sole product of so much effort was merely the two sentences the president read to his cabinet on July 22, there were several texts that he was known to be working on at this time that were concerned with the same subject. One of the most important, at least from Lincoln's point of view, was his appeal to the representatives of the border states.

∾❧

LINCOLN GATHERED THE CONGRESSMEN and senators of the four border states at the White House on July 12. It was a hectic time, nearing the apex of what J. G. Randall called "the painful and crowded summer of 1862." Lincoln had just returned two days earlier from visiting the Army of the Potomac at Harrison's Landing, where, thanks to General Robert E. Lee's brilliant Seven Days counteroffensive, General George McClellan's vaunted Peninsula campaign to capture Richmond was in shambles. To make matters worse, the president's talks with his intransigent commanding general had been maddenly unproductive. McClellan was unrepentant about his military failures, which he blamed on the administration, and he brazenly insisted that the political, as well as the military, policies the president was pursuing had to change. Even worse was the disheartening conclusion Lincoln came to after the meeting, namely, that "McClellan would not fight." Meanwhile, Congress, whose leaders were impatient with the president, was on the verge of passing a second Confiscation Act, partly aimed at freeing the slaves of traitors, but in a way that Lincoln believed was impractical, if not unconstitutional.

In these circumstances, the appeal to the representatives of the border states probably represented more than an attempt to put across his preferred plan of gradual and compensated emancipation, but also an opportunity for something even more desperately needed—a successful initiative that would signal both presidential decisiveness and progress in dealing with the rebellion. Though Lincoln was very adroit at speaking extemporaneously to small groups and individuals, the manuscript evidence indicates that he took the trouble to write out a text in advance, a text he carefully revised and then read to his audience. Such a process may have involved several more drafts than the two that survive, which serves to underscore the importance he attached to the issue at hand. It seems likely that this appeal is one of the texts he worked on in the telegraph office, and at least one report names it as the paper he was working on a few days earlier on the boat back from Harrison's Landing. Interestingly, its failure to produce the desired results—a majority of those present flatly rejected his proposal two days later—is paralleled by the failure of its rhetoric to take flight. In spite of its earnest language and the urgent, beseeching tone of its conclusion (or perhaps because of it), the appeal somehow lacks force.

> Our common country is in great peril, demanding the loftiest views, and boldest action to bring it speedy relief. Once relieved, it's form of government is saved to the world; it's ~~past~~ beloved history, and cherished memories, are vindicated; and it's happy future fully assured, and rendered inconceivably grand. To you, more than to any others, the previlege is given, to assure that happiness, and swell that grandeur, and to link your own names therewith forever._

The themes are sufficiently elevated and Lincolnian, but the phrasing is merely conventional, if not hackneyed, and even his most reliable rhetorical device, parallel construction (happy/happiness, grand/grandeur), here yields lackluster results.

LINCOLN PROBABLY SENSED THE lack of responsiveness in his audience, for even before he heard their verdict he was preparing his cabinet members for a bold new step. His secretary of the navy, Gideon Welles, pinpointed the time that Lincoln, on his way to a funeral, first broached the subject of emancipation by executive order:

> To Mr Seward and myself the President communicated his purpose, and asked our views, on the 13th of July 1862. It was the day succeeding his last unsuccessful and hopeless conference with the representatives in Congress from the border slave states, at a gloomy period of our affairs, just after the reverses of our armies under McClellan before Richmond. The time, he said, had arrived when we must determine whether the slave element should be for or against us.

Welles may not have remembered Lincoln's words precisely, but it is significant that he recalled an emphasis on timing. One of the elements that was just then bearing down on the president was an impending action of Congress. On July 14, the day after Lincoln raised the issue of emancipation with Welles and Seward, he received an advance copy of "An act to suppress treason and rebellion, to seize and confiscate the property of rebels, and for other purposes," whose adoption was imminent. This was the second attempt by Congress to create an effective law that would, among other things, mandate the wresting of slave property from those in rebellion against the government. Lincoln had serious doubts about the practicality of seizing rebel property through court action, as called for in the bill, and grave reservations about its constitutionality. He countered on the same day by sending to Congress a message recommending passage of a compensation bill, which he had taken the liberty of writing out, specifying not only the mode of payment but provisions for action in case of default. While the Senate was passing its "treason" bill on July 15, Lincoln spent much of the day "in his Library writing, with directions to deny him to everybody." He was working on a veto message, the prospect of which caused the congressional leaders to hastily pass resolutions to satisfy his objections. Nonetheless, the president took the unprecedented step of appending his veto message, with its list of objections to the original bill, to his presidential endorsement when he signed the bill.

This message makes interesting reading if only for the example of its tone. It is consistently respectful of a bill whose measures Lincoln does not much welcome or think very helpful. Without archness or irony, he conveys to members of Congress (and the public) what he believes to be the bill's weaknesses and what he has strong objections to, in most cases offering suggestions about how these might be resolved. At least one change in his draft manuscript reveals his impulse to justify his actions by an appeal to general principles, but also his ability to second-guess and restrain himself when the situation calls for it (Fig. 5-4).

To give governmental protection to the property of persons who have ~~left~~ abandoned it, and gone on a crusade to overthrow that same government, is absurd, if considered in the mere light of justice_ The severest justice may not always be the best policy_

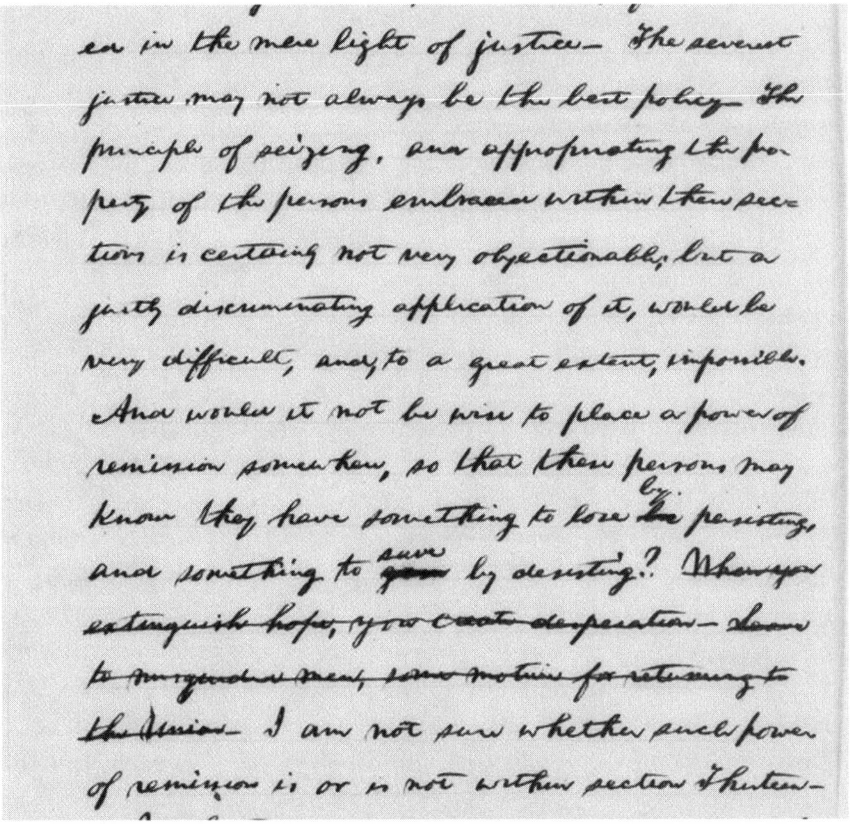

Figure 5-4. Portion of a draft of Lincoln's proposed veto message of the second Confiscation Act of July 17, 1862. Library of Congress.

The principle of seizing, and appropriating the property of the persons embraced within these sections is certainly not very objectionable; but a justly discriminating application of it, would be very difficult, and, to a great extent, impossible. And would it not be wise to place a power of remission somewhere, so that these persons may know they have something to lose ~~be~~ by persisting, and something to ~~gain~~ save by desisting? ~~When you extinguish hope, you create desperation Leave to misguided men, some motive for returning to the Union~~

One reason for striking the last two sentences was surely that it could all too readily be construed as presidential sermonizing, something that many congressmen would be sure to resent. In a different context, Lincoln might have let this stand, for it expresses very well an essential element of his outlook and his characteristic way of handling difficulty.

With the war going badly, with the border states refusing his overtures on compensated emancipation, and now with the Congress trying to deal with slavery by dubious measures, it was time for the president to take the lead and, as David Donald has put it, "to undercut the congressional initiative for emancipation by acting first." This is the way Lincoln put the matter to Francis B. Carpenter, an artist who, in the winter of 1864, had been given permission to work in the White House on an ambitious painting of the first reading of the Emancipation Proclamation. Lincoln told Carpenter: "It had got to be midsummer, 1862. Things had gone on from bad to worse, until I felt that we had reached the end of our rope on the plan of operations we had been pursuing; that we had about played our last card, and must change our tactics, or lose the game!" The morning of decision was apparently drawing near.

Lincoln told Carpenter that he didn't remember the exact date he read his proposed proclamation to the cabinet but that it was "the last of July, or the first part of August 1862." The surviving document consists of two brief paragraphs, the first of which pertains exclusively to the recently passed legislative act (Fig. 5-2 above):

> In pursuance of the sixth section of the act of congress entitled "An act to suppress insurrection and to punish treason and rebellion, to seize and confiscate property of rebels, and for other purposes" Approved July 17. 1862, and which act, and the Joint Resolution explanatory thereof, are herewith published, I, Abraham Lincoln, President of the United States, do hereby proclaim to, and warn all persons within the contemplation of said sixth section to cease participating in, aiding, countenancing, or abetting the existing rebellion, or any rebellion against the government of the United States, and to return to their proper allegiance to the United States, on pain of the forfeitures and seizures, as within and by said sixth section provided_

The second paragraph, which is parallel to the first, announces the imminent arrival of the long-anticipated measure of emancipation. What is most striking here is that the proposed proclamation does not make its appearance as the principal subject to be addressed, but is rather appended to a pro forma proclamation that the president had been required to issue by the recently passed Confiscation Act. This may suggest that Lincoln's strategy at this time was to introduce his momentous measure under the cover of the so-called treason bill. But perhaps a more likely interpretation is that the president hoped his two-sentence statement, offered in parallel, would be seen as trumping the congressional ace: Congress is hereby giving notice that they are going to do *this*, and I am giving notice that I am going to do *that*.

The proposed proclamation itself is rendered in just two sentences, but, curiously, the first could hardly be more inelegant and difficult to follow (Fig. 5-5):

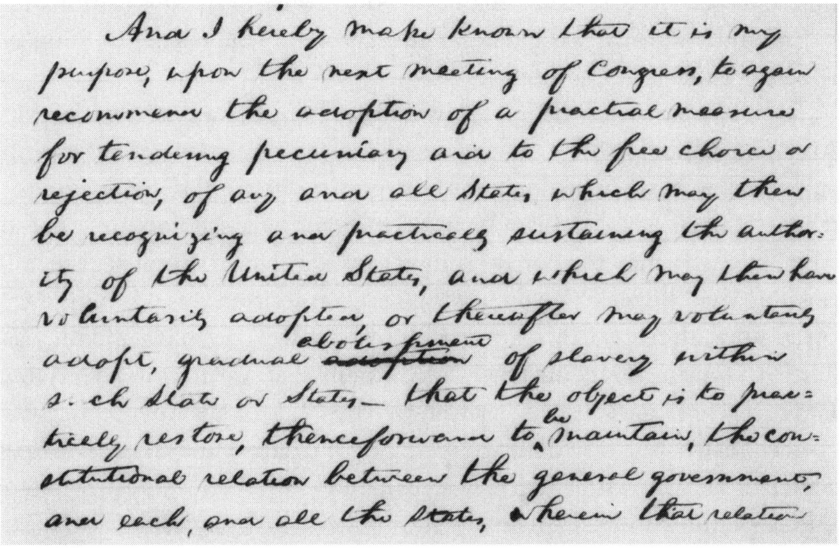

And I hereby make known that it is my purpose, upon the next meeting of Congress, to again recommend the adoption of a practical measure for tendering pecuniary aid to the free choice or rejection, of any and all States which may then be recognizing and practically sustaining the authority of the United States, and which may then have voluntarily adopted, or thereafter may

Figure 5-5. The beginning of the first of two sentences that comprised the earliest text of the Emancipation Proclamation. For the end of this sentence and the whole of the second, see Fig. 5-6. Library of Congress.

voluntarily adopt, gradual ~~adoption~~ abolishment of slavery within such State or States—that the object is to practically restore, thenceforward to be maintain, the constitutional relation between the general government, and each, and all the states, wherein that relation is now suspended, or disturbed; and that, for this object, the war, as it has been, will be, prosecuted.

The ungainliness of this sentence is partly because of its legalistic phraseology, partly a result of the way Lincoln has tried to jam a complicated set of issues into a single utterance. A paraphrase would begin something like this: "I hereby give notice that I intend to again recommend to Congress a scheme for offering compensation to . . ." To what? Eventually we realize that this compensation will be offered to any loyal state that adopts "gradual abolishment of slavery," but the proclamation's convoluted way of saying that this will be a voluntary scheme nearly derails the meaning in midsentence. And this proves to be a sentence, once this difficulty is sorted out, whose work is only half done. The second part is clearly about the "object" of the announced measure, the explicitly acknowledged reason it is being done. But what is it? Again, the sentence seems to insist that we paraphrase it: "The object is to restore and maintain the constitutional relationship between the states and the federal government, which is the basis upon which the war is being fought."

What is going on here? How does it happen, we must ask, that Abraham Lincoln, the acknowledged master of clarity, is serving up such verbal hash in a document of enormous import, a document whose language he has been trying out on various listeners for weeks? Actually, there may be a fairly straightforward answer. Because it seems possible that the paper on which this text was written was not manufactured until after his cabinet meeting, it may well be that Lincoln was here attempting to reconstruct a document that was no longer extant. His endorsement, after all, written on the back of the document, was clearly restrospective, describing it not by date but rather "as first sketched and shown to the Cabinet in July 1862." Perhaps prompted by Carpenter's intense curiosity about the actual physical document, the president, some two years after the fact, still not knowing the exact date, tried to re-create it. In any event, if it was written well after the fact, the tangled language of the first sentence may be one of the results.

But if he had trouble reconstructing the first sentence, the second (and last) apparently presented no such problem (Fig. 5-6), for it is straightforward and emphatic:

And, as a fit and necessary military measure for effecting this object, I, as Commander-in-Chief of the Army and Navy of the United States, do order and declare that on the first day of January in the year of our Lord one thousand, eight hundred and sixtythree, all persons held as slaves within any state or states, wherein the constitutional authority of the United States shall not then be practically recognized, submitted to, and maintained, shall then, thenceforward, and forever, be free.

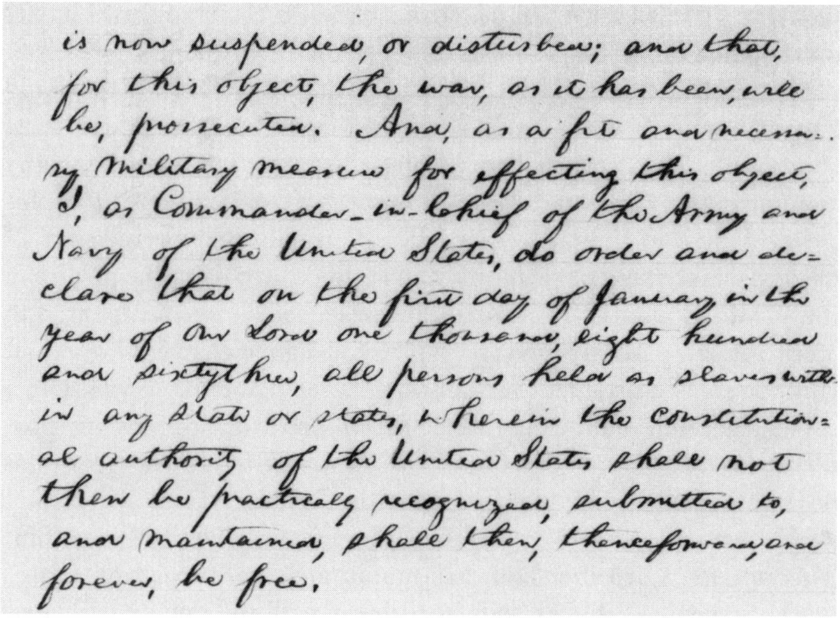

Figure 5-6. Text of the second page of the earliest version of the Emancipation Proclamation. Library of Congress.

Lincoln told Carpenter that when he read his text to the cabinet he was prepared for most of the reactions but that the secretary of state had raised an objection that he confessed he had not considered.

"[Secretary Seward] said in substance: 'Mr. President, I approve of the proclamation, but I question the expediency of its issue at this juncture. The depression of the public mind, consequent upon our repeated reverses, is so great that I fear the effect of so important a step. It may be viewed as the last measure of an exhausted government, a cry for help; the government stretching forth its hands to Ethiopia, instead of Ethiopia stretching forth its hands to the government.' His idea," said the President, "was that it would be considered our last *shriek*, on the retreat."

The prospect of bad timing struck Lincoln "with very great force," and he decided, he told Carpenter, to "put the draft of the proclamation aside, as you do your sketch for a picture, waiting for a victory."

BELIEVING THAT THE EMANCIPATION Proclamation was "an act unparalleled for moral grandeur in the history of mankind," Francis B. Carpenter had conceived the idea of painting "a picture which should commemorate this new epoch in the history of Liberty." As the most appropriate subject for such a painting, Carpenter settled on Lincoln's announcing to his cabinet "that the time for the inauguration of this policy [emancipation] had arrived." Through the intercession of friends, Carpenter gained approval in early 1864 to paint the picture in the White House, where Lincoln promised, as he told Carpenter, to "turn you loose in here, and try to give you a good chance to work out your idea." The president further obliged the painter by giving him a detailed account of how the Emancipation Proclamation was first proposed, so that Carpenter's book, *Six Months at the White House*, has become a prime source of information on the subject.

Carpenter's account, for all its usefulness, has definite limitations. The moment Carpenter hoped to immortalize in his painting turned out to be considerably at odds historically with the one he had envisioned. The meeting itself, as we have seen, proved to be something of a false start, with the president being persuaded to put his emancipation announcement on hold. The artist was apparently unaware that the "immortal document" that Lincoln read on that occasion—what Carpenter called "the most important document submitted to a cabinet during our existence as a nation"—was actually a pro forma proclamation, to which the president had appended a two-sentence statement of his intention to emancipate slaves in certain parts of the country some six months hence. This was, in short, only the germ of what would become the Emancipation Proclamation.

Nonetheless, it was an important step, and once Lincoln had decided on a course of action, he rarely retreated. What is most significant here is that the step, and Lincoln's way of taking it, entailed no small amount of writing. Even as he marked time and waited for a victory in August 1862, his pen was not idle. It seems likely that he carefully worked out the wording of a presentation that he made to the deputation of black leaders, referred to earlier, that he summoned to the White House on August 14, asking for advice and assistance on initiating a pilot program for black colonization in Latin America. Nor was this was the only product of his writing table during this period. When, on August 19, in a public letter by *New York Tribune* editor Horace Greeley titled "The Prayer of Twenty Millions," he was called to task for not implementing provisions of the second Confiscation Act, the president was ready with a prompt reply. In language that would become famous, the letter said, in part: "My paramount object in this struggle *is* to save the Union, and is *not* either to save or to destroy slavery. If I could save the Union without freeing *any* slave I would do it, and if I could save it by freeing *all* the slaves I would do it; and if I could save it by freeing some and leaving others alone I would also do that." This remarkable letter will be considered in more detail in the next chapter, but here it is relevant to note that Lincoln had already written the main body of this "reply" before Greeley's "Prayer" had even appeared. This is not surprising, once we are alerted to Lincoln's habit of constantly working out his ideas and positions on paper. According to a report published two days after Lincoln's reply appeared, the president had read the text of his "reply" to a friend and "said that he had thought of getting some such statement of his position on the Slavery question before the public in some manner. . . . The appearance of Greeley's letter gave him the opportunity he had been looking for."

The heart of the message may well have been another product of the sessions in the telegraph office. We can see clearly in hindsight that the letter was aimed partly at keeping proslavery interests off balance, and partly at preparing the public for what he had already made up his mind to do—freeing some slaves and leaving others alone. This is not duplicity, but it is far from candor, and it illustrates very well the importance of timing. August 22, 1862, was a good time to broach the issue of emancipation as a possibility but far from the right morning for a proclamation. Shortly afterward, the military situation was considerably worsened by a second disastrous defeat at Bull Run, this time at the expense of the Union's newly created Army of Virginia. "Things looked darker than ever," Lincoln told Carpenter, and that fateful morning must have seemed even farther away.

The grim situation got grimmer. On September 5, the Confederate Army crossed the Potomac into Maryland only a short distance upriver from Washington. With the Union forces in disarray, their ability to defend the capital was very much in doubt, and a decisive victory seemed too much to hope for. On September 13, a delegation of Christian ministers from Chicago came to the White House to present a memorial urging a national proclamation of emancipation, to which the beleaguered president demanded: "What *good* would a proclamation of emancipation from me do, especially as we are now situated? I do not want to issue a document that the whole world will see must necessarily be inoperative, like the Pope's bull against the comet! Would *my word* free the slaves, when I cannot even enforce the Constitution in the rebel States?"

As many commentators have pointed out, this is a particularly vivid example of a practice Lincoln had long employed. In discussing habits of mind, he told Indiana congressman Schuyler Colfax "that a peculiarity of his own life from his earliest manhood had been, that he habitually studied the opposite side of every disputed question, of every law case, of every political issue, more exhaustively, if possible, than his own side." No surviving notes or manuscript text of Lincoln's remarks at the meeting with the Chicago ministers are known, but the detailed account reported by the *Chicago Tribune* shows that he came well prepared, giving the full range of arguments against issuing a proclamation, and in carefully chosen language. He began by saying, "The subject presented in the memorial is one upon which I have thought much for weeks past, and I may even say for months," and his reported conversation bears this out. He followed his famous remark about the Pope's bull with another favorite tactic—a series of probing questions:

> Is there a single court, or magistrate, or individual that would be influenced by it there [in the South]? And what reason is there to think it would have any greater effect upon the slaves than the late law of Congress, which I approved, and which offers protection and freedom to the slaves of rebel masters who come within our lines? Yet I cannot learn that that law has caused a single slave to come over to us. And suppose they could be induced by a proclamation of freedom from me to throw themselves upon

us, *what should we do with them*? How can we feed and care for such a multitude?

Clearly, the president had been scouting the issues raised by a proclamation in minute detail.

The object of this line of skeptical questioning, of course, was something Lincoln very much wanted and needed, namely, to prompt the advocates of emancipation to bring forward their best arguments in support. And he gave assurances to the delegation that "whatever shall appear to be God's will I will do." The timing could hardly have been more propitious. Only a few days later, thanks to a misplaced copy of General Robert E. Lee's marching orders falling fortuitously into its hands, the Union Army under McClellan was able to check the Confederates' advance, bring them to battle at Antietam Creek, and force Lee to withdraw his troops back into Virginia. This stunning reversal seemed to many in the North like a miracle, a dramatic answer to their desperate prayers. What is astonishing is that even the religious skeptic Abraham Lincoln seems to have treated it as such. When he told his cabinet a few days later that he was issuing a proclamation of emancipation in keeping with a promise he had made to himself and his Maker, they could scarcely believe their ears, and his secretary of the Treasury Salmon P. Chase asked for confirmation.

To THIS SPECIAL CABINET meeting on September 22 the president had come prepared with a version of his proposed proclamation that was revised and much expanded from the two sentences he had offered in July. Lincoln told Carpenter that even though he had put his original proclamation aside, "From time to time I added or changed a line, touching it up here and there, anxiously watching the progress of events." Then came the disaster with Pope's army at Bull Run at the end of August, and another setback. Allen C. Guelzo has found evidence that Lincoln worked on his draft of a preliminary proclamation intermittently during the two weeks prior to the battle of Antietam, telling George Boutwell that he had "got it pretty much prepared" during that interval. The critical battle, which took place on September 17 at Sharpsburg, Maryland, where the Confederate Army had taken its stand across Antietam Creek, was hardly a clear-cut Union victory, but as soon as the president determined that "advantage was on our side," he told Carpenter he went back to work on his draft. "I was then staying at the Soldiers' Home," where he "finished writing the second draft of the preliminary proclamation." He told Boutwell, "When Lee came over the river, I made a resolution that if McClellan drove him back I would send the proclamation after him." The president, it would seem, had little trouble seeing a presidential proclamation as something of a missile.

Carpenter was under the impression that what Lincoln worked on at the Soldiers' Home and presented to his cabinet on September 22 was the "original draft," that is, the same physical document, the text of which he had read to his cabinet two months earlier. Carpenter would have been well aware when he came to the White House to work on his painting in February 1864 that the four-page document read to the cabinet on September 22 had been sold at public auction at the Army Relief Bazaar in Albany, New York, some months earlier. So the fact that Lincoln showed him the kind of paper he had used in writing what Carpenter thought of as the "original document" probably reflects a misunderstanding. Carpenter believed that Lincoln could not show him the "original document" because he had donated it to the Sanitary Fair, but the president most likely did not produce the true original—the paper he had presented to the cabinet on July 22—because it no longer existed. If this is the case, it would seem a good bet that Lincoln realized the historic importance of the document at Carpenter's insistent prompting, and not being able to locate it, sought to re-create and thus preserve its text.

By the time Carpenter wrote his account two years later, he had seen either the September 22 preliminary proclamation or a facsimile of it, for he described it accurately: "The original draft was written upon one side of four half sheets of official foolscap. . . . [It] is dated September 22d, 1862, and was presented to the Army Relief Bazaar, at Albany, N. Y. in 1864. It is in the proper handwriting of Mr. Lincoln, excepting two interlineations in pencil, by Secretary Seward, and the formal heading and ending, which were written by the chief clerk of the State Department." This document is now one of the most prized possessions of the New York State Library at Albany, where it is carefully preserved in a glass mounting and shown only on special occasions. Known as the Preliminary Emancipation Proclamation, it is *not* the same document Lincoln read from in July.

We know from reliable sources that Lincoln, in addition to the drafting he told Carpenter he did at the Soldiers' Home, worked assiduously on the proposed text of his proclamation at the White House on the day before the cabinet meeting, even refusing to receive visitors. If Carpenter remembered correctly that Lincoln had been making additions and changes to the document that he used in his July meeting with the cabinet, it seems likely that at some point this document was supplanted by one or more others as the new text evolved. What Lincoln brought to the cabinet meeting on Monday, September 22, was a fresh copy of his new text, and none of the drafts or notes that he made along the way seem to have survived. These may have been among the materials William Slade said he collected and destroyed. We can thus only speculate on the amount of effort Lincoln put into the crafting of this four-page document of just under a thousand words, and we are left almost completely in the dark about the various stages that it might have gone through.

Nonetheless, the differences between it and its July predecessor are notable. The language is still legalistic with a vengeance, and some of the points are the same, such as the promise of continued efforts toward compensated emancipation, which is rendered in the same phrase: "a practical measure for tendering pecuniary aid." But there is much that has been added, including a new ordering of elements. Whereas the reconstructed July text began with compensated emancipation, the new version begins with a statement of the object of the war:

> I, Abraham Lincoln, President of the United States of America, and Commander-in-chief of the Army and Navy thereof, do hereby proclaim and declare that hereafter, as heretofore, the war will be prossecuted for the object of practically restoring the constitutional relation between the United States, and each of the states, and the people thereof, in which states that relation is, or may be suspended, or disturbed.

Clearly the aim is to anticipate and counter the reaction that the war would henceforth be prosecuted primarily to abolish slavery. Next in order comes the pledge to push for compensated emancipation, then the promise to free all slaves in rebel territory on January 1, 1863, followed by a definition of what is understood as constituting rebel territory. Next are, in effect, official reminders to the military with respect to two laws passed earlier in the year respecting the treatment of escaped slaves. These were simply clipped from printed documents and pasted onto the manuscript (a common Lincoln technique), and they were aimed at officers like McClellan, who wanted nothing to do with the so-called contrabands and thought they should be returned to their rightful owners.

The ending of the proposed proclamation is noteworthy. It pledges that "all citizens of the United States who shall have remained loyal thereto throughout the rebellion, shall . . . be compensated for all losses by acts of the United States, including the loss of slaves." As a governmental promise this is remarkable, indemnifying loyal citizens against loss of their slave property, but as the note on which to end a military proclamation, it is probably even more indicative. It signals a strong disposition not only to be nonvindictive, but to be generous on the volatile issue of slavery. This was calculated to resonate with slave-holders in the border states, who could be expected to fear the effects on their own situation of any government-sponsored emancipation. But at the same time, such an ending unavoidably prompts other questions: How can a president of the United States promise such a thing? Where does it say, or by what precedent can it be inferred, that the president has any such power?

The power of the American presidency had been debated since the founding of the republic, but with no clear resolution. When the most zealous advocate for a weak executive, Thomas Jefferson, became president, he could not resist buying Louisiana from the French in 1803, even while admitting that, by his own strict-constructionist interpretation, such an act made "waste paper" of the Constitution. Lincoln himself broke into politics during the reign of "King Andrew" Jackson, a strong president whose willful behavior in office prompted his opponents to adopt the name of the British party traditionally opposed to royal power, the Whigs, the party Lincoln joined. In his only term in Congress, Lincoln had protested loudly against President James Polk's arbitrary, unauthorized, and in his view unconstitutional use of military force against Mexico. Now, in adopting the means for dealing with an insurrection of major proportions, President Lincoln had the same criticisms leveled against himself.

So long as his measures had the desired effect, Lincoln was perfectly willing to take this kind of heat, but as a conscientious believer in the Constitution, he had to observe appropriate limits. As a military necessity, to help put down the rebellion by force of arms, he believed that he, as commander in chief, could free slaves and take steps to make sure they were not reenslaved. But he was also keenly aware that for these measures to become permanent, the courts would eventually have to review and approve anything he did. Chief Justice Taney and other members of the Supreme Court were already strongly antagonistic toward his war measures. When the war ended and there was no longer any military necessity, it seemed more than likely that the courts would agree to the return of such property, including slaves.

This is another instance where the legend of the Great Emancipator has worked to obscure an important aspect of Lincoln's actions with respect to emancipation. "Military necessity" was the only constitutional basis that Lincoln thought he could conscientiously invoke for emancipation by presidential fiat. But in proclaiming emancipation as a military necessity, he greatly feared that he was granting freedom that might not be permanent. His position from the beginning of the conflict had been that all the government required was that the rebellious states cease their resistance to the national authority and resume their "constitutional relation" to the United States. Surely it was all too clear that if or when this came about, the first thing the former rebels would do would be to seek to reclaim property seized under a "military necessity" that no longer existed. Lincoln himself had laid out the legal argument for this in the private letter to Orville H. Browning, referred to earlier, at the time of General John C. Frémont's attempt the previous year to liberate the slaves of Missouri rebels by military proclamation:

> If a commanding General finds a necessity to seize the farm of a private owner, for a pasture, an encampment, or a fortification, he has the right to do so, and to so hold it, as long as the necessity lasts; and this is within military law, because within military necessity. But to say the farm shall no longer belong to the owner, or his heirs forever; and this as well when the farm is not needed for military purposes as when it is, is purely political, without the savor of military law about it. And the same is true of slaves. If the General needs them, he can seize them, and use them; but when the need is past, it is not for him to fix their permanent future condition. That must be settled according to laws made by law-makers, and not by military proclamations.

The legend of the Great Emancipator is generally silent about such concerns, but the manuscript of the September 22 Preliminary Emancipation Proclamation presents us with an acute expression of the president's scruples and fears. Carpenter remembered Lincoln's telling him about a change in his draft that Seward had pressed for:

> "When I finished reading [the third] paragraph," resumed Mr. Lincoln, "Mr. Seward stopped me, and said, 'I think, Mr. President, that you should insert after the word "recognize," in that sentence, the words "and maintain." ' I replied that I had already fully considered the import of that expression in this connection, but I had not introduced it, because it was not my way to promise what I was not entirely sure that I could perform, and I was not prepared to say that I thought we were exactly able to 'maintain' this."

But when we look at the manuscript of this passage, we see that more was involved than the addition of the words "and maintain." Carpenter may not have remembered or, indeed, Lincoln may not have revealed anything further, but the manuscript shows that there is more to the story. Lincoln's draft, as presented to the cabinet, read:

> . . . and the executive government of the United States will, during the continuance in office of the present incumbent, recognize such persons, as being free, and will do no act or acts to repress such persons, or any of them, in any efforts they may make for their actual freedom.

Here we can see that what Seward was objecting to was, in large part, the president's constitutional diffidence and the effect it had in undermining the standing and character of the freedom being proclaimed. To imply that the government's recognition of this freedom was somehow connected to the tenure in office of the person proclaiming it opened the door to manifold difficulties. It practically admitted, for one thing, that the ringing phrase "forever free" did not mean permanence, and was therefore hollow, if not hypocritical. It needlessly personalized the measure, rather than giving it the full institutional force of the United States government. It spoke only of passively *recognizing* the freedom of slaves, without affirming that the government would actively *maintain* that freedom. Perhaps worst of all, this way of putting the matter invited an invidious distinction, which James G. Randall described as "a declared or constructive liberation that fell short of 'actual freedom.' "

In this light, Lincoln's defense (as Carpenter remembered it) takes on a broader meaning. Because, as Lincoln said, "it was not my way to promise what I was not entirely sure that I could perform," he had proposed being perfectly aboveboard about the fact that these measures were contingent—not only on the continuance of military necessity but on his own continuance in office. Seward saw in this a major vulnerability, for which the remedy (in Carpenter's account) was the addition of two words, "and maintain." The manuscript (Fig. 5-7) reveals that a more substantial alteration in the text actually took place.

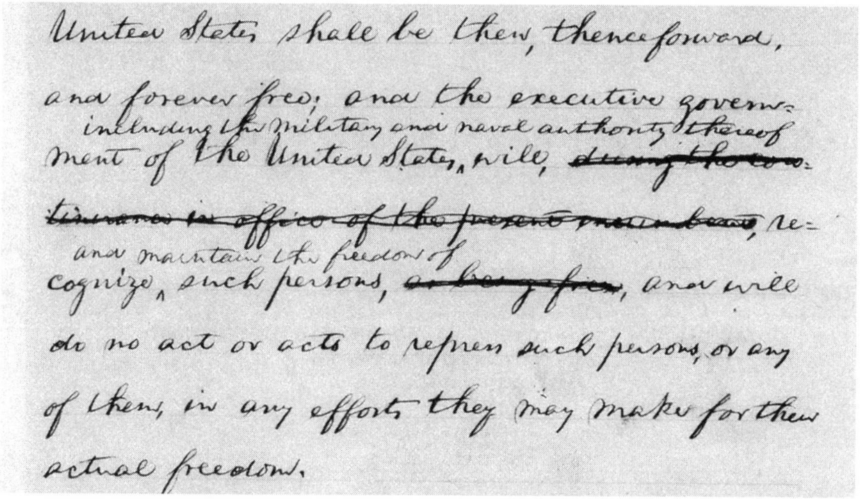
United States shall be then, thenceforward,
and forever free; and the executive govern-
including the military and naval authority thereof
ment of the United States, will, ~~during the con-~~
~~tinuance in office of the present incumbent~~, re-
and maintain the freedom of
cognize, such persons, ~~as being free~~, and will
do no act or acts to repress such persons, or any
of them, in any efforts they may make for their
actual freedom.

Figure 5-7. Manuscript of the Preliminary Emancipation Proclamation of September 22, 1862, showing a change made at the request of Secretary of State Seward. New York State Library.

Here is the passage with both the original construction and changes (additions in angle brackets):

> . . . and the executive government of the United States <including the military and naval authority thereof> will, ~~during the continuance in office of the present incumbent,~~ recognize <and maintain the freedom of> such persons, ~~as being free,~~ and will do no act or acts to repress such persons, or any of them, in any efforts they may make for their actual freedom.

As Randall noted, a critic could "cavil" at this, for a distinction between declared and "actual" freedom can still be made out, but the position being taken by the government was undoubtedly much strengthened by the changes, particularly removing the reference to "the continuance in office of the present incumbent." Carpenter remembered Lincoln representing himself as resisting Seward's proposed change but eventually giving in: " 'But,' said he, 'Seward insisted that we ought to take this ground; and the words finally went in!' " "Take this ground" is certainly a familiar Lincolnian expression, and the implication is that Lincoln agreed to submerge his concern about the reversibility of his actions and put a bolder face on the proclamation.

∾

BOTH THE JULY DRAFT, which was never made public, and the September document, which was duly printed and published by the State Department, were designed as preliminary proclamations, giving fair warning of what was to come on January 1, 1863. This provided the president's various publics—foreign and domestic, friendly as well as hostile—time to get used to the idea of emancipation, which was now no longer a subject of speculation but something that was imminent. He had confessed to his cabinet he could not be sure that he had timed the measure advantageously, saying, "I wish it were a better time. I wish we were in a better condition." Nonetheless, the president had at last rolled the dice and named the day: January 1, 1863.

The antislavery portion of the public was predictably elated by the news, but the president knew better than to entertain false hopes. He replied to a congratulatory letter from Vice President Hannibal Hamlin:

> It is six days old, and while commendation in newspapers and by distinguished individuals is all that a vain man could wish, the stocks have declined, and troops come forward more slowly than ever. This, looked soberly in the face, is not very satisfactory. We have fewer troops in the field at the end of six days than we had at the beginning—the attrition among the old outnumbering the addition by the new. The North responds to the proclamation sufficiently in breath; but breath alone kills no rebels.

Lincoln's caution was not misplaced. In the one hundred days separating the publication of the preliminary proclamation and the first of

January, much more would happen that was "not very satisfactory." As Postmaster General Montgomery Blair had warned, the proclamation gave powerful ammunition to the Democrats, who scored sizable advances across the board in the November elections. The impending proclamation was not the only issue that worked against the Republicans. The discouraging course of the war, as well as the government's curtailing of civil liberties, had helped sink Lincoln's personal popularity to a dismal level. It was widely rumored that lack of confidence in the president was responsible for disaffection and even disloyalty in the Union's officer corps. The bright spot in the picture, turning back the Confederate invasion of Maryland, quickly faded, as McClellan resolutely declined all opportunities (and increasingly strident presidential importunities) to pursue the retreating rebels. There was a serious Indian uprising on the Minnesota frontier, which presented further difficulty for the president when he defied the public outcry for revenge by personally reviewing the charges against the 303 Sioux men condemned to be hanged, and commuting the sentences of all but 39. Dismissing McClellan after the elections, Lincoln hoped to get the war effort back on track by replacing him with General Ambrose Burnside, a successful and well-respected officer. But McClellan's removal was unpopular, especially in the army, and Burnside's conspicuously poor judgment in his first major engagement resulted in the worst Union debacle thus far—the disastrous battle of Fredericksburg.

If this weren't bad enough, the president was beset about this time by leaders of his own party, who believed the desperate situation indicated that high-level changes were needed in the administration. In the Senate, the Republican caucus sent a deputation to the White House to demand the resignation of Seward, but Lincoln so arranged things that Secretary of the Treasury Chase, who had been secretly promoting this confrontation, was forced to admit to the senators that matters in the cabinet were not as he had represented them. When Chase subsequently offered to submit his own resignation, Lincoln fairly snatched it out of his hand. Not, as it turned out, for the purpose of getting rid of him, but as a way of resolving the crisis. He had tried to talk Seward out of resigning, but to little effect; now with Chase's resignation in hand, he saw a way out of his difficulty. By refusing both resignations, he could defuse the explosive animosities within his party and his cabinet and at the same time emphasize that the attention of all sides should be focused on the common task of putting down the insurrection.

❧

THE MOST IMPORTANT PIECE of writing he produced during the one-hundred-day interim between his preliminary and final proclamations was his Annual Message, presented to Congress on the first day of December. Its conclusion is among the most stirring incitements to patriotic commitment on record. It begins, "The dogmas of the quiet past, are inadequate to the stormy present. The occasion is piled high with difficulty, and we must rise with the occasion. As our case is new, so we must think anew, and act anew. We must disenthrall our selves, and then we shall save our country." It is sometimes objected that the nobility of this appeal was undercut by what had preceded it, an elaborated proposal for compensated emancipation and a closely argued brief for its adoption. But the eloquence and force of the passage are palpable and, moreover, are susceptible of a wider application.

The same may be said for the final paragraph, which immediately follows. The difference is that parts of it, especially its concluding two sentences, tie the appeal directly back to the proposal for compensated emancipation and colonization, and for this reason are usually omitted when the passage is quoted. They are included here for reasons that will presently become clear, but with or without them, the appeal is a stellar performance.

> Fellow-citizens, *we* cannot escape history. We of this Congress and this administration, will be remembered in spite of ourselves. No personal significance, or insignificance, can spare one or another of us. The fiery trial through which we pass, will light us down, in honor or dishonor, to the latest generation. We *say* we are for the Union. The world will not forget that we say this. We know how to save the union. The world knows we do know how to save it. We—even *we here*—hold the power, and bear the responsibility. In *giving* freedom to the *slave*, we *assure* freedom to the *free*—honorable alike in what we give, and what we preserve. We shall nobly save, or meanly lose, the last best, hope of earth. Other means may succeed; this could not fail. The way is plain, peaceful, generous, just—a way which, if followed, the world will forever applaud, and God must forever bless.

It is tempting to linger over the allure of this passage and the rhetorical command of the writer, which are everywhere in evidence. Few passages manage to incorporate a more effective combination of energy and earnestness. And few better illustrate Lincoln's distinctive feel for the negative as a basic rhetorical tool. This is apparent in the strategic use of words like "no" and "not," but also in contrasting positive and negative actions or ends—"escape history" or "be remembered"; "honor or dishonor"; "nobly save, or meanly lose." The power of this appeal stands in contrast to the labored effort Lincoln had aimed some five months earlier at the congressional representatives of the border states, though the issue and the argument were much the same. What was missing in the border states appeal, and what makes it seem somewhat limp and ineffective by comparison, is the sternness and resolution conveyed by the tone here: "*We* cannot escape history"; "We—even *we here*—hold the power, and bear the responsibility." It is the difference between pleading and laying down the law.

What is perhaps most important about this final portion of the Annual Message of December 1862 is its close affinity with the forthcoming Emancipation Proclamation. As suggested earlier, the legend of the Great Emancipator does not emphasize, if it even acknowledges, that where emancipation was concerned, Abraham Lincoln was a confirmed gradualist, a firm believer in compensation to slave owners, and a promoter of colonizing freed slaves and other blacks outside of the country—but he was all of these. As noted earlier, in this document he went so far as to propose a federal buyout of slave property (which the states could take as long as thirty-seven years to institute), but he also proposed constitutional amendments to compensate loyal slave owners for loss of slave property as a result of the war and provide funding for "colonizing free colored persons, with their own consent, at any place or places without the United States." Lincoln had been referring to the "gradual abolishment of slavery" in his writings since the recommendation he sent to Congress on March 6, which urged that "the United States ought to co-operate with any State which may adopt gradual abolishment of slavery." The word "abolishment" had raised the eyebrows of the fastidious Charles Sumner when he was given an advanced briefing, no doubt in recognition of the shrewdness of the president in finding an expression, albeit an awkward one, that diplomatically avoided the politically charged word "abolition." He had used the same phrase publicly in his May 19 letter to General Hunter and more conspicuously in the Preliminary Emancipation

Proclamation in September. Thus, what had once been only a somewhat awkward phrase was here expanded into a full-fledged constitutional proposal and was being handed up as part of the president's overall program for emancipation, of which the most conspicuous portion was to be put into place on January 1.

∽❧

BUT WOULD THE PRESIDENT follow through? This question was repeatedly asked as the appointed day approached, and many of those most eager for emancipation were fearful that the president would relent. George Templeton Strong wrote in his diary on December 27: "Will Uncle Abe Lincoln stand firm and issue his promised proclamation on the first of January, 1863? Nobody knows, but I think he will." But just three days later, he asked himself again: "Will Lincoln's backbone carry him through the work he is pledged them to do? It is generally supposed that he intends to redeem his pledge, but nobody knows, and I am not sanguine on the subject." Lincoln himself deliberately contributed to the suspense by refusing to give assurances to some last-minute questioners, but even as Strong was having second thoughts on December 30, the cabinet was reviewing the president's penultimate draft.

If some were worried about whether Lincoln would issue the promised proclamation, others were apprehensive about the form it would take. Given the president's unpredictability and insistence on following his own promptings, could he be relied on to produce a document that was suitable to the gravity of the occasion? Salmon P. Chase, who was already hoping to wrest the Republican nomination for the next presidential term away from Lincoln, went so far as to submit his own draft (of which more later). John Defrees, who seems to have considered it his duty to ride herd on the president's writing, wrote to remind Lincoln's private secretary in mid-December: "Only a few events stand out prominently on the page of the history of each century. The proposed proclamation of the President will be that *one* of this century; and it should be such a document as to justify the act in all coming time." In these circumstances, Defrees foresaw a potential problem: "If the President can only put his whole mind to its composition, it will be done;—but, I fear he will suffer himself to be so perplexed by 'outsiders' that he will not give it proper thought. Can you not gently hint this much to him?"

By this time the members of the cabinet were either actively supporting the president's proclamation or were sufficiently resigned to it as to make very few criticisms or suggestions. Perhaps the most consequential change was the addition of something that had not even been mentioned in September—the decree that the government would begin accepting colored recruits for the military. From all accounts, this was not a major issue in either of the two cabinet meetings where the text of the final draft was reviewed. There is no doubt that the introduction of colored troops was recognized as an important development, and it was probably something Lincoln had in mind from the start. Some of the reports about the decision to proclaim emancipation suggest as much. For example, Gideon Welles reported that when the president first broached the subject to him, he spoke of the time having arrived "when we must determine whether the slave element should be for or against us." The issue of arming blacks was explicitly raised by Chase at the July meeting at which Lincoln announced his decision, the same meeting at which Seward had warned against the public's perception of emancipation as "the last measure of an exhausted government, a cry for help; the government stretching forth its hands to Ethiopia, instead of Ethiopia stretching forth its hands to the government."

Using black troops was obviously a volatile issue, certain to alarm Unionists in the border states and other loyal groups, and Lincoln may have believed it imprudent to introduce it in September. But now, in the long-awaited proclamation, there it was. "And I further declare and make known, that such persons of suitable condition, will be received into the armed service of the United States to garrison forts, positions, stations, and other places, and to man vessels of all sorts in said service." Unlike the freeing of slaves behind the rebel lines, no one could dispute that this measure would have immediate and practical consequences, and in the months to come, Lincoln would vigorously defend it as such. In fact, he would come to represent it as virtually indispensable to the survival of the Union. As he is reported to have said to Governor Andrew Curtin of Pennsylvania the following year, "We had reached the point where it seemed that we must avail ourselves of this element, or in all probability go under."

This important addition to the proclamation promised in September was part of the final draft that Lincoln distributed to members of his cabinet on December 30, but a second notable change was not. All known versions of his proposed proclamation had used the word "forever" to describe the freedom being conferred upon slaves in rebel territory.

Reconstructed Draft (July)
... all persons held as slaves within any state or states, wherein the constitutional authority of the United States shall not then be practically recognized, submitted to, and maintained, shall then, thenceforward, and forever, be free.

Preliminary EP (September)
... all persons held as slaves within any State or designated part of a State, the people whereof shall then be in rebellion against the United States, shall be then, thenceforward, and forever free.

Draft of Final EP (December)
... all persons held as slaves within said designated States, and parts of States, are, and henceforward forever shall be free

In the first two versions, which were both designed as preliminary, the core statement was encumbered by geographical considerations, but disposing of these matters in the previous paragraph enabled the final version to achieve an economy of phrase that made for clarity and emphasis.

So matters stood on December 31, but on the morning of January 1, when the president wrote out his final text, he included a number of modest changes suggested by members of his cabinet, and introduced one of his own (Fig. 5-8):

... all persons held as slaves within said designated States, and parts of States, are, and henceforward shall be free.

There would appear to be no other way to understand so dramatic a change as the elimination of the word "forever," laden as it was with the promise of permanence, than as an expression of Lincoln's deep-rooted distaste for promising what he "was not entirely sure that [he] could perform." The troubling prospect of what a federal court might rule in the future could not, alas, be banished by a rhetorical flourish. Perhaps reluctantly, at the last minute he removed the word "forever"

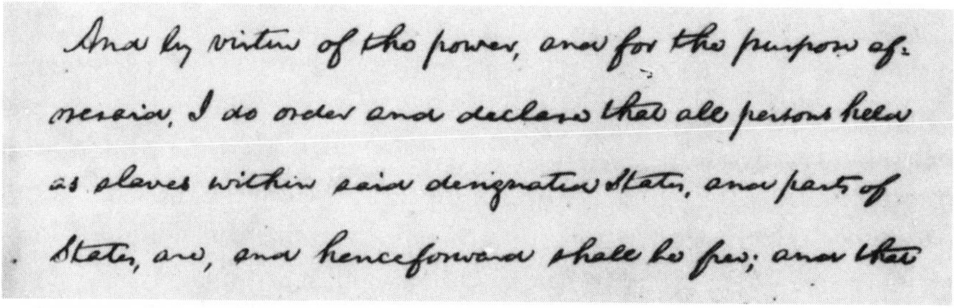

Figure 5-8 From a lithograph of the final manuscript version of the Emancipation Proclamation. The original was lost in the Chicago fire of 1871. Library of Congress.

from his text, as Allen C. Guelzo has written, "rather than give the judges even one spike to hang the Proclamation on."

One further change in the final version of the Emancipation Proclamation should be noted, one that came at the urging of Chase. Chase believed that inasmuch as the proclamation would signal a momentous new direction, and one with humanitarian and religious implications worldwide, it should be couched in more appropriate language. He even went so far as to propose his own substitute draft, which begins, "When in obedience to the will of the People I assumed the duties of Chief Magistrate I expressly declared my purpose to refrain from the invasion of any State and from all bloodshed unless compelled by the criminal madness of those who were then endeavoring to subvert the Government & dismember the Republic." Nothing could better illustrate how widely Chase's view of what constituted appropriate language differed from Lincoln's. Whereas Chase would refer to "bloodshed" and "criminal madness" in the very first sentence, Lincoln's drafts and other evidence show that he labored over the language at all stages and that one of his clearest motives in doing so was to neutralize its emotional impact. In deference to Chase, he finally agreed to add a concluding sentence that the secretary had submitted, but not without some minor editorial surgery. Eliminating one of Chase's phrases, he substituted in its place one more to the point (shown here in italics): "And upon this act, sincerely believed to be an act of justice, warranted by the Constitution, *upon military necessity,* I invoke the considerate judgment of mankind, and the gracious favor of Almighty God."

❧

ABRAHAM LINCOLN'S EMANCIPATION PROCLAMATION constituted a special problem in writing. As conceived by its author over a period of many months and through numerous trials, the problem was to find not only the right formula of ingredients and the most advantageous order of presentation, but to employ highly disciplined language. Most of all, it had to be emotionally chaste; it must avoid words and phrases that would appeal only to partisans and be land mines for others. Unlike almost any other kind of purposeful writing, it would be enhanced by its rhetorical barrenness. Its ultimate appeal would consist largely in its *lack* of linguistic or rhetorical appeal.

In taking note of the integral connection between the emancipation proposals contained in the president's Annual Message and the Proclamation itself, we passed over a surprising incongruity, if not a paradox. To antislavery proponents, to much of the Northern public at the time, and to most observers ever since, nothing about Lincoln's overall program for emancipation has ever had much appeal, except the Proclamation. Ironically, it appeals in spite of its uninviting "bill of lading" language, whereas the balance of his emancipation program—gradualness, compensation, and colonization—lacks appeal in spite of having been urged in some of its author's most spirited and memorable prose: "The fiery trial through which we pass, will light us down, in honor or dishonor, to the latest generation." The moral would seem to be that ideas and actions are more important than the language used to express them. But what does it say that those spirited phrases that could not induce the public to embrace the rest of Lincoln's emancipation package are still remembered and still resonate with modern readers? Perhaps this: that well-crafted language, particularly if flexible and adaptable, can outlive the ideas it was created to promote and can even take on a life of its own. Of course, it would be a mistake to ignore completely the affinity that existed between the parts of the program, for when Lincoln wrote, "Fellow-citizens, *we* cannot escape history," he *was* talking about the necessity of ending slavery. Whatever we make of it, the Emancipation Proclamation, which has taken its place as one of history's most celebrated documents, was an unlikely literary triumph. It succeeded not by eloquence, but by inexquisite language exquisitely suited to the occasion.

CHAPTER SIX

Public Opinion

Lincoln's deft maneuvering in December 1862, in fending off the attempt by leaders of his own party to force changes in his cabinet, was worthy of a seasoned diplomat, but it was characteristic of the president to explain the way the resignations of Seward and Chase canceled each other out by a colorful metaphor from his rural past. "I can ride on now," he told a visitor. "I've got a pumpkin in each end of my bag!"

It was just this kind of folksy expression that gave his visitors their strongest impression of the prairie president, something of which he was doubtless fully aware. There was nothing inauthentic about this kind of behavior, for the colorful colloquialisms and stories were a residue of his hoosier upbringing, something he had never relinquished and, in fact, had systematically used to advantage. It seems clear from the experience of many observers that, when in the presence of stylish visitors who came to size him up, Lincoln regularly resorted to homespun language and stories. To give the flavor of the president's talk, George Templeton Strong recorded in his diary a story Lincoln had recently told in his presence.

> "Wa-al," says Abe Lincoln, "that reminds me of a party of Methodist parsons that was travelling in Illinois when I was a boy thar, and had a branch to cross that was pretty bad—ugly to cross, ye know, because of the waters was up. And they got considerin' and discussin' how they should git across it, and they talked about it for two hours, and one on 'ed thought they had ought to cross one way when they got there, and another another way, and they got quarrellin' about it, till at last an old

brother put in, and he says, says he, 'Brethren, this here talk ain't no use. I never cross a river until I come to it.' "

Such performances persuaded sophisticated visitors like Strong that their president was "a barbarian." And Strong *liked* him. The impression of Lincoln as an incorrigible rube in manner and expression was so widely publicized and became so thoroughly ingrained with the public that recognition of his extraordinary abilities as a writer was slow in arriving. Undeniably apt or obviously able passages in his state papers were often assumed to be the work of Seward or Chase. Some months after Edwin M. Stanton arrived in the cabinet, he met a former associate at the bar, George Harding, who thought Stanton more able than either Seward or Chase. Years earlier, when Lincoln had been hired as part of the same legal team on an important patent case in Cincinnati, Harding had been the Philadelphia lawyer who had helped Stanton callously humiliate the Illinois "gorilla," Abraham Lincoln. Referring to one of Lincoln's recent state papers, Harding told Stanton that he knew who had actually authored it—Stanton. "Not a word of it, not a word of it," was Stanton's answer. Lincoln, he said, wrote "every word of it; and he is capable of more than that. Harding, no men were ever so deceived as we at Cincinnati."

Not everyone was blind to Lincoln's writing ability. As noted, his very first presidential effort, the First Inaugural, had found notable admirers, and four months later, his Message to Congress of July 4 made a keen impression on certain skeptics, such as the editor of the leading national magazine, *Harper's Weekly*. But even with such discerning supporters, the national crisis was too grave, and the focus on preconceived issues and antagonisms was too intense, for serious attention to the president's literary skills. His critics and enemies were already persuaded that he had none, and would not have pointed them out in any case. Even if his allies and defenders had recognized his skills for what they were, they could have made little headway by praising them, and generally did not.

The truth is that Lincoln's writing, while frequently given credit for its clarity, did not rate high by the prevailing standards of eloquence, which, like the architecture of the day, valued artifice and ornament. Like his contemporaries Herman Melville, Nathaniel Hawthorne, Walt Whitman, Henry David Thoreau, and Emily Dickinson, Lincoln was effectively forging a new, distinctively American instrument. Less self-consciously than some of these, perhaps, but no less diligently, Lincoln was in his own way perfecting a prose that expressed a uniquely American way of apprehending and ordering experience. His all-consuming purpose was, of course, not literary, but political—to find a way to reach a large and diverse American audience, and to persuade them to support the government in its efforts to put down the rebellion.

◈

As an experienced politician and, more particularly, one who had spent his career in minority parties, Lincoln was acutely aware of the importance of public opinion. "Public opinion in this country," he had once said expansively, "is everything." That was in 1859, when he was trying to persuade his party to lay the necessary groundwork for a successful presidential campaign. Three years earlier, he had given this idea a more focused treatment, telling a gathering of Illinois Republicans: "Our government rests in public opinion. Whoever can change public opinion, can change the government, practically just so much." If public opinion was thus malleable, then politicians with the power of office and the gift of persuasion could potentially do as much harm as good, especially if they could effect a change in basic American ideals and values. All of this, he maintained, had a practical application for the new Republican Party in the political turmoil of the 1850s.

In the campaign of 1858, which featured the famous series of debates with Stephen A. Douglas, Lincoln made the influencing of public opinion a primary issue. If the public had been led to believe by the actions of the founders and subsequent developments that slavery had been placed on a course of ultimate extinction, then Douglas and his Democratic cohorts, Lincoln argued, had been deliberately trying to undermine that sentiment. In the first debate, at Ottawa, Lincoln punctuated his claim with a memorable example of antithesis that we know from his manuscripts he had carefully composed in advance:

> With public sentiment, nothing can fail; without it nothing can succeed. Consequently he who moulds public sentiment, goes deeper than he who enacts statutes or pronounces decisions. He makes statutes and decisions possible or impossible to be executed. This must be borne in mind, as also the additional fact

that Judge Douglas is a man of vast influence, so great that it is enough for many men to profess to believe anything, when they once find out that Judge Douglas professes to believe it.

Later, in the fifth debate, at Galesburg, Lincoln stressed this charge, arguing that Douglas was "in every possible way preparing the public mind, by his vast influence, for making the institution of slavery perpetual and national."

Lincoln alleged in that campaign the existence of a provocative but largely fanciful conspiracy to this end, in which two presidents (Pierce and Buchanan), the chief justice of the Supreme Court (Taney), and Douglas were secretly in league. But few doubt that the fear behind it—that another Supreme Court decision in the willful spirit of *Dred Scott* could make slaveholding legal in Northern states and thus national—was quite real. This helps to account for the way he energized his language the following year, urging in several speeches that Douglas's arguments and actions were aimed at a "gradual and steady *debauching* of public opinion" (emphasis added). As we have seen, Lincoln used this harsh term again in his Message to Congress of July 4, 1861, to characterize the efforts of Southern extremists. Their attempts to "sugar-coat" secession so that it would be swallowed by otherwise loyal citizens he there labeled "an insidious debauching of the public mind."

So what, then, could or should be done legitimately to influence or change public opinion? One thing that Lincoln apparently would not consider doing was what people like Horace Greeley often did, which was to attempt to bully others into submission under the pretense of speaking, like a Roman tribune, for the general public. As early as 1842, Lincoln had laid it down as a principle in his Temperance Address that to "assume to dictate to [someone's] judgment, or to command his action, or to mark him as one to be shunned and despised" is counterproductive, for the person so admonished "will retreat within himself, close all the avenues to his head and his heart; and tho' your cause be naked truth itself, transformed to the heaviest lance, harder than steel, and sharper than steel can be made, and tho' you throw it with more than Herculean force and precision, you shall no more be able to pierce him, than to penetrate the hard shell of a tortoise with a rye straw." Although he had reformed his oratorical diction since that time, his views on persuasion had remained essentially the same. A prime consideration was still what it had been in 1842: "If you would win a man to your cause, first convince him that you are his sincere friend."

Very much in the forefront of Lincoln's calculations was the obverse of what he regarded as "debauchery," namely the gradual *education* of public opinion. "No one had greater responsibility for defining and directing democracy than the president," writes a leading historian of Lincoln's presidency, Phillip S. Paludan, "and Abraham Lincoln may have been the most qualified man in the nation for the job. For over a quarter century, as both lawyer and politician, Lincoln had been in the persuading business in the most democratic society in the world."

As we have seen, even in his early speeches there are glimpses of a theory of persuasion that he operated by. Except for the passages on rhetoric in the textbooks he read as a young man, it is doubtful that Lincoln ever studied the art of persuasion as a formal discipline or read Aristotle's *Rhetoric*. But as Ronald C. White Jr. has suggested, Lincoln's practice in many respects embodies the principles of Aristotle. For example, Lincoln's endorsement in his 1842 Temperance speech of the sympathetic reform efforts of the Washingtonians over the harsh denunciations of the clergy accords perfectly with Aristotle's precept that "our judgements when we are pleased and friendly are not the same as when we are pained and hostile."

In the same way, Aristotle's formulations shed light on Lincoln's various ways and means of bringing his audience around. George Templeton Strong concluded on the basis of his first meeting with Abraham Lincoln that he was a "Scythian, yahoo, or gorilla, in respect of outside polish (for example, he uses 'humans' as English for *homines*), but a most sensible, straightforward, honest old codger." Strong was an extremely well educated Wall Street lawyer, whose public-spirited work for the Sanitary Commission brought him several times into meetings with Lincoln. The detailed entries in his diary show him to have been a discerning observer, but he seems never to have grasped that the president's "yahoo" persona might have been, at least in part, a means to an end—a means, for example, of convincing sophisticated strangers like Strong that he was sensible, straightforward, and honest.

"Persuasion," writes Aristotle, "is achieved by the speaker's personal character when the speech is so spoken as to make us think him credible. We believe good men more fully and more readily than others; this is true generally whatever the question is, and absolutely true where exact certainty is impossible and opinions are divided." Lincoln seems to have understood this instinctively, and from a very early period. An account of a speech he gave in Quincy, Illinois, in 1841 reports: "As a speaker, he is characterized by a sincerity, frankness and evident honesty calculated to win attention and gain the confidence of the hearer." When he became president, Lincoln seems to have behaved accordingly. Rather than trying to convince strangers to alter their preconceptions, he understood that he would be better served by simply giving them reason to believe that, whatever his faults, he was essentially honest and trustworthy.

⤜

IN AUGUST OF 1862, this was about all Lincoln had going for him. This particularly anguished period in Lincoln's administration has to rate, in hindsight, as one of the lowest points in his presidency. The public, as Strong reported in his diary, was generally disheartened and disillusioned with its honest but ineffective commander in chief: "Most honest and true, thoroughly sensible, but without the decision and energy the country wants." But when the president's determination to meet this situation dramatically with a proclamation of emancipation had to be postponed until the deteriorating military situation improved, he looked for other ways to make his presence felt. Not surprisingly, he took up his pen.

Horace Greeley was a notorious gadfly. As the editor of the *New York Tribune*, he had long occupied a prominent pulpit from which he issued his opinions forcefully and at high volume. At every turn of events, Greeley could be counted on for emphatic pronouncements about what was needed and what must be done. Now he was seemingly incensed that the president had not acted promptly on the provisions of the second Confiscation Act, and on August 20 published a long, nine-part indictment in the form of a public letter to the president with the eye-catching title "The Prayer of Twenty Millions." Presuming, in characteristic fashion, to speak for all those loyal to the Union, Greeley intoned:

> We require of you, as the first servant of the Republic, charged especially and preeminently with this duty, that you EXECUTE THE LAWS. Most emphatically do we demand that such laws as

have been recently enacted, which therefore may fairly be presumed to embody the *present* will and to be dictated by the *present* needs of the Republic, and which after due consideration
have received your personal sanction, shall by you be carried
into full effect, and that you publicly and decisively instruct your
subordinates that such laws exist, that they are binding on all
functionaries and citizens, and that they are to be obeyed to the
letter.

Since the second Confiscation Act had been passed scarcely a
month earlier, Greeley's indignation about delay in its execution was
arguably overdrawn, but there may well have been more to it. News of
Lincoln's decision in July to proclaim some form of emancipation was
no secret to insiders in Washington, and the chances are good that
Greeley knew what was coming. In this light, "The Prayer of Twenty
Millions" may well have been the egotistic Greeley's attempt, as one
writer has suggested, "to beat Lincoln to the draw on emancipation
and thus win for himself a portion of the reflected glory."

But Greeley, as it turned out, had misjudged his man. He had
known the president since they served together in Congress in the
1840s, and he was persuaded that "the power of Mr. Lincoln is not in
his presence or in his speech, but in the honesty and gloriously refresh-
ing sincerity of the man." If Greeley's "Prayer" was intended as a pre-
emptive strike, it had the misfortune of being aimed at one who was
not only a superior writer, but one who, at that very moment, was cast-
ing about for an occasion to publish something he had already written.
Lincoln's reply to Greeley appeared promptly on August 23, and the
next day the *New York Times* reported: "Several days ago the President
read to a friend a rough draft of what appears this morning as a letter to
Horace Greeley. He said that he had thought of getting some such
statement of his position on the Slavery question before the public in
some manner, and asked the opinion of his friend as to the propriety of
such a course, and the best way of accomplishing it." Lincoln had
merely been doing what he often did in times of difficulty—putting his
thoughts down on paper. That he had tried the result out on a friend
was typical and perhaps an indication that he regarded his brief statement as a finished product; that he was taking soundings on the propriety of publication suggests remarkable confidence, if not downright
audacity.

Greeley's ostensible objective was to smoke the president out on the question of emancipation, but he could hardly have anticipated a public reply, much less one printed in another newspaper. It is important to recognize that Lincoln's public response to Greeley was unprecedented. Presidents in the past may have been sorely tempted to defend or explain their views directly to the people through the medium of the newspapers, but it was considered undignified for a chief executive to do so and had, so far as contemporary commentators were aware, never been done. Thomas Jefferson, the only president whose writing ability rivaled Lincoln's, had, in fact, composed at least one such letter, but he had done it entirely in secret and under the fictitious guise of a concerned citizen.

Predictably, Lincoln's precedent-breaking letter caused a stir. Whitelaw Reid, the brilliant young reporter for the *Cincinnati Gazette*, told his readers: "So novel a thing as a newspaper correspondence between the President and an editor excites great attention. Mr. Lincoln does so many original things that everybody had ceased to be surprised at him, and hence the violation of precedent in this matter did not provoke so much comment as might be expected." Going public with his response to Greeley was clearly a risk. It is possible to argue, of course, that Lincoln had little to lose and that his taking such an unprecedented step was a measure of his desperation. But this would obscure the fact that he made a shrewd calculation, especially after seeing Greeley's wordy and ill-tempered letter, that his brief but pithy message would carry the day.

If the fact that Lincoln had carefully prepared his statement in advance helps to explain its aptness and quiet eloquence, the first paragraph shows that he could also write effectively on short notice. Greeley's "Prayer" was an ill-disguised harangue, and one that showed scant respect for the president. Lincoln's strategy was to open on the opposite tack:

> Dear Sir: I have just read yours of the 19th, addressed to myself through the New York Tribune. If there be in it any statements, or assumptions of fact, which I may know to be erroneous, I do not now and here controvert them. If there be in it any inferences which I may believe to be falsely drawn, I do not now and here argue against them. If there be perceptible in it an impatient and dictatorial tone, I waive it in deference to an old friend whose heart I have always supposed to be right.

This opening proves to be a piece of ingenious jujitsu, using his opponent's own strength against him. Righteous impatience and a domineering tone were Greeley's editorial stock in trade. It was largely the aggressive use of these tools that had made him a formidable national presence and had given him a hearing on all the great questions of the day. In another perspective, Lincoln's stategy in replying to Greeley has a lot in common with his legendary courtroom gambit of yielding points for which an argument or rejoinder might ordinarily be expected. The difference is that here, under the guise of cordially waiving these issues, he manages to imply that Greeley's "Prayer" contains erroneous assumptions of fact, as well as inferences that are falsely drawn. He more than implies that the tone of Greeley's letter is "impatient and dictatorial," but all of this, he insists, is to be overlooked because the writer is an old friend whose heart is (or is *supposed* to be) right.

Lincoln's choice of a newspaper in which to reply to Greeley is indicative. The *National Intelligencer* had long been a leading paper in the nation's capital, having been for many years the main source of detailed accounts of congressional speeches and debates. Although pro-Union, the *National Intelligencer* was not a staunch supporter of the president, and it was decidedly unfriendly to the idea of emancipation. Placing his unprecedented public letter in this newspaper was thus something of a defiant gesture toward Greeley, inviting the implication that Lincoln's position on emancipation would be more welcomed by status quo conservatives than by radicals and abolitionists. In gauging the effect of Lincoln's letter to Greeley on the public, it is important to focus on the text that appeared in the *National Intelligencer* on August 23, but as is often the case, Lincoln's manuscript tells us even more about the letter, and especially about Lincoln as a writer.

As we have seen, the main portion of Lincoln's letter consisted of something he had already written when Greeley's "Prayer" fortuitously appeared on August 20. The only surviving manuscript of the letter (see Figs. 6-1, 6-2, 6-3) contains evidence of this and a number of other interesting things as well.

The portion of the letter that Lincoln had presumably written in advance is transcribed below from the manuscript; the inserted material is shown in angle brackets:

I would save the Union. I would save it the shortest way under the Constitution. The sooner the national authority can be

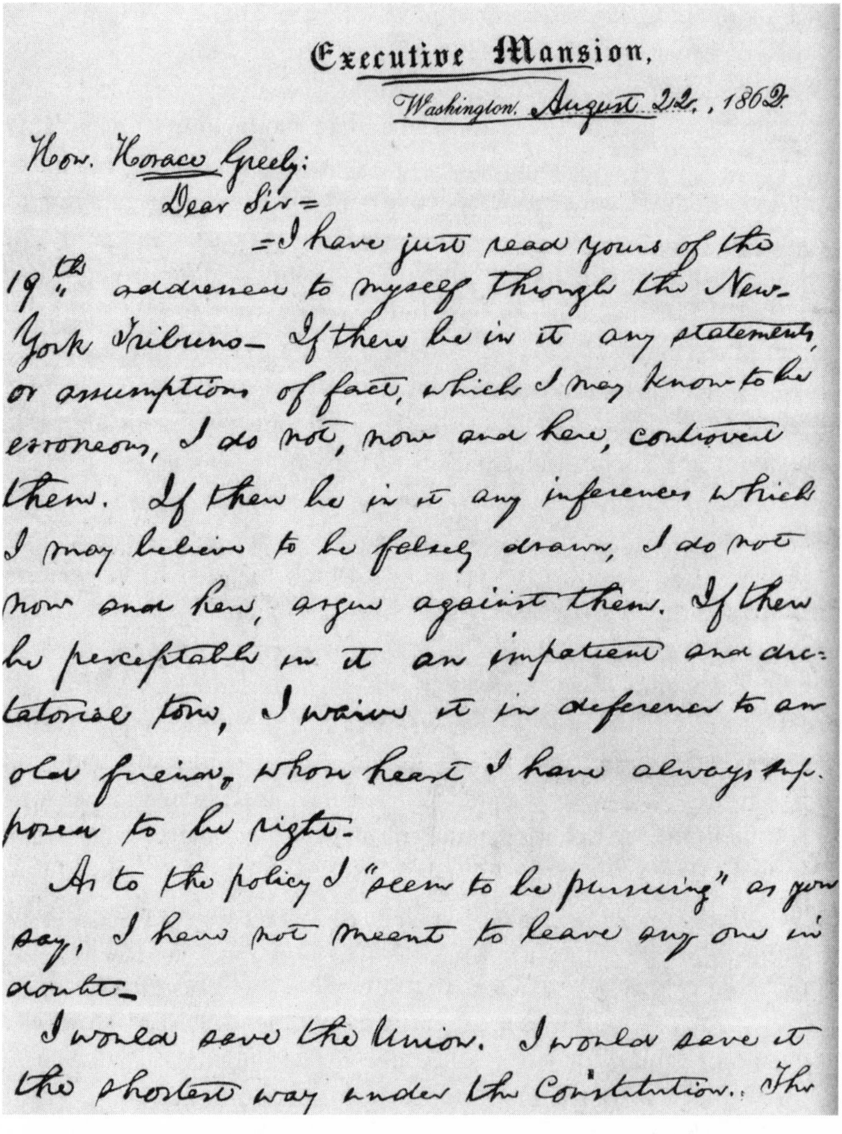

Figure 6-1. Lincoln's reply to Greeley, page one. The underlining on this page was done by the editors of the *National Intelligencer.* Wadsworth Atheneum.

restored, the nearer the Union will be "the Union as it was." Broken eggs can never be mended, and the longer the breaking proceeds the more will be broken_ If there be any <those> who would not save the Union, unless they could at the same time

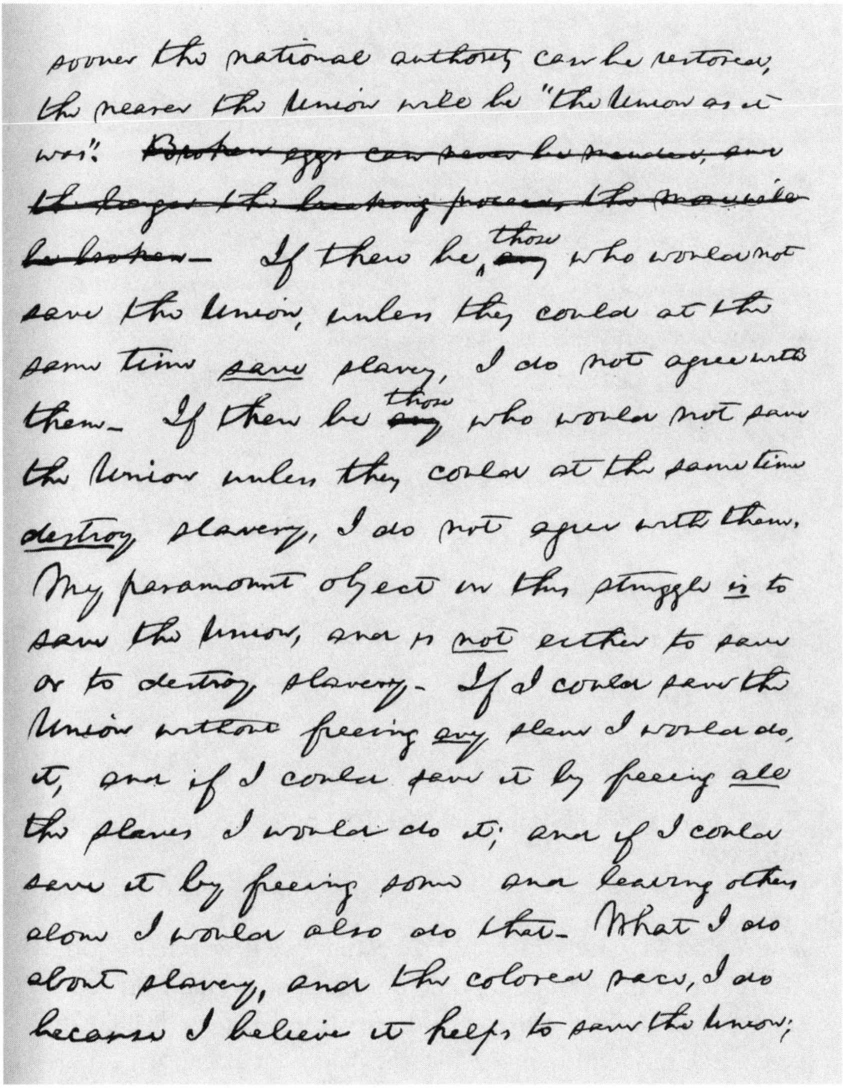

Figure 6-2. Lincoln's letter to Greeley, page two. The underlining on this and the next page was done by Lincoln. Wadsworth Atheneum.

save slavery, I do not agree with them— If there be ~~any~~ <those> who would not save the Union unless they could at the same time *destroy* slavery, I do not agree with them. My paramount object in this struggle *is* to save the Union, and is *not* either to save or to destroy slavery— If I could save the Union without freeing *any* slave I would do, it, and if I could save it by freeing *and what I forbear, I forbear because I do not believe it would help to save the Union. I shall do less whenever I shall believe what I am doing hurts the cause, and I shall do more whenever I shall believe doing more will help the cause— I shall try to correct errors when shown to be errors; and I shall adopt new views so. fast as they shall appear to be true views—*

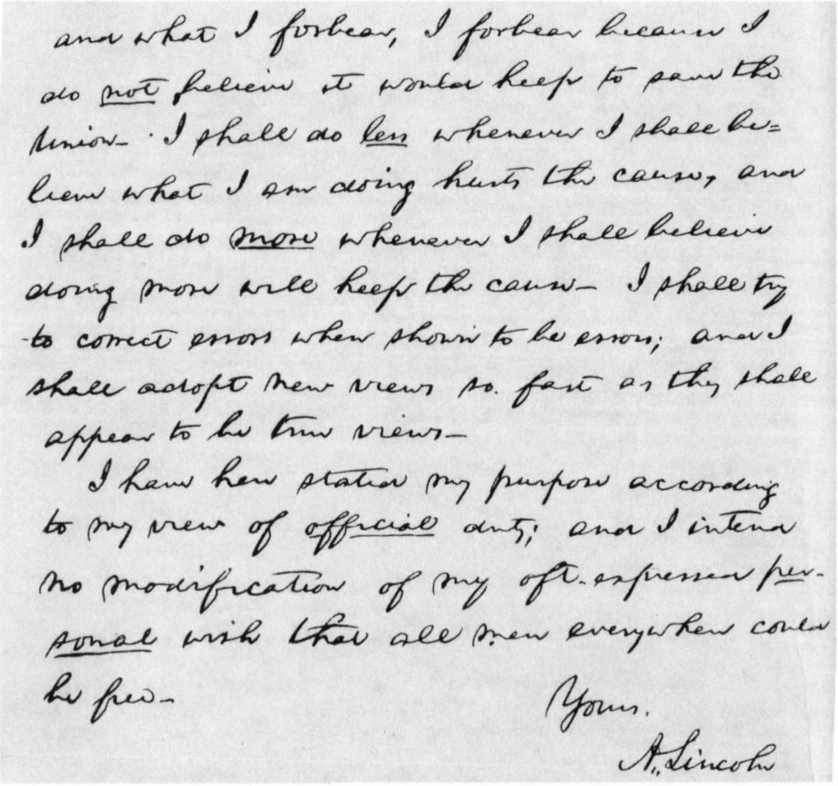

I have here stated my purpose according to my view of official duty; and I intend no modification of my oft-expressed personal wish that all men everywhere could be free—

Yours.
A. Lincoln

Figure 6-3. Lincoln's reply to Greeley, page three. Wadsworth Atheneum.

all the slaves I would do it; and if I could save it by freeing some and leaving others alone I would also do that_ What I do about slavery, and the colored race, I do because I believe it helps to save the Union; and what I forbear, I forbear because I do *not* believe it would help to save the Union_ I shall do *less* whenever I shall believe what I am doing hurts the cause, and I shall do *more* whenever I shall believe doing more will help the cause_ I shall try to correct errors when shown to be errors; and I shall adopt new views so fast as they shall appear to be true views_

I have here stated my purpose according to my view of *official* duty; and I intend no modification of my oft-expressed *personal* wish that all men everywhere could be free_

The most noticeable revelation here is, of course, the elimination of an entire sentence: "Broken eggs can never be mended, and the longer the breaking proceeds the more will be broken_" This is a strong image, a compact and forceful way of acknowledging the destructive and irreversible violence of the war, while at the same time amplifying the theme of saving the Union by the "shortest" way permitted by the Constitution. This figurative expression was much on Lincoln's mind, for he had used it in a private letter a few weeks earlier, and in a similar context: "Broken eggs cannot be mended; but Louisiana has nothing to do now but to take her place in the Union as it was, barring the already broken eggs. The sooner she does so, the smaller will be the amount of that which will be past mending." Lincoln would use the metaphor again in another private letter, written five months later, in January 1863: "Still, to use a coarse, but an expressive figure, broken eggs can not be mended. I have issued the emancipation proclamation, and I can not retract it."

But why did Lincoln strike this very same "expressive figure" from his public letter to Greeley? Did he consider it too "coarse" for this context? James C. Welling, who was political editor of the *National Intelligencer* at the time, later described the circumstances.

> The letter came into my hands from the fact that I was one of the editors of the *Intelligencer*, to which Mr. Lincoln sent it for publication. The omitted passage—"Broken eggs can never be mended, and the longer the breaking proceeds the more will be broken"—was erased, with some reluctance, by the President, on the representation, made to him by the editors, that it seemed somewhat exceptionable on rhetorical grounds, in a paper of such dignity.

In other words, Lincoln removed this sentence from his letter to Greeley, not because he thought better of it, but because of pressure from the editors at the *National Intelligencer*, who thought it undignified.

The manuscript also reveals something about Lincoln's attention to details. If we ask, for example, why he changed his parallel phrases "if there be any" to "if there be those," there would seem to be at least two reasons. First, the habit of parallel construction was so deep-seated that he probably did not at first realize, in copying his prewritten material into his letter, that he had used the same "if there be" construction in his more recently composed opening paragraph. Overexposure can weaken, so changing "any" to "those" corrected for the problem of repetition. But it is important to recognize that it also worked to strengthen, in a culminating passage a few sentences later, the contrast of *any* and *all*. "If I could save the Union without freeing *any* slave I would do it, and if I could save it by freeing *all* the slaves I would do it." Because it is not part of his iconic persona, Lincoln's self-conscious and discriminating treatment of seemingly minor details in his writing catches most people by surprise, but it is everywhere apparent in his manuscripts.

This letter calls our attention to another telling aspect of Lincoln's writing, namely, his adroit placement of emphasis. Especially when drawing distinctions—something that is often a characteristic of his best writing—Lincoln often sought to guide the reader's understanding by placing emphasis on certain words. Some instances, such as the pairing of "any" and "all" of the last example, are reasonably straightforward, but others are much more subtle and unexpected. A good example is the famous sentence cited in the previous chapter: "Fellow citizens, *we* cannot escape history." In the Greeley letter, consider the pattern of emphasis in the passage following the stricken sentence about "broken eggs." The next sentence emphasizes the word "save" and the following sentence, the word "destroy," both words referring, of course, to slavery. But then comes the riveting sentence about the president's principal goal: "My paramount object in this struggle *is* to save the Union, and is *not* either to save or to destroy slavery." Here another writer might have emphasized "Union" and "slavery," which would have been perfectly in keeping with the meaning. But by underlining "is" and "not," Lincoln pairs the words that refer back to, and thus amplify, his "paramount object." In the final sentence, the message the president is trying to send—that he is going to do whatever will get the job done, regardless of his own personal view of things— uses emphasis to sharpen the contrast between "*official* duty" and "*personal* wish." His early editors eliminated these and all other indications of authorial emphasis when they printed the letter.

The letter to Greeley has been widely admired for its eloquence and, in Allen C. Guelzo's phrase, its "economy of expression." The heart of the letter—the part that was written in advance—is only 295 words. Putting his message in so narrow a compass was, of course, a way of concentrating his meaning and focusing his readers' attention. Its fluidity and succinctness of phrasing proved doubly effective in that he was able to successfully reply to Greeley's wordy artillery barrage with a well-placed rifle shot. Though this was partly fortuitous, being able to take advantage of what comes along is one sure mark of ability. And yet, for all its apparent singularity of purpose, there is in the letter, especially when viewed in its context, a measure of real complexity.

Harper's Weekly welcomed the president's message, which it interpreted as sensible and straightforward: "While distinctly avowing his personal wish that 'all men every where could be free,' the President declares that his sole exclusive aim is to restore the Union, without reference to slavery; and that while he would not hesitate to proclaim emancipation if he were satisfied that that would restore the Union, neither would he scruple to save the Union with slavery." The letter properly took issue, said *Harper's*, with the extremists on the Union side—"the pro-slavery half-and-half Union men of the Border States who object to the restoration of the Union at the cost of their peculiar institution," and "the fanatical ultraists of the North who object to the restoration of the Union unless slavery be destroyed." Nothing could have pleased Lincoln more than to have his letter interpreted as showing that he had not been distracted by the special pleading of vocal minorities, but rather had steadfastly fixed his attention on the goal embraced by the mainstream of public opinion.

The editors of *Harper's* may or may not have known that Lincoln was already committed to issuing a proclamation of emancipation at the earliest favorable opportunity. Word was said to have leaked out, and there are indications in their editorial that they may have been privy to the secret. Nonetheless, they were satisfied with the president's position in the Greeley letter because, as they said, they believed that "whatever be the issue of the war, slavery has already received a death-blow from which it can never recover." Lincoln's view about the outcome of the war was surely very different, for he knew all too well that a rebel victory, at least in the short term, would give the institution of slavery a new lease on life. But he probably did see the survival of the Union and the destruction of slavery as linked.

Don E. Fehrenbacher has urged that the Greeley letter "will be misunderstood if it is read as a straightforward statement of Lincoln's political and ethical priorities, with the union counting for everything and slavery, nothing. Lincoln's ostensible neutralism about slavery was misleading—and intentionally so." Fehrenbacher argued that by this time saving the Union and abolishing slavery "were already bound together as twin purposes of the Civil War," and that Lincoln was grappling with a more complex situation than his readers were aware of. "Saving the Union had become more than an end in itself. It was also the indispensable means of achieving emancipation. But Lincoln, for reasons of political strategy, had to put it the other way around, viewing emancipation as a means, and very likely a necessary means of saving the Union."

If Fehrenbacher is right, Lincoln had by this time accepted that the outcome of the war would have to be something other than what he had pleaded for in his inaugural address and pledged himself to many times thereafter—the straightforward restoration of the national authority and a resumption of things as they were, slavery included. In such a context, the third sentence in his letter takes on considerable significance: "The sooner the national authority can be restored, the nearer the Union will be 'the Union as it was.' " The parallel construction one might have expected here—"the *sooner* . . . the *sooner*"—is deliberately passed over. What is offered instead is a quiet but clear implication that the best that can be gained by acting expeditiously is a state of affairs that will not be the same as, but only *nearer* to, the way things used to be. As we have seen, this point was originally driven home by what its author regarded as a "coarse, but an expressive figure": "Broken eggs can never be mended, and the longer the breaking proceeds the more will be broken_" Removing the "broken eggs" figure effectively blunts the meaning of the previous sentence. This may well have been the intention of James C. Welling and his fellow editors when they requested its removal. There is little doubt, in any case, that this was the effect.

Because what follows in the letter resonated so powerfully with contemporary readers and has remained so resonant and quotable, the third sentence is rarely noticed. If Lincoln had not agreed to delete his "broken eggs" metaphor, his hint about hopes for "the Union as it was" would likely have stirred more comment and concern. But even though he removed the figure, we can be reasonably sure of Lincoln's meaning, for he spelled it out in the private letter of July 31 cited earlier regarding the Louisiana situation: "The sooner she does so, the smaller will be the amount of [broken eggs] which will be past mending. This government cannot much longer play a game in which it stakes all, and its enemies stake nothing. Those enemies must understand that they cannot experiment for ten years trying to destroy the government, and if they fail still come back into the Union unhurt. If they expect in any contingency to ever have the Union as it was, . . . 'Now is the time.' "

This same message was to be the burden of the Preliminary Emancipation Proclamation that he was working on at the time and would issue in exactly one month: if you want to return to the Union as it was, you can get most of it back by giving up the rebellion before January 1, 1863. From this point forward, the issue of not being able to reestablish "the Union as it was" would weigh on all Lincoln's deliberations, for he continued to be fearful that the war might terminate in such a way that liberated blacks would face reenslavement as the rightful property of former belligerents. Not until the Thirteenth Amendment to the Constitution was safely launched in 1865 would he breathe easier on this crucial point.

LINCOLN'S PUBLIC LETTER TO Greeley dates from one of the darkest periods of the war for his administration, and it came at a time when the president had already made up his mind to invoke a desperate remedy—emancipating rebel slaves and using them as troops. This measure seems so logical and inevitable to modern readers that historians find it endlessly necessary to assure their audiences that such an action was, at the time, a very risky venture. Emancipation was not generally popular in the North, and no one could be sure how the loyal Democrats, or the loyalists in the border states, or the officer corps, or the soldiery, or the Northern public at large would react to it. Strong resistance from any of these quarters would present serious difficulties for prosecuting the war; broad opposition would be ruinous. Nonetheless, Lincoln determined to risk it. The public letter to Greeley, coming just one month after Lincoln revealed his intention to his cabinet, was the first of its kind and played a key part in his calculated efforts to prepare the country for a change in direction.

While not universally approved, there is little doubt that the letter, and thus the president's initial gambit, succeeded. "Those who insist on precedent, and Presidential dignity, are horrified at this novel idea of Mr. Lincoln's," the sympathetic *New York Times* admitted, "but there is unanimous admiration of the skill and force with which he has defined his policy." Even Greeley got the message. "I have no doubt," he wrote years later, "that Mr. Lincoln's letter had been prepared before he ever saw my 'Prayer,' and that this was merely used by him as an opportunity, an occasion, an excuse, for setting his own altered position—changed not by his volition, but by circumstances—fairly before the country." While it is ironic in the extreme that Greeley, who changed his mind about the war repeatedly, should treat Lincoln's "altered position" as an implicit criticism, the charge was essentially true. A week after its publication, Lincoln reportedly told Isaac N. Arnold "that the meaning of his letter to Mr. Greeley was this: that he was ready to declare emancipation when he was convinced that it could be made effective and that the people were with him." What he did not say, but what is clear in retrospect, is that the public letter to Greeley was part of a conscious effort to bring these things about.

❧

THOMAS JEFFERSON HAD CONSIDERABLE experience at shaping public opinion, but he knew that the public was often unresponsive or actively resisted measures that he believed were necessary. He wrote to a friend that he had come to see "the wisdom of Solon's remark, that no more good must be attempted than the nation can bear." Lincoln was probably as little acquainted with Solon as he was with Aristotle, but he had read Jefferson's own works with care. That he was familar with the substance of Solon's remark and that he acted accordingly as president is evident in a number of instances. In the case of the reply to Greeley, the first of his unprecedented public letters, he was trying to prepare the way for the acceptance of a highly controversial measure. Unable to be certain that he had properly gauged the situation, Lincoln himself was unsure, when he issued the Preliminary Emancipation Proclamation a month later in September 1862, that the public was ready for it. He confessed as much to his cabinet at the time, but he followed his instincts and took a chance. When it proved successful, he characteristically admitted to a visitor, "When I issued that proclamation, I was in great doubt about it myself. I did not think the people had been quite educated up to it."

But there could be little doubt that the Greeley letter had helped enormously in the process of educating the public up to the point of accepting emancipation. A public letter from a president, even if considered an undignified gesture, cannot be ignored. If its arguments are pithy and provocative, they will be noticed and will generate widespread public discussion, especially if they are timely. Indeed, what this episode suggests in retrospect is that one of the things Lincoln was most criticized for by members of his own party—his slowness to act—was in reality a superior sense of timing. But the publication of the Greeley letter was the unveiling of what would prove to be an even greater asset, his ability to shape public opinion with his pen.

CHAPTER SEVEN

Rising with Each New Effort

I F THERE IS CONCLUSIVE evidence that Lincoln was a careful and conscientious reviser of his own writing, a *re*writer, there is also considerable evidence that he was what might be called a *pre*writer. His personal papers contain many drafts and fragments that show him trying out ideas and arguments, and once we are alerted to it, there is a fair amount of eyewitness testimony relating to this practice. We have already seen that his son Robert, his law partner Herndon, his servant William Slade all bore witness to his practice of writing on slips and scraps of paper. His private secretary, John G. Nicolay, took this one step further by calling this part of Lincoln's "process of cumulative thought." Nicolay remarked the "habit [Lincoln] had acquired of reducing a forcible idea or an epigrammatic sentence or phrase to writing, and keeping it until further reasoning enabled him to add other sentences or additional phrases to complete or supplement the first. . . . There were many of these scraps among his papers, seldom in the shape of mere rough notes, but almost always in the form of a finished proposition or statement."

Unfortunately, most of these have disappeared, but the evidence is clear that Lincoln's prewriting, writing in anticipation, was habitual and is thus a revealing aspect of his presidency. If nothing else, it illustrates a certain quality of mind that is a clue, if not a key, to his success—a quality of mental alertness, of always looking ahead, of actively trying to anticipate the future and not being caught off guard. This quality is closely allied with another that Lincoln amply displayed, that of being patient and being prepared to take full advantage of opportunities that may present themselves. His activity as a prewriter is also an unmistakable indication of the prominence and, increasingly as president, the priority that he gave to writing as a prime tool in the conduct of his office. Such glimpses as we have of Lincoln's prewriting offer a kind of window on his imagination at work. Taken in conjunction with his other exceptional talents, his prewriting would seem to be an essential ingredient in the rare quality for meeting adversity that Shakespeare sums up as "readiness."

The reports cited above come from people who knew Lincoln well and who have no known reason to offer misleading testimony on such a subject. There is, however, at least one account that gives a description of Lincoln's practice of prewriting that purports to come from Lincoln himself.

James F. Wilson was a Civil War congressman from Iowa, and his claim to have had many conversations with Lincoln about suspension of the writ of habeas corpus may be exaggerated, just as his long account of what Lincoln said thirty years earlier must be regarded as a reconstruction or paraphrase, rather than as a verbatim account. But there is little reason not to credit the substance of what he says Lincoln told him about saving up ideas with which to answer his critics. Wilson says he told Lincoln on one occasion that he regarded his reply some months earlier to a petition from a group of Albany, New York, Democrats as his "best paper," and that the president agreed. "He then explained how the paper had been prepared. Turning to a drawer in the desk at which he was sitting and pulling it partly out, he said: 'When it became necessary for me to write that letter, I had it nearly all in there,' pointing to the drawer, 'but it was in disconnected thoughts, which I had jotted down from time to time on separate scraps of paper.' "

AFTER THE PUBLICATION OF the Emancipation Proclamation, on January 1, 1863, the substantial wing of the Democratic Party that opposed the war—the Peace Democrats—became more vocal and more vehement. A majority of Northerners supported the government, but one issue that raised widespread concern, and that the Peace Democrats were able to use to attract sympathetic attention, was the curtailment of civil liberties. From the earliest days of the war, Lincoln had not hesitated to support the arrest and detention of civilians considered dangerous by the military and to authorize the temporary suspension of the writ of habeas corpus at certain designated times and places. Americans were no less zealous about their liberties in that era than at other periods, and many pro-Union loyalists were concerned about the line being drawn, especially by the military authorities, between patriotism and protest. Especially troublesome was the distinction between political speech that was merely critical of the government and speech that constituted disloyalty, giving aid and comfort to the enemy.

One of the most fearlessly outspoken critics of the administration and the war was Clement Vallandigham, who had been a congressman from Ohio since 1856. When the military commander of the District of Ohio, General Ambrose Burnside, issued Order No. 38 in April 1863 forbidding the expression of sympathy with the enemy, Vallandigham promised defiance and, after making a fiery speech on May 1 in Mount Vernon, Ohio, was arrested by the military and jailed. Vallandigham was a handsome, self-assured man and a persuasive speaker. He insisted that he was very much committed to the Constitution and the Union, which, he argued, were being destroyed by the war and could be preserved only by making peace with the rebellious Southern states. Although he had been denied a fourth term in Congress by his constituents in the fall of 1862, he exhibited great confidence in the rightness and patriotism of his position and continued to speak out vehemently against the war and the policies of the government. Because there were many who shared his doubts about the war, and more who believed in the citizen's right to express them, his case became what J. G. Randall called the "*cause célèbre* of the Lincoln administration."

Part of the trouble was that the Emancipation Proclamation, issued on January 1, had seemed to prove what Vallandigham and the Peace Democrats had been claiming all along—that a Republican administration had been the cause of a sectional war for the express purpose of abolishing slavery. The controversial provision of the proclamation that called for the enlistment of black soldiers only added to the disenchantment and political turmoil that followed. As always, the situation on the battlefield had much to do with the mood of the country, and things were not going well. In the West, Grant had been trying for months, without success, to capture Vicksburg and reestablish control of the Mississippi River. Between the time Vallandigham made his speech at Mount Vernon and was arrested four days later, the Army of Northern Virginia, under the daring generalship of Robert E. Lee, had outmaneuvered the invading Union Army and its new commander, Fighting Joe Hooker, at Chancellorsville. When Lincoln learned that Hooker, with greatly superior numbers, had abandoned his offensive and retreated back across the Rappahannock River, he was visibly shaken and was heard to say, "My God! My God! What will the country say? What will the country say?"

For Union loyalists, it was a profoundly discouraging time. "Northern morale," notes James M. McPherson, "descended into the slough of despond in the spring of 1863." It was at the depth of this despondency that the news of Vallandigham's arrest became known. From the public's perspective, the military that could not stand up to the Confederate Army (Burnside had been the general who presided over the Union's humiliation some months earlier at Fredericksburg) had broken down the door of a prominent politician in the middle of the night and hurriedly hauled him off to jail before his neighbors could come to his aid. And for what? For criticizing the administration and its war policies.

Censure of what seemed like a blatant denial of civil liberties was immediate and widespread. Lincoln's secretaries noted in their biography, "No act of the Government has been so strongly criticized, and none having relation to the rights of an individual created a feeling so deep and so widespread." Public meetings were quick to convene. One such meeting in Albany, New York, was composed of loyal Democrats and chaired by prominent businessman and former congressman Erastus Corning. The tone of the meeting was set by a message from New York's Democratic governor, Horatio Seymour, who wrote: "If this proceeding [Vallandigham's prosecution] is approved by the Government, and sanctioned by the people, it is not merely a step toward revolution—it is revolution; it will not only lead to military despotism—it establishes military despotism." The aroused Democrats sent the president a bristling petition of protest on May 19. It was the receipt of this petition that Lincoln used as the occasion for offering, in the form of a public letter to Corning, his defense of the government's actions, the ammunition for which he had been saving up in his desk drawer.

"Often an idea about it [his power to restrict civil liberties] would occur to me which seemed to have force and make perfect answer to some of the things that were said and written about my actions," Lincoln told James F. Wilson. "I never let one of those ideas escape me, but wrote it on a scrap of paper and put it in that drawer." Wilson's recollection of what Lincoln said next may be somewhat harder to credit at such a distance in time, but it is, especially for our purposes, provocative: "In that way I saved my best thoughts on the subject, and you know, such things often come in a kind of intuitive way more clearly than if one were to sit down and deliberately reason them out." This may be Wilson's own gloss on the process Lincoln had described, but its authenticity is an intriguing possibility. It would suggest a lesson that a thoughtful and experienced writer had learned over time—that it is easier to capture illuminating insights and aphorisms on the fly, when and as they occur, than to attempt to generate them on demand.

Trusting his intuition to spontaneously provide ideas and arguments may appear unsurprising, especially given the pervasive spirit of the Romantic age in which the president had grown up, but it is not be confused with another pervasive phenomenon of Lincoln's time and place known as "spread-eagle oratory." In scrutinizing Lincoln's First Inaugural for indications of the new president's mettle, George Templeton Strong noted in his diary: "The absence of fine writing and spread-eagleism is a good sign." Lincoln was definitely an opponent of "fine writing," and Nicolay told how the president delighted in repeating on several occasions a satiric description of a prototype practitioner of "spread-eagle" speech making: "He mounted the rostrum," Lincoln said, "threw back his head, shined his eyes, opened his mouth, and left the consequences to God."

Lincoln's mockery of this method is perfectly in keeping with his own practice, for increasingly as a politician in the 1850s, he had spoken in public only on well-deliberated themes, using carefully prepared arguments, and leaving as little as possible to the inspiration of the moment. As president, he had, it seemed, almost a phobia about speaking without a prepared text. From the time of his election, whenever he was asked for some extemporaneous public remarks, he kept insisting that too much was at stake to run the risk of inadvertently misspeaking. He told a crowd of serenaders the night before his speech at Gettysburg, for example: "In my position it is somewhat important that I should not say any foolish things." Here a voice from the crowd inserted, "If you can help it," to which the president replied, "It very often happens that the only way to help it is to say nothing at all." This is the mark of a man who had a profound appreciation for the power of words, and who would rather pass up an opportunity to gratify his public than to express himself with less than precision. In this connection, Richard J. Carwardine makes an especially telling point: "His enforced near-silence made him all the more attentive to the quality of his prose, which he sought to imbue with color, life and energy."

LINCOLN'S PROBLEM IN REPLYING to Corning and the Albany Democrats was compounded by the fact that he himself did not approve of Burnside's action in arresting Vallandigham. The president had not been consulted in the matter and had learned of it only through newspaper accounts. While he believed that military arrests and the suspension of the writ of habeas corpus were at times necessary, he was keenly aware of what people like Governor Seymour were saying and highly sensitive to the charge that the government had misused its constitutional powers, a circumstance that made supporting Burnside's actions all the more difficult. In defending the suspension of the writ of habeas corpus in his Message to Congress of July 4, 1861, he had denied that he had exceeded his constitutionally authorized powers, but he had nonetheless posed a hard question for those who thought he had: "are all the laws, *but one*, to go unexecuted, and the government itself go to pieces, lest that one be violated?" But that defense related to the arrest of a civilian actively engaged in raising troops to fight against the government. How could the seizing of a high-profile Democratic politician making a political speech be justified?

Lincoln's letter to Corning must be read in its entirety to be properly appreciated, but his remarkable ability to size up a situation is immediately apparent in the way he begins, by shrewdly resolving the petition into three major "propositions." The first is that the petitioners have pledged themselves "to sustain the cause of the Union" and "support the administration in every constitutional, and lawful measure to suppress the rebellion"; the second, he concedes, is "a declaration of censure upon the administration for supposed unconstitutional actions such as the making of military arrests." From these propositions, Lincoln says, "a third is deduced," which is that the petitioners "are resolved on doing their part to maintain our common government and country, despite the folly or wickedness ... of any administration." That being the case, it only remained for the president to "thank the meeting" and to assure its members that "my purpose is the same" and that they "can have no difference, except in the choice of means or measures for effecting that object."

Neatly done, but, of course, Lincoln has more to say. His masterfully concise introductory paragraph is intended to emphasize the points of basic agreement on the larger issues and, perhaps just as important, to establish a respectful disposition and a responsive tone. Then comes the transition: "And here I ought to close this paper, and would close it, if there were no apprehension that more injurious consequences than any merely personal to myself might follow the censures systematically cast upon me for doing what, in my view of duty, I ~~can~~ could not forbear." The charges must be responded to because more is at stake in this issue than Lincoln's merely personal culpability. It is, he goes on to make clear, an issue of whether any United States president can, under the Constitution, legally do what has been done on his authority. The petitioners, he says, "assert and argue, that certain military arrests and proceedings following them for which I am ultimately responsible, are unconstitutional. I think they are not."

The issue is thus sharply joined, but Lincoln does not wade into his opponents. He first allows them to wade into him. He begins by paraphrasing and then quoting directly the charges made against him in the petition—that he had violated the Constitution by ignoring the definition of treason and by ignoring the "safe-guards of the rights of the citizen against the pretentions of arbitrary power." Lincoln quotes the language in which the petitioners trace the history of American civil liberties to their English origins: "They were secured substantially to the English people, *after* years of protracted civil war, and were adopted into our Constitution at the *close* of the revolution."

But here is the "nub" that Lincoln has been looking for. He asks, in a courteous, nonbelligerent tone (deftly letting his underlining make his point):

> Would not the demonstration have been better, if it could have been truly said that these safe-guards had been adopted, and applied *during* the civil wars and *during* our revolution, instead of *after* the one, and at the *close* of the other_ I too am devotedly for them *after* civil war, and *before* civil war, and at all times

"except when, in cases of Rebellion or Invasion, the public Safety may require" their suspension_

The words Lincoln puts in quotation marks are from the Constitution and go to show, as he emphasizes presently, that "the arrests complained of were not made for treason," but "on totally different grounds," as a constitutional means of dealing with a rebellion.

Promising to "consider the real case with which we are dealing, and apply to it the parts of the Constitution plainly made for such cases," Lincoln briefly rehearses the lead-up to the Civil War as a way of putting the Vallandigham incident in context. After demonstrating that the South had gotten the jump on the federal government before the outbreak of hostilities by seizing its forts and arms, Lincoln draws attention to the fact that the rebels had counted on using the Constitution as a shield for their insurgency. "It undoubtedly was a well pondered reliance with them that in their own unrestricted effort to destroy Union, Constitution, and law, all together, the government would, in great degree, be restrained by the same Constitution and law, from arresting their progress." They knew they would eventually face restriction of their civil liberties, such as the denial of the writ of habeas corpus,

> . . . but they also knew they had friends who would ~~raise a squabble~~ make a question as to *who* was to suspend it; meanwhile their spies and others might remain at large to help on their cause. Or if, as has happened, the executive should suspend the writ, without ruinous waste of time, instances of arresting innocent persons might occur, as ~~always do in~~ are always likely to occur in such cases; and then a ~~howl~~ clamor could be raised in regard to this, which might be, at least, of some service to the insurgent cause.

Here the only known manuscript (see Fig. 7-1) helps us better understand the process whereby Lincoln crafted and fine-tuned his letter. The first change was made on the fly, as he set down the sentence about arresting innocent persons. He had started to admit flatly that, in such situations, the innocent "always" suffer. Thinking better of that in midsentence, he makes it say that instances of such arrests "are always likely to occur." In revising what he had earlier written, we

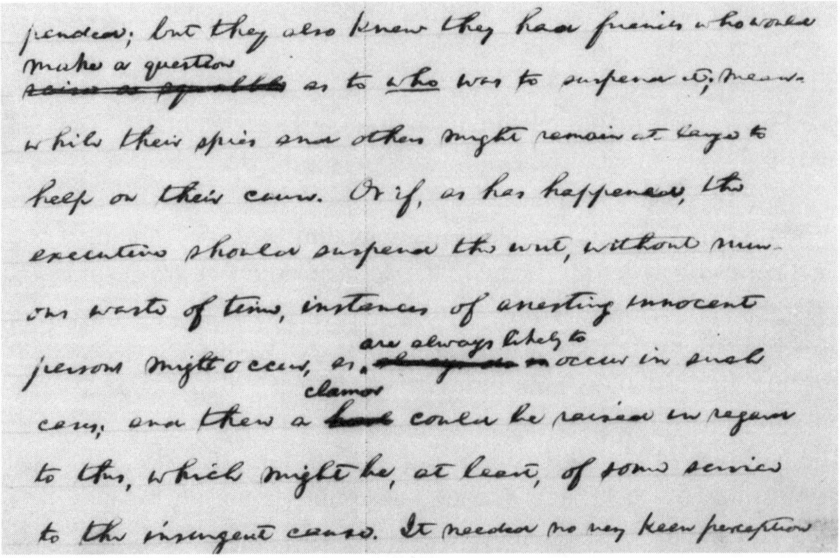

Figure 7-1. Passage from the manuscript draft of Lincoln's reply to Erastus Corning, page six. Library of Congress.

can see that he made two further changes to this passage. He replaced the colorful petulance of "raise a squabble" with the more sober and statesmanlike "make a question," just as he replaced the raucous "howl" with the slightly more civilized "clamor." One gets the impression that this illustrates a significant aspect of Lincoln's method, to let the energized language flow as much as possible in drafting (or, as with brief notes, *pre*drafting), knowing that it can always be reconsidered and toned down, if necessary, in revision.

Lincoln had been "slow," he insists, "to adopt the strong measures, which by degrees I have been forced to regard as being within the exceptions of the constitution." Part of the difficulty was that ordinary courts "are utterly incompetent to such cases." Speaking from long experience, he urged that "a jury can scarcely be empannelled, that will not have at least one member, more ready to hang the panel than to hang the traitor." On reflection, he toned this down to the more discreet observation that "too frequently" are juries so constituted (see Fig. 7-2). And some actions that are seriously harmful in times of rebellion may not even be recognized by the courts as wrongful, for, as Lincoln writes, "he who dissuades one man from volunteering or induces one soldier to desert, weakens the Union cause as much as he who kills a union soldier in battle. Yet this dissuasion, or inducement,

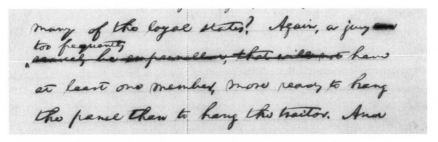

Figure 7-2. Passage from the manuscript draft of Lincoln's reply to Erastus Corning, page seven. Library of Congress.

is may be so conducted as to be no defined crime of which any civil court would take cognizance." Lincoln would return to this point before concluding.

"Ours is a case of Rebellion—so called by the resolutions before me—in fact, a clear, flagrant, and gigantic case of Rebellion." Even the petitioners, Lincoln points out, agree that the armed hostilities against the government constitute a rebellion. What does the Constitution say about such cases? " 'The previlege of the writ of Habeas Corpus shall not be suspended, unless when in cases of Rebellion or Invasion, the public Safety may require it' is *the* provision which specially applies to our present case." Moreover, Lincoln says, the provision "plainly attests the understanding of those who made the Constitution that ordinary Courts of justice are inadequate to 'Cases of Rebellion' " and that persons may be held in custody in such circumstances whom the courts, "acting on ordinary rules," would discharge. A substantial portion of the text is given over to spelling out what this distinction means in practice and why, particularly in terms of the "public safety," it is important. Arrests in times of rebellion "are made, not so much for what has been done, as for what probably would be done." They are "more for the preventive, and less for the vindictive" than arrests in ordinary criminal cases.

Eventually, having laid down the constitutional basis for making military arrests, Lincoln takes up the case of Vallandigham as though it were a convenient example: "Take the particular case mentioned by the meeting." If the charge made by the petition—that Vallandigham was arrested "for no other reason than words addressed to a public meeting, in criticism of the course of the administration, and in condemnation of the Military orders of that general"—then, Lincoln says, with disarming magnanimity, "I concede that the arrest was wrong." But this, he insists, is not the case. "He was not arrested because he was damaging the political prospects of the administration, or the personal interests of the commanding general; but because he was damaging the army, upon the existence, and vigor of which, the life of the nation depends." Moreover, the president wrote, "If Mr. Vallandigham was not damaging the military power of the Country, then his arrest was made on mistake of fact." In revision (see Fig. 7-3), the writer decided to add "which I would be glad to correct, on reasonably satisfactory evidence."

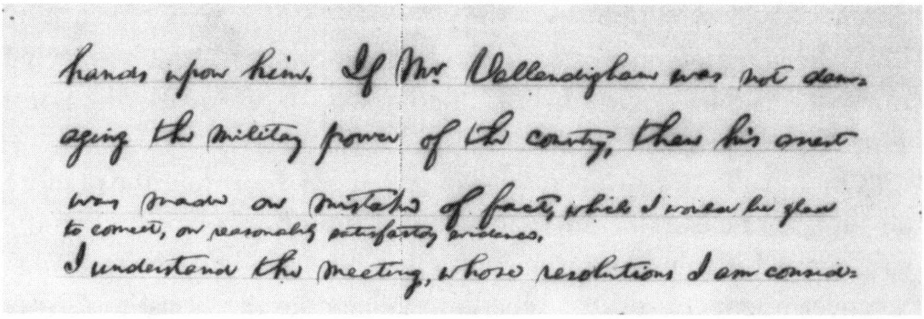
hands upon him. If Mr. Vallandigham was not dam-
aging the military power of the country, then his arrest
was made on mistake of fact, which I would be glad
to correct, on reasonably satisfactory evidence.
I understand the meeting, whose resolutions I am consider-

Figure 7-3. Passage from the manuscript draft of Lincoln's reply to Erastus Corning, page fourteen. Library of Congress.

It was at this point, after having made some very significant concessions, that Lincoln unleashed the idea that he had probably conceived in advance as a crushing argument against "agitators," an idea that was to produce the most striking and memorable passage in the entire letter. What makes it doubly interesting in our context is that the manuscript (see Fig. 7-4) enables us to see the role played by revision in shaping the sentence that would resonate with literally millions of readers. If the original version was jotted down on a scrap of paper, it has not come to light, so that the earliest form of the passage we have reads:

> Must I shoot a simple-minded soldier boy who deserts, while I must not touch a hair of a wiley agitator who induces him to desert by getting his father, or brother, or friend, into a public meeting, and there working upon his feelings, till he is persuaded to write the soldier boy, that he is fighting in a bad cause, for a wicked administration of a contemptable government, too weak to arrest and punish him if he shall desert.

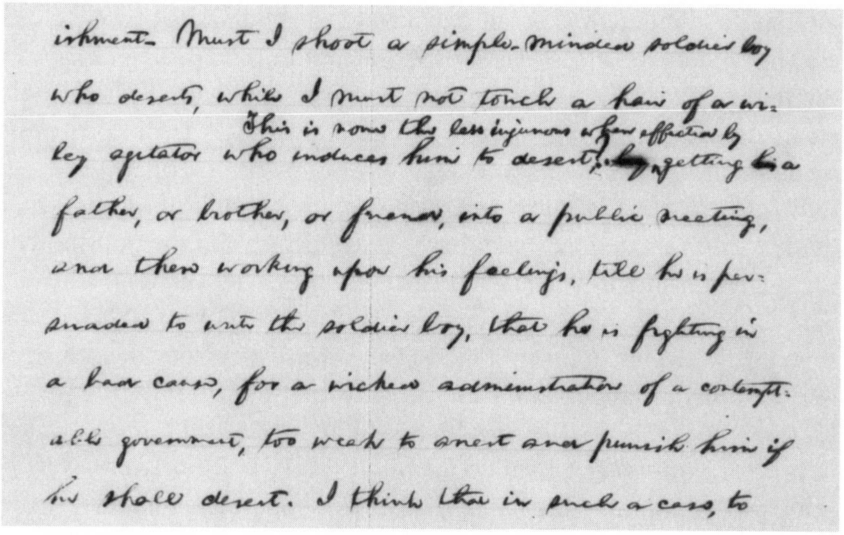

Figure 7-4. "Must I shoot a simple-minded soldier boy" passage from the manuscript draft of Lincoln's reply to Erastus Corning, page fourteen. Library of Congress.

In this form, the potential force of the idea is effectively dissipated by the momentum of the sentence, which carries the reader past the arresting sentiment too quickly. The solution, which Lincoln applies in revision, is elegantly simple—a full stop in the form of a question mark:

Must I shoot a simple-minded soldier boy who deserts, while I must not touch a hair of a wiley agitator who induces him to desert?

The sentence is thus rescued from wordiness and brought sharply into focus by the simple expedient of separating it from its much longer original and giving the remaining part a new beginning. By means of a touchingly sympathetic image, an appealing argument is packed into a single sentence and becomes the nineteenth-century equivalent of a sound bite. The mood thus created sets the stage for what follows in the rest of the original sentence, which is the connective tie between the soldier's desertion and death and the public meetings at which "wiley" agitators like Vallandigham do their work.

The line about the soldier boy has lived on, and its power is still felt, but the image of the deserting soldier who is subject to execution carried an especially potent emotional charge for the immediate audience at which Lincoln's letter was aimed, loyal Northerners, most of whom had a husband or son or nephew or sweetheart or neighbor in the Union Army. The newly established draft was unpopular; overstaying leave was treated by the military as desertion; and the punishment for desertion in time of war was execution. All of this was painfully familiar to the readers of this letter, as well as to its author, who was by this time well-known for his disposition toward clemency in such situations. Thus his appeal on these grounds had a credibility that made his apparent anguish at being forced to approve such a grim verdict more real. And this, in turn, made his argument more effective. "It is not true," Aristotle wrote, "that the personal goodness revealed by the speaker contributes nothing to his power of persuasion; on the contrary, his character may almost be called the most effective means of persuasion he possesses."

The final sentence in the passage functions as a kind of clincher and is a good example of Lincoln's more consciously literary manner, where his usually transparent artfulness shows through.

> I think that in such a case, to silence the agitator, and save the boy, is not only Constitutional, but, withal, a great mercy.

Linking the silencing of the agitator and saving the boy by alliteration is effective, although the inclusion of the Shakespearian "withal" is the kind of literary flourish that calls attention to itself and does not wear well. But the manuscript reveals that this sentence was originally even more self-consciously artful and that its author, in revision, took steps to rein it in.

The sentence's original ending was "but, withal, a great mercy, and a great merit." Lincoln wisely struck the last four words (see Fig. 7-5), adhering to the principle that, in certain cases, less is more.

Of all the points Lincoln made in his letter, perhaps the one most likely to have been the first conceived in advance was his story about President Andrew Jackson. Lincoln had begun his political career as a very young man by declaring his opposition to "Old Hickory," the hero of New Orleans, who was president at the time. Opposition to Jackson, who was enormously popular in backwoods

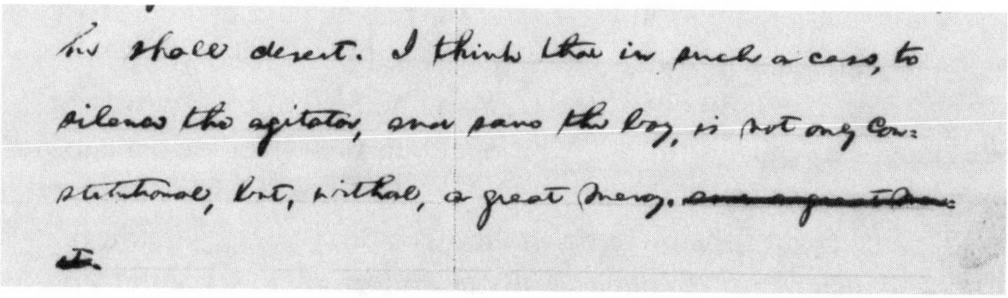

Figure 7-5. Passage from manuscript of Lincoln's reply to Erastus Corning, page fourteen. Library of Congress.

America, was thus a defining gesture for Lincoln, who had spent his subsequent political life in opposition to Jackson's Democratic Party. But, characteristically, Lincoln had studied Jackson's history in detail and knew how to draw on it to confound and embarrass his Democratic opponents. For example, when Stephen A. Douglas criticized him in their 1858 debates for opposing a decision of the Supreme Court (the infamous *Dred Scott* decision), Lincoln pointed to Jackson's defiance of the same court's ruling on the constitutionality of a national bank. The letter to Corning was to be another prime example.

The manuscript tells us that the anecdote about Jackson was drafted separately and inserted near the end of the letter, a circumstance that adds weight to the notion that it was conceived in advance. The placement near the end of the letter could hardly have been more advantageous. Making a point of regretting that the Albany petitioners represented themselves by party, as Democrats rather than as Unionists, Lincoln uses this as an opening for observing that the general who ordered Vallandigham's arrest was a Democrat, and that the judge "who rejected the constitutional view expressed in these resolutions, by refusing to discharge Mr. V. on Habeas Corpus, is a democrat of better days than these, having received his judicial mantle at the hands of President Jackson."

Having thus set the stage, Lincoln retells the story of Jackson's ordeal in maintaining martial law in New Orleans after the great victory over the British in January 1815. To quell a public outcry against the continuance of martial law, the general was obliged to make a series of military arrests, which become the highlight of Lincoln's narrative:

Among other things a *Mr. Louiallier*, published a denunciatory newspaper article_ Gen. Jackson arrested him_ A lawyer by the name of *Morel*, procured the U. S. Judge *Hall* to order a writ of Habeas Corpus to release Mr Louaillier. Gen. Jackson arrested both the lawyer and the judge_ A Mr. Hollander ventured to say of some part of the matter that "it was a dirty trick." Gen. Jackson arrested him_ When the officer undertook to serve the writ of Habeas Corpus, Gen. Jackson took it from him, and sent him away with a copy.

Lincoln then concluded the story so that it drew its own moral. When word of the peace was finally received, Jackson withdrew martial law and permitted himself to be fined $1,000 by the same judge, a fine which Jackson magnanimously paid, but which the American Congress many years later, at the instigation of Democrats, voted to repay. "The permanent right of the people to public discussion," Lincoln wrote, "the liberty of speech and the press, the trial by jury, the law of evidence, and the Habeas Corpus suffered no detriment whatever by that conduct of Gen. Jackson, or its subsequent approval by the American Congress." There was a further message in this anecdote that, while it was important, was so obvious to his readers, especially Democrats, that Lincoln did not even have to utter it. Edward Everett, to whom Lincoln sent a copy, could not resist pointing it out: that Vallandigham "would not have got off so cheaply under General Jackson."

At least one other portion of the Corning letter was quite likely conceived in advance, an extended analogy that involved the indelicate subject of emetics. Here the president declared himself unable "to appreciate the danger" that had been voiced by the petitioners

that the American people will, by means of military arrests during the rebellion, lose the right of public discussion the liberty of speech and the press, the law of evidence, trial by jury, and Habeas Corpus, throughout the indefinite peaceful future which I trust lies before them, any more than I am able to believe that a man could contract so strong an appetite for emetics while temporarily sick during temporary illness, as to persist in feeding upon them through the remainder of his healthful life.

This is an interesting passage in the letter, for it is precisely the kind of indecorous simile that fit the public stereotype of Lincoln as a crude, unpolished politician who was a stranger to the sensitivities requisite to statesmanlike behavior. Here it is offered forthrightly, almost, given the circumstances, defiantly. Why? Probably because the analogy is so apt and so forceful, it does not disrupt the argument and was not widely objected to. It is hard to believe that Lincoln did not employ this analogy quite deliberately, fully aware of what a circumspect editor like Welling or Defrees might say, but knowing that the analogy was fitting, expressive, and ultimately effective. Surely a good part of what observers saw as the "oddity" of his literary manner was just such insistence on expressions and similes that he knew others would avoid.

Finally, having made a series of detailed arguments showing that the curtailment of civil liberties practiced by his administration was constitutional and appropriate, Lincoln admitted forthrightly that he had serious reservations about the arrest of Vallandigham. "And yet, let me say that in my own discretion, I do not know whether I would have ordered the arrest of Mr. V. While I can not shift the responsibility from myself, I hold that, as a general rule, the commander in the field is the better judge of the necessity in any particular case_" Responding directly to the appeal of the petitioners that Vallandigham be released, Lincoln was disarmingly frank. "In response to such appeal I have to say it gave me pain when I learned that Mr. V. had been arrested, and that it will afford me great pleasure to discharge him so soon as I can, by any means, believe the public safety will not suffer by it." Before having his letter printed and distributed, Lincoln revised this admission so as to qualify it somewhat: "that is, I was pained that there should have seemed to be a necessity for arresting him"—but he soon made good on the promise to free his adversary from prison, banishing him instead beyond the Union lines.

AS AN ILLINOIS ATTORNEY, Lincoln had been a successful advocate at the bar, but he had the reputation of being strangely ineffective when he thought his client was in the wrong. As his second law partner, Stephen T. Logan, phrased it, Lincoln "had this one peculiarity: he couldn't fight in a bad case." Yet the Corning letter, which defends an arrest he didn't think appropriate, is, and certainly was considered at the time, a brilliant defense. There are reasons for this. For one thing, the Corning letter was not just about the Vallandigham case, though the hue and cry over the former congressman's arrest had called it forth. It confronted the whole question of civil liberties and the president's constitutional powers in time of rebellion. Another reason was surely Lincoln's foresight. Being able to employ ideas and material that he had been accumulating for just such a purpose meant that he was, as he might have expressed it, loaded for bear. "Burnside's unfortunate act caused Lincoln to fight on ground not of his own choosing," Mark E. Neely Jr. observed, "but he fought exceedingly well."

The potential of Lincoln's letter for raising much-needed public support for his administration's policies was immediately recognized by his cabinet, to whom he read a draft on June 5. Gideon Welles, himself a journalist, listened approvingly and noted in his diary, "It has vigor and ability and with some corrections will be a strong paper." By June 12 the letter had been printed and was sent off to newspapers around the country. The president also sent printed copies of the letter directly to a variety of influential persons, which may have been partly an act of pride but was also an effective way to spread the message and generate action.

In short order, his mail was filled with animated responses. They noted enthusiastically that the letter was particularly timely, that it "hit the nail on the head," and was written "in the right spirit." Francis Lieber, at Columbia University, wrote to say he was going to "propose to our Loyal Publication Society to print some 10000 copies" of the letter. Others apparently had the same idea, for it was an age in which political pamphlets were widely distributed and read. David Herbert Donald has traced the outlines of a fairly vast readership for this letter. "Published in the *New York Tribune*, reissued as a pamphlet, and given further distribution as a publication of the Loyal Publication Society, at least 500,000 copies of the Corning letter were read by 10,000,000 people."

What Lincoln needed, and what the Corning letter seems to have secured for him, was a measure of favorable public opinion—a very timely vindication of the government's actions with its supporters and the mollification of others who were subject to appeal. Given the somber mood and high level of concern for civil liberties demonstrated by the public at large, this was a highly significant accomplishment. One of the principal reasons the letter succeeded so well probably owed much to the difficulty ordinary citizens had in fathoming the intricacies of constitutional law. This was the consideration pointed out in a letter from Horace Maynard, a Tennessee Unionist, who wrote, "They have been so much beclouded in the discussions of lawyers, that the people despaired of ever understanding them, & took sides, according to their partisan predilections." Quieting the fears of large numbers of loyal Democrats, whose support Lincoln desperately needed, was probably the most consequential result that he could hope for, but Maynard's letter spelled out another consideration that Lincoln and his cabinet were surely aware of. "Some of the ablest of your own party journals, & party men," Maynard went on, "lent their influence to your opponents, & helped to procure a very wide spread popular impression that you had committed some acts of maladministration, that could not well be defended. This letter will go far to correct that impression."

⤚

ONE OF THE PEOPLE who received a copy of the Corning letter sent out by the president was Hugh McCulloch, an Indiana banker who was comptroller of the currency and who would later serve in Lincoln's cabinet. He wrote in his letter of response, "You were kind enough to read to me, last Friday evening, your reply to the Albany Resolutions upon the subject of Military Arrests." When Lincoln read a draft of his letter to his cabinet a week before it was sent off, it was for the purpose of getting its reactions and suggestions. But when he read the letter for McCulloch, it had already been printed and was being sent out by Lincoln's secretaries. About thirty-eight hundred words in length, the letter would have taken a reader like Lincoln perhaps as much as twenty-five minutes to read aloud. Why would he choose to take this much time to read his letter to someone like McCulloch, who was, after all, about to get his own printed copy and could read it for himself?

This takes us into one of Lincoln's most distinctive and, perhaps, for our purposes, most instructive idiosyncrasies. There is no doubt that Lincoln liked to read aloud. It was one of the ways he had learned at an early age to amuse his friends and make himself the center of attention. He had a variety of other ways to achieve the same end, such as telling jokes and stories, reciting poetry from memory, and mimicking familiar speakers. But reading aloud had always been a favorite practice, and it was something he did with great frequency as president, with texts that ranged from the humorous sketches of the "phunny phellows" of the day—such as Artemus Ward and Petroleum V. Nasby—to some of the most somber passages in Shakespeare. He read, sometimes by the hour, to entertain visitors, and there are instances where he seems to have been reading aloud for strictly personal reasons, as a form of self-therapy, to ease his depression or purge his emotions.

Returning to the Soldiers' Home at the end of a particularly fatiguing day at the end of June 1862, when nothing was going well, he excused himself from his other guests and took Orville H. Browning out to the porch. There he unburdened himself on the cause of his vexations, and then, without explanation, began reading aloud. "He then took from his pocket a copy of Hallack's poems," Browning noted in his diary, "and read to me about a dozen stanzas concluding the poem of Fanny. The song at the end of the poem he read with great pathos, pausing to comment upon them, and then laughed immoderately at the ludicrous conclusion." Here reading aloud from a poem he admired seems clearly to have been intended to help him regain his emotional equilibrium.

As we have noted, Lincoln seems to have read virtually every important piece he wrote as president to someone or some group before issuing or presenting it to the public. He read his much-altered First Inaugural Address to the elder Francis Blair the night before it was given. He read his Message to Congress of July 4, 1861, to Browning the night before its submission. He read what were apparently various drafts of his earliest attempts at a preliminary proclamation of emancipation to Vice President Hannibal Hamlin and several other friends in June and July 1862. The following month, he read the body of his "reply" to Greeley to a friend even before Greeley's own letter was published. When he could have handed out individual copies of his presidential documents to members of his cabinet, he almost invariably elected to read them aloud, as he did in the case of the letter to Corning. In some cases, such as the latter, he seems to have invited suggestions, but in most instances he asked only for reactions. It is hard to escape the conclusion that all of this reading aloud must have served some purpose. It lends credence to the recollection of one of his law clerks that Lincoln had told him in the 1840s: "I write by ear. When I have got my thoughts on paper, I read it aloud, and if it sounds all right I just let it pass." Only a year after his death, one of his White House clerks reported that it was Lincoln's "custom to read his manuscript over aloud, 'to see how it sounded, as he could hardly judge of a thing by merely reading it.' " This and much other evidence suggests that Lincoln had a profoundly aural sense of the language, that he thought he needed to hear it to critically engage it.

A truly striking instance of this phenomenon involves his old and trusted legal colleague Leonard Swett, whom he summoned to Washington by telegram from his home in Bloomington, Illinois, in 1862. Swett caught a train and presented himself at the White House as soon as he could. Upon arrival, he was asked by the president simply to listen as he read from letters he had received, expressing a full range of opinion on the wisdom of declaring emancipation. After reading Swett these letters, the president then went over the details of each argument and the implications of every position. Swett's description of Lincoln's demeanor in this incident was related to Ida Tarbell by one of his friends: "[Lincoln's] manner did not indicate that he wished to impress his views *upon* his hearer, but rather to weigh and examine them for his own enlightenment in the presence of his hearer." When Lincoln finished his presentation, he asked for no response but merely thanked Swett for coming, sent best regards to his Bloomington friends, and wished him a safe journey home.

Encouraged by the success of the Corning letter in June, Lincoln sent off another a few weeks later to the Democrats of Vallandigham's home state of Ohio, but the boldest of all his public letters, and the one that was probably the most consequential, was addressed two and a half months later to a meeting in his hometown, Springfield, Illinois. Unlike the Greeley or Corning letters, the Springfield letter was written to be read aloud by his old friend James C. Conkling. When he finished composing it in late August, Lincoln looked around the White House for someone to read it to. As luck would have it, all of his principal aides were away. At last locating a clerk, he invited him into his office. Years later, the clerk, William O. Stoddard, recalled the scene.

"Sit down. I can always tell more about a thing after I've heard it read aloud, and know how it sounds. Just the reading of it to myself doesn't answer as well, either."

"Do you wish me to read it to you?"

"No, no; I'll read it myself. What I want is an audience.

Nothing sounds the same when there isn't anybody to hear it and find fault with it."

"I don't know, Mr. President, that I'd care to criticise anything you'd written."

"Yes, you will. Everybody else will. It's just what I want you to do. Sit still now, and you'll make as much of an audience as I call for."

❧

THE SUMMER OF 1863 witnessed the great Union victories at Gettysburg and Vicksburg during the same week in July, but little more than a week later it saw the eruption of the bloody riots in New York City that rampaged for several days, resulting in massive destruction and over a hundred deaths. The Conscription Act had been passed in March, instituting a draft that was immediately unpopular. Many New Yorkers considered it inequitable, especially as it applied to their state, and the riots were largely initiated in protest against the draft. But they were also blatantly and murderously antiblack. Not accidentally, this was also the summer that newly recruited black troops were first being employed in important engagements, and in spite of the fact that they were showing that they could fight effectively, which many had doubted, their deployment was still unpopular. By August, Lincoln was at work on another public letter, this time defending both the draft and the decision to enlist former slaves and free blacks into the armed forces.

His opportunity to use it—or perhaps the opportunity that he decided to seize—came from Springfield. In spite of its being his own state, Illinois was a difficult one for the administration. The Democrats were numerous and their opposition to the war was strong and disruptive. Conkling and his friends had projected plans for a huge gathering in Springfield that would attempt to bring together all those, regardless of party, who favored the Union cause. On August 14, Conkling wrote to the president,

> The unconditional Union men of all parties in our State are to hold a Grand Mass Meeting at Springfield on the 3rd day of September next. It would be gratifying to the many thousands who will be present on that occasion if you would also meet with them. . . . Many of the most distinguished men in the country

have been, and will be invited to attend and I know that nothing could add more to the interest of the occasion than your presence.

Lincoln seriously considered making the trip. He telegraphed Conkling on August 20: "Your letter of the 14th. is received. I think I will go, or send a letter—probably the latter." He knew that his presence would help dramatize his concern to win over vacillating and disaffected Unionists, but he also knew he had been getting very good results with his public letters. He probably decided that he could not be away from his office for so long a time as a trip to Springfield would take, but he may well have concluded, in addition, that writing out his speech and having it printed for all to read was an even more effective way to shape public opinion. His secretaries wrote in their joint biography: "Modest as he was, he knew the value of his own work, and when a friend called to ask him if he was going to Springfield he replied, 'No, I shall send them a letter instead; and it will be a rather good letter.'"

Lincoln knew it would be a good letter because he had already written it. Or at least he had written a draft of what would become the main body of the letter. We can't be certain when he began this first version, but he had probably been working on it for some time. In early August, he had written a forceful letter to New York governor Horatio Seymour rejecting his request that the draft be suspended in his state. On August 10, the president had his first meeting with Frederick Douglass, who was helping to recruit black soldiers and had come to Washington to urge measures in their behalf, such as equal pay and promotions. There is little doubt that this meeting brought the efforts of black soldiers to Lincoln's attention, but by Douglass's own testimony, he was already well primed on the subject. "Upon my ceasing to speak [the president] proceeded with an earnestness and fluency of which I had not suspected him, to vindicate his policy respecting the whole slavery question and especially that in reference to employing colored troops."

The earliest version we have of what became the Conkling letter is a manuscript that was originally eleven pages long, the first six pages of which are now missing. The text that would become the body of the letter is on the remaining five pages, beginning on page seven (see Fig. 7-6).

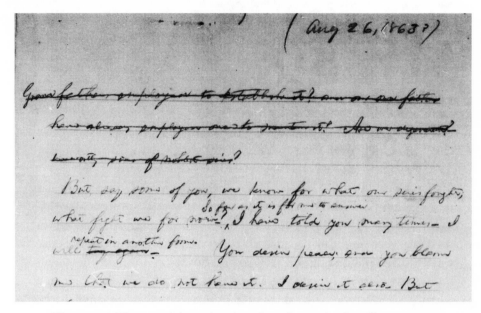

Figure 7-6. First surviving page (numbered seven) of an eleven-page manuscript containing an early version of the text that would constitute the body of Lincoln's August 26, 1863, letter to James C. Conkling. Library of Congress.

Though now lost, we can be reasonably sure of what was on the first six pages. This is indicated by the fragment of a sentence that carried over from the previous page: "Grand fathers employed to establish it? and our own fathers have already employed one to maintain it? Are we degenerate?—unworthy sons of noblest sires?" This is undoubtedly an earlier version of a sentence that appears in a paper on the draft that Lincoln would read to his cabinet a few weeks later: "Shall we shrink from the necessary means to maintain our free government, which our grand-fathers employed to establish it, and our own fathers have already employed once to maintain it? Are we degenerate? Has the manhood of our race run out?"

The fragmentary sentence at the top of page seven tells us a great deal. It tells us, for one thing, that Lincoln's original paper began with a strong defense of the draft, which after the riotous events of a month earlier in New York was the most volatile issue he was facing at the time. It also tells us that Lincoln had contemplated using, in this connection, a provocative emotional appeal that would, quite uncharacteristically, attempt to shame and humiliate those Unionists opposing conscription by directly calling their manhood into question. But perhaps most important, it tells us that in framing his letter to Conkling, he determined not to use the first six pages of his text, which in turn indicates that he had decided, in this letter, to avoid dealing with the issue of the draft altogether.

Why Lincoln decided to pass over the draft is not clear, but he may have resolved to concentrate on the issue of black soldiers because it was a positive development and one that needed to be publicly highlighted and put into perspective. In spite of the kind of difficulties that Frederick Douglass had spoken of—discrimination in promotion, a lower rate of pay, prejudiced treatment threatened by the Confederacy if captured—recruitment of black soldiers had been highly successful, and the so-called colored regiments had begun to distinguish themselves with hard fighting at such recent engagements as Milliken's Bend, Port Hudson, and Fort Wagner. With his usual keen sense of timing, Lincoln decided to use the occasion to confront the critics of emancipation and arming blacks.

And confront them he did. The most notable thing about the Conkling letter is the boldness and directness of its tone. Perhaps because he had sidestepped the draft, he was straightforward on the issues of emancipation and black soldiers. Reversing the tactic of the Corning letter, he waded right into his critics:

> There are those who are dissatisfied with me. To such I would say: You desire peace; and you blame me that we do not have it. But how can we attain it? There are but three conceivable ways.

As he spells out the three ways, he begins asking very pointed questions:

> First, to suppress the rebellion by force of arms. This I am trying to do. Are you for it? If you are, so far we are agreed_ If you are not for it, a second way is to give up the Union_ I am against this_ Are you for it? If you are, you should say so plainly_ If you are not for *force*, nor yet for *dissolution*, there only remains some imaginable *compromise*.

Putting aggressive questions is used repeatedly as a rhetorical pressure tactic in the Conkling letter.

Each topic is taken up in a similar way:

But, to be plain, some of you are dissatisfied with me about the colored man— Quite likely there is a difference of opinion between some of you and ~~me~~ myself upon that subject— I certainly wish that all men, ~~every where~~, could be free; while I suppose many of you do not.

Or again:

You dislike the emancipation proclamation; and, perhaps, would have it retracted. You say it is unconstitutional. I think differently. I think the Constitution invests it's Commander-in-Chief, with the laws of war, in time of war—

By the time he comes to the issue of using black soldiers, which he saves for last, Lincoln has laid the groundwork for his hardest sell by carefully creating a distinct feeling, a tension between himself and a skeptical listener, that is not hostile, but is nonetheless firm and resolute, and that puts the listener on the defensive. In the earliest draft, he had proposed to open the subject like this:

You say you will not fight to free negroes— Very well, fight exclusively to save the Union—

But he reinforced this in revision by inserting a sentence:

You say you will not fight to free negroes. Some of them seem willing to fight for you; but, no matter. Fight you, then exclusively to save the Union.

That strategic "but, no matter" is necessary to rescue the inserted sentence from sounding like recrimination, which could only cause resentment. The argument culminates with a passage that has been carefully reworked from its earlier stage and copied fair onto a separate page (see Fig. 7-7)—a well-deliberated pattern of assertions and questions, followed by a rationale:

I thought that ~~that~~ in your struggle for the Union, to whatever extent the negroes should cease helping the enemy, to that

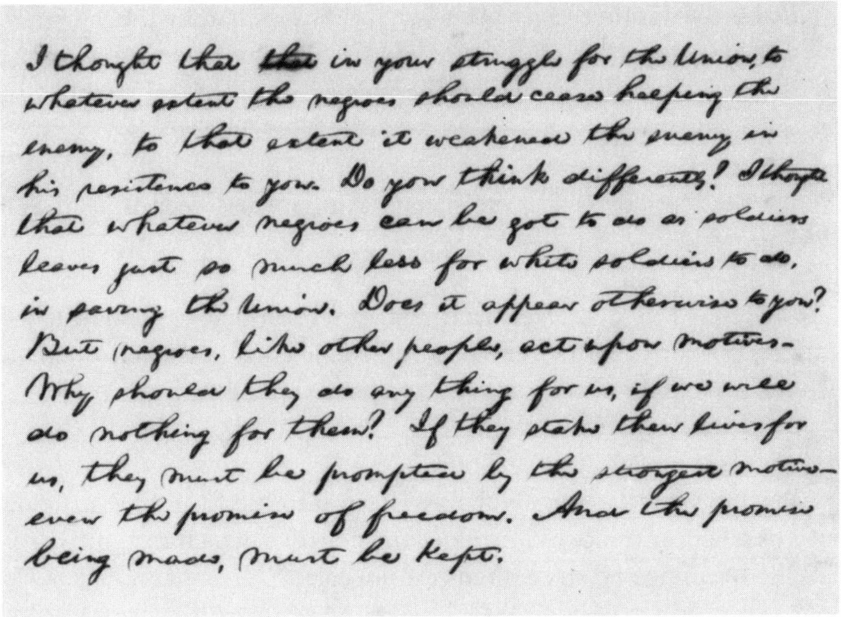
I thought that ~~that~~ in your struggle for the Union, to
whatever extent the negroes should cease helping the
enemy, to that extent it weakened the enemy in
his resistence to you. Do you think differently? I thought
that whatever negroes can be got to do as soldiers
leaves just so much less for white soldiers to do,
in saving the Union. Does it appear otherwise to you?
But negroes, like other people, act upon motives.
Why should they do any thing for us, if we will
do nothing for them? If they stake their lives for
us, they must be prompted by the strongest motive—
even the promise of freedom. And the promise
being made, must be kept.

Figure 7-7. Passage from the manuscript draft of Lincoln's letter of August 26, 1863, to James C. Conkling, page six. Library of Congress.

> extent it weakened the enemy in his resistence to you_ Do you think differently? I thought that whatever negroes can be got to do as soldiers leaves just so much less for white soldiers to do, in saving the Union. Does it appear otherwise to you? But negroes, like other people act upon motives_ Why should they do any thing for us, if we will do nothing for them? If they stake their lives for us, they must be prompted by the strongest motive—even the promise of freedom. And the promise being made, must be kept.

Because the overall tone is so forceful and relentless, Lincoln wisely softens some of his strongest wording. The "charges and intimations" that he had originally labeled "utter humbuggery, and falsehood" are more tactfully described in the revised version as "deceptive and groundless."

Lincoln's credentials as a careful, discriminating craftsman are often evident in small, almost invisible details. In the earliest draft, by way of arguing the military necessity of emancipation, he first wrote:

Is there—has there ever been—any question that, by the law of war, property both of enemies and friends, may be taken when needed? And it is needed whenever taking it helps us, or hurts the enemy_

But in the revised version the second sentence has been framed as a question:

Is there—has there ever been—any question that by the law of war, property, both of enemies and friends, may be taken when needed? And is it not needed whenever taking it, helps us, or hurts the enemy?

Putting what had been a flat assertion into the form of a question affords an opportunity to introduce the negative, which tactfully hardens the meaning and strengthens the appeal.

WHEN HE HAD EXHAUSTED the points laid out in his prewritten defense and turned to drafting a suitable conclusion to his letter, Lincoln did something that is not, at first glance, easy to explain but impossible to overlook. Into a letter of great earnestness, in which he had every reason to believe he had been cogently answering the grave misgivings of doubters and adversaries, he now introduced a strain of whimsy. The fact that such a whimsical strain is interwoven with more dignified language gives this transitional paragraph (see Fig. 7-8) a strangely anomalous character:

The signs look better. The Father of Waters again goes unvexed to the sea. Thanks to the great North-West for it. Nor yet wholly to them. Three hundred miles up, they met New-England, Empire, Key-Stone, and ~~the Jerseys'~~ <Jersey,> hewing their way right and left. The Sunny South too, in more colors than one, also lent a hand. On the spot their part of the history was jotted down in black and white. The job was a great national one; and let none be banned who bore an honorable part in it. And while those who have cleared the great river may well be proud, even that is not all. ~~Nothing~~ <It is hard to say that any-thing> has been more bravely, and well done, than at Antietam,

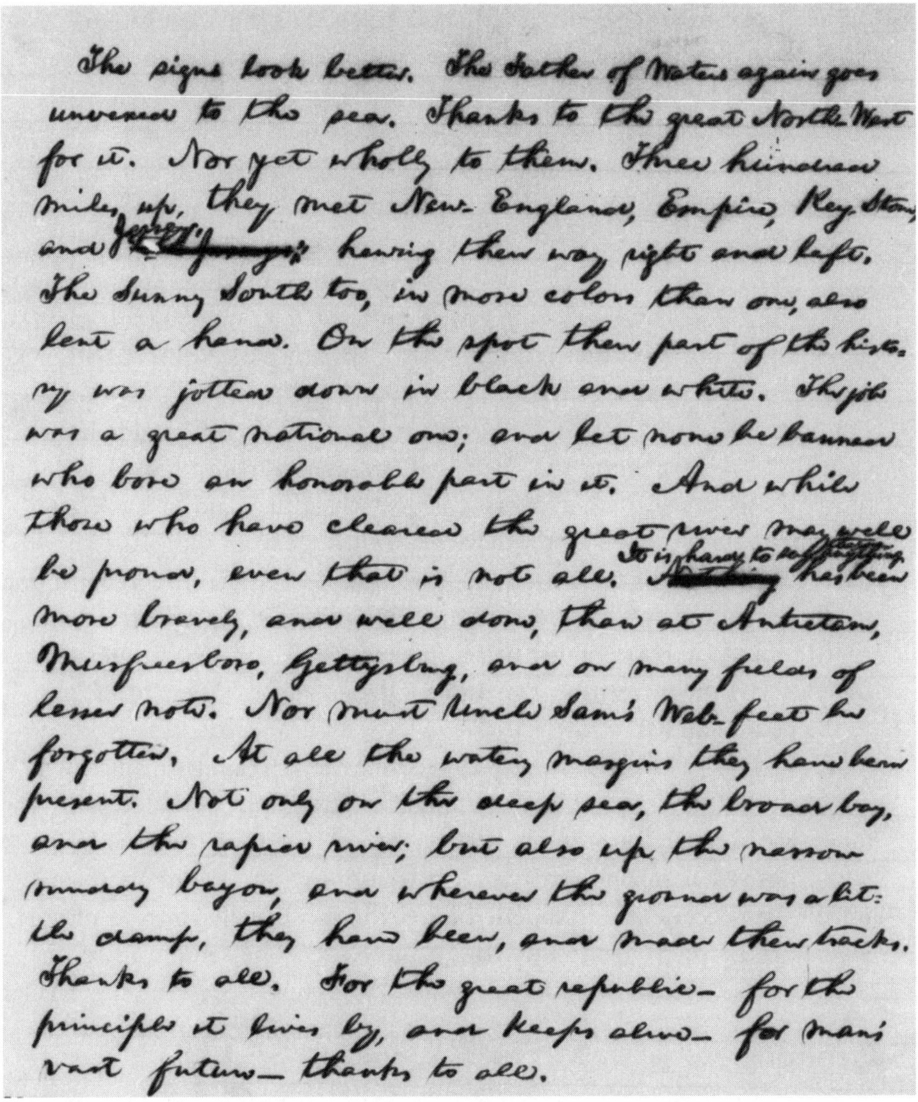

Figure 7-8. Paragraph from the manuscript draft of Lincoln's August 26, 1863, letter to James C. Conkling, page seven. Library of Congress.

Murfreesboro, Gettysburg, and on many fields of lesser note. Nor must Uncle Sam's Web-feet be forgotten. At all the watery margins they have been present. Not only on the deep sea, the broad bay, and the rapid river; but also up the narrow muddy bayou, and wherever the ground was a little damp, they have

been, and made their tracks. Thanks to all. For the great republic—for the principle it lives by, and keeps alive—for man's vast
future—thanks to all.

Though Lincoln's message zigzags, the direction is easy enough to
plot, and the paragraph, from the point of view of its writing, starts
well. After a series of confrontations, the writer clearly wants to con-
clude on a brighter note. The best news for people in Illinois is that the
Mississippi River has been opened, and it has been done by an Illinois
general. But not wanting to run the risk of slighting the efforts of other
important contingents, such as units from New England, New York,
Pennsylvania, and New Jersey, he gestures in their direction. Then the
contribution to opening the river that originated from New Orleans
must be acknowledged, especially since it featured both black and
white troops. But once all these accolades for clearing the Mississippi
have been handed out, notice must be taken of all the other battle-
fronts, large and small. And with all this praise for the efforts of the
army, those of the navy must be acknowledged. Finally, with a general
thanks from the government to all its citizens, must come a brief bow
to the goal of all this effort.

How did such a promising start get so far out of hand? In spite of a
confident beginning, the direction of the paragraph is suddenly dictated by a series of ricocheting references, and the tone is increasingly
compromised by feeble attempts at wit and low-grade humor. If one
were to try to say what happened here, the most likely starting place
would be the reference to the Mississippi River. The sentence itself is
memorable: "The Father of Waters again goes unvexed to the sea." As
a poetic collage of sounds and images, it is ingenious and affecting. But
referring to the Mississippi with the familiar stock phrase "Father of
Waters" surely precipitated the chain effect that resulted in "Empire"
for New York, "Keystone" for Pennsylvania, and the ultimate clunker,
"Uncle Sam's Web-feet" for the navy. Like the glancing references to
events and actors that seem to take on a life of their own, the whimsical naming and wordplay seem out of place and much too close to
clowning for such a context.

Especially in a discussion of his literary skill, the question presents
itself: why would Lincoln, after surveying what he had written, let such
a paragraph stand? Its mixed modes have raised eyebrows and drawn
unfavorable comment from the time the paragraph first appeared.
Even the clerk that Lincoln recruited as a listener in the White House,

when the president insisted on criticism, claimed he timorously pointed to "Uncle Sam's Web-feet." Lincoln reportedly only chuckled and said, "I reckoned it would be some such place as that. I'll leave it in just as it is."

But was this really the result of a tin ear? To imagine that Lincoln was blind to these objections would defy most of what we know about his care and sensitivity in rendering his text. The weight of the evidence is that he knew perfectly well what he was doing, that, like it or not, he was deliberately seeking the effect he succeeded in producing. So what was that effect? It was certainly not to impress sophisticated readers, but it may well have been something much more practical—to change the mood and thereby to ease the argumentative pressure he had brought to bear on his audience. And he knew that his principal audience, both at the meeting in Springfield and as newspaper readers throughout the North, would not object to the whimsical character of the paragraph, but, on the contrary, would probably respond favorably. As he reportedly told Chauncey Depew, he believed that ordinary people "are more easily influenced and informed through the medium of a broad illustration than in any other way, and as to what the hypercritical few may think, I don't care." George Templeton Strong seemed to understand as much, for he wrote in his diary of the Conkling letter, "There are sentences that a critic would like to eliminate, but they are delightfully characteristic of the 'plain man' who wrote it and will appeal directly to the great mass of 'plain men' from Maine to Minnesota."

That Lincoln felt the strategic necessity for such a paragraph is suggested by the fact that he had one more strong message he wanted to deliver. Its potential impact was such that both he and his audience needed breathing space before taking it up. Here it is:

> Peace does not appear so distant as it did. I hope it will come soon, and come to stay; and so come as to be worth the keeping in all future time—It will then have been proved that, among free men, there can be no successful appeal from the ballot to the bullet; and that they who take such appeal are sure to lose their case, and pay the cost. And then, there will be some black men who can remember that, with silent tongue, and clenched teeth, and steady <eye,> and well ~~borne~~ <poised> bayonet, they have helped mankind on to this great consummation; while <I fear,> there will be some white ones, unable to forget that, with

malignant hearts, and deceitful speech, they have strove to hinder it.

This is the only draft we have of this part of the letter, and it probably represents the result of a certain amount of prior drafting and revision, but what is interesting in the extant draft (see Fig. 7-9) is that all Lincoln's final revisions are concentrated in the extraordinarily vivid depiction of the black soldier disciplining himself to fight. The literary strategy of this paragraph is masterful. It is to first *tell* us that peace, when it comes, will prove the truth of a proposition, which the writer states in a catchy, alliterative synecdoche about the ballot and the bullet. But then we are not told but *shown*, graphically, what else will be proved by the coming of peace—that there were black men who had faced death to save democracy while some whites would live to regret that they had tried actively to undermine the effort.

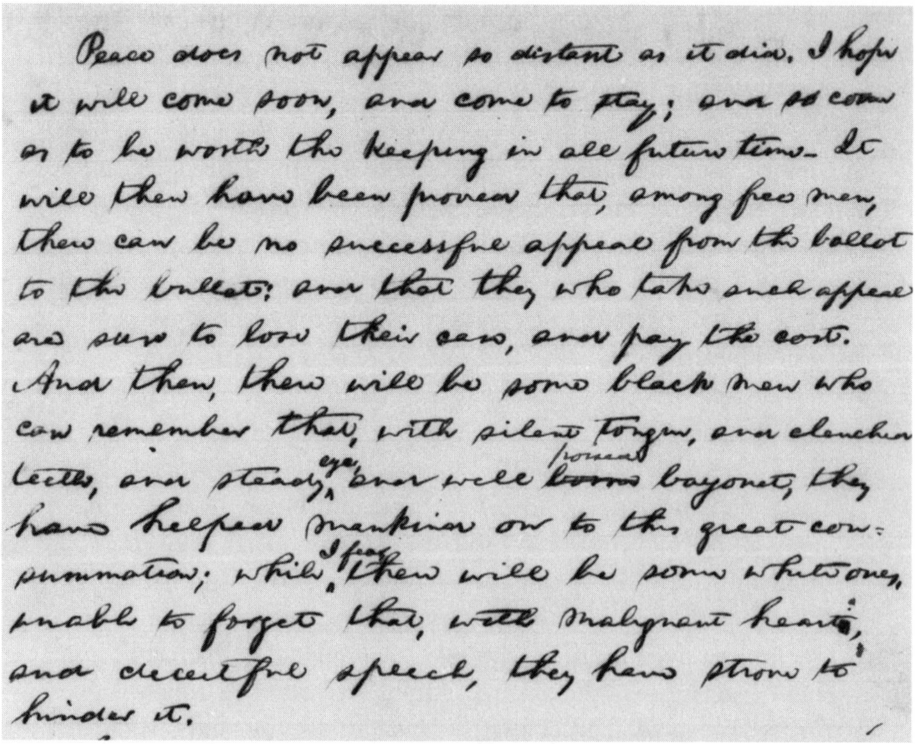

Figure 7-9. Next-to-last paragraph of the manuscript draft of Lincoln's August 26, 1863, letter to James C. Conkling. Library of Congress.

Nicolay and Hay wrote of the Conkling letter: "Among all the state papers of Mr. Lincoln from his nomination to his death this letter is unique. It may be called his last stump-speech, the only one made during his Presidency." In the sense that they meant it, this is perhaps just: "It was, like most of his speeches, addressed principally to his opponents, and in this short space he appealed successively to their reason, to their sympathies, and to their fears." True enough. But in other ways the Conkling letter was unlike a stump speech, which is why Lincoln wanted it read in a certain way. "You are one of the best public readers," he wrote Conkling. "I have but one suggestion. Read it very slowly." Not slowly, but *very* slowly. It had been carefully crafted for nuance of expression, and it was packed with meaning. Its themes and expressions were broad enough to engage listeners but at the same time rich and deep enough to repay readers. The letter managed to address a broad spectrum. The abolitionists had been given reason to rejoice; the moderates, reason to believe. The more conservative loyalists had been given arguments that directly challenged their doubts and misgivings.

THE CONKLING LETTER WAS duly presented to the mass meeting in Springfield on September 3, 1863. Although it was prematurely printed in some newspapers, and thus not entirely fresh, the president's letter was enthusiastically received by the Springfield meeting, estimated by Conkling at fifty to seventy-five thousand. Much to the gratification of the administration, the reception across the country was nearly the same. "Nothing he ever uttered had a more instantaneous success," Nicolay and Hay remembered. Praise poured in through the mails, some of it from hard-to-please critics, like the austere Massachusetts senator Charles Sumner. "I must begin what I have to say by my thanks for yr true & noble letter, which is an historic document. The case is admirably stated, so that all but the wicked must confess its force. It cannot be answered."

With the publication and general success of the Conkling letter, there began to be some wider recognition that the president, even with his idiosyncrasies, was an effective writer. It dawned on some of those open to the idea that their unpolished, self-educated chief magistrate, "Honest Old Abe," was developing a literary track record, having produced not one or two able papers but what was beginning to look like a whole series of them. One of the editors of the *New York Times*, probably Henry J. Raymond, printed an article on the subject a few days after the Conkling letter appeared. Under the headline "The Right Man in the Right Place," the *Times* writer extolled the aptness and effectiveness of Lincoln's public letters. "In his own independent, and perhaps we might say very peculiar, way, he invariably gets at the needed truth of the time. When he writes, it is always said that 'he hits the nail upon the head,' and so he does; but the beauty of it is that the nail which he hits is sure to be the very nail of all others which needs driving." The Greeley and Corning letters came in for special recognition. "His letter to Mr. GREELEY, odd as it seemed at first blush, was, as everybody now admits, perfectly adapted to that stage of the war. His letter to the intercessors for Mr. VALLANDIGHAM utterly annihilated the case they thought they had made so strong; and yet it was done in so genial a way that the victims themselves felt like joining in the general applause."

The *Times* writer wasn't simply being partisan, for a measure of astonishment is evident in his tone. Lincoln's public letters were actually having a decided impact on the way the war was being perceived. Just when it looked as if the concern for the curtailment of civil liberties was going to bring on a general crisis of confidence, Lincoln had produced the Corning letter, noticeably quieting the public's fears and restoring the government's credibility. A few months later, when doubts about emancipation and the use of black soldiers became a serious issue for large numbers of Union loyalists, the president produced yet another persuasive letter. In large part because of their assumptions about Lincoln's abilities, even his supporters were unprepared for this kind of sustained literary performance.

The *Times* was not alone in recognizing that the Conkling letter was only the latest in a series of notable letters. A New York publisher and its Boston affiliate soon brought out a twenty-two-page pamphlet entitled *The Letters of President Lincoln on Questions of National Policy*. In addition to the Greeley, Corning, and Conkling letters, the pamphlet included letters written to General McClellan, former New York mayor Fernando Wood, and New York governor Horatio Seymour. The latter three were not written as public letters but had been previously disclosed by the press, and they constituted evidence of a shrewd politician and forceful writer dealing with a headstrong general, a meddling Southern sympathizer, and a fractious and uncooperative governor. In a brief preface, the publisher allowed that the president's letters "though peculiar in style, are marked by very high ability and statesmanship."

Charles Eliot Norton was a classically trained scholar who would soon become editor of the prestigious *North American Review* and one of the founders of the *Nation*. Norton thought he had seen Lincoln's shortcomings revealed in his style the initial year of his presidency, when he wrote of Lincoln's first annual message: "We are very serious over the President's message. We think it very poor in style, manner and thought—very wanting in pith, and exhibiting a mournful deficiency of strong feeling and of wise forecast in the President." Like most of his fellow Brahmins, Norton agreed that the Emancipation Proclamation had been "an important step," but he worried that its stylistic failings might be an ominous sign. "His style is worse than ever; and though a bad style is not always a mark of bad thought—it is at least proof that thought is not as clear as it ought to be." But the public letters of 1863 turned Norton completely around. Writing to George William Curtis shortly after the appearance of the Conkling letter, Norton told his friend,

> We might congratulate each other on the extraordinary excellence of the President's letter. He rises with each new effort, and his letters are successive victories. Indeed the series of his letters since and including the one to the Albany Committee are, as he says to General Grant of Vicksburg, 'of inestimable value to the country'—for they are of the rarest class of political documents, arguments seriously addressed by one in power to the conscience and reason of the citizens of the commonwealth.

Another formidable literary presence, Harriet Beecher Stowe, was likewise converted. "Sooth to say," she wrote of Lincoln, "our own politicians were somewhat shocked with his state-papers at first. Why not let *us* make them a little more conventional, and file them to a classified pattern? 'No,' was his reply, 'I shall write them myself. *The people will understand them.*' 'But this or that form of expression is not elegant, not classical.' '*The people will understand it,*' has been his invariable reply." Mrs. Stowe, the author of *Uncle Tom's Cabin*, had met Lincoln at the White House and probably had a source of inside information, for this is exactly what he had told both Defrees and Stoddard. But whatever may be said of his writing, she insisted, "there are passages in his state-papers that could not be better put; they are absolutely perfect. They are brief, condensed, intense, and with a power of insight and expression which make them worthy to be inscribed in letters of gold. Such are some passages of the celebrated Springfield letter, especially that masterly one where he compares the conduct of the patriotic and loyal blacks with that of the treacherous and disloyal whites." This is high praise indeed, and it explains, to some extent, another opinion that she shared with her readers, that "the state-papers of no President have more controlled the popular mind."

A sticking point for the intelligentsia with respect to Lincoln, perhaps *the* sticking point, had always been the question of whether he was really a "gentleman." Stuffy and irrelevant as that sounds to twenty-first-century ears, it was an important consideration to highly educated and cultivated men and women of that time, especially those who understood their education and cultivation as having been acquired for the purpose of the improvement, if not the salvation, of the world. This issue is always present when Lincoln's accomplishments are being weighed, and it duly appeared in the *Times* article. "Men talk about a courtly felicity of speech, and term it a rare accomplishment. So indeed it is. Nothing but high culture and the most patient practice confers it. Here [in the Conkling letter] is a felicity of speech far surpassing it, yet decidedly uncourtly." The *Times* writer is here touching on what was in effect a major reason that Lincoln's qualities as a superior writer had been so little recognized—because everyone knew that he conspicuously lacked "high culture," the courtly refinement that was presumed to be necessary for the felicitous use of language. But here, for all to see, was felicitous speech that was decidedly "uncourtly." "The most consummate rhetorician never used language more pat to the purpose," noted the *Times* writer, "and still there is not a word in the letter not familiar to the plainest plowman."

A measure of how stubborn the "gentleman" issue was at the time can be seen in the attitude of Ralph Waldo Emerson. America's most prominent man of letters had been much disappointed by Lincoln's nomination, and only with the announcement of the Emancipation Proclamation the previous September did he begin to endorse the president with enthusiasm. Emerson had been calling much of his adult life for a distinctively American language and literature that would eschew the courtliness of European models and search out, instead, the latent eloquence of authentic American speech. But where Lincoln's writing was concerned, Emerson remained strangely tone-deaf. He was still reconciling himself to Lincoln's rough edges and lack of refinement, when sometime after the Conkling letter he wrote in his journal:

> Lincoln.—We must accept the results of universal suffrage, and not try to make it appear that we can elect fine gentlemen. We shall have coarse men, with a fair chance of worth and manly ability, but not men to please the English or French.
>
> You cannot refine Mr. Lincoln's taste, or extend his horizon; he will not walk dignifiedly through the traditional part of the President of America, but will pop out his head at each railroad station and make a little speech, and get into an argument with Squire A. and Judge B. He will write letters to Horace Greeley, and any editor or reporter or saucy party committee that writes to him, and cheapen himself.

Lincoln's public letters had made a strong impression and contributed greatly to his stature as a leader and to public support for the Union cause, but where his literary ability and its power to produce results were concerned in the fall of 1863, not everyone had seen the light.

CHAPTER EIGHT

The Gettysburg Address

I believe the declaration that "all men are created equal" is the great fundamental principle upon which our free institutions rest.

ABRAHAM LINCOLN, 1858

I. THE ELECTRIC CORD

JOHN HAY WAS ONLY twenty-three years old when appointed assistant personal secretary to President Lincoln, but he quickly became a trusted aide. Intelligent, loyal, and discreet, Hay's powers of observation and ready wit made him an ideal companion for a beleaguered president to whom it became increasingly important to see the humor in things and find occasions to indulge his innate sense of fun. With Hay, the president could let his hair down without fear of being compromised, which is why Hay's letters and diary are such a mine of inside information on Lincoln's private sayings and personal views. A delightful conversationalist and storyteller, Hay had another asset that made him valuable to this particular president—his special affinity for wordplay and literature. It was Hay who often accompanied Lincoln to the theater and listened to his readings from Shakespeare and other poets by the hour.

In fact, John Hay was himself an aspiring writer, a budding versifier who had been the class poet at Brown. It was probably this that prompted Lincoln to present him with some comic verses he wrote in July 1863. And therein lies a story. What most Americans could not have known at the time was that their president, while publicly celebrating the great victory at Gettysburg, had actually been in deep despair. As Hay well knew, the president had been mortified and almost beside himself when, during the two weeks following the battle of Gettysburg, the Union forces had not moved decisively to prevent the defeated army's escape across the Potomac River. Characteristically, he had tried to explain his frustration in writing—a letter on July 14 to the victorious general, George G. Meade—but uncharacteristically he lost control of his message and allowed his extreme disappointment to overwhelm his gratitude. "Again, my dear general, I do not believe you appreciate the magnatude of the misfortune involved in Lee's escape. He was within your easy grasp, and to have closed upon him would, in connection with our other late successes, have ended the war." Ultimately sensing that giving voice to such sentiments would do more harm than good, he quietly filed the letter, unsigned and unsent.

It was not like the president to remain in a funk for long, for as a long-suffering depressive, he was experienced at bringing himself around. On Saturday, July 18, he put in a grueling six-hour session reviewing court-martial proceedings, looking, as Hay wryly recorded in his diary, for "any fact that would justify him in saving the life of a condemned soldier." In the course of reviewing the grim sentences, he leavened the atmosphere with humor, allowing, for example, that men convicted of cowardice must not be condemned to death for "it would frighten the poor devils too terribly to shoot them." The next morning, Hay reported, the president was "in very good humor" and presented his poet assistant secretary with the following verses (see Fig. 8-1):

Gen. Lees invasion of the North written by himself—

> In eighteen sixty three, with pomp
>   and mighty swell,
> Me and Jeff's Confederacy, went
>   forth to sack Phil-del,
> The Yankees they got arter us, and
>   giv us particular hell,
> And we skedaddled back again,
>   and didn't sack Phil-del.

Another man in Lincoln's situation might understandably have made General Meade the subject of his verses and given *him* particular

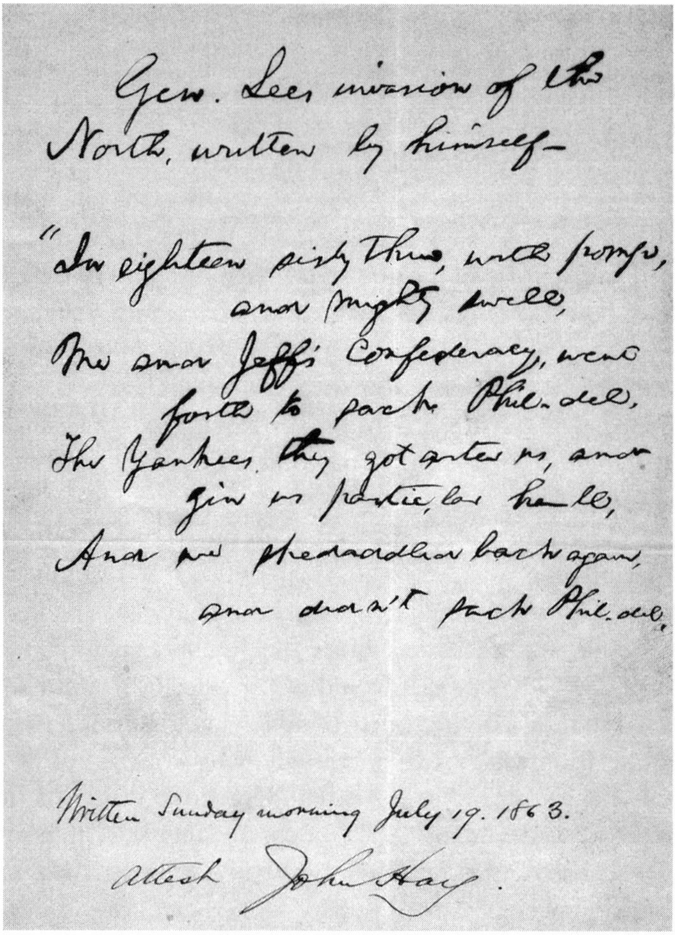

Figure 8-1. Manuscript of verses on Lee's invasion of Pennsylvania by Abraham Lincoln. Courtesy of John Hay Library, Brown University.

hell. But Lincoln's instincts were nonvindictive; he looked for spirit-raising humor and found it by versifying in comic dialect the improbable musings of the dignified Southern general Robert E. Lee.

Lincoln knew well enough that it did little good to moan about his misfortunes and berate his subordinates. It was more fruitful to acknowledge the positive side and get on with your work, which is what he did. Giving expression to the "skedaddling" of General Lee and his army marked the passing of the president's funk. A few weeks later, on August 7, Hay wrote to the vacationing John G. Nicolay, "The Tycoon is in fine whack. I have rarely seen him more serene &

busy. He is managing this war, the draft, foreign relations, and planning a reconstruction of the Union, all at once." When Nicolay had left the White House in mid-July, the "Tycoon" had been very much *out* of whack, but Hay's remark suggests that their chief had resumed his accustomed manner and was more productive than ever. A month later, Hay wrote again to tell Nicolay that their boss was still going strong. "The old man sits here and wields like a backwoods Jupiter the bolts of war and the machinery of government with a hand equally steady & equally firm."

This period of renewed presidential energy and activity presumably produced most of the prewriting, and all of the drafting, that went into the Conkling letter of August 26, as well as other memoranda on reunion and the draft. Hay offered Nicolay his appraisal, both literary and political, of the merits of the letter to Conkling, probably the most successful of the president's unprecedented public letters: "His last letter is a great thing. Some hideously bad rhetoric—some indecorums that are infamous—yet the whole letter takes its solid place in history, as a great utterance of a great man. The whole cabinet could not have tinkered up a letter which could have been compared with it. He can snake a sophism out of its hole, better than all the trained logicians of all schools."

THE CONKLING LETTER WAS thus, by Hay's lights, a product of Lincoln working at the top of his form, but there was also another speech gestating in Lincoln's mind and perhaps on scraps of paper during the same period. The draft, the emancipation of slaves, the deployment of black troops, like the curtailment of civil liberties, were all public opinion issues that had to be dealt with to keep the war effort going successfully, and for these, public letters had proved gratifyingly effective. But what, at this point, did the Northern public think the war itself was about? What was all the killing and dying for? Could it at least be understood as having a noble purpose, not just for idealistic abolitionists, but for ordinary Americans? These were questions that grew more pressing as the war ground on. In his first Annual Message to Congress back in December 1861, Lincoln had stressed that he was particularly anxious that suppressing the insurrection should "not degenerate into a violent and remorseless revolutionary struggle." But it had taken far longer for the government to gain the upper hand in the rebellion than the president and most Unionists had anticipated, and such success as had been gained was far from unmixed. The Union Army, it was true, had exacted a fearful price for the Confederate attempt to operate North of the Mason-Dixon Line—twenty-eight thousand casualties at Gettysburg alone—but the Union losses of twenty-three thousand had been almost as bad, and the end was scarcely in sight.

It did not require the president's keen sense of timing to know that a "remorseless revolutionary struggle" would inevitably weary and sicken its supporters, causing them to seek or accept some means of relief short of military victory. The longer the list of casualties, the greater became the need for some galvanizing purpose to bolster and sustain the military effort. "Once it became clear that the war would be a protracted struggle," Richard J. Carwardine has written, "Lincoln knew that superior military force would not alone secure victory. Essential to the Union's success was the nourishing of popular patriotism in the face of the ravages of war." In resorting to the image of ballots over bullets in the Conkling letter, Lincoln had invoked perhaps his strongest and most basic argument for resisting the rebellion—that it would undermine and ultimately destroy the American experiment, and with it, popular government itself. But to much of his audience such a goal must have seemed somewhat abstract and impersonal, and arguments, by their nature, can do only so much. They may convince or placate or give pause, but to what extent do they reach the public's deepest feelings? And how, without engaging these, was public opinion to be molded and mobilized?

Lincoln had a theory about public opinion. He told a meeting of his fellow Republicans in 1856 that public opinion "always has a '*central idea*,' from which all its minor thoughts radiate. That 'central idea' in our political public opinion, at the beginning was, and until recently has continued to be, 'the equality of men.' And although it [h]as always submitted patiently to whatever of inequality there seemed to be as matter of actual necessity, its constant working has been a steady progress towards the practical equality of all men." What had changed by 1856 was that the defenders of slavery had begun either to deny that this assertion from the Declaration of Independence was meant to apply to blacks, as Stephen A. Douglas would do in his debates with Lincoln, or to disparage it as a "self-evident lie."

Lincoln had discovered in his campaigning in the 1850s, if not previously, that the Declaration's theme of the equality of all men had an especially powerful effect on ordinary citizens, appealing, it would seem, to something deeper than parties or policies, something, perhaps, having to do with ordinary people's sense of themselves. In his breakthrough speech at Peoria in 1854 he had said, "Near eighty years ago we began by declaring that all men are created equal; but now from that beginning we have run down to the other declaration, that for SOME men to enslave OTHERS is a 'sacred right of self-government.' " Even with immigrants, who could claim no direct relationship to the American Revolution or to the founding fathers, the Declaration's principle retained its special appeal. In a speech in Chicago on July 10, 1858, Lincoln undertook to explain why this was so:

> . . . they cannot carry themselves back into that glorious epoch and make themselves feel that they are part of us, but when they look through that old Declaration of Independence they find that those old men say that "We hold these truths to be self-evident, that all men are created equal," and then they feel that that moral sentiment taught in that day evidences their relation to those men, that it is the father of all moral principle in them, and that they have a right to claim it as though they were blood of the blood, and flesh of the flesh of the men who wrote that Declaration, and so they are. That is the electric cord in that Declaration that links the hearts of patriotic and liberty-loving men together, that will link those patriotic hearts as long as the love of freedom exists in the minds of men throughout the world.

By contrast with most of his recorded speeches of this period, which typically show evidence of carefully deliberated phrasing, there is an uncharacteristic lack of restraint in the conclusion of this Chicago speech: "Let us discard all this quibbling about this man and the other man—this race and that race and the other race being inferior, and therefore they must be placed in an inferior position—discarding our standard that they have left us. Let us discard all these things, and unite as one people throughout this land, until we shall once more stand up declaring that all men are created equal." It was a heady moment on a hot July night in 1858, and Abraham Lincoln was perhaps somewhat carried away, but there is little doubt that he was giving vent to a passionately held political precept. In the debates to follow, his opponent, Stephen A. Douglas, made Lincoln pay dearly for this unguarded moment by quoting what he had said to unsympathetic audiences in more conservative parts of Illinois as evidence of Lincoln's abolitionist extremism. Since no politician of that day could be elected to statewide office in Illinois if he was even suspected of advocating social or political equality for blacks, Lincoln was forced, in effect, to backtrack and issue disclaimers in subsequent speeches. Although he clung tenaciously throughout the debates to the Declaration and its assertion of human equality as an inalienable natural right, forcing Douglas to restrict and qualify its application, he never repeated the suggestion that racial distinctions were mere "quibblings" that should be discarded.

Lincoln's attachment to the Declaration was neither temporary nor merely expedient, but after the debates with Douglas, he began to be more circumspect in his references to its assertion of human equality. In the year following the debates, he seized an opportunity to claim its author and Democratic hero, Thomas Jefferson, as a surprise political ally of the Republican Party. Invited to a commemoration of Jefferson in Boston, Lincoln used his reply to make a political statement that would be published by his friends and circulated nationally. It concluded: "All honor to Jefferson—to the man who, in the concrete pressure of a struggle for national independence by a single people, had the coolness, forecast, and capacity to introduce into a merely revolutionary document, an abstract truth, applicable to all men at all times, and so to embalm it there, that to-day, and in all coming days, it shall be a rebuke and a stumbling-block to the very harbingers of re-appearing tyranny and oppression." Without naming it, Lincoln had called attention to the Declaration's "self-evident" truth that all men are created equal.

On his way to Washington to assume the presidency two years later, Lincoln paid a visit to the birthplace of the Declaration, Independence Hall in Philadelphia. Still hopeful of keeping several key Southern states from joining the burgeoning Confederacy, he was, in his remarks, careful not to make the Declaration a source of contention. But he did not disguise his deep personal feeling for the revolutionary struggle and his strong attachment to the much-revered document that gave it expression:

I have often inquired of myself, what great principle or idea it was that kept this Confederacy so long together. It was not the mere matter of the separation of the colonies from the mother land; but something in that Declaration giving liberty, not alone to the people of this country, but hope to the world for all future time. It was that which gave promise that in due time the weights should be lifted from the shoulders of all men, and that *all* should have an equal chance. This is the sentiment embodied in that Declaration of Independence.

This was as close to an endorsement of the assertion that "all men are created equal" as the festering political circumstances would permit him to come—that the Declaration of 1776 gave not only liberty to the colonists but hope to the world that the future would see the burdens of oppression lifted and all people set on an equal footing. "Now, my friends," the president-elect then asked, "can this country be saved upon that basis? If it can, I will consider myself one of the happiest men in the world if I can help to save it. If it can't be saved upon that principle, it will be truly awful." Perhaps sensing that this was a weak note to end on, he added dramatically, "But, if this country cannot be saved without giving up that principle—I was about to say I would rather be assassinated on this spot than to surrender it." This was an emphatic endorsement, indeed, of the basic "sentiment embodied in the Declaration of Independence" and an early precursor of the opening lines of a more famous speech to come.

Four months later, in his first Message to Congress, Lincoln would make another strategic reference to the Declaration, observing, "Our adversaries have adopted some Declarations of Independence; in which, unlike the good old one, penned by Jefferson, they omit the words 'all men are created equal.' Why? They have adopted a temporary national constitution, in the preamble of which, unlike our good old one, signed by Washington, they omit 'We, the People,' and substitute 'We, the deputies of the sovereign and independent States.' Why? Why this deliberate pressing out of view, the rights of men, and the authority of the people?"

Pointed questions were a mark of Lincoln's most provocative writing, and here they set the stage for the message's most memorable passage, which conspicuously redeploys the imagery he had used at Independence Hall. "This is essentially a People's contest. On the side of the Union, it is a struggle for maintaining in the world, that form, and substance of government, whose leading object is, to elevate the condition of men—to lift artificial weights from all shoulders—clear the paths of laudable pursuit for all—to afford all, an unfettered start, and a fair chance, in the race of life. Yielding to partial, and temporary departures, from necessity, this is the leading object of the government for whose existence we contend." The last sentence, which is often omitted when this passage is quoted, is nonetheless a reminder of the affinity of this 1861 statement with his 1856 theory about the "central idea" of American political opinion, which spoke of its submitting "patiently to whatever of inequality there seemed to be as matter of actual necessity" and its emphasis on "the practical equality of all men."

❧

HAVING BEEN VICTIMIZED BY his unbuttoned Chicago remarks in 1858, Lincoln, once elected to the presidency, stubbornly refused to make unscripted, impromptu speeches. Fearful of saying something inadvertently that might be susceptible of an adverse interpretation, he persisted, when unprepared, in saying little more than "thank you," even to the crowds of well-wishers who came to the White House to serenade him. But the night of July 7, 1863, was to be a notable exception. The great victories at Gettysburg and Vicksburg, coming at or near the Fourth of July, brought crowds of celebrants to the White House, and for once the president gratified them with a speech. Martin P. Johnson, who has recently discovered a more complete and telling text of this speech, adduces evidence that Lincoln probably prepared for it and notes that this was "the longest extemporaneous speech to a serenading party of his presidency, well over twice as long as the average of his fourteen other serenade speeches for which there was no written draft."

There can be little doubt what was foremost on the president's mind, for in his brief remarks he mentioned it three times. "How long ago is it?" he asked the crowd. "Eighty-odd years, since upon the Fourth of July, for the first time in the world, a union body of representatives was assembled to declare as a self-evident truth that all men were created equal." After noting that both Thomas Jefferson, the chief author, and John Adams, the chief supporter of the Declaration, had died on the same Fourth of July, an "extraordinary coincidence" that may be understood as providential, Lincoln then says, "and now on this Fourth of July just past, when a gigantic rebellion has risen in the land, precisely at the bottom of which is an effort to overthrow that principle that all men are created equal, we have a surrender of one of their most powerful positions and powerful armies forced upon them on that very day." This is followed immediately by the third reference to the Declaration's equality theme, a reference which, by its phrasing and humor, was likely prepared in advance and may even have been the kernel from which the idea for a brief speech was formed. "And I see in a succession of battles in Pennsylvania, which continued three days, so rapidly following each other as to be justly called one great battle, fought on the first, second, and third of July, and on the *fourth* the enemies of the declaration that all men are created equal had to turn tail and run."

Lincoln's depiction of the Confederates as the enemies of the Declaration was more than just an idle or invidious characterization. His former congressional colleague from Georgia, Alexander H. Stephens, after being elected vice president of the Confederacy, had made a point of proclaiming *inequality* as a founding principle of his new government:

> The prevailing ideas entertained by [Jefferson] and most of the leading statesmen at the time of the formation of the old Constitution, were that the enslavement of the African was in violation of the laws of nature; that it was wrong in *principle*, socially, morally and politically. . . . Our new government is founded upon exactly the opposite idea; its foundations are laid, its corner-stone rests upon the great truth, that the negro is not equal to the white man; that slavery—subordination to the superior race—is his natural and normal condition.

This "cornerstone" doctrine, which was widely publicized North and South, came as a vindication of what Lincoln had argued about the beliefs of the founders in his debates with Douglas. Now, in July of 1863, the president had decided to use the Union victories, coming in conjunction with the nation's birthday, as the occasion for emphasizing that the war against the Union was being waged by the enemies of the Declaration. But after Lincoln stated his thesis to the serenaders, his reticence about speaking extemporaneously returned, and he promptly declined to follow it up. "Gentlemen," he told the crowd, "this is a glorious theme and a glorious occasion for a speech, but I am not prepared to make one worthy of the theme and worthy of the occasion." The implication, especially seen in hindsight, is that he would *like* to make such a speech on such a glorious theme. And, given time, he would.

&

WHAT THE FOREGOING SUGGESTS is that the "glorious theme" and the famous speech at Gettysburg that was to give it expression had a very long gestation period indeed, predating even the presidency. Lincoln's response to the serenaders on July 7, 1863, was thus not so much the origin of the speech he would give five months later as a sign that the elements of such a speech had begun to crystallize in his mind. If the Greeley, Corning, and Conkling letters suggest a pattern, it is that when Lincoln seized upon a theme, he began making notes and looking for a suitable occasion. Unfortunately, no notes have survived to indicate the permutations that the "glorious theme" might have undergone, but we know enough about Lincoln's way of working to be reasonably sure he was making notes on the subject as ideas occurred to him. His son Robert simply took that for granted, for he wrote a correspondent that he had no knowledge of "what became of the original notes."

The dedication was set for November 19, but the formal invitation for the president to speak at Gettysburg was not sent by David Wills until November 2. Wills had been put in charge of developing a cemetery to accommodate the burial of soldiers who had been killed at Gettysburg, a scheme that was originally authorized by Governor Andrew Curtin of Pennsylvania but was eventually sponsored jointly by all the Northern states whose soldiers had died on the Gettysburg battlefield. It has long been suspected that Lincoln had heard about this project much earlier from Curtin, who had been to Washington in August and October, and who presumably discussed with the president the possibility of his participation. Little-noted accounts in Pennsylvania newspapers make it virtually certain that the president was already being included in the official arrangements in early October, at least three weeks before his invitation was sent. For example, on October 11, Wills told a correspondent for the *Philadelphia Inquirer* that "President Lincoln is expected to perform the consecrational service." This would mean Lincoln had significantly more time to prepare than previously believed. While we can't be sure that he actively sought the invitation, everything we know about the way Lincoln worked suggests that once he was committed to participating, he would have been thinking about and making notes on what he was going to say.

Although we have none of the president's notes, we can see, in retrospect, that there were other factors at work that would draw him toward the Gettysburg dedication. Across the road from the Soldiers' Home, where he lived during the summer and fall of 1863, was a graveyard for the "inmates," retired and disabled soldiers from the regular army. Because Washington had become the principal place that sick and wounded soldiers were brought during the war, and because there was no other government burial place available, the Soldiers' Home graveyard became the scene of large numbers of burials on a daily basis. By the end of 1863, the number of graves was approaching five thousand and the available ground nearly exhausted, which led directly to the establishment the next year of Arlington National Cemetery. The effect of these incessant burials on a president long haunted by the idea of human mortality, and openly anguished by his own role in the deaths of thousands of young men, can well be imagined. There is at least one account that places him on the scene. A visitor to the Soldiers' Home reported walking over to the cemetery and gazing upon "numberless graves—some without a spear of grass to hide their newness." As the party viewed this somber spectacle, the report continued, "Mr. Lincoln joined us and stood silent, too, taking in the scene.

> 'How sleep the brave, who sink to rest
> By all their country's wishes blest,'—

he said, softly."

~∾

THE DETAILS OF DAVID WILLS'S letter of invitation are worth noting:

> The several States having soldiers in the Army of the Potomac, who were killed at the Battle of Gettysburg, or have since died at the various hospitals which were established in the vicinity, have

procured grounds on a prominent part of the Battle Field for a Cemetery, and are having the dead removed to them and properly buried.

These Grounds will be Consecrated and set apart to this sacred purpose, by appropriate Ceremonies, on Thursday, the 19th instant,—

Hon Edward Everett will deliver the Oration.

I am authorized by the Governors of the different States to invite You to be present, and participate in these Ceremonies, which will doubtless be very imposing and solemnly impressive.

It is the desire that, after the Oration, You, as Chief Executive of the Nation, formally set apart these grounds to their Sacred use by a few appropriate remarks.

The late date and other evidence has often been taken to mean that Lincoln's invitation had been an afterthought. Clark E. Carr, who represented the state of Illinois on the commission over which Wills presided, believed this to be the case, and his account makes clear that the members of the commission had doubts about Lincoln's suitability for such an assignment. The implication left by Carr is that the invitation was urged upon the commission by someone else, presumably Governor Curtin. When the prospect of the president's speaking had been proposed, Carr testified, there had been misgivings among the commission members "as to [Lincoln's] ability to speak upon such a grave and solemn occasion as that of the memorial services." Thus a fear that the president might lack the requisite sensitivity, or worse, might seize the occasion to make a political speech, may well have been reflected in the letter's careful limitation of the president's role—to make "a few appropriate remarks."

None of this, of course, would have been lost on Lincoln, especially if he himself had planted the idea of a presidential speaking role, and there is certainly no doubt that he welcomed the invitation. This in itself is notable, for it was a particularly busy time for his administration, with the fall elections still shaking out, the new Congress about to convene, and the president's Annual Message being due the first of December. As the date of the ceremony drew near, his son Tad became quite ill, and his wife, who had already lost two sons, was understandably distraught. The press of government business was such that, in spite of being solicited by the president himself, a majority of the cabinet members declined to make the two-day trip. Secretary of War Stanton had planned to go but was forced to cancel just before departure by urgent business. Lincoln was aware, as he later told James Speed, that something of the kind might intervene to keep him from attending, "but he was anxious to go—and desired to be prepared to say some appropriate thing." That the president, who rarely gave a speech in public and even more rarely left Washington, was eager to go to Gettysburg and to speak at the dedication ceremony under such circumstances seems a clear indication that he had something important to say for which this was the right occasion.

Possibly the earliest indication on record of the existence of a draft of the forthcoming speech came some days before the event, when the president spoke of it to the journalist Noah Brooks. "In reply to a question as to the speech having been already written, he said that it was written, 'but not finished.' " Brooks used versions of this striking phraseology—written, but not finished—more than once in telling this story, and it would seem to indicate a speech that had either been fully conceptualized but not yet fully written out, or one that had been fully drafted but not perfected. In either case, the implication is that the president knew what he wanted to say and was taking pains with exactly how to say it.

The first actual sighting of the speech, or some version of it, may have come at about the same time. On November 12, a week before the dedication, Lincoln sent a note to John Defrees: "Please see this girl who works in your office, and find out about her brother, and come and tell me." When Defrees called on the president, probably a few days later, he was asked his opinion of what proved to be "the famous Gettysburg speech." Ward Hill Lamon, Lincoln's longtime friend and associate, had a similar experience. Lamon been designated chief marshal and master of ceremonies at the dedication in Gettysburg. In a draft for a memoir that was later printed in slightly different forms, Lamon wrote of his encounter with the anxious author:

> Just before the dedication of the national cemetary at Gettysburg Mr. Lincoln told me he would be expected to make a speech on the occasion—that he was extremely busy and had no time to prepare himself for it and feared he would be unable to do himself and the subject justice
>
> He took out of his hat (the general receptacle of his notes

and memoranda) a page of fools cap, closely written and read
me, what he called a memorandum of what he intended to say,
which proved to be in substance and [(] I think,) in *haec verba*
what was printed as his Gettysburg speech. He remarked that
if he got time he would try to write something worthy of the
occasion

For students of the composition of the Gettysburg Address,
Lamon's testimony contains an intriguing suggestion—that Lincoln
had composed something that he represented only as "memorandum,"
presumably an abstract of what he wanted to say, and then used it, or
something very like it, for the speech itself. But the fact that he read it
to Lamon probably tells us that it was more than a memorandum. As a
man who habitually read things aloud to hear how they sounded and
who needed a live audience to get the right effect, Lincoln was more
likely trying out a portion of an incomplete speech in order to hear its
all-important intonations and rhythms. That Lamon recognized many
of the same words Lincoln used at Gettysburg probably tells us that he
had at least part of the speech well in hand. This would accord with the
recollection of his second attorney general, James Speed, to whom
Lincoln later gave an account of "the preparation and delivery of the
speech." Speed understood the president to say that "before he left
Washington he found time to write about half of a speech."

Like much of the testimony about this famous document and event,
the accounts of Brooks, Defrees, Lamon, and Speed are not entirely
congruent, but they are nonetheless quite credible and yield a fairly
consistent and recognizable picture of an author approaching his dead-
line while still in the throes of composition. All of this is in keeping
with what Lincoln's private secretary believed, that the speech was partially written, but only partially, in Washington.

LAMON'S RECOLLECTION THAT LINCOLN read to him from a single sheet of foolscap would, if accurate in this respect, be quite noteworthy. "Foolscap" traditionally referred to larger paper of a certain
size, but it was commonly used in Lincoln's day to refer to writing
paper that was larger than letter-size stationery. Lincoln regularly
used, for drafting, foolscap that was similar to what is now called
"legal" length (eight and a half by fourteen inches), but the document

that most scholars regard as the earliest of the surviving manuscripts of the Gettysburg Address is on letter-size presidential stationery. The implication is clear that if what Lincoln took from his hat to read to Lamon was actually "a page of foolscap," it was, in all likelihood, a document that Lincoln students have never seen.

The earliest surviving manuscripts of the Gettysburg Address referred to above belong to the Nicolay copy, so named from the belief that this two-page document was presented by the president to John G. Nicolay. The first of its two pages (see Fig. 8-2) is letter-size engraved office stationery, is written in ink, and does not appear to be a composition draft, but rather one that was copied out fair from another draft.

Therefore, even if we didn't have Lamon's testimony about a "page of foolscap," we could reasonably infer the existence of a composition draft that preceded the first page of the Nicolay copy. Because its last line ends in midsentence, it seems clear that there must have been another page that went with this one, written in ink and continuing this sentence: "It is rather for us, the living, to stand here. . . ." Unfortunately, this second page is missing, so that what may be the earliest known draft of the address consists of a single leaf, and its text is incomplete.

The second page of the Nicolay copy is not written in ink but rather in pencil, and it does not continue the sentence left hanging on the first page, but rather begins in the middle of a different sentence, and in midword: "ted to the great task remaining before us" (see Fig. 8-3).

Like the first page, this does not appear to be a composition draft but rather a fair copy, but unlike the first page, its paper is foolscap-size. In fact, it proves to be a "half-sheet"—one half of a double-size sheet folded down the middle that has been separated at the fold.

Why are these two nonmatching pages customarily treated as constituting a single draft? Basically, for two reasons. The first and most important is that the last line of the text of the first page has been altered, in pencil and in what appears to be Lincoln's hand, to create an awkward conjunction with the text of the second: "It is rather for us, the living, to stand here" has been changed by crossing out "to stand here" and writing in pencil above it the ungrammatical "we here be dedica" (see Fig. 8-2). The second reason is that Nicolay said he was present when his boss completed his drafting of the speech, which was

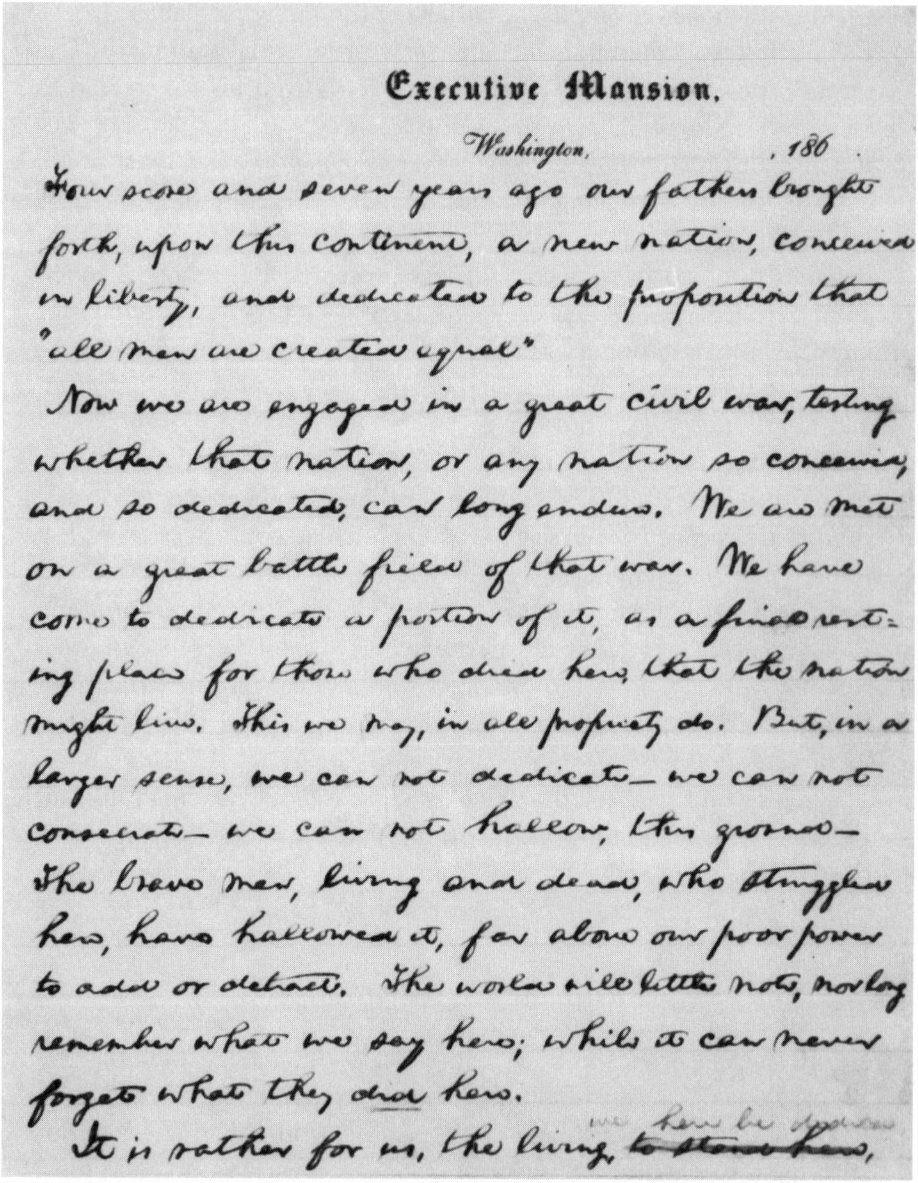

Executive Mansion,

Washington, , 186 .

Four score and seven years ago our fathers brought forth, upon this continent, a new nation, conceived in liberty, and dedicated to the proposition that "all men are created equal"

Now we are engaged in a great civil war, testing whether that nation, or any nation so conceived, and so dedicated, can long endure. We are met on a great battle field of that war. We have come to dedicate a portion of it, as a final resting place for those who died here, that the nation might live. This we may, in all propriety do. But, in a larger sense, we can not dedicate — we can not consecrate — we can not hallow, this ground — The brave men, living and dead, who struggled here, have hallowed it, far above our poor power to add or detract. The world will little note, nor long remember what we say here; while it can never forget what they did here.

It is rather for us, the living, we here be dedica ~~to stand here~~,

Figure 8-2. The first page of the Nicolay copy, written in ink on engraved letter-size stationery, usually thought to be the oldest surviving manuscript of the Gettysburg Address. Library of Congress.

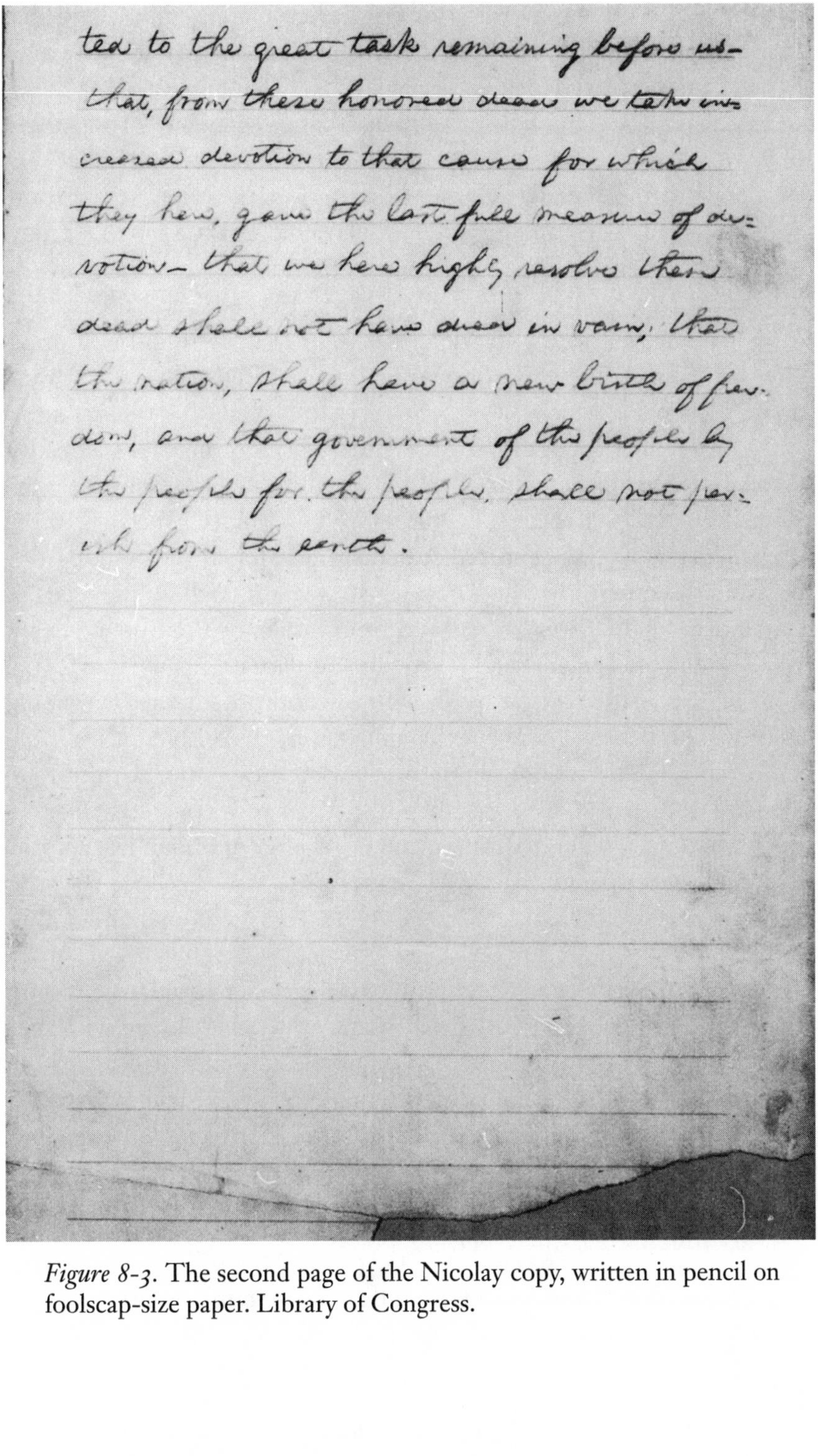

ted to the great task remaining before us—
that, from these honored dead we take increased devotion to that cause for which
they here gave the last full measure of devotion— that we here highly resolve these
dead shall not have died in vain; that
the nation, shall have a new birth of freedom, and that government of the people by
the people for the people, shall not perish from the earth.

Figure 8-3. The second page of the Nicolay copy, written in pencil on foolscap-size paper. Library of Congress.

done in pencil on the morning of the dedication ceremony, and that these two pages constituted the manuscript that the president held in his hand on the platform at Gettysburg.

There are many reasons for thinking that Nicolay was wrong about this, not the least of which is that what Lincoln famously said on that platform was, as Nicolay himself admitted, very different from the awkwardly conjoined and apparently incomplete text formed by joining these two pages. But these objections are less important in the present context than getting at what, if anything, the two manuscript leaves have to tell us about the creation of the Gettysburg Address. They both are on paper that Lincoln regularly used at his office in the White House and may well have been written there. No one seems to doubt that the first page was written in Washington, and except for Nicolay's belief to the contrary, there seems to be no reason why the second page could not have been also. Judging by the versions of the text that Lincoln was reported to have uttered at the ceremony and that he subsequently wrote out after the event, both pages seem to contain early, predelivery versions. For example, by the time he delivered his address Lincoln had decided to replace "This we may, in all propriety do" with "It is altogether fitting and proper that we should do this." The ending, of course, underwent a conspicuous change before delivery by the addition of the phrase "under God." Contrary to Nicolay's contention, it seems quite likely that these two leaves represent parts of two separate drafts—the beginning of one in ink and the closing of one in pencil.

NOAH BROOKS RECALLED THAT the president told him before leaving for Gettysburg that he had written his address "two or three times," which may represent a considerable amount of drafting. In addition to this rather vague description, we have evidence of at least three separate drafts of the Gettysburg Address prior to delivery:

- The "memorandum" on a "page of foolscap" that Lincoln took from his hat and read to Lamon

- The first page of a multipage draft written in ink on presidential stationery (page one of the Nicolay copy)

- The second page of a multipage draft written in pencil on foolscap (page two of the Nicolay copy).

It is possible, as many have conjectured, that the third item could have been part of a draft written in Gettysburg. Lincoln arrived there about sundown on the day before the dedication and was escorted to the house of David Wills, where he stayed overnight. After dinner and some socializing, the president excused himself and went up to his room to work on his address. In so doing, he gave the impression to some of those present that he was going to begin work on his speech for the first time, testimony that would later fuel the notion that the address was dashed off quickly. Indeed, there is a battery of testimony, most of it highly problematical, that he had worked on his address on the train, which he may have done.

His host, David Wills, subsequently testified that later in the evening he had seen the president in his room either writing or preparing to write, and that when the president went next door to confer with Secretary Seward, he carried the paper he was writing with him. Governor Curtin, who was delayed and arrived about eleven o'clock, also saw the president at his writing table and also saw him carry what he was writing with him to Seward's quarters. Curtin was sure that Lincoln had been writing on a large yellow envelope before visiting Seward, and that there were notes in the envelope. When the governor later came back to the room, he said the president "seemed to be copying from the notes on the sheet of foolscap paper, and I have no doubt that was the address." If, as Curtin believed, these were notes that pertained to Lincoln's forthcoming speech, this is the first time we see them. What Curtin saw Lincoln copying may have included the third item above, or something like it.

Both Wills and Curtin surmised that Lincoln visited Seward to confer about his address, and they were probably right. Lincoln, as we have seen, valued Seward's advice and had consulted him about other important speeches. Lincoln probably had another motive for conferring with Seward, for he had been told earlier in the evening by the Pennsylvania politician Wayne MacVeagh about a speech Seward had given to the same serenaders that Lincoln himself had largely evaded. Lincoln surely knew that Seward had been asked to speak in the event the president could not, and so had come prepared. Nothing is known about what was said in that conference, although it is almost a certainty that Lincoln read Seward his draft, such as it was. It is also a good bet that he quizzed Seward about his own speech, and possibly asked to see it.

Seward's remarks make an interesting contrast to Lincoln's, for

Seward touched on many of the themes that one might have expected a president to talk about on such an occasion—the horrors of "fratricidal war," the pitiable errors of the "misguided" rebels, the evil of slavery, and the necessity for its removal. What is especially interesting is that Seward had concluded his speech with essentially the same idea on which Lincoln would end his, the need to preserve democratic government: "But with that principle [majority rule] this government of ours—the purest, the best, the wisest, and the happiest in the world—must be, and, so far as we are concerned, practically will be, immortal." It is, to say the least, an intriguing possibility that the ending of the Gettysburg Address came about in parallel to the conclusion of the First Inaugural, with Lincoln taking his cue from Seward's very different example. We would know more about this possibility had Governor Curtin only followed his larcenous impulse. He told Nicolay that when he returned to Lincoln's room in the Wills house and saw him writing out from his notes what Curtin believed was the text of his address, "I could have picked up from the table the notes that he then made, and have regretted it 1000 times that I did not do it."

❧

THE NEXT MORNING LINCOLN presumably worked on his speech again, although the testimony of Nicolay, who claimed to have been present, is somewhat misleading. In his 1894 essay "Lincoln's Gettysburg Address," he appears to describe Lincoln in the act of writing:

> But when, at Gettysburg on the morning of the ceremonies, Mr. Lincoln finished his manuscript, he used a lead pencil, with which he crossed out the last three words of the first page, and wrote above them in pencil "we here be dedica," at which point he took up a new half sheet of paper—not white letter-paper as before, but a bluish-gray foolscap of large size with wide lines, habitually used by him for long or formal documents, and on this he wrote, all in pencil, the remainder of the word, and of the first draft of the address, comprising a total of nine lines and a half.

But this description does not depend on Nicolay's having been present. Its details, in fact, are all drawn from the condition of the Nicolay copy, which he had in front of him, and from his assumptions about its origin and role. Anyone who had seen the manuscript and shared these assumptions could have written much the same.

Nicolay had not been with the president in his room the night before. His research files show he was familiar with what Wills, Curtin, and others had said about the work done then on the address, all of which he carefully ignored in his version of how the address got written. Apart from his description of the manuscript, Nicolay's account is actually quite hazy about what transpired in Lincoln's room that morning, and when. He reports merely that "it was after the breakfast hour" that he went to the president's room and that he "remained with the President while he finished writing the Gettysburg address. . . . The time occupied in this final writing was probably about an hour, for it is not likely that he left the breakfast table before nine o'clock, and the formation of the procession began at ten."

Nicolay does not claim he was with the president for all of this time and probably was not, for we know from other sources that Lincoln had already toured the grounds with Seward earlier that morning and that he was busy writing in his room before nine o'clock. James A. Rebert, a soldier, was detailed as an orderly to the president and was sent to wait on him in his room at nine. Rebert made no mention of Nicolay in describing his encounter with the president.

> He requested me to wait a few minutes until he finished his writing, which I found him engaged in on entering the room. He had several sheets of note paper in front of him written in pencil, and several that he was just finishing. Both looked more like notes for reference than articles for publication. After finishing them he folded them all together and placed them in his pocket.

Are these sheets of paper the notes Curtin saw the night before and/or early drafts for the Gettysburg Address? Or was Lincoln perhaps working on other presidential business? We have no way of knowing for sure, but Rebert's next sentence might indicate the latter: "He then wrote an order for me to deliver to Marshal Lamon, of Washington, D. C., whose headquarters were at the Eagle Hotel." Rebert's straightforward testimony, which is definite as to time and offers details about Lincoln's activity and manuscripts, makes Nicolay's account appear vague and insubstantial by comparison.

FORSAKING, FOR THE MOMENT, the issue of manuscripts and pre-pared texts, we come to the question of what Lincoln actually said on the platform at Gettysburg. What words did those present hear him utter? There were, of course, a number of newspaper reporters present, some of whom were on the platform with the speakers and other dignitaries. Most newspaper accounts of public speeches at this time were not strictly verbatim, as most reporters could not write short-hand. By writing quickly and noting down key phrases, they could then reconstruct or paraphrase the speaker's statements afterward from their notes. Inevitably, some reports were more faithful than others, particularly in an era when newspapers were openly partisan and often made little effort to be objective in reporting political matters. Consider, in the light of the familiar final text, the beginning of the address as reported by the *Chicago Tribune*, a paper that had long supported Abraham Lincoln.

> Four score and seven years ago, our fathers established upon this continent a Government subscribed in liberty and dedi-cated to the fundamental principle that all mankind are created equal by a good God, and now we are engaged in a great contest. We are contesting the question whether this nation, or any nation so conceived, so dedicated can longer remain.

While obviously trying to be faithful to the president's sentiments, the reporter was having trouble getting his exact words, which reminds us how essential they are to the speech's effect. The *Philadelphia Inquirer* reporter, on the other hand, rendered this passage in language that appears nearly faultless:

> Four score and seven years ago our fathers brought forth upon this continent a new nation, conceived in liberty and dedicated to the proposition that all men are created equal. Now we are engaged in a great civil war, testing the question whether this nation or any nation so conceived, so dedicated, can long endure.

But further on, this same reporter seems to falter:

The number of men, living and dead, who struggled here have consecrated it far above our poor attempts to add to its consecration. The world will little know and nothing remember of what we see here, but we cannot forget what these brave men did here.

But for this passage, the *Chicago Tribune* correspondent comes closer to the mark:

The brave men lying dead, who struggled here, have consecrated it far above our poor power to add or to detract. The world will little heed, nor long remember, what we say here; but it will not forget what they did here.

In short, speeches taken down by reporters were rarely accurate, which is why Edward Everett took the trouble to have his oration printed and distributed in advance.

Joseph L. Gilbert, who represented the Associated Press, had been chosen to cover the Gettysburg dedication for his shorthand skills, but it turned out that he didn't need them. Because Gilbert was known to have been given access to Lincoln's manuscript after the address, his report has often been described as having been taken "partly from his shorthand notes and partly from Lincoln's manuscript." But this is not what Gilbert said when he described his coverage many years after the address: "Before the dedication ceremonies closed, the President's manuscript was copied with his permission; and as the press report was made from a copy no transcript from shorthand notes was necessary." The clear implication of Gilbert's testimony is that he did not need to transcribe whatever notes he had taken and that they did not figure in his "press report."

Strange as it may seem, Gilbert's report of the address, widely distributed to newspapers by the Associated Press, has come down to us in an imperfect form. The large New York daily newspapers were apparently among the first to receive the initial AP dispatch, and the text that they rushed into print was subsequently adopted by the editors of Lincoln's *Collected Works* as the standard newspaper account. But this is misleading. The version of the AP text that the New York newspapers all printed on November 20, the day after the Gettysburg dedication, contained at least one obvious error: Lincoln's word "unfinished" had apparently been garbled in telegraphic trans-mission—a common occurrence—and was printed in the New York papers as "refinished." The AP dispatch that appeared in many other papers (recognizable by its inclusion of identical reports of applause), especially those that were printed a few days later, corrected this error, as well as two others from its first transmission. The most conspicuous of these is the inclusion of a word previously omitted, the word "poor" in the president's phrase "our poor power to add or detract." Versions of the later AP dispatch containing "poor" and "unfinished" also contain another correction, the phrase "these dead" where the earlier transmission had "the dead." Therefore, the AP dispatch first printed in the major New York newspapers, which sub-sequently found its way into the *Collected Works* and Lincoln schol-arship generally, contains three errors that did not originate with Gilbert.

Another reporter who was capable of making a verbatim report of the address was Charles Hale of the *Boston Daily Advertiser.* Hale was present as part of a three-man delegation representing the governor and state of Massachusetts, and his verbatim transcription appeared not in his newspaper but in the report of his commission. William E. Barton brought attention to Hale's version by pronouncing it the only text that faithfully reported "what Lincoln actually said at Gettys-burg." Here, side by side, are Gilbert's corrected AP text and Hale's, with differences in boldface type.

GILBERT TEXT	HALE TEXT
Four score and seven years ago our fathers brought forth upon this conti-nent a new nation, conceived in liberty and dedicated to the proposition that all men are created equal. Now we are engaged in a great civil war, testing whether that nation, or any nation so conceived and so dedicated, can long endure. We are met on a great battle-field of that war. We are met to dedicate a portion of it as the final resting-place of those who **here gave**	Fourscore and seven years ago, our fathers brought forth upon this conti-nent a new nation, conceived in liberty and dedicated to the proposition that all men are created equal.
	Now we are engaged in a great civil war, testing whether that nation—or any nation, so conceived and so dedi-cated—can long endure.
	We are met on a great battle-field of that war. We are met to dedicate a por-tion of it as the final resting-place of

their lives that that nation might live. It is altogether fitting and proper that we should do this. But, in a larger sense, we cannot dedicate, we cannot consecrate, we cannot hallow this ground. The brave men, living and dead, who struggled here have consecrated it far above **our poor power** to add or detract. The world will **little note** nor long remember what we say here; but it can never forget what they did here. It is for us, the living, rather to be dedicated here to the unfinished work that they have thus far so nobly carried on. It is rather for us to be here dedicated to the great task remaining before us; that from these honored dead we take increased devotion to that cause for which they here gave the last full measure of devotion; that we here highly resolve that these dead shall not have died in vain; that the nation shall, under God, have a new birth of freedom; and that **Governments** of the people, by the people, and for the people, shall not perish from the earth.

those who **have given** their lives that that nation might live.

It is altogether fitting and proper that we should do this.

But, in a larger sense, we cannot dedicate, we cannot consecrate, we cannot hallow, this ground. The brave men, living and dead, who struggled here, have consecrated it, far above **our power** to add or detract.

The world will **very little note** nor long remember what we say here; but it can never forget what they did here.

It is for us, the living, rather, *to be dedicated*, here, to the unfinished work that they have thus far so nobly carried on. It is rather for us to be here dedicated to the great task remaining before us; that from these honored dead we take increased devotion to that cause for which they here gave the last full measure of devotion; that we here highly resolve that these dead shall not have died in vain; that the nation shall, under God, have a new birth of freedom, and that **government** of the people, by the people, for the people, shall not perish from the earth.

Ignoring differences in punctuation, capitalization, and paragraphing—which were all subject to editorial intervention and which Hale could not have gleaned aurally—there are only four verbal differences between these two texts.

Gilbert Text / Hale Text

1. "here gave" / "have given"
2. "our poor power" / "our power"
3. "will little note" / "will very little note"
4. "Governments" / "government"

The inclusion of "poor" in such non-AP versions as those of the *Chicago Tribune* and the *Philadelphia Inquirer* confirms that Hale failed to catch it, while the absence of the word "very" in all other reports and manuscript versions makes it reasonably certain that Hale's account is here mistaken. At the same time, Hale's may be virtually the only text that accurately records the way Lincoln began his final clause: "that government of the people . . ." In spite of these minor differences, the relatively close correspondence of these two texts would seem to indicate that what Gilbert copied out from Lincoln's manuscript and what Hale heard and recorded were very close to being the same.

The upshot of all this is that we can be reasonably certain what Lincoln said on the platform at Gettysburg. As the phrase "under God" does not appear in the predelivery draft of this part of the address, there is a tradition that he improvised it on the platform as he spoke, but that seems refuted by its presence in the Gilbert text. In the same way, otherwise credible testimony that Lincoln said he improvised on the platform is put in doubt by the virtual identity between the 266-word text Gilbert copied from Lincoln's delivery manuscript and what was taken down from his spoken words by Charles Hale.

II. An Architecture of Its Own

In describing the events at Gettysburg, many historians and biographers indulge in the harmless fiction of having the president deliver from the platform a different text from the one we have been considering, one consisting of 272 words. But that text was not perfected until several months after the ceremony. Before becoming president, Lincoln often took advantage of opportunities to revise his spoken text so as to enhance its effectiveness with readers when it appeared in print. This was the process we encountered with the Farewell Address, which was offered spontaneously but then recast in writing. In the case of his Gettysburg speech, of course, Lincoln started with a written text, and he would have a good deal more leisure in which to reconsider it. Noah Brooks, the man said to have been chosen to replace Nicolay as Lincoln's private secretary, noted on several occasions the attention Lincoln devoted to his writing. "The same [painstaking] care which Lincoln bestowed on his messages and letters was given to his speeches," Brooks wrote, "though it is not likely that any of these was elaborated as much as the Gettysburg address." "I found, afterward," he said, "that the Gettysburg speech was actually written and rewritten a great many times."

David Wills wrote the president on November 23, four days after the ceremony: "On behalf of the States interested in the National Cemetery here, I request of you the original manuscript of the Dedicatory Remarks delivered by you here last Thursday. We desire them to be placed with the correspondence and other papers connected with the project." The president probably saw no reason not to oblige him, but he was also bedridden with a mild version of smallpox by the time he received the request, and he may have authorized sending his delivery copy to Wills before realizing that his only remaining text was the incomplete Nicolay copy. This would explain why he asked his secretaries to make copies of the newspaper reports, which he then consulted in working out a new, revised text for his address. Nicolay himself was absent from the White House during this period, but in telling the story of the revision, he associates the Wills request with the copies made of the newspaper texts and with Lincoln's creation of what he called "a new autograph copy—a careful deliberate revision—which has become the standard text."

Readers of Nicolay's 1894 essay were not misinformed about the "careful deliberate revision" that resulted in the "standard text," but they were somewhat misled. Nicolay left the impression that Lincoln had revised his text shortly after returning from Gettysburg and then simply made copies to gratify later requests. Nothing is said about the fact that all the surviving copies of the address in Lincoln's hand are different or that the period over which these changes were being made amounted to four months. The differences, which are considered in detail in an appendix, prove to be much more about texture than meaning, but they are evidence of a serious literary craftsman laboring to perfect an important work.

The picture of Lincoln considering numerous revisions to his already delivered speech raises the much-disputed issue of whether he considered his address a "failure." This, in turn, is entangled in another controversy about the reception of the speech at the ceremony. As with almost every issue involving the Gettysburg Address, there is contradictory testimony to be confronted and sorted out. We have highly credible testimony that the crowd listened to the speech without interrupting applause and that there was an awkward silence at the end, before the crowd realized that the speech was over. But there is also testimony to the effect that Lincoln's speech was warmly or even enthusiastically received by the crowd. Frequently pointed to in this regard is the most prominent newspaper dispatch—that of Gilbert of the Associated Press—which indicated that the president was applauded no less than five times during his speech and that he was greeted at its conclusion with "long-continued applause." In cases of such disparate data, one has no alternative but to weigh the testimony and try to determine where the preponderance of the evidence lies, taking into account not only the relative amount but also its credibility.

In this case, the weight of the evidence would seem to indicate that the crowd was relatively undemonstrative and that the extreme brevity of Lincoln's speech took the audience and those on the platform by surprise, creating an awkward moment after the speech's conclusion. Most of the testimony on both sides is reminiscence, provided long after the event, but a recently discovered letter, written at the time by a Union officer who was present, reports that when Lincoln "finished speaking the people were silent for a time[:] many not knowing his speech was finished." Gilbert himself later testified that he heard no interrupting applause: "Narratives of the scene have described the tumultuous outbursts of enthusiasm accompanying the President's utterances. I heard none. There were no outward manifestations of feeling." Gilbert thus disowned that aspect of his AP press report as printed. Another prominent reporter, John Russell Young of the *Philadelphia Press*, who was seated on the platform, also claimed that he heard no applause during the speech. He added: "To my surprise, almost it seemed before Mr. Lincoln had begun to speak, he turned and sat down. Surely these five or six lines of shorthand were not all. Hurriedly bending over the aisle I asked if that was all. 'Yes, for the present,' he answered." Clark E. Carr, the delegate to the commission from Illinois and a political associate of Lincoln, was also on the platform. Many years later he confessed that he had been surprised the next day upon reading the newspaper report of the interrupting applause, which he was sure he had not heard. What he did hear, he wrote, were numerous indications of disappointment. "So short a time was Mr. Lincoln before them that the people could scarcely believe their eyes when he disappeared from their view. They were almost dazed. They could not possibly, in so short a time, mentally grasp the ideas that were conveyed, nor even their substance. Time and again expressions of disappointment were made to me. Many persons said to me that they would have supposed that on such a great occasion the President would have made a speech."

None of this, of course, speaks to the reaction of the president himself, and whether he thought his speech had been a "failure." That suggestion is largely based on the account of Ward Hill Lamon, cited earlier. After relating what the president said to him before the event—that he was concerned that his speech might not suit the occasion—Lamon continued: "After he delivered his speech, he said he greatly regretted not having been better prepared. Said he to me on the stand, that speech wont *scour*—it is a flat failure—and the people are disappointed!—He seemed more than ordinarily concerned about what the people would think." What has attracted attention, along with no little doubt and disbelief, is the emphatic language attributed to Lincoln, but one must bear in mind that these words are Lamon's colorful approximation of what Lincoln said, reported many years later. The substance of the president's comment, which is all that can claim credibility, is to the effect that the misgivings that he had expressed to Lamon earlier had proved well founded and that he felt chagrin at what he sensed was the crowd's disappointment.

All of this, in retrospect, makes sense. Lincoln knew better than anyone that, appropriate as his remarks might be to his assignment and official role, the audience would not be expecting so abbreviated a speech. He knew from long experience that to get the undivided attention of a large audience, to set the desired tone, and to bring one's message into proper focus—all take a certain amount of time. Thus he could hardly have been surprised at the crowd's reaction, for what he had offered had been constructed on an entirely different principle. But even if he was not surprised, it would be only natural to feel some measure of regret.

John Hay referred to the president's speech in his diary, where he summarized the entire afternoon's activities in a single sentence: "And Mr Stockton made a prayer which thought it was an oration—and Mr Everett spoke as he always does perfectly—and the President in a firm free way, with more grace than is his wont said his half dozen ~~words~~ lines of consecration and the music wailed and we went home through crowded and cheering streets." From Hay's point of view, his boss had performed his modest assignment admirably. Nicolay, writing much later, observed that the crowd was "totally unprepared for what they heard." William E. Barton, who conducted an extensive investigation of the event, and at a time when it was still possible to interview actual spectators, was convinced that crowd's reaction was subdued and that "Lincoln did not think he had succeeded." But acknowledging that Lincoln felt regret that the people in the audience seemed disappointed with his speech is quite different from saying that he was ready to write it off as a "failure."

～

LINCOLN'S EXPRESSION OF CONCERN to Lamon a day or two before the event must have been partly related to the fact that his speech was, as he told Noah Brooks, "written, but unfinished." Whatever this meant, the implication is that he already knew what he wanted to say. Brooks apparently understood as much, for he recalled Lincoln saying that "what he had ready to say was very short, or, as he emphatically expressed it, 'short, short, short.' " Apart from its eloquence, brevity is perhaps the most notable quality of the Gettysburg Address. Not surprisingly, it was a key element in its "failure" with the crowd, for it proved too brief to be effective under the conditions that prevailed at the dedication ceremony. Readjusting its attention after a two-hour address by Everett, the audience was unprepared for a speech that was over so quickly.

But as its author undoubtedly calculated, its brevity was an important key to its potential success. Lincoln certainly knew what he was risking with his immediate audience by offering such a short speech, but it does not follow that he had the same kind of misgivings about its appeal to readers. The crowd within his hearing at the Gettysburg ceremonies was in the thousands, but it was the reading audience of many millions that he was ultimately trying to reach. Arguably the single most important means of achieving such a goal was to be brief.

But if Lincoln deliberately fashioned his speech to be eye-catchingly brief, what does this say about the notion that he had been laying the basis for this speech months in advance? Here an old, seemingly paradoxical concept comes into play. The seventeenth-century philosopher Pascal perhaps put it most succinctly: "I have made this letter longer than usual, because I lack the time to make it short." This is sometimes regarded as merely a witticism, but serious writers know better. The conscientious literary craftsman Henry David Thoreau once wrote to a friend: "Not that the story need be long, but it will take a long while to make it short." One of Lincoln's successors in the presidency, and one of its best writers, Woodrow Wilson, once applied this maxim directly to his public speeches: "If I am to speak for ten minutes, I need a week for preparation; if fifteen minutes, three days; if half an hour, two days; if an hour, I am ready now." Thus, while its extreme brevity has suggested to many a layman that the Gettysburg Address must have required little time to compose, the opposite is a much safer surmise.

~

IF LINCOLN HAD REGRETS about the reception of his address as a live performance, he was certainly aware as he returned to Washington that the verdict of real consequence, the reaction of readers across the country, was yet to come. One of the advantages of a very short speech was that it would be sure to be reported in many newspapers in its entirety, and on the front page. And as it had every appearance of being nonpartisan and merely ceremonial, it had a good chance of being printed in Democratic newspapers, of which there were a very sizable proportion. Some of these, such as the president's old nemesis the *Chicago Times*, would offer predictably demeaning comments: "The cheek of every American must tingle with shame as he reads the silly, flat and dish-watery utterances of the man who has to be pointed out to intelligent foreigners as the President of the United States." But even this pictures the address being read, which is all a writer can hope for.

The first reader that Lincoln heard from was probably Edward Everett, who wrote to him the next day and offered a ringing compliment. After thanking the president for some personal favors, he wrote: "Permit me also to express my great admiration of the thoughts expressed by you, with such eloquent simplicity & appropriateness, at the consecration of the Cemetery. I should be glad, if I could flatter myself that I came as near to the central idea of the occasion, in two hours, as you did in two minutes." There is evidence that, like many others, Everett had not, at first, been impressed with Lincoln's brief presentation, not even mentioning it, for example, in his diary. But he had been somewhat disappointed in his own performance, and may have been thinking about that while Lincoln was speaking. Reading Lincoln's text in papers the next day had doubtless given him a new perspective on it. His praise brightened the spirits of the ailing president, who, in spite of being afflicted by the onset of varioloid, replied immediately. "Your kind note of to-day is received. In our respective parts yesterday, you could not have been excused to make a short address, nor I a long one. I am pleased to know that, in your judgment, the little I did say was not entirely a failure." Lincoln was unusually proud of this letter, telling James Speed that "he had never received a compliment he prized more highly."

While the immediate response to the Gettysburg Address by readers was not overwhelming, the speech was recognized at once by some discerning observers as something notable. A Massachusetts editorial writer at the *Springfield Republican* (probably Josiah G. Holland) is often credited with being the first in what would eventually become a long line of public admirers: "Surprisingly fine as Mr. Everett's oration was in the Gettysburg consecration, the rhetorical honors of the occasion were won by President Lincoln. His little speech is a perfect gem, deep in feeling, compact in thought and expression, and tasteful and elegant in every word and comma." This is, understandably, a writer's compliment, paying tribute not only to the effect on the reader but the craft that the work exhibits. But the key to the success that the address was ultimately to have with so many readers was brought out by another early admirer, George William Curtis, the editor of *Harper's Weekly*, whose notice appeared on December 5. "The few words of the President were from the heart to the heart. They can not be read, even, without kindling emotion. 'The world will little note nor long remember what we say here, but it can never forget what they did here.' It was as simple and felicitous and earnest a word as was ever spoken."

Curtis's praise in a national weekly called wide attention to Lincoln's address, and for us it calls attention to a key point. Relatively few listeners at Gettysburg seem to have had a strong emotional response to the president's words, although different conditions might have produced a better result. But as Curtis points out, and more and more readers discovered, the written words on the page can be so affecting they cannot even be read without emotion. This was particularly true for its first readers, whose feelings about the war were intricately bound up with the fate of family members. But because it has remained true for succeeding generations of readers, increasingly far removed from the Civil War's agonies and issues, its ability to kindle emotion is undoubtedly why the Gettysburg Address has been so widely and persistently admired. By contrast, many orators of Lincoln's day could excite powerful emotions in listeners, but very few of their speeches can do the same for readers today. How such kindling is effected is never easy to specify, but it is surely related to the things that Curtis lists as the most important attributes of the address—that it was simple, felicitous, earnest. These are all qualities that arise from its language, but they also depend, as Lincoln understood and his painstaking revisions attest, on the sound and rhythm of its sentences.

❧

ABRAHAM LINCOLN WAS KEENLY aware that public opinion, while it ultimately determined what could be done politically, was nonetheless malleable. It could be educated and modified. Though he had begun, as most politicians, by promising to do the bidding of his constituents, he eventually saw things in a different light. "Instead," as Richard J. Carwardine has written, "he came to work by the rule that public sentiment was to some degree plastic and that elected representatives had the power to shape it, as well as the moral responsibility to improve it. Opinion-forming was the most potent of all the politician's activities, for it provided the means of changing the government." In an illuminating study of Lincoln and the shaping of public opinion, Phillip Shaw Paludan makes the case that Lincoln was "self consciously a propagandist" whose efforts largely succeeded, not by demonizing his adversaries or by deluding and manipulating his constituents, but by appealing to "the better angels of our nature."

There is little doubt that by the summer of 1863 Lincoln had come to see opinion forming as a primary presidential task. His public letters were popular, and he was becoming more self-confident with each successive outing. His Conkling letter in late August had made the strongest impression of all, but the man who frequently likened his presidency to a card game had not yet played his ace.

What he had glimpsed in July and shared cryptically with his audience of serenaders was a connection between the fighting and "the father of all moral principle," the dictum of the Declaration of Independence that "all men are created equal." In his remarks to the serenaders, as Martin P. Johnson observes, Lincoln was "perhaps more boastful of Union successes than on any other occasion," but trumpeting military victories was not what he was interested in. He was not a boastful man by nature, but more important, he was in search of something that would go deeper than boasting, something whose positive appeal could counter the disheartening effect of war. If equality was, as he had said in Chicago, "the electric cord in [the] Declaration that links the hearts of patriotic and liberty-loving men together," it could perhaps be employed in creating the sense of patriotism and common purpose so urgently needed.

In many ways the dedication at Gettysburg came at the wrong time, but it was the right occasion, and Lincoln seized it. Jefferson's words had been timeless and universal, almost cosmic in scope. The challenge was to make them timely, and applicable to the struggle at hand. Treating this kind of opposition—the past and present—seemed to come naturally to Lincoln. "The dogmas of the quiet past are inadequate to the stormy present," he had written in an Annual Message. "As our case is new, so we must think anew, and act anew." Here it would be important to make the point in a different way, to emphasize the need to prevent the total destruction of the nation established by the forefathers and to vindicate the noble and far-reaching ideals upon which it was founded. And to this it would be necessary to add one more thing: that to persist and prevail would be to transform the nation and bring it nearer to its founding ideals.

If we judge in terms of what Lincoln was presumably trying to accomplish at Gettysburg—to forge a galvanizing and durable expression of war's purpose—the genius of the famous first sentence is less in the stately quality of its language, which is admittedly superlative, than the way in which the sentence is so worded as to command assent to what was then, for a good portion of its audience, a highly disputable contention. So ingenious was its combination of elements that the sentence not only commanded the assent of any self-respecting, patriotic American, but it fairly defied contradiction. Its deliberate, measured phrasing conveys the sense of a solemnly judicious account of the nation's founding:

> Four score and seven years ago our fathers brought forth, upon this continent, a new nation, conceived in liberty, and dedicated to the proposition that "all men are created equal."

But truth to tell, it was nothing of the kind. That it should seem so to twenty-first-century American readers is, to a large degree, a tribute to the literary ability and persuasiveness of Abraham Lincoln.

Even the wariest and most mistrustful Civil War–era reader—and where Abraham Lincoln was concerned, there were a great many of these—might have read the first sentence without suspicion or disagreement, but the second sentence, at least for the more ideological readers, might well have set off an alarm.

> Now we are engaged in a great civil war, testing whether that nation, or any nation so conceived, and so dedicated, can long endure.

Wait a minute! The war is about a national commitment to the equality of all men? Granted that one of the things declared to be a self-evident truth in the great Declaration was that "all men are created equal," but there is wide disagreement about what that meant and how far it extended. Isn't the principal idea of the Declaration the right of self-government? And come to think of it, isn't that what the Confederate states are claiming for themselves, just as the American colonists had claimed it in 1776? Such reservations may have been (and may still be) well grounded, but they are effectively one sentence too late. The genie is already out of the bottle. As Frederick Douglass observed many years later, Lincoln had "a happy faculty of stating a proposition, of stating it so that it needed no argument."

The famous conclusion, like the opening, may well have been part of what was prepared in advance of the Wills invitation, for Lincoln had long acknowledged that equality and self-government were linked. As far back as his 1854 Peoria speech, he had said, "Allow ALL the governed an equal voice in the government, and that, and that only is self government." He was talking about slavery then, and how it violated the first principle of self-government. He was talking about slavery now, and a good deal more.

> . . . that the nation, shall have a new birth of freedom, and that government of the people by the people for the people, shall not perish from the earth.

Consider, for a moment, the possibility that the opening and closing portions, both quoted above in their earliest known form, were not conceived and written after the invitation to Gettysburg but before, and that they constitute a kind of template of the ideas Lincoln most wanted to engage. This, obviously, is the Gettysburg Address without Gettysburg. In this perspective, we see a configuration of three related ideas, all from the Declaration—equality, freedom, and self-government. Equality was the premier self-evident truth, and liberty, or human freedom, was a natural right that came from God. Lincoln's political position, here and elsewhere, was that these two were ultimately interrelated, and that without a full accommodation of both, true self-government was seriously compromised.

This somewhat rarified level of abstraction was not something novel for Lincoln, but was rather, as his law partner more than once pointed out, the intellectual world he was most at home in. In the 1850s, this Declaration-based line of thinking lay behind his opposition to the Kansas-Nebraska Act and the extension of slavery, but after the Southern states rebelled and renounced the idea of human equality, it found a new focus. The unwanted war, which was necessary to preserve self-government, was now also necessary to sustain the venerated principle of equality. And in moving inexorably toward the destruction of slavery, the war would be a victory for freedom as well, not just for people in bondage, but for a nation "so conceived, and so dedicated."

In many respects, the linchpin of that extraordinary first sentence is surely the word "proposition." To the discriminating eye, it seems at first to be a word out of place, which is why both Seward and Senator Charles Sumner were said to have objected to it. Matthew Arnold is supposed to have refused to read any further. But as Sumner eventually saw, there is no other word for what Lincoln wanted to say. It perfectly conveys the sense in which the most revolutionary of American ideals, however revered, was not a universally accepted principle, but was instead something that needed to be demonstrated. If Lincoln had already formulated this template by the time he heard about the memorial cemetery being established at Gettysburg, the word that would have helped to make the connection was "dedication." That the "new nation" in his Euclidean version of the founding is *dedicated* to the ideal of equality provides an opportunity to connect it linguistically with a ceremony to dedicate a national cemetery for fallen soldiers. How a talented writer might exploit such a connection is given a definitive illustration in the Gettysburg Address.

⟡

"WE DO NOT FIRST see, and then define," Walter Lippmann observed; "we define first, and then we see." That so many Americans have been brought to see the Declaration's affirmation of equality the way Lincoln presented it at Gettysburg is no accident. Jefferson's greatest distinction is not that he originated the idea of human equality or that he introduced it into our political vocabulary but that he framed it at such a time and in such a way as to capture the American imagination. Lincoln grew up at the very time when the Declaration was being canonized as a sacred American text, but by the time he reached his political maturity, the issue of equality had become a major fault line in a nation dividing over slavery, and the proposition that "all men are created equal" was being openly derided as a "self-evident lie."

Lincoln's spectacular rise to political prominence in the 1850s would be punctuated by his responses to this trend. He had tried to infuse new life into the promises of the Declaration's preamble in those years, using them to oppose the repeal of the Missouri Compromise, the Kansas-Nebraska Act, the *Dred Scott* decision. With the secession crisis precipitated by his own election, he would continue to speak of them, if indirectly, referring to "something in that Declaration giving liberty, not alone to the people of this country, but hope to the world for all future time." It was that something, he said, "which gave promise that in due time the weights should be lifted from the shoulders of all men." In his first address to Congress as an embattled president, he would assert that the "leading object of government is, to elevate the condition of men . . . to afford all, an unfettered start, and a fair chance in the race of life." But with the victory at Gettysburg, coming almost exactly on the Fourth of July, Lincoln saw something like the hand of fate and determined to look for an opportunity to reinvoke the spirit and emotional resonance of Jefferson's own inspiring words.

Having crafted and condensed his message and adapted it to an occasion ideally suited to a receptive hearing, Lincoln had maximized his chances for success. Once it gained wide readership, the Gettysburg Address would gradually become ingrained in the national consciousness. Neither an argument nor an analysis nor a new credo, it was instead a moving tribute incorporated into an alluring affirmation of the nation's ideals. "This was the perfect medium for changing the way most Americans thought about the nation's founding act," Garry Wills has written. "Lincoln does not argue law or history, as Daniel Webster did. He *makes* history."

IN *LINCOLN AT GETTYSBURG*, a book that has shed more light on its subject than any other, Wills has shown that Lincoln's address bears an uncanny similarity to the highly formalized funeral oration of the ancient Greeks. Yet far from being an imitation or an attempt to follow a classic formula, Lincoln's speech is an American original, like the man himself. Although he began his career as a public speaker using the current conventions of oratory, he soon gave them up and followed his own bent. "He could act no part but his own," his friend Joshua Speed observed. "He copied no one either in manner or style." This is perhaps one reason he abandoned poetry as a serious enterprise in middle age. Like many great prose writers before and since, Lincoln considered himself a failed poet, principally, it would appear, because of his limited success in communicating powerful feelings in standard verse forms. While the world has long since taken for granted that poetry need not be confined to traditional metric patterns, this idea was novel in Lincoln's time and defended by few literary authorities. An exception, and a consequential one, was Ralph Waldo Emerson, who argued that "it is not metres, but a metre-making argument, that makes a poem." Because of its poignant language and distinctive rhythms, and perhaps because its length is more like that of a lyric than a speech, Lincoln's address is often called a prose poem. By Emerson's definition, the Gettysburg Address would surely qualify, for it would be hard to find a piece of American writing that better fits Emerson's description of a meter-making argument: "a thought so passionate and alive, that, like the spirit of a plant or an animal, it has an architecture of its own, and adorns nature with a new thing."

> Four score and seven years ago our fathers brought forth on this continent, a new nation, conceived in Liberty, and dedicated to the proposition that all men are created equal.
>
> Now we are engaged in a great civil war, testing whether that nation, or any nation so conceived and so dedicated, can long endure. We are met on a great battle-field of that war. We have come to dedicate a portion of that field, as a final resting place for those who here gave their lives that that nation might live. It is altogether fitting and proper that we should do this.
>
> But, in a larger sense, we can not dedicate—we can not consecrate—we can not hallow—this ground. The brave men, living and dead, who struggled here, have consecrated it, far above

our poor power to add or detract. The world will little note, nor long remember what we say here, but it can never forget what they did here. It is for us the living, rather, to be dedicated here to the unfinished work which they who fought here have thus far so nobly advanced. It is rather for us to be here dedicated to the great task remaining before us—that from these honored dead we take increased devotion to that cause for which they gave the last full measure of devotion—that we here highly resolve that these dead shall not have died in vain—that this nation, under God, shall have a new birth of freedom—and that government of the people, by the people, for the people, shall not perish from the earth.

CHAPTER NINE

A Truth That Needed
to Be Told

T HE DISTANCE BETWEEN THE comic verses about General
Lee and the Gettysburg Address is a measure of the remarkable
range of Lincoln's writing. Although one is a mere jeu d'esprit
and the other an undoubted masterpiece, each has a functional place in
the overall economy of his imagination. While we have here been
mainly concerned with some of his most notable presidential writings,
Lincoln's personal papers are surprisingly replete with incidental writings called forth by a variety of provocations, many of them incomplete or otherwise not intended for general consumption.

A small cluster of such writings survives, for example, from the
closing days of his first campaign for the presidency in the fall of 1860.
After his nomination in May, Lincoln observed a nearly complete public silence, refusing to make speeches or even to publicly clarify his
positions in writing, arguing that between the Republican platform
and his own published speeches, he had already put on record what the
public needed to know. Neither did he permit himself to correspond
very extensively, especially considering that he was a candidate at the
center of a widely dispersed national campaign. Yet his papers reveal
that at the climax of that campaign he busied himself with at least three
behind-the-scenes literary efforts.

The first was a reply to a political attack from a Democratic newspaper editor in nearby Petersburg, Illinois, John Hill, who was well
known to Lincoln as the son of one of his old New Salem friends.
Writing in the guise of someone else, Lincoln undertakes to defend
"Mr. Lincoln" from Hill's charges by showing that they contain errors

and falsehoods, but perhaps because of the relentless particularity of the argument, it never strikes fire. This surely helps to explain why the letter is unfinished and apparently unsent, but it also may have dawned on the candidate that, stung as he was to have been attacked from such a quarter, there was little, if anything, to be gained by following through with a reply.

The second effort is considerably more lighthearted. It consists of an imaginary dialogue between Stephen A. Douglas and John C. Breckenridge, both of whom were running for president against him, each representing a portion of the fragmented Democratic Party. By the time Lincoln wrote this dialogue in late September, it was becoming clear that this split in the opposition would assure Lincoln's election, a circumstance that may well have prompted the exercise. The dialogue ends on a comic note, with Douglas having highmindedly charged Breckenridge and his supporters with being disunionists:

> Breck—Bah! You have known us long, and intimately; why did you never denounce us as disunionists, till since our refusal to support *you* for the Presidency? Why have you never warned the North against our disunion schemes, till since the Charleston and Baltimore sessions of the National convention? Will you answer, Senator Douglas?
>
> Doug—The condition of my throat will not permit me to carry this conversation any further—

Douglas's obvious dodge is humorous enough, but for Lincoln and his closest friends it privately referenced a fabled episode in the 1854 campaign when Lincoln had apparently agreed to cancel a scheduled joint appearance at the town of Lacon because of Douglas's professed hoarseness and inability to be heard.

The third piece that Lincoln wrote out as he awaited the conclusion of the 1860 election was much more earnest, surprisingly so considering that its subject had apparently nothing to do with the presidential campaign. Its first paragraph (see Fig. 9-1) reads:

> It is now less than three weeks to the election— For months we have been trying to get an unequivocal declaration from democratic newspapers and democratic candidates for the Legislature,

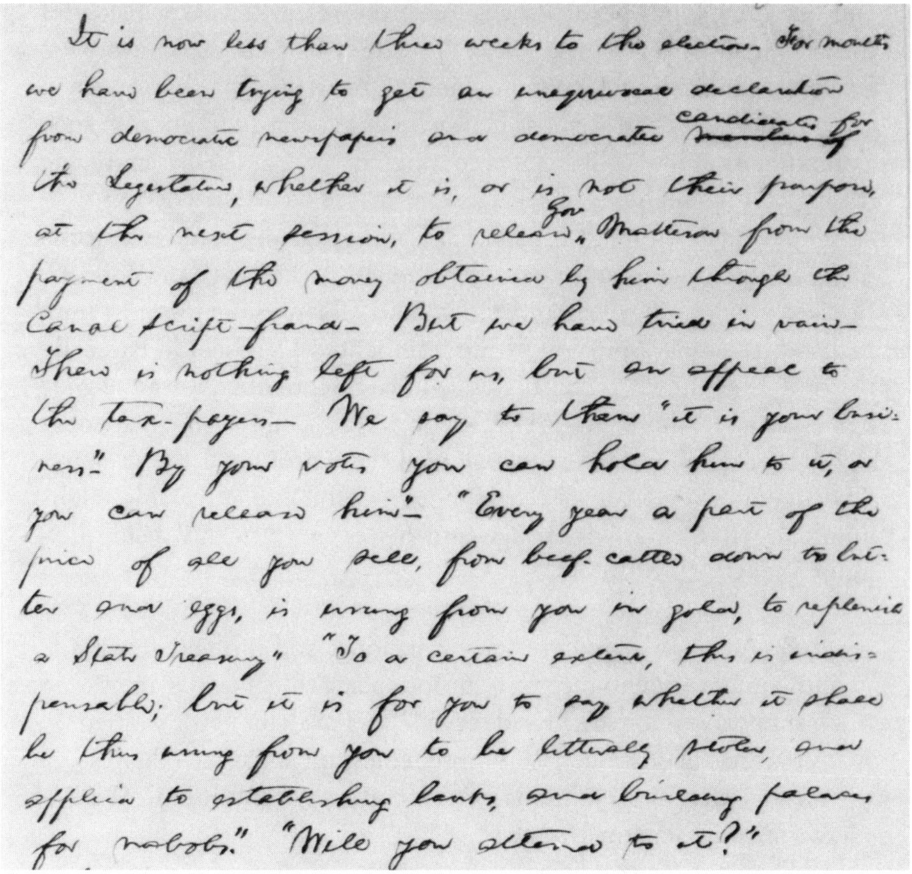

Figure 9-1. Beginning of a draft of an unpublished editorial by Lincoln, written in October 1860. Library of Congress.

whether it is, or is not their purpose, at the next session, to release Gov Matteson from the payment of the money obtained by him through the Canal script-fraud_ But we have tried in vain_ There is nothing left for us, but an appeal to the tax-payers_ We say to them "it is your business"_ By your votes you can hold him to it, or you can release him"_ "Every year a part of the price of all you sell, from beef-cattle down to butter and eggs, is wrung from you in gold, to replenish a State Treasury" "To a certain extent, this is indispensable; but it is for you to say whether it shall be thus wrung from you to be litterally stolen, and applied to establishing banks, and building palaces for nabobs." "Will you attend to it?"

We know from his law partner that Lincoln had been writing this kind of anonymous editorial matter for the local newspaper for years, but what would possess the front-running presidential candidate, three weeks before the election, to interest himself so intensely in the fate of the schemes of the slippery ex-governor Joel A. Matteson? While it is certainly true that such an issue might help to attract votes to the local Republican ticket, where support for Lincoln's own candidacy was lagging, there were presumably other means that would help more, and this piece does not even seem to have been published.

The answer to this puzzle may lie partly in Lincoln's rare ability to put a complicated case into a brief and coherent form. That is, it might be a practical answer to the question local Republicans were asking themselves: "How do we explain a complicated multiple swindle to the ordinary citizen, and what do we ask him to do about it?" Lincoln's characterization of the complex fraud, whereby scrip issued when the state was bankrupt was subsequently redeemed and then fraudulently recycled for further redemptions, is the subject of a long second paragraph not given here, but the incident recommends itself to our attention for its example. Along with the other two instances of behind-the-scenes writing just referred to, it suggests that the man about to become president of the United States was never too busy or too preoccupied to write. That none of these pieces seem to have been put into print or otherwise employed for a practical purpose further suggests that its author wrote them not on demand but rather on impulse—to refute a charge, to capture a perspective, to demonstrate how to pursue a scoundrel. He instinctively reacted to political phenomena with his pen.

Because we have so many of his manuscripts, we are able to see that during his presidency, this happened over and over again. Something would occur, and almost his first reaction would be to write something in response. Here is an example from the summer of 1864, when Lincoln's presidency was in the doldrums, with depressing news on nearly every front. In these circumstances, the president received a letter of resignation from a lackluster appointee, a solicitor in the Court of Claims named Charles Gibson, who had the effrontery, in his transmitted letter of resignation, to complain about Lincoln's renomination and to add, "I accepted the office solely as a patriotic duty, & at considerable personal & pecuniary sacrifice." The clerk of the court, who had forwarded Gibson's resignation, was sent the following letter over the signature of John Hay.

According to the request contained in your note, I have placed
Mr Gibson's letter of resignation in the hands of the President.
He has read the letter, and says he accepts the resignation, as he
will be glad to do with any other which may be tendered, as this
is, for the purpose of taking an attitude of hostility against him.
He says he was not aware that he was so much indebted to Mr
Gibson for having accepted the office at first, not remembering
that he ever pressed him to do so, or that he gave it otherwise
than as was usual, upon request made on behalf of Mr Gibson.
He thanks Mr Gibson for his acknowledgment that he has been
treated with personal kindness and consideration; and he says he
knows of but two small draw-backs upon Mr Gibson's right to
still receive such treatment, one of which is that he never could
learn of his giving much attention to the duties of his office, and
the other is this studied attempt of Mr. Gibson's to stab him.

It is clear from Hay's letter that the president felt insulted by Gibson's letter and that the secretary had been authorized to pass along the
general tenor of the chief magistrate's pique, but the original draft
shows that the president had been sufficiently aroused by the occasion
(in conjunction with his other woes) to write the letter himself (see
Fig. 9-2).

One final example. The journalist Noah Brooks described being
sent for by the president in December 1864 "to hear a story." Still writing when Brooks came into his library, Lincoln finished and then read
aloud the following:

On thursday of last week two ladies from Tennessee came before
the President asking the release of their husbands held as prisoners of war at Johnson's Island. They were put off till friday,
when they came again; and were again put off to saturday. At
each of the interviews one of the ladies urged that her husband
was a religious man. On saturday the President ordered the
release of the prisoners, and then said to this lady "You say your
husband is a religious man; tell him when you meet him, that I
say I am not much of a judge of religion, but that, in my opinion,
the religion that sets men to rebel and fight against their government, because, as they think, that government does not sufficiently help *some* men to eat their bread on the sweat of *other*

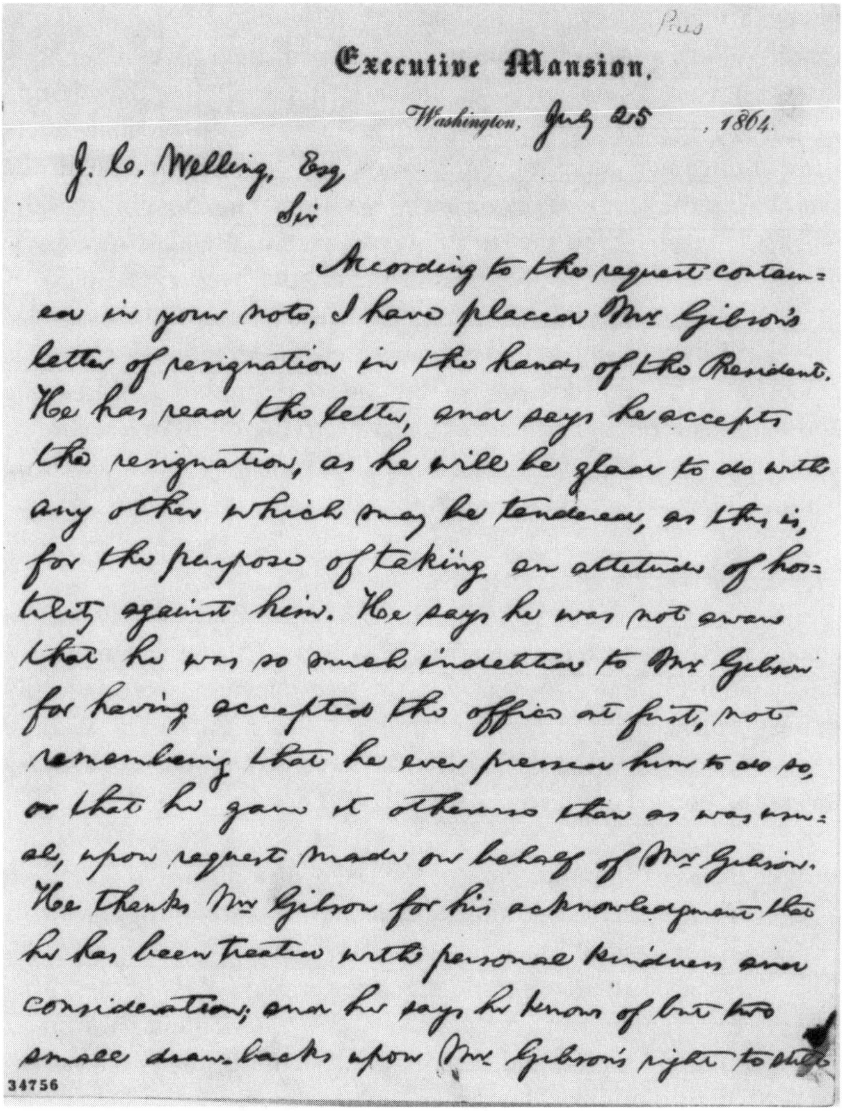

Figure 9-2. Letter written by Lincoln over John Hay's signature. Library of Congress.

men's faces, is not the sort of religion upon which people can get to heaven!"

Appending the caption "The President's last, shortest, and best speech," Lincoln asked that Brooks not send it to his paper in California but arrange to have it published in the *Washington Chronicle*, saying candidly, "I've a childish desire to see it in print right away."

In the case of the offending solicitor, it seems clear that writing functioned as a safety valve. Where some would swear and others throw things in exasperation, Lincoln reached for his pen. With the "speech" to the religious soldier's wife, whose caption possibly makes a whimsical reference to the shortness of a certain previous speech, he gave vent to another source of impatience, the hypocritical piety of those fighting on the side of oppression. It is hard to avoid the conclusion that Lincoln's impulse to write had become an integral part of his personality. He needed to put his response to things into words, to see and hear his thoughts articulated. Was he trying to make a record of his thoughts, or merely to express them? In a way, it matters little because he was effectively doing both.

৯

By 1864, THE FOURTH year of Lincoln's presidency, things had changed. Not only was there reason to believe that the Union had finally gained military advantage in the war, but there was an equally dramatic turnaround in Northern public opinion on slavery. George Templeton Strong, whose diary had followed this issue since the war's inception, poured out his astonishment on February 24, 1864:

> The change of opinion on this slavery question since 1860 is a great historical fact, comparable with the early progress of Christianity and of Mahometanism. Who could have predicted it, even when the news came that Sumter had fallen, or even a year and a quarter afterwards, when Pope was falling back on Washington, routed and disorganized? I think this great and blessed revolution is due, in no small degree, to A. Lincoln's sagacious policy. But I do wish A. Lincoln told fewer dirty stories.

Here it is evident that Strong still cannot think about the president, whose official conduct he clearly admired, without somewhat mixed feelings. Nonetheless, in assaying the primary cause of the "blessed revolution," he credited Lincoln's efforts, dirty stories and all. Having made a general observation about the altered situation, Strong proceeded to dramatize it with revealing, close-to-home examples.

What a marvelous change it is! Henry Clitz, Walter Cutting, and Jem Ruggles avowing themselves damn Abolitionists, and my little Louis singing after dinner, Sundays: "John Brown's bodies lies a-modrin' in the graves" just as if it were "The Star-Spangled Banner." Abolitionism established in Maryland and Missouri! *Mirifica Opera Tua.* God pardon our blindness of three years ago! But for our want of eyes to see and of courage to say what we saw, the South would never have ventured on rebellion.

Shortly after Strong entered the above in his diary, an editorial in *Harper's Weekly* marveled at the progress the president had made in spite of being constantly criticized from all sides. *Harper's* had no hesitation in seeing Lincoln's public utterances as the key to his success:

> He wrote the Greeley letter, the Vallandigham letter, the Springfield letter, simple, plain, direct; letters which the heart of every man in the land interpreted, and, unlike any other instance in our political annals, every letter he wrote, every speech he made, brought him nearer to the popular heart.

Thanks to the president's persuasive public offerings, and to countless other measures, military and otherwise, public sentiment in the loyal states had undergone a profound change. As Strong pointed out, two of the all-important border states, Maryland and Missouri, had taken the incredible step of abolishing slavery. While the radicals of his own party, unhappy with the president's perceived lack of zeal and efficiency in dealing with emancipation and the war, still hoped to deprive him of a second term, it was becoming increasingly difficult to put their case convincingly when they had to measure verbal swords with him.

In late April, one of his most persistent critics, Horace Greeley, grudgingly offered the president his due. "President Lincoln is not generally esteemed a man of signal ability," he began, "yet he has no adviser, and (since Jefferson) has had no predecessor, who surpassed him in that rare quality, the ability to make a statement which appeals at once, and irresistibly, to the popular apprehension—what we may call the shrewdly homely way of 'putting things.'" This was high praise indeed, but Greeley was not finished. "As we are known not to favor his re-nomination, we cannot be blinded by partiality in our judgment that few men have ever lived who could have better explained and commended his course and attitude with regard to slavery, than he has done in his late letter to Mr. Hodges of Kentucky."

Greeley was referring to a letter that Lincoln had sent in early April to a Kentucky newspaper editor, Albert G. Hodges. Hodges had come to Washington in March with a delegation of Kentuckians headed by Governor Thomas Bramlette to present their views to the president, in particular their grave objections to the deployment of blacks as soldiers in the Union Army. Orville H. Browning noted in his diary what the president had told him about the meeting:

> He said when they were discussing the matter he asked them to let him make a little speech to them, which he did and with which they were much pleased. That afterwards Mr Hodges came back to him, and asked him to give him a copy of his remarks to take with him to Ky_ He told Mr Hodges that what he had said was not written, and that he had not then time to commit it to paper—but to go home and he would write him a letter in which he would give, as nearly as he could all that he had said to them orally.

If Lincoln did not write out his speech and memorize it, Hodges apparently thought he did, which suggests it had a certain finished quality when delivered. That Lincoln had prepared can hardly be doubted, but he probably thought it advisable not to bring a text to the meeting so that, if things did not go well, nothing could be carried away and used against him. By this time the reader of these pages can pretty well predict why Lincoln was telling Browning all this: he wanted to read him the letter he had written to Hodges.

Lincoln had met with the Kentuckians on March 26 and read his letter to Browning on April 4, the date of the letter. In the intervening eight days, he apparently did a good deal more than write down what he had prepared in advance or remembered saying. On April 3, one of his appointees, Joseph H. Barrett, received a note from Lincoln to come to the White House for a political assignment. Barrett says he found the president "in his office with scattered pieces of manuscript before him, out of which he was making up his noted letter to Mr. Hodges, which bears the date of April 4, 1864." This is not surprising, for Lincoln carefully packed into his speech and its literary counterpart a detailed narrative of presidential restraint—his own—that he had likely been wanting to rehearse for a long time. The resulting defense of his conduct contains some of his most memorable and often-quoted utterances.

I am naturally anti-slavery. If slavery is not wrong, nothing is wrong. I can not remember when I did not so think, and feel. And yet I have never understood that the Presidency conferred upon me an unrestricted right to act officially upon this judgment and feeling. It was in the oath I took that I would, to the best of my ability, preserve, protect, and defend the Constitution of the United States. I could not take the office without taking the oath. Nor was it my view that I might take an oath to get power, and break the oath using the power. I understood, too, that in ordinary civil administration this oath even forbade me to practically indulge my primary abstract judgment on the moral question of slavery. I had publicly declared this many times, and in many ways. And I aver that, to this day, I have done no official act in mere deference to my abstract judgment and feeling on slavery. I did understand ~~hower,~~ however, that my oath to preserve the Constitution to the best of my ability, imposed upon me the duty of preserving, by every indispensable means, that government—that nation—of which that Constitution was the organic law. Was it possible to lose the nation, and yet preserve the Constitution? By general law life *and* limb must be protected; yet often a limb must be amputated to save a life; but a life is never wisely given to save a limb. I felt that measures, otherwise unconstitutional, might become lawful, by becoming indispensable to the preservation of the Constitution, through the preservation of the nation. Right or wrong, I assumed this ground, and now avow it. I could not feel that, to the best of my ability, I had even tried to preserve the Constitution, if, to save slavery, or any minor matter, I should permit the wreck of government, country, and Constitution all together. When, early in the war, Gen. Fremont attempted military emancipation, I forbade it, because I did not then think it an indispensable necessity. When a little later, Gen. Cameron, then Secretary of War, suggested the arming of the blacks, I objected, because I did not yet think it an indispensable necessity. When, still later, Gen.

Hunter attempted military emancipation, I again forbade it, because I did not yet think the indispensable necessity had come. When, in March, and May, and July 1862 I made earnest, and successive appeals to the border states to favor compensated emancipation, I believed the indispensable necessity for military emancipation, and arming the blacks would come, unless averted by that measure, They declined the proposition; and I was, in my best judgment, driven to the alternative of either surrendering the Union, and with it, the Constitution, or of laying strong hand upon the colored element. I chose the latter. In choosing it, I hoped for greater gain than loss; but of this, I was not entirely confident. More than a year of trial now shows no loss by it in our foreign relations, none in our home popular sentiment, none in our white military force,—no loss by it any how, or any where. On the contrary, it shows a gain of quite a hundred and thirty thousand soldiers, seamen, and laborers. These are palpable facts, about which, as facts, there can be no cavilling—. We have the men; and we could not have had them without the measure.

And now let any Union man who complains of the measure, test himself by writing down in one line that he is for subduing the rebellion by force of arms; and in the next, that he is for taking these hundred and thirty thousand men from the Union side, and placing them where they would be but for the measures he condemns. If he can not face his case so stated, it is only because he can not face the truth.

This was the president's artful redaction of the "little speech" he had given the Kentuckians. By all accounts, he was very persuasive in a face-to-face encounter. Putting his visitors at ease came naturally to him; he was a good listener; he had a way of making his visitors feel important, that he valued their opinions, and that his response was candid and sincere. Many leaders are effective precisely because they have this special gift for dealing creatively with criticism and complaint. But Lincoln had something else that is much rarer: he could translate this kind of face-to-face communication into a written form that worked just as well publicly as privately.

Albert G. Hodges may have requested a written version of Lincoln's argument, as is usually assumed, for the purpose of sharing its force and appeal with his fellow Kentuckians. But if he secretly hoped for the opposite result—that the president's privately conveyed message would seem lame and ineffective if translated into writing—his request would ordinarily have been a very promising gambit. But not in the case of Abraham Lincoln. Even without the aura of the presidency, the atmosphere of the president's private office, the friendliness and personal deference of the chief magistrate himself—even without such tools of personal persuasion, Lincoln had a publicly effective weapon. This is what Greeley, who was anxious to undercut the president politically, thought was important to acknowledge up front. "We consider [the president's] course, that attitude, open to criticism; but none but a besotted partisan can fail to see that both are honestly and candidly set forth in the letter to Hodges, and that Whoever shall hereafter charge the President with being impelled by 'fanaticism' in his official action respecting slavery must sin against the clearest light."

LINCOLN'S LETTER TO HODGES included a final paragraph that was not part of the redaction of his speech but which nonetheless contains some of the letter's most notable elements. It begins with an attempt to counter any impression his "little speech" to the Kentuckians might have given that he had manipulated events so as to bring about the result in question—the arming of black soldiers. "I add a word which was not in the verbal conversation. In telling this tale I attempt no compliment to my own sagacity. I claim not to have controlled events, but confess plainly that events have controlled me." This last sentence has become a battleground in the struggle to understand the character of both Lincoln and his presidency, for there is a clear sense in which it is disingenuous, especially for historians who know much more about Lincoln's activities than did his 1864 audience, public or private. If we judge that Lincoln here attempted to convey the impression that he had passively accepted the course of events and had made no effort to influence them, then the statement is unquestionably misleading, and deliberately so. Lincoln's was a demonstrably energetic presidency, and he, himself, an untiring worker. He constantly urged greater exertion in all aspects of the Union war effort, and the evidence is clear that, in order to get results, he was willing to experiment and to take risks.

On the other hand, there was an aspect of Lincoln's distinctive makeup that suggested passivity. He was, for example, extraordinarily patient, willing and able to withhold action until he could discern the direction events were taking, when most others thought it necessary to act. He was philosophically disposed to accept adversity as unavoidable, his favorite saying being "What is to be will be, and no prayers of ours can arrest the decree." It was such pronounced qualities as these that led his law partner Herndon to characterize him as "passive."

But the context of the famous sentence in the Hodges letter tells us that Lincoln was there addressing a larger issue than mere human instrumentality. In fact, this paragraph marks the introduction into the president's public discourse of a whole new dimension of meaning for the war, the x-factor over which he had been privately brooding for some time. "Now, at the end of three years struggle," the paragraph continues, "the nation's condition is not what either party, or any man devised, or expected. God alone can claim it." Lincoln may well have been quietly glossing over the issue of his personal responsibility for current realities, but there can be little doubt that he wanted to use the occasion and the context to start an idea about the operation of the divine will. "Whither it is tending seems plain. If God now wills the removal of a great wrong, and wills also that we of the North as well as you of the South, shall pay fairly for our complicity in that wrong, impartial history will find therein no cause to question the justice or goodness of God."

This is what Lincoln first set down in the fair copy of his letter that he had copied out for sending to Hodges (see Fig. 9-3). But the last sentence, whose substance would become the major thesis of his Second Inaugural, did not quite satisfy him. In essence, he decided to reverse the polarity of this sentence, changing it from negative to positive, so that it would finally read: "impartial history will find therein new cause to attest and revere the justice and goodness of God." His fretting over the most suitable polarity for this sentence is, in retrospect, a signal that he was preparing the ground for a public pronouncement far more profound and far-reaching than anything he had previously attempted.

∾

ABRAHAM LINCOLN WAS WHAT Ralph Waldo Emerson called a "causationist." According to Emerson, all successful men fit this description, by which he meant, "They believed that things went not

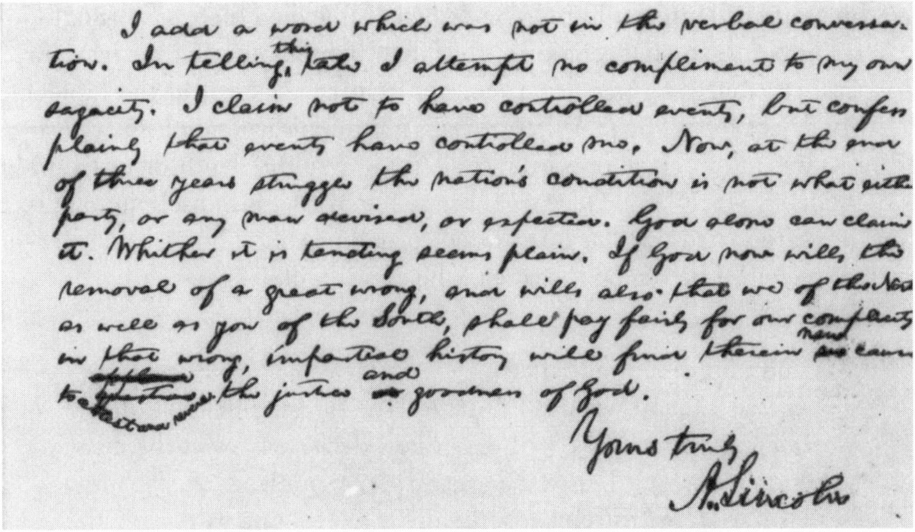

Figure 9-3. Final paragraph of Lincoln's draft for his letter to Albert G. Hodges. Library of Congress.

by luck, but by law." Herndon testified repeatedly that his law partner was, indeed, such a man. Lincoln's settled view, according to Herndon, was something like this: "God starts causes, & effects follow those causes; & those Effects are at once, in the ages, causes as well as Effects—Hence the universal chain of causation." This belief owed much to Lincoln's early acceptance of eighteenth-century rationalism and was evidently colored, to some extent, by the Calvinistic religious outlook of the community in which he was raised. Lincoln was a fatalist from first to last, but for him that did not imply that human events had no purpose or meaning, for he also endorsed the view expressed by the familiar Shakespearean line he was fond of quoting: "There is a divinity that shapes our ends, Rough-hew them how we will." It was this last perspective—that there is a divine will operating, and possibly discernible, in human affairs—that seems to have increasingly haunted his thinking as president.

Lincoln had never been religious in the conventional sense of belonging to a church or subscribing to a recognized religious creed. As his wife told Herndon in a famous interview, "Mr Lincoln had no hope & no faith in the usual acceptation of those words: he never joined a Church." And yet she believed, as did Herndon, that in some sense "he was a religious man always, as I think." She said she detected

an awakened interest in religion "when Willie died [February 1862]—
never before. he felt religious More than Ever about the time he went
to Gettysburg: he was not a technical Christian: he read the bible a
good deal about 1864." What perhaps neither his wife nor his law partner was allowed the opportunity to grasp was the depth of Lincoln's
theological thinking. Orville H. Browning, who was himself quite religious, reported that "in the summer or fall of 1861," he had a conversation with Lincoln on the role of the divine will.

> I said to him substantially:
> "Mr. Lincoln we can't hope for the blessing of God on the
> efforts of our armies, until we strike a decisive blow at the insti-
> tution of slavery. This is the great curse of our land, and we must
> make an effort to remove it before we can hope to receive the
> help of the Almighty."
> I remember being much impressed by his reply, because it
> caused me to reflect that perhaps he had thought more deeply
> upon this subject than I had.
> "Browning, suppose God is against us in our view on the
> subject of slavery in this country, and our method of dealing
> with it?"

This conversation, which Browning recalled for John G. Nicolay in
1875, was not mentioned in his diary, and he may have been mistaken
about the date, but he did record in his diary something Lincoln confided to him in the grim days of December 1862: "We are now on the
brink of destruction. It appears to me the Almighty is against us, and
I can hardly see a ray of hope." But however much it may have occupied his thoughts in the interim, it was not until the Hodges letter of
April 4, 1864, that Lincoln chose to speak of the will of God publicly.
To a twenty-first-century reader, such speculation may seem strange,
but for Lincoln's contemporaries it was not at all unexpected. Horace
Greeley observed in his response to the Hodges letter, "As he is a poor
natural philosopher who ignores the law of gravitation, so that statesmanship is shallow which fails to count God's justice among the forces,
which it is far safer and wiser to conform to than to resist." Less than a
year later, Lincoln would make the question of God's justice in the
Civil War the centerpiece of his Second Inaugural Address.

LINCOLN'S PREOCCUPATION WITH THE issue of God's will and the providential meaning of the nation's calamitous ordeal is particularly evident throughout the last year of his life. The concentration of so many indicators from the time of the Hodges letter in April 1864 to the delivery of the Second Inaugural on March 4, 1865, is quite notable. The day after he sent his letter to Hodges he addressed another to Mary Mann, the author of a petition signed by 195 schoolchildren from Concord, Massachusetts, asking the president to free "all the little slave children in this country." He replied, "Please tell these little people I am very glad their young hearts are so full of just and generous sympathy, and that, while I have not the power to grant all they ask, I trust they will remember that God has, and that, as it seems, He wills to do it." This, as he well knew, was the kind of private communication that would soon find its way into the newspapers, and it seems, in retrospect, motivated by a wish to begin preparing the ground for the vision that would be presented in the Second Inaugural.

A much more pointed and more public remark was incorporated into a brief speech he gave a few weeks later at the Baltimore Sanitary Fair on April 18:

> When the war began, three years ago, neither party, nor any man, expected it would last till now. Each looked for the end, in some way, long ere to-day. Neither did any anticipate that domestic slavery would be much affected by the war. But here we are; the war has not ended, and slavery has been much affected—how much needs not now to be recounted. So true is it that man proposes, and God disposes.

The way in which this anticipates the Second Inaugural's lead-in to the issue of the war and the divine will is quite striking, both in the similarities and differences:

> All knew that this interest [slavery] was, somehow, the cause of the war. . . . Neither party expected for the war, the magnitude, or the duration, which it has already attained. Neither anticipated that the *cause* of the conflict might cease with, or even before, the conflict itself should cease. Each looked for an easier

triumph, and a result less fundamental and astounding. Both read the same Bible, and pray to the same God; and each invokes His aid against the other.

One way to gauge the richness and complexity of what many consider Lincoln's greatest speech is by comparison with such earlier versions of his ideas and language. In a real sense, these forerunners function as early, if partial, drafts of the master work, each giving a trial exposure to a part or an expression of what would become an impressively articulated and integrated whole.

At the intellectual core of the Second Inaugural is a logical exercise, whose starting point is that whatever was happening in the Civil War, however difficult to understand and painful to endure, was precisely what God wanted to happen. Lincoln clearly brooded over this premise for a long time, occasionally touching on it privately, as we have seen. His most direct confrontation of the premise on record is in a manuscript fragment called by Lincoln's secretaries "Meditation on the Divine Will" (see Fig. 9-4), a document whose language and logic are equally austere.

> The will of God prevails_ In great contests each party claims to act in accordence with the will of God. Both *may* be, and one *must* be wrong. God can not be *for*, and *against* the same thing at the same time. In the present civil war it is quite possible that God's purpose is something different from the purpose of either party—and yet the human instrumentalities, working just as they do, are of the best adaptation to effect ~~his~~ <His> purpose. I am almost ready to say this is probably true—that God wills this contest, and wills that it shall not end yet_ By his mere quiet power, on the minds of the now contestants, He could have either *saved* or *destroyed* the Union without a human contest_ Yet the contest began_ And having begun He could give the final victory to either side any day_ Yet the contest proceeds_

Part of the wonder in the extraordinary case of Abraham Lincoln is that, while a man of down-to-earth practicality, he constantly worried his problems at philosophical levels. All the time he was devising and experimenting with strategies to win or simply to end the war, he was brooding on its meaning, and the closely related matter of why, given

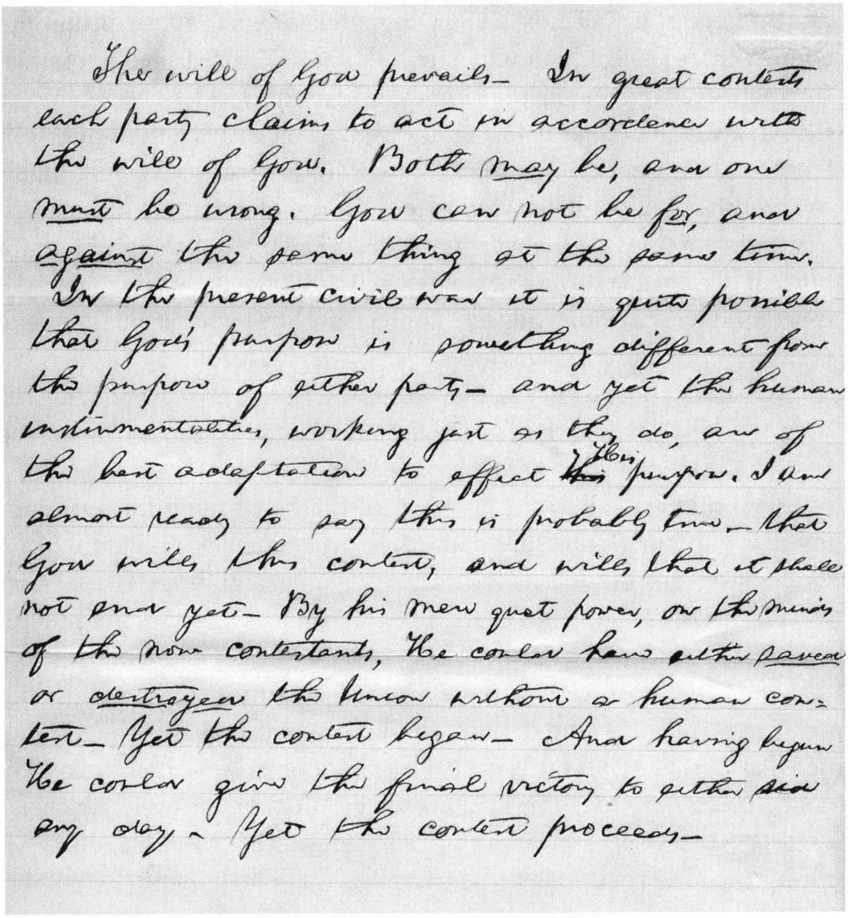

Figure 9-4. This undated manuscript, known as the "Meditation on the Divine Will," undoubtedly reflects Lincoln's thinking about the role of Providence in the Civil War and may have been written in or near the year 1864. John Hay Library, Brown University.

its horrific human cost, it had to last so long. This famous meditation is undated but was placed by his secretaries and all subsequent editors in the summer or early fall of 1862, when its author was anguished at the deteriorating military situation and desperate for an opportunity to begin a general emancipation by presidential proclamation. But there are problems with this date (which are duly discussed in the notes) and good reasons for thinking that the "Meditation" is chronologically much closer to, and perhaps even belongs to, the year 1864. Certainly it fits seamlessly into the series of references to the divine will under review here. Furthermore, 1864 arguably offers a more propitious context than 1862, which was, after all, a time when Lincoln was reasonably sure why the Union forces, under the feckless leadership of General McClellan, were losing. By 1864, even with a determined military and vastly superior resources, the Union forces were still unable to end the rebellion. This would seem a more likely time for the president's sitting down at his writing table and laying out the problem for himself in its starkest form: since the will of God necessarily prevails, it must follow that "God wills this contest, and wills that it shall not end yet_"

And that conclusion raises yet another objection to placing the writing of the "Meditation" in the summer or fall of 1862. Hay argued that the "Meditation" reflected the anguish of a leader beset by repeated military failures and unsure of the best timing for proclaiming emancipation, a measure that might prove the biggest failure of all. The editors of the *Collected Works*, using the same basis as Lincoln's secretaries, speculatively assigned the writing of the "Meditation" to the day on which Lincoln was reported by a cabinet member as saying that "he felt almost ready to hang himself." But the document does not seem to reflect this kind of anguish. The conclusion that Lincoln says he is "almost ready to say is probably true" points to a different kind of concern, namely that the prolonged duration of the war, which far exceeds the expectation of both parties, indicates that God is using it for his own inscrutable purposes.

⁓

TWO ANECDOTES FROM LINCOLN'S residence at the Soldiers' Home point up his preoccupation in 1864 with the idea that whatever happens is an expression of the will of God. The first is a story he told in the summer to the Pennsylvania volunteers assigned to guard him, who were "grumbling around the campfire that their talents were being wasted on this unnecessary duty." Lincoln reportedly said, "with a twinkle in his eye":

> You boys remind me of a farmer friend of mine in Illinois, who said he could never understand why the Lord put the curl in a pig's tail. It never seemed to him to be either useful or ornamental, but he reckoned the Almighty knew what he was doing when he put it there.

As with many of Lincoln's stories, what appears on the surface to be a homely or even benighted observation of an unsophisticated farmer contains, on reflection, surprising depth and acuity. Just because we can't understand the purpose of things, however insignificant, doesn't mean that there is none.

The second anecdote relates to an unannounced evening visit in the fall from a traveling Englishman, George Borrett, who reported that the president obligingly came downstairs in good humor and talked knowledgeably on a variety of subjects.

> The conversation next turned upon English poetry, the president saying that when we disturbed him he was deep in Pope. He seemed to be a great admirer of Pope, especially of his "Essay on Man;" going so far as to say that he thought it contained all the religious instruction which it was necessary for a man to know. Then he mused for a moment or two, and asked us if we could show him any finer lines than those ending, as he quoted them without hesitation—
>
> > "All nature is but art, unknown to thee;
> > All chance, direction, which thou canst not see;
> > All discord, harmony not understood;
> > All partial evil, universal good:
> > And, spite of pride, in erring reason's spite,
> > One truth is clear, whatever is, is right."

This passage from Pope is, of course, the classic eighteenth-century characterization of the divine will, the concept whose application to the Civil War Lincoln had been contemplating for months. It indicates, perhaps, a concern with the moral edge that Pope gives to the idea that whatever is, is the will of God. This is further suggested by what Lincoln said when Borrett remarked on the beauty of Pope's verses: "Yes, that's a convenient line, too, that last one. You see, a man may turn it, and say, 'Well, if whatever *is* is right, why, then, whatever *isn't* must be wrong.' " For a president trying to decide how to frame a volatile moral issue, this remark betrays a mind acutely aware of the need to make a case in such a way that it cannot be easily evaded by a facile reply.

ANOTHER CLEAR INDICATION THAT the divine will was very much
on Lincoln's mind in the fall of 1864 is found in a letter he wrote on
September 4 to a noted Quaker activist, Eliza P. Gurney. She had visited Lincoln in the White House two years earlier and was a strong
supporter, partly because of his considerate handling of the issue of
Quaker pacifism. Lincoln's letter to Gurney is one of his most sensitive
and revealing, and we are fortunate in having his composition draft,
which he retained as a file copy. Just looking at the changes he made,
best seen in the illustration (see Fig. 9-5), gives a sense of the care that
went into the writing.

> My ~~dear~~ <esteemed> friend.
>   I have not forgotten—probably never shall forget—the very
> impressive occasion ~~of the visit of~~ <when> yourself and friends
> ~~to~~ <visited> me on a Sabbath forenoon two years ago, Nor has
> your kind letter, written nearly a year later, ever been forgotten.
> In all, it has been your purpose to strengthen my reliance on
> God. I am much indebted to the good Christian people of the
> country for their constant prayers and consolations; and to no
> one of them more than to-yourself_ The purposes of ~~God~~ <the
> Almighty> are perfect, and must prevail, though we erring mor-
> tals may fail to accurately perceive them in advance. We hoped
> for a happy termination of this terrible war ~~ere~~ <before> this;
> but God knows best, and has ruled otherwise. We shall yet ~~per-
> ceive his~~ <acknowledge> His wisdom, and our own error
> therein_ Meanwhile we must work earnestly ~~by~~ in the best lights
> He gives, <us,> trusting <that> so working still conduces to the
> great ends He ordains_ Surely He intends some great good to
> follow this mighty convulsion, which no mortal could make, and
> no mortal could ~~hinder~~ stay.

The account of Lincoln's recitation of Pope at about the same time
throws considerable light on this letter and on the status of Lincoln's
ruminations on these questions. "We shall yet acknowledge His wisdom, and our own error therein" is the rough equivalent, inversely
stated, of "And, spite of pride, in erring reason's spite, One truth is
clear, whatever is, is right."
     In a final paragraph of his letter to Gurney, Lincoln raises another
dilemma presented by the war.

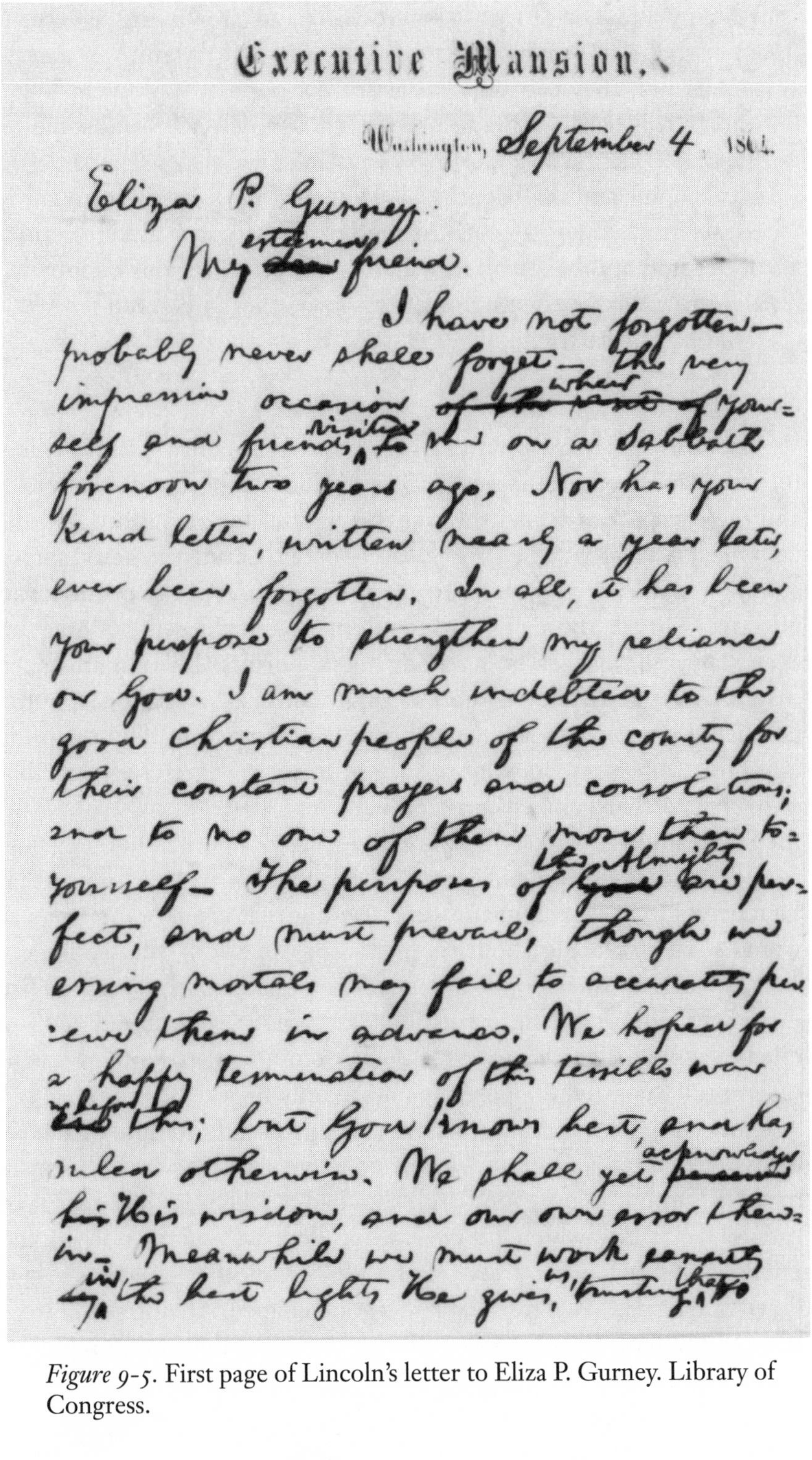

Figure 9-5. First page of Lincoln's letter to Eliza P. Gurney. Library of Congress.

Your people—the Friends—have had, and are having a very great trial. On principle, <and faith,> opposed to both war *and* oppression, they can only <practically> oppose oppression by war. In this hard dilema some have chosen one horn and some the other. For those appealing to me on conscientious grounds, I have done, and shall do, the best I <could and> can, in my own conscience, under my oath to the law. That you believe this I doubt not; and believing it, I shall still receive, for our country and myself, your earnest prayers to our Father in Heaven,

Your sincere friend,

A. Lincoln

Written on the day after he learned that Atlanta had fallen, the letter may have been prompted by the revival of his hopes for reelection and the prospect of seeing the war through to its conclusion. As Lincoln must have recognized immediately upon hearing the news, such a stunning victory would go far to change the mood of the country and effectively break the dam of discontent that had been building up against him all summer, even among his supporters. This circumstance may throw a spotlight on the exquisitely phrased passage about the conflicted situation of Quakers in the last paragraph. The dilemma faced by pacifists, as Lincoln well knew, to some degree reflected that of many Northern citizens, particularly Democrats, who did not want the South to separate but who were reluctant to support what they perceived as an ill-advised, ill-managed Republican war. While radical Democrats like Vallandigham were arguing that abandoning the war would somehow bring about reunion with the South, the Confederacy's strong insistence on independence made such a possibility extremely doubtful, and realistic Northerners were faced with a dilemma much like that of the Quakers: opposed to both war and separation, they could oppose separation only by war.

This said, it is by no means clear precisely what prompted Lincoln to write to Eliza P. Gurney. Her personal visit in 1862 had obviously made a strong impression, and she had spoken in her letter of August 18, 1863, which he clearly recalled, of "submission to the Divine will." It is a good bet that he wanted another occasion to put down in writing, in a letter that had a good chance of being publicized, a formulation of the role of Providence in view of the stubborn persistence of the war: "The purposes of the Almighty are perfect, and must prevail, though we erring mortals may fail to accurately perceive them in advance. We hoped for a happy termination of this terrible war before this; but God knows best, and has ruled otherwise." This is very close in meaning to what he said in the "Meditation on the Divine Will," and is paired with his equally incisive formulation of the role to be played by mortals: "Meanwhile we must work earnestly in the best lights He gives us, trusting that so working still conduces to the great ends He ordains_" For those who wonder how a fatalist who believes that God is controlling events finds a place for human agency, here, in a nutshell, is Lincoln's answer. In Joshua Wolf Shenk's telling metaphor, while Lincoln believed he was not the captain of the ship that "carried him on life's rough waters," neither did he regard himself as an "idle passenger but a sailor on deck with a job to do."

THESE REFERENCES TO THE divine will that bear so directly on the biblical judgment he would render in his Second Inaugural Address inevitably raise the question of Lincoln's religious beliefs and how they may have informed his thinking on this subject. Lincoln, as we have seen, was not conventionally religious, and people like Herndon, who had known him intimately but had little contact with him as president, found it hard to believe that he could have changed. His private secretary, John G. Nicolay, did not think he had. He told Herndon: "Mr. Lincoln did not, to my knowledge, change his religious ideas, opinions or beliefs from the time he left Springfield to the day of his death. I do not know just what they were, never having heard him explain them in detail; but I am very sure he gave no outward indication of his mind having undergone change in that regard while here." Nicolay here identified a large part of the problem, for Lincoln was not in the habit of discussing such things, making it difficult even for those around him to measure any alteration.

Nonetheless Mary Lincoln told Herndon that she noticed a change in her husband's thinking about religion during his presidency, and so had many others. Indeed, it is difficult to peruse his presidential writings and reported remarks chronologically without being struck by the numerous appeals to God and religion generally, over and above the preoccupation in 1864 that we have been tracing. Richard Carwardine has recently made a strong case for what he calls "Lincoln's new religious position." This, Carwardine argues, was "expressed in his search to discover God's purposes" and was "inextricably entwined with his developing emancipation policy." If we start with the notion that Lincoln always believed in an overruling Providence, as seems to have been the case, his new position may be understood as something like an extension or amplification brought about by the transforming pressures of office. If he had not been accustomed to talking about such things as the divine will, even to confidants like Herndon, he had nonetheless endorsed the concept of a moral universe set out in the Declaration of Independence, whose creator was acknowledged to have endowed human beings with inalienable natural rights, such as life, liberty, and the pursuit of happiness. It was not such a long step from that position to affirming that the war and its duration were governed by the will of the same creator.

But we must also take into consideration that Lincoln was at the same time on another presidential mission. Having enjoyed considerable success answering his critics and winning over the public to his policies with his public writings, he had ventured further afield at Gettysburg, seeking to justify the trials and sacrifices of the war as the cost of realizing such deep-seated and interrelated ideals as human equality, freedom, and meaningful self-government. When the probability of a Union victory began to take shape in early 1864, it seems likely that Lincoln was already searching for an effective means of conveying to his Northern constituency what he considered a necessary message—that the war had been about the violation of those inalienable rights spoken of in the Declaration, and that complicity in the offense of slavery was not confined to the Confederacy, but rather extended to the entire country, North and South. This hard message was akin to Old Testament prophecy, not in the sense of foretelling the future but of interpreting the divine will. The message was necessary not only for its moral truth but also the hoped-for effect of tempering the vengeful spirit that was already abundantly in evidence and that would predictably plague postwar reconstruction.

To render such an unwelcome message effectively, one had to consider the dispositions of the audience and the most promising ways to which it might be appealed. As Carwardine has aptly shown, Lincoln as president had well understood the importance of gaining the support of religious groups and denominations, which he worked at by actively cultivating their leaders. He thus had reason to believe that a very large and influential portion of his audience, which was thoroughly Christian and largely Protestant, would be susceptible to the prophetic mode and a theological theme.

To fully appreciate what Lincoln decided to do in his Second Inaugural, it is necessary to recognize that notwithstanding his susceptible audience, he was taking a considerable risk. Having had what appear to be profound intimations about the role of Providence and the mysterious operations of the divine will in connection with the war and slavery, he had to make a conscious and calculated decision about whether or not to incorporate them into the inaugural, his most prominent presidential message. The same was true for assuming a prophetic mantle. In a lifetime of public speaking and writing, he had rarely, if ever, offered his audience anything that could be classified as prophecy or an interpretation of divine purpose. To do so would constitute a distinct and noticeable departure, and if less than effective, a rather jarring one. Considering the risks involved, Lincoln's decision to take the course he did in the Second Inaugural was nothing if not bold.

FRANCIS B. CARPENTER, THE painter who spent six months in the White House in 1864 painting Lincoln and his cabinet, wrote that he had seen the manuscript of the Second Inaugural several days before the address was delivered on March 4, 1865.

> I was sitting in the President's office with Mr. G. B. Lincoln, of Brooklyn, and the Hon. John A. Bingham, of Ohio,—who were there by appointment with the President,—the Sunday evening before the reinauguration, when Mr. Lincoln came in through the side passage which had lately been constructed, holding in his hand a roll of manuscripts.
>
> "Lots of wisdom in that document, I suspect," said he; "it is what will be called my 'second inaugural,' containing about six hundred words. I will put it away here in this drawer until I want it."

This is an example of the kind of testimony that both tantalizes and exasperates historians. There is so much specific "factual" information here—the precise location, the names of those present, the exact date (February 26), the reference to the newly constructed passageway between Lincoln's office and the family library, the number of words in the speech—that it can readily lull one into uncritically accepting it as reliable. But given what we know about the foibles of human memory, this passage might very well prove to be a jumble of "facts" that actually belong to different occasions and have differing degrees of accuracy. Even if everything else in the testimony could be verified, we could still not be certain that Lincoln's speech, six days before delivery, contained about six hundred words, but the story will perhaps do as a starting point.

Unlike the case of the Gettysburg Address, no preliminary draft of the Second Inaugural is known. The only existing manuscript is a fair copy, written out by Lincoln in a large, clear hand, and well spaced, as though it were intended as a reading copy (see Fig. 9-6). It originally contained 694 words, but at some point Lincoln decided to change the ending. To accomplish this, he pasted a slip over the last two lines and inscribed on it the new ending (see Fig. 9-7), adding seven more words, for a grand total of 701.

If Carpenter's memory and Lincoln's remembered remark were both accurate, during the week preceding its delivery Lincoln increased the overall length of his speech by nearly twenty percent.

A Washington newspaper reported that the president had announced he would not receive callers that week "for any purpose whatever, between the hours of three and seven o'clock p.m." But if the president was using some of this time to revise his speech and write out a fair copy, this was not all he was doing. Perhaps mindful of the errant newspaper reports of his Gettysburg speech, Lincoln decided to have his inaugural printed for distribution to the press. Though it has received little notice and seems to have escaped the attention of the editors of the *Collected Works* altogether, the Second Inaugural first appeared in print on a folded leaflet that was distributed to reporters immediately after delivery (see Fig. 9-8). This process proved consequential, for when the president received the printer's proof sheets for the prospective press handout, he decided to fashion his delivery text from the uncorrected proof sheets. The resulting document is of great interest as a distinctively Lincolnian creation (see Fig. 9-9).

Lincoln occasionally resorted to the expedient of clipping printed matter and pasting it directly into a manuscript he was drafting, thus saving time and preserving the accuracy of the text. But in this case he clipped the entire text of the galley proof, sentence by sentence, and then pasted these twenty-five sentences, individually, in two col-

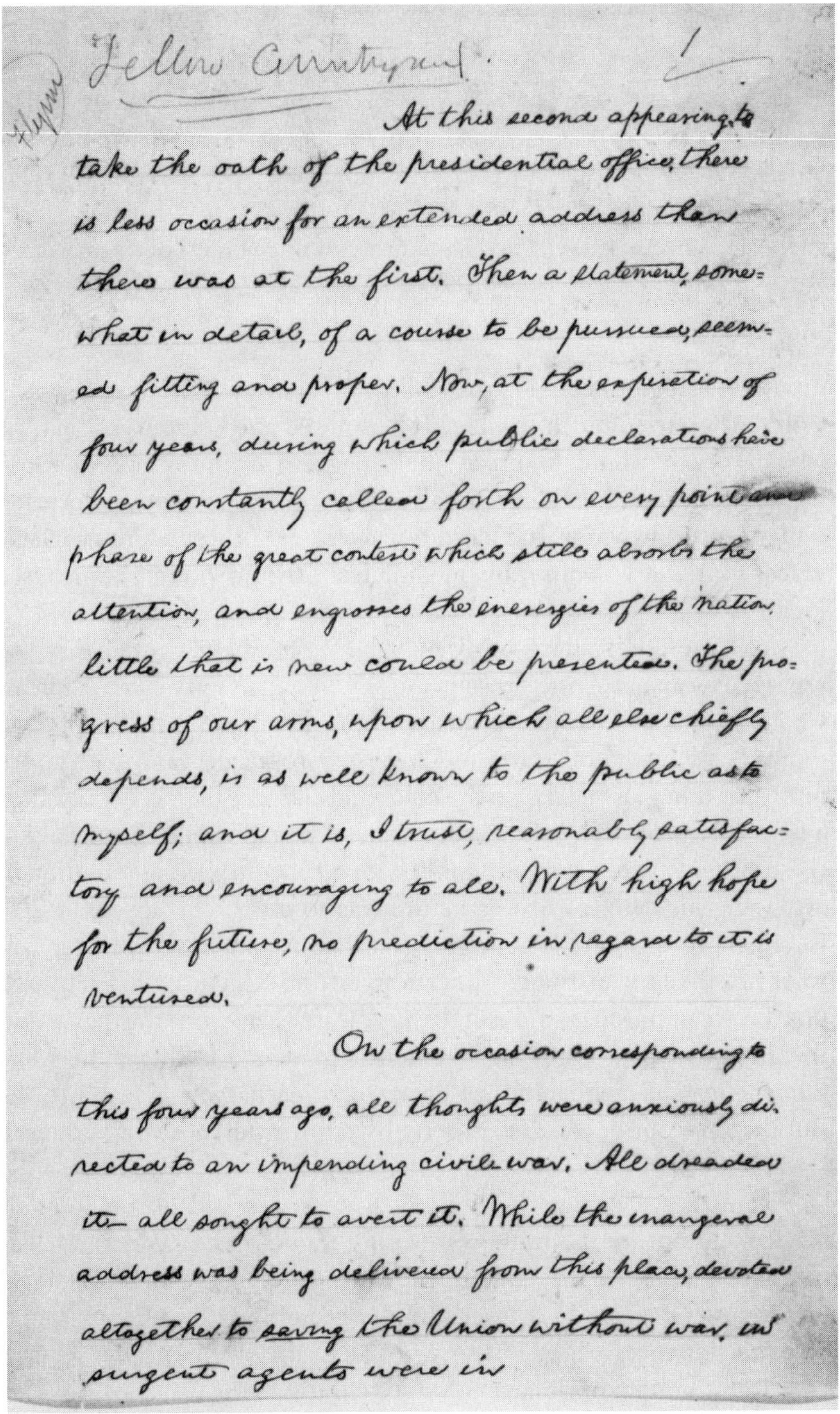

Fellow Countrymen.

At this second appearing to take the oath of the presidential office, there is less occasion for an extended address than there was at the first. Then a statement, somewhat in detail, of a course to be pursued, seemed fitting and proper. Now, at the expiration of four years, during which public declarations have been constantly called forth on every point and phase of the great contest which still absorbs the attention, and engrosses the energies of the nation, little that is new could be presented. The progress of our arms, upon which all else chiefly depends, is as well known to the public as to myself; and it is, I trust, reasonably satisfactory and encouraging to all. With high hope for the future, no prediction in regard to it is ventured.

On the occasion corresponding to this four years ago, all thoughts were anxiously directed to an impending civil war. All dreaded it— all sought to avert it. While the inaugural address was being delivered from this place, devoted altogether to saving the Union without war, insurgent agents were in

Figure 9-6. First page of the manuscript of Lincoln's Second Inaugural. Note typesetter's name (Flynn) and salutation in pencil, possibly in another hand. Library of Congress.

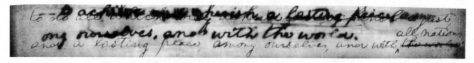

Figure 9-7. The original last two lines of text (darker text) of the manuscript of Lincoln's Second Inaugural are shown in this special photograph. The revised version (lighter text) is written on a slip pasted over the original lines. Library of Congress.

umns on a single sheet. This was his delivery copy. Why, we must ask, would he go to so much trouble? If he wanted two columns so that the whole speech would fit on a single page, why not simply cut out the whole text and divide it in half? Why a separate clipping for each sentence, and why, for that matter, place each of those individual sentences so that it was offset by one line from the previous sentence (see Fig. 9-10)?

Like the Gettysburg Address, the Second Inaugural may be regarded as an authentic prose poem. Unlike the Gettysburg Address, which begins with a quietly magical and memorable first sentence, the Second Inaugural starts much more prosaically, and with more restraint. It begins to take on the color and cadence of poetry only after a fair amount of straightforward, businesslike exposition. Especially in these circumstances, it seems unlikely that Lincoln's initial intention in arranging his delivery text as he did was to create the appearance of versified prose. There is no suggestion that he sought to call attention to or preserve the distinctive lineation, or line structure, that resulted. His original purpose was surely to create space on the page and thereby produce a visual arrangement that would facilitate the vocal sequencing and deliberate presentation of each successive sentence. But that, of course, is not so different from the purposes that underlie traditional versification.

Even so, the convention by which poetry is laid out in lines or verses may not be the most compelling model. The address itself is infused with biblical language and ends up generating a kind of biblical and prophetic ethos. Whatever impulse prompted the author to separate the sentences of his text and set them off on the page, however practical in origin, must have owed something to the essentially oracular character of the address and to the prophetic voice he wanted to project.

INAUGURAL ADDRESS.

MARCH 4, 1865.

FELLOW-COUNTRYMEN: At this second appearing to take the oath of the presidential office, there is less occasion for an extended address than there was at the first. Then, a statement, somewhat in detail, of a course to be pursued, seemed fitting and proper. Now, at the expiration of four years, during which public declarations have been constantly called forth on every point and phase of the great contest which still absorbs the attention and engrosses the energies of the nation, little that is new could be presented. The progress of our arms, upon which all else chiefly depends, is as well known to the public as to myself; and it is, I trust, reasonably satisfactory and encouraging to all. With high hope for the future, no prediction in regard to it is ventured.

On the occasion corresponding to this four years ago, all thoughts were anxiously directed to an impending civil war. All dreaded it—all sought to avert it. While the inaugural address was being delivered from this place, devoted altogether to *saving* the Union without war, insurgent agents were in the city seeking to *destroy* it without war—seeking to dissolve the Union, and divide effects, by negotiation.

Figure 9-8. First page of the text of Lincoln's Second Inaugural printed in advance for distribution to the press. Lincoln prepared the copy from which he read at the inaugural ceremony from the uncorrected printer's proof of this text (see Fig. 9-9). Library of Congress.

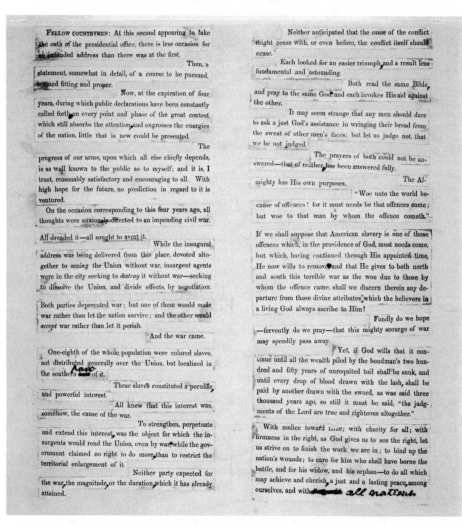

Figure 9-9. The copy of his Second Inaugural that Lincoln prepared from the uncorrected printer's proof and from which he read at the inaugural ceremony. Library of Congress.

❧

As is sometimes pointed out, the Second Inaugural is remarkable for what it *doesn't* say. Lincoln makes a point of listing at the outset the things he is not going to talk about. More surprisingly, he says that there is "less occasion for an extended address" than when he first took his presidential oath, even suggesting, as Garry Wills has phrased it, that "there was nothing useful to say about the war."

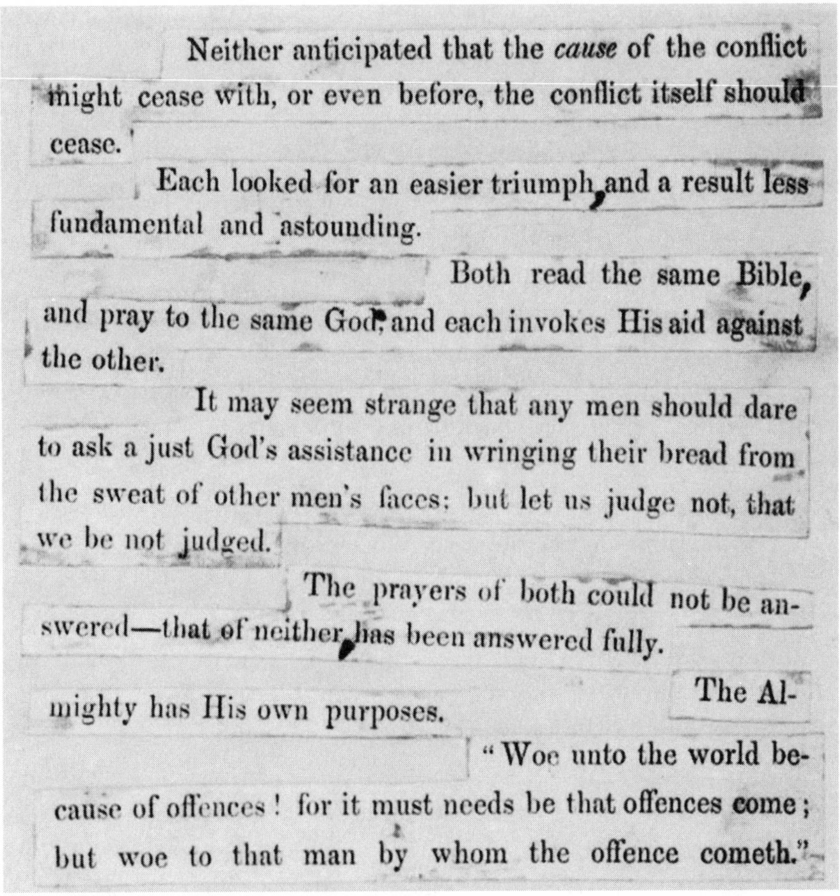

Neither anticipated that the *cause* of the conflict might cease with, or even before, the conflict itself should cease.

Each looked for an easier triumph, and a result less fundamental and astounding.

Both read the same Bible, and pray to the same God, and each invokes His aid against the other.

It may seem strange that any men should dare to ask a just God's assistance in wringing their bread from the sweat of other men's faces; but let us judge not, that we be not judged.

The prayers of both could not be answered—that of neither has been answered fully.

The Almighty has His own purposes.

"Woe unto the world because of offences! for it must needs be that offences come; but woe to that man by whom the offence cometh."

Figure 9-10. Close-up view showing the way the sentences of the uncorrected printer's proof of Lincoln's Second Inaugural have been individually clipped and pasted onto a paper backing to create his delivery copy. Library of Congress.

Now, at the expiration of four years, during which public declarations have been constantly called forth, on every point and phase of the great contest which still absorbs the attention, and engrosses the energies of the nation, little that is new could be presented.

The progress of our arms, upon which all else chiefly depends, is as well known to the public as to myself; and it is, I trust, reasonably satisfactory and encouraging to all.

The fateful note—the harbinger of the speech's true subject—is not struck until the very end of the second paragraph, about a third of the way into the speech, where a sentence of four simple words produces an ominous intonation.

> Both parties deprecated war; but one of them would *make* war rather than let the nation survive; and the other would *accept* war rather than let it perish.
>
>   And the war came.

The note having been struck, the narrative appears to revert to a matter-of-fact rehearsal of background information.

> One-eighth of the whole population were colored slaves, not distributed generally over the Union, but localized in the southern part of it.

But here something begins to happen. With the mention of slavery, there is the initiation of a scarcely perceptible shift away from plain exposition and in the direction of elevated language.

> These slaves constituted a peculiar, and powerful interest.
> All knew that this interest was, somehow, the cause of the war.
> To strengthen, perpetuate, and extend this interest was the object for which the insurgents would rend the Union, even by war;

Here an emerging cadence begins to be felt, while the use of the word "rend," with its violent and accusatory overtones, effectively raises the emotional register. The character of the speech is about to be transformed.

The next sentence initiates what turns out to be a crucial device, the pairing of the North and South as warring "parties," so as to emphasize that what is true of one is true of the other. Here, too, the language becomes more distinctly cadenced and more intense. These elements are being combined to produce a gradually heightened effect.

Neither party expected for the war, the magnitude, or the duration, which it has already attained.

Neither anticipated that the <u>cause</u> of the conflict might cease with, or even before, the conflict itself should cease.

Each looked for an easier triumph, and a result less fundamental and astounding.

Both read the same Bible, and pray to the same God; and each invokes His aid against the other.

It may seem strange that any men should dare to ask a just God's assistance in wringing their bread from the sweat of other men's faces; but let us judge not, that we be not judged.

The prayers of both could not be answered—that of neither, has been answered fully.

The Almighty has His own purposes.

"Woe unto the world because of offences! for it must needs be that offences come; but woe to that man by whom the offence cometh."

For a speech addressed to an audience comprised of one of the warring parties, this is astonishingly evenhanded, and of course, intentionally so. The address up to this point, with its prosy beginning and gradual movement toward biblical language, has been artful preparation for what comes next—an unexpected and unorthodox theological interpretation of the war. Had Lincoln wanted to embrace a popular interpretation—for example, that the Union's success proved that God was on its side—he could have counted on nearly universal approval. But his meditations seem to have convinced him that this could not be an accurate reading of the divine will, because the duration of the war had proved that great suffering on both sides was part of God's plan. That much was hard to argue with. But what Lincoln wanted to add, albeit conditionally, was a vexing and unwelcome supposition—that the war was a punishment for the offense of slavery, an offense for which both sides, North as well as South, were to blame and to whom punishment was therefore due.

The master rhetorical stroke of this masterly address is surely the way the idea of Northern complicity in the offense of slavery is so smoothly and unobtrusively, almost painlessly presented.

> If we shall suppose that American slavery is one of those
> offenses which, in the providence of God, must needs come,
> but which, having continued through His appointed time,
> He now wills to remove; and that He gives to both north
> and south this terrible war as the woe due to those by
> whom the offense came, shall we discern therein any de-
> parture from those divine attributes which the believers in
> a living God always ascribe to Him?

The special qualities of this formulation become apparent when compared with its earlier counterpart in the Hodges letter, where he wrote:

> If God now wills the removal of a great wrong, and wills also
> that we of the North as well as you of the South, shall pay fairly
> for our complicity in that wrong, impartial history will find
> therein new cause to attest and revere the justice and goodness
> of God.

As expressions of an idea, the two passages are roughly equivalent, but the differences are considerable. The "removal of a great wrong" in the earlier passage is quite stark, whereas in the Second Inaugural this idea has been carefully prepared for, so that slavery becomes one of the offenses whose time, "in the Providence of God," has come. Even more impressive is that the idea of Northern complicity is carefully withheld in the Second Inaugural, so that a listener or reader has no notion that the blame for slavery will be placed anywhere but on the South until these words: "He gives to both north and south this terri-ble war as the woe due to those by whom the offense came." It may be doubted that many in the massive crowd that heard their president utter these words felt either a rush of resentment at the imputation or the immediate sting of guilt. Nonetheless, the message had been deliv-ered, and it would be there for all to see, and for all time.

Nor was the prophet quite finished with his divination.

> Fondly do we hope
> —fervently do we pray—that this mighty scourge of war
> may speedily pass away.
>> Yet, if God wills that it con-
> tinue until all the wealth piled by the bondman's two hun-
> dred and fifty years of unrequited toil shall be sunk, and
> until every drop of blood drawn with the lash, shall be
> paid by another drawn with the sword, as was said three
> thousand years ago, so still it must be said, "the judg-
> ments of the Lord are true and righteous altogether."

Perhaps for obvious reasons, this was the favorite passage of the former slave Frederick Douglass, who could quote it from memory. Like the previous passage, it is unremitting in its moral judgment yet entirely free of vindictiveness. This certainly reflects Lincoln's own personal inclinations, but its success on the page is directly related to his handling of figures of speech. The "scourge of war" in the first sentence initially seems to be nothing more than a fairly conventional metaphor, but in the next sentence the "scourge" (historically, a whip) has become a "lash" that draws blood, a powerful synecdoche for the cruelest form of tyranny. By using the instrument to represent the wielder, Lincoln describes the war symbolically and thus avoids having to name or depict either the victors or the vanquished, while emphasizing the role of divinity and justice.

The last of the four paragraphs comprising the speech is also the shortest—a single sentence of sixty-two words. One of the most memorable he ever wrote, this sentence was designed to perform multiple functions, which largely accounts for its unconventional structure. Its main clause—"let us strive on to finish the work we are in"—borrows from a prominent theme in the Gettysburg speech, but this is rarely noticed because, somewhat oddly, this main clause does not reflect the sentence's most important message, which is conveyed by what comes before and after. It proves, nonetheless, to be an ingeniously crafted sentence, which may bear some relationship to the drafting of the earlier address. Given what we know about Lincoln's propensity for prewriting, it would not be hard to imagine it having been written first.

But if it was, it was still a work in progress when he copied the text out fair during the week before the inaugural, for it is the only sentence in the existing manuscript that he significantly altered. As originally copied out, this famous sentence read (line for line):

With malice toward none;
with charity for all; with firmness in the
right, as God gives us to see the right,
let us strive on to finish the work we
are in; to bind up the nation's wounds;
to care for him who shall have borne the battle, and for his widow, and his orphan—
to achieve and cherish a lasting peace among ourselves, and with the world.

To revise his ending, Lincoln pasted a slip over the last two lines and wrote out a new ending (see Figs. 9-7 and 9-11):

to do all which may achieve and cherish a just,
and a lasting peace, among ourselves, and with the world.

When the galley proof came back from the printer, this is the way the text ended, but Lincoln subsequently changed both the manuscript

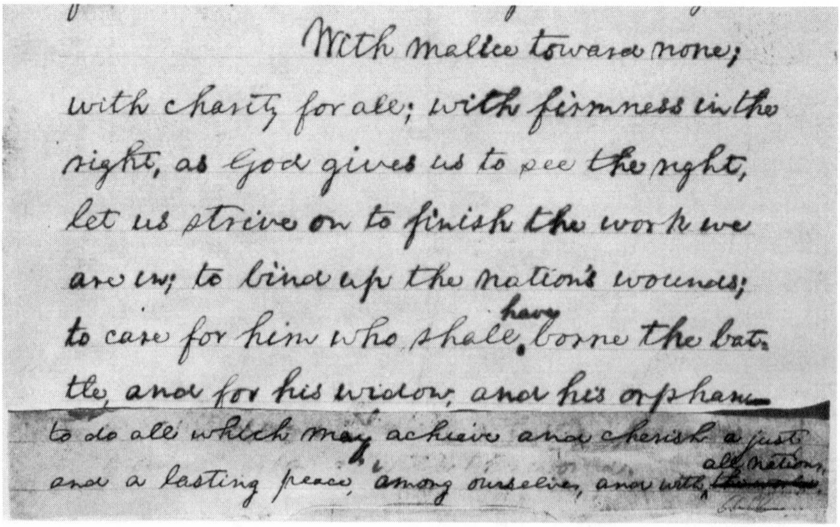
With malice toward none;
with charity for all; with firmness in the
right, as God gives us to see the right,
let us strive on to finish the work we
are in; to bind up the nation's wounds;
to care for him who shall have borne the battle, and for his widow, and his orphan—
to do all which may achieve and cherish a just
and a lasting peace, among ourselves, and with ~~the world~~ all nations.

Figure 9-11. The final page of the manuscript of Lincoln's Second Inaugural, showing the slip pasted over the two lines forming the original conclusion (see Fig. 9-7) and the revised text written on the slip. Library of Congress.

and the proof by substituting "all nations" for "the world." Like many of the changes observable in his manuscripts, those he made here have less to do with literal meaning than with a close attention to rhythm and feel. The incorporation of seven additional words in the last two lines is obviously aimed at giving the conclusion a more fluent feel and a more graceful finish.

This is a noble ending, but the sentence has an even more noble beginning. It succeeds, characteristically, by anticipation, by posing, in the silence that follows prophecy, a response to an unspoken question: what do we do now? Lincoln's answer, like his overall strategy, is pre-emptive. Before the celebrations begin, he wants to establish the mood, to somehow calibrate the tone for what is to come. He turns, not surprisingly, to the rhetorical device he has most perfectly mastered over the years, the measured antithesis. "With malice toward none; with charity for all." The humanity and generosity of this is transparent, but it must not be mistaken for weakness, so another antithesis is in order, one that acknowledges the difficulty of the task: "with firmness in the right, as God gives us to see the right." Those elements comprise the ideal by which the victorious nation should be guided—magnanimity.

MORE THAN ANYTHING HE would write as president, Lincoln's Second Inaugural emerges as the product of a resourceful and probing mind at work. No other case so aptly displays him as energetically engaged in finding and communicating perspective on a public issue. This is partly because there is such a clearly marked trail showing the direction and persistence of his thinking on one particular theme, but also because of the penetration and originality of his thinking and the difficulty of the task. Although he lived in an age that set great store by religion and its precepts, Lincoln's own delving into theological questions seems to have been distinctively his own. In this respect, he had little to learn from the theologians of his time, and much, apparently, to teach them. A leading historian of American religion finds the contrast remarkable. "None of America's respected religious leaders mustered the theological power so economically expressed in Lincoln's Second Inaugural," writes Mark Noll. "None penetrated as deeply into the nature of providence." Noll also notes that the best American theologians, north and south, were busy throughout 1864 explaining what the war signified, but while their writings have virtually ceased to be read, Lincoln's short address "remains an object of intense study and admiration."

Coming, as it does, at the end of his presidency, the Second Inaugural calls our attention to a remarkable aspect of his presidential writing, namely, his willingness to accept increasingly greater challenges and to perform at successively higher levels. Lincoln was a talented writer when he assumed the presidency, but discharging the obligations of the office made him a far better one. "Lincoln had been growing as a writer and deepening as a thinker under the pressure of the war," Garry Wills has observed, "which made him weight every word with the fateful events impending on it." It is no accident that his last great effort has often been considered his best.

Lincoln was far from a vain man, but he occasionally betrayed an author's pride in his literary efforts, if only in his eagerness to know how they had been received. After waiting more than two weeks to hear back from Albert G. Hodges about his letter of April 4, 1864, he sent the Kentucky editor a telegram asking if he had received it. What he had sent Hodges was clearly too valuable a document to be pigeon-holed, as Greeley's response, which appeared a few days after the letter's publication, clearly shows. In acknowledging a compliment from the New York politician Thurlow Weed, Lincoln offered some revealing thoughts on his Second Inaugural and its likely effect.

> Every one likes a compliment. Thank you for yours on my little notification speech, and on the recent Inaugeral Address. I expect the latter to wear as well as—perhaps better than—any thing I have produced; but I believe it is not immediately popular. Men are not flattered by being shown that there has been a difference of purpose between the Almighty and them. To deny it, however, in this case, is to deny that there is a God governing the world. It is a truth which I thought needed to be told; and as whatever of humiliation there is in it, falls most directly on myself, I thought others might afford for me to tell it.

Frederick Douglass was in the crowd when the Second Inaugural was delivered and later attended the public reception at the White House. He very nearly didn't get in, being blocked by policemen at the door as an inadmissible black man, but when finally admitted he was greeted warmly by the president. "Here comes my friend Douglass," he reported the president as saying; "I am glad to see you. I saw you in the crowd to-day, listening to my inaugural address; how did you like it?" Douglass protested that there were too many waiting in line, but the president insisted. "No, no, you must stop a little, Douglass; there is no man in the country whose opinion I value more than yours. I want to know what you think of it?" Douglass says he replied, "Mr. Lincoln, that was a sacred effort."

Lincoln was eager to know what this black abolitionist thought of his speech, and Douglass assured him, with two well-chosen words, that he had fully understood the president's message and mode of address. Six weeks later, Abraham Lincoln was assassinated. Douglass, who had come from being a harsh critic to a strong supporter and personal admirer of the president, declared in a memorial lecture: "Whosoever else have cause to mourn the loss of Abraham Lincoln, to the colored people of the country his death is an unspeakable calamity." In the same lecture, he renewed his tribute to the Second Inaugural.

> The last days of Mr Lincoln were his best days. If he did not control events he had the wisdom to be instructed by them. When he could no longer withstand the current he swam with it. What he said on the steps of the Capitol four years ago did not determine what the same lips should utter four years afterward. No two papers are in stronger contrast—than his first and his last Inaugural addresses. The first was intended to reconcile the rebels to the Government by argument and persuasion. The Second was a recognition of the operation [of] inevitable and universal Laws. In this he was willing to let justice have its course.

Epilogue:
A Notable Elevation of Thought

WHEN ABRAHAM LINCOLN WAS assassinated, everything changed. So great was the shock and so huge and unexpected was the void suddenly created in the nation's sense of itself, that his enemies were silenced, his critics converted, and the public at large impulsively rushed to embrace him as a martyr. One day, an honest and likable politician with a mixed record and much baggage; the next, a national hero to be ranked with Washington. In one important respect, Ralph Waldo Emerson exemplified this phenomenon. Not that he had been unsympathetic to the president or unmindful of his good works, but as we have seen, he had been surprisingly unresponsive to the extraordinary qualities of Lincoln's writing.

Emerson was, after all, the acknowledged prophet of America's literary promise, having urged American writers to abandon traditional models and create new, authentically American forms of expression. He, of all people, might have been expected to have recognized Lincoln's literary gifts for what they were, or at least for what they had become. But not until the stirring eulogy that Emerson delivered to his Concord, Massachusetts, neighbors on April 19, 1865, just four days after Lincoln's death, did the shock of recognition manifest itself. After first admitting the disappointment that had been felt at Lincoln's nomination and then describing the steady emergence of admirable qualities in his performance as president, Emerson crowned his tribute by acknowledging the virtues of Lincoln's writings: "What pregnant definitions; what unerring common sense; what foresight; and, on great occasion, what lofty, and more than national, what humane tone! His brief speech at Gettysburg will not easily be surpassed by words on any recorded occasion."

"Humane tone," like many of Emerson's characterizations, is richly suggestive, and it has the virtue of laying stress on precisely the aspect of political writing that Lincoln himself emphasized in his own eulogy of his idol, Henry Clay.

> Mr. Clay's eloquence did not consist, as many fine specimens of eloquence [do], of types and figures—of antithesis, and elegant arrangement of words and sentences; but rather of that deeply earnest and impassioned tone, and manner, which can proceed only from great sincerity and a thorough conviction, in the speaker of the justice and importance of his cause. This it is, that truly touches the chords of human sympathy.

In a statement that came as close as Lincoln ever would to theorizing about what made for true eloquence, he directs our attention not to rhetorical devices, of which both he and Clay were masters, but to something more fundamental—the impassioned tone that comes from sincerity and conviction.

Lincoln had this ability to a considerable extent as a stump speaker in the 1850s, as a colorful anecdote told by Noah Brooks illustrates. Brooks told of "once meeting a choleric old Democrat striding away from an open-air meeting where Lincoln was speaking, striking the earth with his cane as he stumped along and exclaiming, 'He's a dangerous man, sir! a d——d dangerous man! He makes you believe what he says, in spite of yourself!' " But having the same effect on the page is a different matter, and Lincoln, in the course of his presidency, became more "dangerous" there than he had been on the stump. It seems clear in retrospect that one of the things Lincoln strove for in his writing, especially on great occasions, was to emulate his idol and attempt to touch the chords of human sympathy by the same means, through the tone or manner of expression. This meant using language that, in its rhythms as well as its connotations, carried conviction. What is interesting is that Henry Clay, who was enormously successful as a speaker addressing the issues of his day, ceased to be read when those issues receded, whereas Lincoln's writings live on.

❧

IN ADDITION TO SINCERITY AND CONVICTION, Lincoln knew his words must carry something else to be widely effective—the flavor of common experience and speech. This constituted an important difference between himself and his counterpart in the Confederacy, Jefferson Davis, as is colorfully demonstrated in James M. McPherson's classic essay on Lincoln's use of figurative language, "How Lincoln

Won the War with Metaphors." Davis, as McPherson shows, was highly educated and thoroughly proficient in the learned graces. "He could write with vigorous logic, turn a classical phrase, quote the leading authorities on many a subject, and close with a rhetorical flourish." Yet he had considerable trouble communicating successfully with other Confederate leaders and with his own constituents. His austere diction and manner left his various audiences cold. This stood in utter contrast with Lincoln, whose homespun stories and expressions drew the public to him. One might object that each was simply doing what came naturally, but the presidency is not only an office but a persona, and each occupant must decide how his part is to be played. Classical education or not, Davis's capabilities were not up to the demands of the role, whereas Lincoln's linguistic assets, which McPherson holds reflected his bottom-up life experiences, helped to make him an authentic star.

What is most astonishing about Lincoln's performance in this regard is that he managed to bring his language within the range of ordinary vocabularies without cheapening his expression and, if anything, lending it even greater dignity. That this was recognized at the time is implicit in a remark of Charles Francis Adams Jr., whose father was Lincoln's minister to Great Britain, and whose family tended to look askance at their ill-bred president. Writing to his father, Adams asked:

> What do you think of the inaugural? That rail-splitting lawyer is one of the wonders of the day. Once at Gettysburg and now again on a greater occasion he has shown a capacity for rising to the demands of the hour which we should not expect from orators or men of the schools. This inaugural strikes me in its grand simplicity and directness as being for all time the historical keynote of this war; in it a people seemed to speak in the sublimely simple utterance of ruder times.

This was a great deal for an Adams to admit, but, tellingly, it also betrays, in what Adams goes on to say, signs of a grudging national pride in the feat of the rail-splitting lawyer. "What will Europe think of this utterance of the rude ruler, of whom they have nourished so lofty a contempt? Not a prince or minister in all Europe could have risen to such an equality with the occasion."

What confounded Adams was what had been confounding much of the Northern intelligentsia all along, namely, how a man with no formal education, scant familiarity with polite society, and a "peculiar" way of expressing himself could be, at the same time, so unorthodox and so effective. This was no Andrew Jackson, who wore his coarseness as a badge of honor; and Jackson's writing ability was just what people like Adams expected—nil. But in Abraham Lincoln they were forced to come to terms with a man who read lowbrow comic writers to his cabinet and had a reputation for telling dirty stories, yet could write better, nobler, and more inspiring prose than any of them.

By the end of his first term, however, Lincoln's "peculiar" way of doing things, including his writing, was being more generally recognized as efficacious and, as noted, earning him plaudits and support. A Cincinnati journalist who had not always been friendly toward the Lincoln administration, Whitelaw Reid, was very favorably struck by the president's Annual Message to Congress in December 1864, praising it extravagantly and calling attention to "the most striking peculiarity which separates this from all previous documents of the kind in our history—a peculiarity which may be best explained by saying that is the most purely American message ever delivered to Congress." Reid even displayed a positive reaction to something that earlier might have been seen as another indication of Lincoln's unsuitability, the "peculiar" way in which the message was composed. "It may be interesting to put in print the fact that the President wrote the Message on stiff sheets of a sort of cardboard, which he could lay upon his knee and write upon as he sat with his feet on the table and his chair tilted back in the 'American attitude.' " Here Reid communicates a sense of what Lincoln was coming to represent—a writer who composes in an unconventional, unself-conscious way but with brilliant and brilliantly original results. A distinctively American writer.

❧

THE JUDGMENT OF CHARLES SUMNER, the forceful and egotistical senator from Massachusetts, posed a much more severe test for Lincoln's writing. Sumner and Lincoln held widely different views on vital issues, yet each had cultivated the other over the course of four years and, in spite of strong disagreements, had achieved something approaching a friendship toward the end. Like Horace Greeley, Sumner believed that Lincoln's leadership had been unsteady and his performance as president inept, and also like Greeley, he viewed the Second Inaugural with grave misgivings, and its conciliatory overtones as an augury of trouble. But Sumner, high-minded and overbearing as he was, understood the political process and recognized, in his own way, Lincoln's signal achievements. To a correspondent who shared his criticisms of the president, he wrote: "But the late Presdt. put his name to Emancipation—made speeches that nobody else could have made—& early dedicated himself to the support of Human Rights as announced in the Decltn of Indep. Therefore, we honor him, & Fame takes him by the hand." Sumner's telling phrase, "made speeches that nobody else could have made," echoes something William H. Seward was reported as saying when asked what he thought of the speech at Gettysburg—that "no one but Abraham Lincoln could have made that address."

Sumner was a deeply learned man with aristocratic tastes, which makes his judgments of Lincoln's writing all the more interesting. Realizing this, Lincoln's friend Joshua F. Speed made a point in his reminiscences of reporting a conversation with Sumner about Lincoln's style:

> I wish here to record what I heard Senator Sumner say of him and of his style: He said "He had read with great interest, all of Lincoln's published speeches, and particularly the volume of debates with Douglas. That while there is no speech in that book artistic from its base to summit, there is no speech of his in which you will not find gems of English excelled by none. But," said he, "of all the speeches he ever read, in any language, by any man living or dead, he thought Lincoln's Gettysburg speech was the greatest." Lincoln said, "The world will little note, nor long remember what we say here, but it never can forget what they did here." Sumner said "the speech would live when the memory of the battle would be lost, or only be remembered because of the speech."

❧

EMERSON HAD DELIVERED an address in 1837, "The American Scholar," which would prove to be a landmark in American letters. The title referred not to an academic distinction but rather to what Emerson called the "delegated intellect" of humankind, or "Man Thinking." In Emerson's Platonic projection, it was through the scholar and his delegated function that meaning came into the world. "The scholar of the first age received into him the world around; brooded thereon; gave it the new arrangement of his own mind, and uttered it again. It came into him life; it went out from him truth. It came to him, short-lived actions; it went out from him, immortal thoughts. It came into him, business; it went from him, poetry."

Especially as it pertained to American life, if Emerson's idea of the American scholar ever applied to anyone, it applied to Abraham Lincoln. In Emerson's parable, the transformation of life into truth, actions into thoughts, and business into poetry is offered as magical or mystical, but in Lincoln's case, we have been witness to a process that was much more deliberate and painstaking. We saw earlier an instance of this in the story told by Leonard Swett of being summoned to Washington for the sole purpose of listening to the president read and recite various opinions and positions on the subject of emancipation. Swett told his friends with whom he shared the story that it was "an instance of stating conclusions aloud, not that they might convince another, or be combatted by him, but that the speaker might see for himself how they looked when taken out of the region of mere reflection and embodied in words." The region of reflection was a place Lincoln was long familiar with, but it was the process of embodying things found there in words that set him apart.

George Santayana, the cosmopolitan Spanish philosopher who grew up in America and taught for a time at Harvard, offered many shrewd observations on American culture, including one on the role played by eloquence, which he insisted was a republican, as opposed to an aristocratic, art. In a country where the important issues had to be aired and decided on a broad basis, it was by eloquence—in the pulpit or in public meetings or in the press—that the community could sometimes attain "a notable elevation of thought." This experience was itself, according to Santayana, an important aspect of American life. "Although Americans, and many other people, usually say that thought is for the sake of action, it has evidently been in these high moments, when action became incandescent in thought, that they have been most truly alive."

This may help to explain the way millions of Americans, and a surprising number of people around the world, are affected by Abraham Lincoln's most inspired writing. It perhaps illuminates what visitors commonly experience at the Lincoln Memorial in Washington, where they typically stand in silence and read the words of the Gettysburg Address and the Second Inaugural, both of which are inscribed in their entirety on facing marble walls. Although shrines in the form of Greek temples and monumental statues are increasingly unlikely attractions for modern-day pilgrims, the Lincoln Memorial is an exception and continues to exercise a powerful emotional appeal. In experiencing these two "high moments," something important is somehow affirmed. For Americans, to be sure, this is an affirmation about themselves, their country, their history, their common values and beliefs, both realized and unrealized. But in a larger sense, and one that was surely part of Lincoln's larger purpose, these "high moments" manage to reflect and symbolize all human striving. On one wall it says there must first be ideals, then dedication, then a willingness to sacrifice and to persevere. On the other wall it says that even in triumph, the victors share complicity with the vanquished.

Appendix

Lincoln's Postdelivery Revisions
of the Gettysburg Address

ABRAHAM LINCOLN DELIVERED HIS famous address on November 19, 1863, but he was far from finished with its text. In spite of being ill upon his return to Washington, he began a process of revision that was not finally concluded until four months later, a process that is recorded in four known manuscripts. It has recently come to light that Nicolay, at the time he wrote his *Century Magazine* essay "Lincoln's Gettysburg Address" in 1894, knew of but failed to mention a manuscript that helps us visualize this postdelivery revision of his address. Martin P. Johnson has recently called attention to a letter written by Nicolay in 1885 containing a heretofore unnoticed reference to "the revision which Lincoln made after his return to Washington." In addition to having what he called "the original ms.," by which he meant the Nicolay copy, the secretary told his correspondent, "I have also the ms. notes of the revision before me." Johnson argues convincingly that the "ms. notes" Nicolay refers to must be what has traditionally been known as the Hay copy, "as there is no fragment, note, or writing of any kind in Lincoln's hand of the Gettysburg Address aside from the five well-known holograph versions of the Address."

The Hay copy (see Fig. App-1), sometimes referred to as the second draft, has been called "the most inexplicable of the five copies Lincoln made." It surfaced only after Hay's death in 1905 and has long been thought to have been a gift to Hay from the president himself. Having been seriously put forward by different interpreters in a variety of roles—as the earliest of Lincoln's drafts, as the second draft, as the delivery draft, as a souvenir of the occasion—the Hay copy has proved the hardest of all versions for scholars to account for. Because Nicolay failed to mention it in his essay, it has always been considered that he must have been ignorant of its existence, but thanks to Johnson, we now have reason to believe differently. Nicolay's strategy in explaining the creation of the Gettysburg Address was to simplify, and bringing this manuscript into view would only have complicated his task. Robert Todd Lincoln

Figure App-1. Pictured here are the first two paragraphs of the Hay copy of the Gettysburg Address, a document that records a stage of the revision process Lincoln engaged in after the delivery of his speech. Library of Congress.

was probably right when he allowed that this copy "was not regarded as important by Nicolay, being merely a step in the revision process." Robert even ventured the opinion, based on his knowledge of his father's habits, that it was "more probable that several drafts of a revision were made before one was adopted." Johnson's conclusion, which probably agrees with that of Nicolay, is that "the Hay text is an intermediate draft, part of Lincoln's revision process when reworking the speech after his return to Washington."

The physical condition of the document bears this out. It has been observed by others that the Hay copy, ostensibly a two-page document, shows no creasing or other indication of ever having been folded for carrying, something that strongly argues against its having been in Lincoln's coat pocket at Gettysburg prior to delivery. Another notable aspect of its condition, which I observed when transcribing it, is that the Hay copy was written on a single sheet of paper, folded in the middle. This is the form in which the "foolscap" commonly used by Lincoln seems to have come from the supplier, which meant that to make individual sheets of foolscap from this stock, it was necessary to tear or cut the sheet at the fold. The leaves thus created were sometimes referred to as "half-sheets." This is why one edge of each of the four pages of Lincoln's manuscript of the Second Inaugural, for example, is rough from having been separated by tearing. (The second page of the Nicolay copy shows the same condition.) That the Hay copy text is written on a single bifold sheet—and one that has never been folded further—not only argues against its having been carried by Lincoln in his pocket but points, instead, to its having been created and then filed away in an office.

Seen as a stage in the revision process, the Hay copy has important things to tell us. It shows, first of all, the care Lincoln took with the details of a speech that had already been delivered and reported. Some of the manuscript's changes, as Garry Wills has shown, were probably no more than corrections of copying mistakes. Others appear to be reversions back to an earlier wording. The omission of the word "poor," which Lincoln then inserts above the line, may simply be an indication that his secretaries had copied from an early version of the AP text in making their compilations. Some changes are quite subtle, such as the one altering the rhythm of the passage "which they have thus far so nobly carried on" by setting off the phrase "thus far" with commas. Lincoln used commas to indicate pauses, and what we see here in the Hay copy is an experimental look at the same words in a different rhythm. That the experiment would continue in the next known draft is testimony to his persistence in pursuit of the most effective sound in a sentence. Dropping the word "it" in the phrase "but it can never forget what they did here," as the Hay copy does, may have been accidental, and it may also be another such rhythm experiment, but with a different result.

Some of the changes Lincoln considers in the Hay copy are quite consequential. An obvious instance is that he experiments with dropping the phrase "under God," which is actually a return to an earlier version (see Fig. App-2). We can only speculate why he would consider this, but we know from other sources that he was always uncomfortable with anything that smacked of claiming that God was on the Union side. But perhaps the weightiest change he contemplated in this version is making the ending specific to the United States: "that this government of the people . . . shall not perish from the earth." As we have seen, this is virtually the reverse of the general statement about popular government that appears in some versions of the speech and that he would ultimately settle on in his final drafts. The phrase "*this* government," especially coming on the heels of "*this* nation" (another change), made for a stronger and more emphatic statement, but at the price of a narrower application. And although this wording was ultimately not to prevail, it stands as a reminder that Lincoln experimented not just with minor but with fairly bold changes during the evolution of the address.

for us to be here dedicated to the great task remaining before us— that from these honored dead we take increased devotion to the cause for which they here gave the last full measure of devotion— that we here highly resolve that these dead shall not have died in vain; that this nation shall have a new birth of freedom, and that this government of the people, by the people, for the people, shall not perish from the earth.

Figure App-2. The second page and conclusion of the Hay copy of the Gettysburg Address. Library of Congress.

⤙

THE TEXT THAT CONCERNS us most, of course, is the one that Nicolay described as "a new autograph copy—a careful deliberate revision—which has become the standard text." But like his description of how the address was written, Nicolay's seemingly straightforward explanation of the revision process is problematic, for he neglects to mention that before writing out the "standard" text, Lincoln wrote out for publication at least two others, each of which was slightly different.

The first was sent to Edward Everett on February 4, 1864, and it included interesting changes, some of which were previewed in the experimental Hay copy. The first substantial change in the Everett copy comes in the fourth sentence, which had been delivered as: "We are met to dedicate a portion of it as the final resting-place of those who here gave their lives that that nation might live." In the Hay copy Lincoln had reverted to his earlier beginning for this sentence, "We have come," and here in the Everett copy he reinstates much of the rest of the earlier form (emphasis added): "*a* resting place *for* those who here gave their lives." In expanding "it" to "that field," he adds specificity but also, and possibly even more important, he fills out the sound and enhances the rhythm. Though these changes are admittedly small, they contribute to a noticeable improvement in the revised sentence. "We have come to dedicate a portion of that field, as a final resting place for those who here gave their lives, that that nation might live."

The Everett copy is the first text we have that includes the phrase "who fought here" (see Fig. App-3), and it occurs in the same sentence in which Lincoln, in the experimental Hay copy, introduced commas to alter the rhythm. As delivered, the sentence had read:

> It is for us, the living, rather to be dedicated here to the unfinished work that they have thus far so nobly carried on.

Putting commas around "thus far" in the Hay copy obviously didn't satisfy him. By the time he crafted the text of the Everett copy, he had decided the sentence needed more words, not so much, it would seem, for the sake of the meaning as for the sound.

> It is for us, the living, rather, to be dedicated here to the unfinished work which they who fought here, have, thus far, so nobly advanced.

Here, in a single transitional sentence, is a painstaking artist at work.

Difficult as it may be for those familiar with the final form of the Gettysburg Address to explain why or how "advanced" is an improvement over "carried on," we sense immediately that it is. "Advanced" is, to be sure, the word we are familiar with, but familiarity aside, it has some clear advantages. As diction, it is more on a level with its modifier "nobly," and it was arguably more in keeping with the occasion that the action be raised than that the modifier be lowered. Another advantage is again a matter of rhythm. Whereas "carried on" has three syllables, "advanced" has only two. This makes for a stronger word and a more decisive sound with which to end the sentence—a more pronounced stop. Speaking the alternatives aloud, as Lincoln undoubtedly did, helps make the rhythmical advantage of the change apparent:

> . . . the unfinished work that they have thus far so nobly carried on.
> . . . the unfinished work that they have, thus far, so nobly carried on.
> . . . the unfinished work which they who fought here, have, thus far, so nobly advanced.

The Everett copy text, in fact, introduces a number of new commas, most of which do not appear in other versions, with the result that, if read with due

Figure App-3. Portion of the Everett copy of the Gettysburg Address. Courtesy of the Abraham Lincoln Presidential Library and Museum.

attention to the pauses indicated by commas, it sounds the most deliberate and ponderous of all the handwritten texts.

Having contemplated removing the phrase "under God" during the revision process, Lincoln decided to retain but reposition it. He moved it back by one word, so that instead of following "shall," which was somewhat disruptive of the rhythm, it would follow "nation," a word newly reinforced during the revision process by the more forceful adjective "this." The new wording—"that this nation, under God, shall have a new birth of freedom"—lends this passage a euphony, an emphasis, and a cadence that contribute markedly to the effect.

Finally, Lincoln resolved the vacillation between general and particular meaning for "government," again by settling on his earlier wording (albeit with an unaccountable comma after "government"). It is hard to believe, given his strong and often-stated view that popular government itself was at stake in the war, that Lincoln even considered ending with a wording that restricted his meaning to the United States. But this is one of the intriguing things we learn from a study of the revision process.

❧

EDWARD EVERETT WAS NOT the only distinguished public figure to ask for a manuscript copy of Lincoln's brief speech at Gettysburg. George Bancroft was easily the most famous American historian of the day, long identified with the Democratic Party and, like Everett, initially quite skeptical of Lincoln's abilities. Both Everett and Bancroft asked for manuscripts, it is true, to benefit charities, but the fact that both were quite willing, if not eager, to be personally associated with Lincoln's address only a few months after its delivery is an indication of its rapidly growing stature.

Lincoln sent Bancroft his manuscript copy on February 29, 1864, just one month after sending Everett his, and its text is notable in our context for quietly canceling many of the new commas introduced in the Everett text and the pauses they created. It is also notable for making the only verbal change made to the first three sentences of the address—the substitution in the first sentence of "on" for "upon." Although very minor, this is an interesting and perhaps indicative change in that the original phrase, "upon this continent," is not essential to the meaning Lincoln wants to convey and seems to function primarily as a kind of pregnant pause, a means of heightening the anticipation of what comes next—"a new nation."

Bancroft loaned his manuscript copy of the Gettysburg Address to his son-in-law, Alexander Bliss, so that it could be lithographed and included in a collection of facsimiles to be printed and sold to the Baltimore Sanitary Fair. But Lincoln's manuscript did not fit the format of the proposed volume, and he was persuaded to rewrite and resubmit it, the new copy eventually becoming the property of Colonel Bliss and known subsequently as the Bliss copy. As the last known copy in Lincoln's own hand, its rendering has become accepted as the "standard" text of the address. Aside from the fact that it is dated and signed, there are only two noticeable differences between the Bancroft and the Bliss texts. Whether there should be a comma after the word "forth" in the first sentence is, in one regard, the point about which the mind of the author was most divided. If we look at the handwritten drafts in the order in which they were composed and include, in its proper place, the delivery text, we see that in the first, third, and fifth versions Lincoln placed a comma after "forth" and in the second, fourth, and sixth versions left it out. The more significant change, and perhaps the most puzzling of all Lincoln's changes, is the elimination of the word "here" from the phrase "that cause for which they here gave the last full measure of devotion."

It would be easy to argue that Lincoln simply decided that his piece contained just too many instances of the word "here." But every other version in Lincoln's hand, as well as the delivery text, included the phrase "that cause for which they here gave the last full measure of devotion," of which the word "here" seems (at the risk of a pun) an inherent part. It is possible, at least, that in copying out the Bliss text, Lincoln simply overlooked this word and thus altered his text unintentionally. While documentary editions are committed to rendering the text strictly as it appears, the editor of a critical edition of this work, believing this omission to be accidental, would be justified in restoring the word to the text.

To do so would, of course, require a cogent argument, but there can be little dispute that "here" is no ordinary word in the Gettysburg Address. Because we have parts of two preliminary (predelivery) drafts, we are able to get some sense of how "here" started out as an ordinary word but took on, in the course of composition, a more important role. The first page of the Nicolay copy actually shows this process in action (see Fig. App-4).

Figure App-4. Portion of the first page of the Nicolay copy of the Gettysburg Address. Library of Congress.

The initial occurrence of the word is in the bland phrase "those who died here," followed three sentences later by a more evocative parallel reference to the brave men "who struggled here." But it is in the famous sentence about the world's not long remembering "what we say here" but never forgetting "what they did here" that the word assumes a new importance and becomes quietly incantatory.

The next sentence of the Nicolay copy was completed on a page that has not survived, but it is clear from the first part of the sentence that the position and role of the word "here" will be changed. "It is rather for us, the living, to stand here" is what Lincoln first wrote at the end of his page (see Fig. App-4), and we cannot be sure how this sentence originally ended. Nor can we understand with certainty what circumstances might have led him to strike out "to stand here" and substitute something that simply does not fit: "we here be dedica[ted]." But this doesn't alter the evident fact that Lincoln's sentence was subsequently recast so as to take better advantage of the resonance that the word "here" had already acquired.

By the time the delivery text was written, the word "here" had attained a new status, which is immediately evident in the fourth sentence, with the transformation of "those who died here" into the more memorable "those who here gave their lives." In the postdelivery revision process recorded in the Hay copy, we glimpse Lincoln experimenting with inserting "here" even earlier in his text by changing "We are met on a great battle-field" to "We are met here on a great battle-field." But this doesn't quite work, and the insertion is not repeated in subsequent versions. The Everett text, which is not so much a draft as the first iteration of the final text, adds another "here" in the new phrase "who fought here," thus making the complement of incantatory "heres" complete. In this context, it seems clear that Lincoln would not alter this pattern of meaning without good reason, but how the address is made better by eliminating the "here" that is missing from the text of the Bliss copy is difficult to say. Its absence does not mar the felicity of the lines, and the eliminated word is not likely to be missed until one's attention is called to it. But whether the word was dropped intentionally or inadvertently still seems an open question.

The differences between the Gilbert/Hale delivery text and the final text of the Bliss copy are somewhat difficult to put into perspective. In the sense that the speech as delivered was already a masterpiece and would have achieved its high standing without further alteration, the subsequent changes may be considered minor. But for the light they shed on the sensibility and literary craftsmanship of the author—his attention to small differences in sound and rhythm, his concern for verbal resonance and texture, his seemingly tireless efforts to perfect his work in all its details—they remain invaluable.

Acknowledgments

To MY LONGTIME COLLEAGUE at Knox College and partner in the Lincoln Studies Center, Rodney O. Davis, I owe an immense debt that I can never repay. Were it not for my association with him in teaching and research, I would never have been able to undertake such a study as this.

A number of Lincoln scholars have given me the benefit of their knowledge and advice in various ways, and I am pleased to be able to acknowledge their help: Gabor Boritt, Steven L. Carson, David Herbert Donald, Allen C. Guelzo, Harold Holzer, Richard Lawrence Miller, William Lee Miller, Philip S. Paludan, and Matthew Pinsker.

I am indebted to a former student, Bill Barnhart, who came to me for guidance on the subject of Lincoln as a writer and ended up helping me to see things I might never have noticed on my own.

For an idyllic residency at its Bellagio Study Center, I am forever grateful to the Rockefeller Foundation. For continuing research and travel support, I am pleased to acknowledge the long and steadfast backing of Knox College, and in particular its very supportive dean, Lawrence Breitborde. Also providing travel support, through a grant to the Lincoln Studies Center, was the Lincoln Institute, whose assistance is gratefully acknowledged.

In spite of all the accommodations on the Internet and other places, research of the kind that went into this book is heavily dependent on libraries, and I am pleased to acknowledge here those to which I am most indebted. At the Library of Congress, the repository of Abraham Lincoln's personal and presidential papers, I was fortunate to have the constant and capable assistance of a true friend, John R. Sellers, who is in effect the curator of those papers. His colleagues in the Manuscript Division reading room, the late Mary Wolfskill and Jeffrey Flannery, have been exceeding helpful and considerate. In the Rare Books and Special Collections Division, Clark Evans provided invaluable assistance. Examining Lincoln's most famous manuscripts means working in the Conservation Division, where these are held, and I am grateful for very able and valuable assistance in this regard from Maria Nugent and Sylvia Rodgers Albro.

At the Knox College Library, I am indebted, as always, to the usual suspects, who I am pleased to salute: Jeffrey Douglas, Laurie Sauer, Sharon Clayton, Ann Giffey, Carley Robison, Kay Vander Meulen, and Matthew Norman.

At the Abraham Lincoln Presidential Library, I am especially obligated for assistance from Cheryl Schnirring, Thomas F. Schwartz, and Kim Bauer. At the Huntington Library, John Rhodehamel was, as always, very considerate and helpful. At the John Hay Library of Brown University, I am grateful to Holly Snyder and Ann Morgan Dodge. At the Wadworth Athenaeum, I enjoyed the courtesy and assistance of Librarian John Teahan, Archivist Eugene R. Gaddis, and Adria Patterson. For help in accessing and examining the Preliminary Emancipation Proclamation at the New York State Library, I am pleased to acknowledge Curator Kathi Stanley and J. Van der Veer Judd. I am also under obligation to Leslie Hunt of the Historical Society of Pennsylvania, and to Randy L. Bixby and Danny Stockdale, Southern Illinois University Library. John Adler of HarpWeek was kind enough to make his invaluable Web site on Lincoln and the Civil War readily available. Jeffrey S. Cramer graciously supplied needed information.

I am grateful to Richard J. Carwardine of Oxford University for an advance look at an unpublished paper. Joseph J. Ellis Jr. read drafts of several chapters and offered sterling advice. Doris Kearns Goodwin did the same and kindly supplied material she had uncovered in her own research. Conversations with Garry Wills have long been a stimulating resource, and I am particularly indebted to him for reading and reacting to my chapter on the Gettysburg Address. Donald Ritchie, of the Historian's Office in the U.S. Senate, is a mine of information, and I am grateful to him for sharing some of it with me. Michael Burlingame, whose knowledge of Lincoln sources is without peer, very kindly read the entire manuscript in draft and provided numerous leads, for which I am much in his debt.

I want to warmly acknowledge the inestimable help of my resourceful agent, Lydia Wills. I have been fortunate in having a wise and exceedingly patient editor at Alfred A. Knopf, Ashbel Green, whose assistants, Luba Ostashevsky and Sara Sherbill, have also been very helpful. I would be remiss if I did not gratefully acknowledge the unfailing interest and support that Cynthia A. Wilson and Timothy C. Wilson both give to their father and his projects. Finally, the dedication names the person to whom I am irredeemably indebted, and who, for encouragement, inspiration, and support, is in a class by herself—Sharon E. Wilson.

Notes

AL   Abraham Lincoln

ALP   Abraham Lincoln Papers, Library of Congress,
      accessible on the Library of Congress Web site

Prologue

3   *"frivolous and uncertain"*: Quoted in Doris Kearns Goodwin, *Team of Rivals: The Political Genius of Abraham Lincoln* (New York: Simon & Schuster, 2005), 310, citing Adams's diary, Feb. 20, 1861.

4   *"to express it"*: John G. Nicolay, "Lincoln's Literary Experiments," *Century Magazine* 47:6 (April 1894), 823, 825.

4   *"political kind"*: Edmund Wilson, *Patriotic Gore: Studies in the Literature of the American Civil War* (New York: Oxford University Press, 1962), 122.

5   *"a very deliberate writer"*: Robert Todd Lincoln to Isaac Markens, June 18, 1918, in Paul M. Angle, ed., *A Portrait of Abraham Lincoln in Letters by His Oldest Son* (Chicago: Chicago Historical Society, 1968), 62.

6   *"every body else is tired out"*: Joshua F. Speed to William H. Herndon, May 8, 1866, in Douglas L. Wilson and Rodney O. Davis, eds., *Herndon's Informants: Letters, Interviews, and Statements About Abraham Lincoln* (Urbana: University of Illinois Press, 1998), 255.

7   *"part of the sentence"*: Joshua F. Speed, *Reminiscences of Abraham Lincoln and Notes of a Visit to California: Two Lectures* (Louisville: John P. Morton, 1884), 25.

7   *"treasure of the nation"*: Don E. Fehrenbacher, "The Words of Lincoln," *Lincoln in Text and Context: Collected Essays* (Stanford: Stanford University Press, 1987), 285.

8   *"obstinate will"*: Wilson, *Patriotic Gore*, 123.

9   *"man of letters"*: John G. Nicolay and John Hay, *Abraham Lincoln: A History*, 10 vols. (New York: Century Co., 1904), 10:351.

Chapter One: Springfield Farewell

10   *"a single word"*: *New York Herald*, Feb. 12, 1861. This account was written by Henry Villard.

10   *reach the train*: See the testimony of two eyewitnesses, John Bunn and Louis H. Zumbrook, included in an appendix of a new edition of Jesse W. Weik, *The Real Lincoln*, ed. Michael Burlingame (Lincoln: University of Nebraska Press, 2002), 322–23, 387–88.

10 **"emotions of the hour":** *Chicago Tribune*, Feb. 12, 1861. According to Victor Searcher, this account was written by Henry Martin Smith. See Victor Searcher, *Lincoln's Journey to Greatness: A Factual Account of the Twelve-Day Inaugural Trip* (Philadelphia: John C. Winston Company, 1960), 6.

11 **changed his mind:** Lincoln's private secretary, John G. Nicolay, described the situation to Jesse W. Weik. "Mr. Nicolay related that on the day before Lincoln departed he caused the newspaper correspondents gathered about the hotels to be notified that nothing warranting their attention would take place at the railroad station when he embarked on his journey; in other words, that speechmaking, so far as he was concerned, would not begin till after he had left Springfield. But the next morning when he looked into the faces of the neighbors gathered about his car he forgot the assurances to the newspaper men made the night before and indulged in a brief but appropriate farewell speech" (Burlingame, *The Real Lincoln*, 311–12).

11 **"sufficiently to commence":** James C. Conkling to Clinton L. Conkling, Feb. 12, 1861, in *Concerning Mr. Lincoln: In Which Abraham Lincoln Is Pictured as He Appeared to Letter Writers of His Time*, comp. Harry E. Pratt (Springfield, Ill.: Abraham Lincoln Association, 1944), 50.

11 **"My friends":** Roy P. Basler, et al., eds., *The Collected Works of Abraham Lincoln*, 9 vols. (New Brunswick: Rutgers University Press, 1953), "Farewell Address at Springfield, Illinois," "A" version, 4:190; hereafter *Collected Works*. Because Nicolay and Hay took editorial liberties with Lincoln's text, I present here the more faithful transcription of the *Collected Works*. For Nicolay and Hay's version, see *Century Magazine* 30:38 (December 1887), 265. Note that the editors of *Collected Works* failed to correct the transcription error referred to below on p. 16.

12 **accounts vary:** The version that appeared in Lincoln's friendly hometown paper, the *Illinois State Journal*, was printed by some biographers even after Lincoln's manuscript was made public, most notably by his law partner, William H. Herndon, in 1889, and by Carl Sandburg as late as 1926. But the *Journal*'s version of the speech seems a wordy and unlikely approximation of Lincoln's distinctive language. While there is no doubt it was reported by someone actually present and taking notes, it is conspicuous for its lack of the kind of verbal economy that was Lincoln's trademark, being, at 245 words, over 60 percent longer than the 152 words in the text Lincoln wrote out. In addition to being too verbose, the *Journal* reporter used at least one word—"chequered"—that was not in Lincoln's known vocabulary. Another version by a reporter undoubtedly present, which appeared the next day in the Quincy, Illinois, paper, errs in the opposite way—of being, at 122 words, too brief and elliptical. See *Quincy Daily Whig and Republican*, Feb. 12, 1861. The version that appeared most frequently and is probably the closest to what Lincoln actually said on the platform (*Collected Works*, 4:190, "B" version) has 161 words.

12 **afterward, on the train:** Harold Holzer has wittily observed that this "is not the speech Lincoln would have delivered had he taken the time to write it beforehand. So he did the next best thing. He wrote it afterward." " 'Avoid Saying Foolish Things': The Legacy of Lincoln's Impromptu Oratory," *Lincoln Seen and Heard* (Lawrence, Kan.: University Press of Kansas, 2000), 167.

13 **"We will do it":** *New York Herald*, Feb. 12, 1861.

13 **"We will pray for you":** *New York Times*, Feb. 12, 1861. This account, both its

description and its text of the speech (*Collected Works*, "B" version), appeared word for word in the majority of the newspapers consulted for this study. It is sometimes attributed to the Associated Press.

13 **on-the-scene accounts:** The relevant passages are these: "I hope you, my friends, will all pray that I may receive that Divine assistance without which I cannot succeed" (*Collected Works*, "B" version); "permit me to ask that with equal s[incer]ity and faith, you all will invoke His wisdom and guidance for me" (*Collected Works*, "C" version); "so let me, so let all of *you, for* me, pray that I, too, may be led in that course which will lead to the welfare of our beloved country" (Quincy text). The *Illinois State Journal* was probably referring to the same phenomenon in reporting, "When he said, with the earnestness of a sudden inspiration of feeling, that *with God's help he should not fail,* there was an uncontrollable burst of applause." Not included in this calculus are the texts, such as those of the *New York Herald* and the *Chicago Tribune,* that derive directly from Lincoln's manuscript text.

13 **"He never would have succeeded":** *Collected Works,* "B" version, 4:190. Note that this text is the closest to Lincoln's written text in length, style, organization, and vocabulary.

14 **comment at the time:** "So little was the man's character understood that his simple and earnest request that his neighbors should pray for him was received by many as an evidence both of his weakness and his hypocrisy. No President had ever before asked the people, in a public address, to pray for him." J. G. Holland, *The Life of Abraham Lincoln* (Springfield, Mass.: Gurdon Bill, 1866), 254.

15 **"never returning":** Jacques Barzun, *Lincoln the Literary Genius* (Evanston, Ill.: Schori Private Press, Evanston Publishing Company, 1960), 45, 47. This is a reprint of an article in the *Saturday Evening Post* in 1959, at the time of sesquicentennial of Lincoln's birth.

15 **"I feel that I":** *Collected Works,* "B" version, 4:190.

15 **"Without the assistance":** *Collected Works,* "A" version, 4:190.

16 **"Here I have lived":** *Collected Works,* "B" version, 4:190. The bracketed material is taken from the "A" version.

16 **"Here I have been":** "Farewell Address," Feb. 11, 1861, ALP (#7280).

16 **detected until recently:** In transcribing this passage in the year 2000 for the Library of Congress Web site of its Abraham Lincoln Papers, the Lincoln Studies Center editorial team, of which I was a member, first transcribed this word as "lived." In studying the document more closely and intensively in 2002, I concluded that the word was "been." This reading has been further confirmed by the independent findings of the staff of the Papers of Abraham Lincoln, which supplied a transcription of the document for an appendix in Ronald C. White Jr., *The Eloquent President: A Portrait of Lincoln Through His Words* (New York: Random House, 2005), 310.

16 **Lincoln gave him:** Villard's version of this episode in his *Memoirs* is misleading. In writing his recollection of this event some thirty years later, he testified that he had asked Lincoln for a copy of his remarks and that he had carried this copy, in Lincoln's own hand, around with him as a souvenir until he lost it. But his memory apparently failed him, for because he thought he had covered the event for the Associated Press, he mistakenly printed in his memoir the *Collected Works* "B" version, which is not the one that appeared in his coverage of the

event in the newspaper he was working for at the time, the *New York Herald.* Except for one line, the *Herald* text is virtually identical to that of Lincoln's manuscript. See Henry Villard, *Memoirs of Henry Villard, Journalist and Financier, 1835–1900* (Boston and New York: Houghton, Mifflin and Company, 1904), 149.

17   *"I know not how":* Collected Works, "B" version, 4:190.

17   *"I now leave":* Collected Works, "A" version, 4:190.

Chapter Two: A Long Foreground

19   *"their own proportions":* Ralph Waldo Emerson, "Power," *Essays and Lectures* (New York: Library of America, 1983), 976.

19   *"a great career":* Emerson to Walt Whitman, July 21, 1855, *The Selected Letters of Ralph Waldo Emerson,* ed. Joel Myerson (New York: Columbia University Press, 1997), 384.

20   *"to wide fame":* Ralph Waldo Emerson, "Abraham Lincoln: Remarks at the Funeral Services Held in Concord, April 19, 1865," *Miscellanies,* in *The Complete Works of Ralph Waldo Emerson* (Boston: Houghton Mifflin Company, 1906), 11:333.

20   *"for such a start":* Emerson to Whitman, July 21, 1855, *Selected Letters of Emerson,* 384.

20   *"capacity for writing":* John Locke Scripps, *Life of Abraham Lincoln,* ed. Roy P. Basler and Lloyd A. Dunlap (Bloomington: Indiana University Press, 1961), 28–29. The importance Scripps placed on Lincoln's early writing experience is amplified when one considers (as he explained in a letter to Lincoln) that he was forced to cut his original biography from ninety-six to thirty-two pages: "Of course I have been compelled to omit much that I would have got in had we published a larger pamphlet" (*Life,* 11).

21   *"clear and forcible language":* Ibid., 32.

21   *"sure to get it":* Sarah Bush Lincoln interview, Douglas L. Wilson and Rodney O. Davis, eds., *Herndon's Informants: Letters, Interviews, and Statements About Abraham Lincoln* (Urbana: University of Illinois Press, 1998), 106–7.

21   *"this preserved them":* Ibid., 107.

22   *"wanted to convey":* Ibid.

22   *"could not understand":* Cited in Francis B. Carpenter, *Six Months at the White House* (New York: Hurd and Houghton, 1866), 312.

22   *"knew to comprehend":* Ibid., 313.

22   *"People to Abe intellectually":* Joseph C. Richardson interview, Sept. 14?, 1865, *Herndon's Informants,* 120.

22   *newspaper in Ohio:* William Wood interview, Sept. 15, 1865, *Herndon's Informants,* 123–24. See the discussions below of the Lyceum speech (1838) and the Temperance speech (1842).

23   *"Abraham Lincoln/his hand and pen":* Roy P. Basler, et al., eds., *The Collected Works of Abraham Lincoln,* 9 vols. (New Brunswick: Rutgers University Press, 1953), 1:1; hereafter *Collected Works.*

23   *roundly acknowledged:* See the testimony of Joseph C. Richardson and William Wood cited above.

23   *"pensive in tone":* Gibson William Harris, "My Recollections of Abraham Lincoln," *Farm and Fireside,* Jan. 15, 1905, 24.

23   *"have it known"*: Ibid., 24.

24   **Journal *in 1838*:** See Richard Lawrence Miller, "What Is Hell to One Like Me . . . ?" *American Heritage* 55:4 (August/September 2005), 50–55.

24   *"quite another question"*: AL to Andrew Johnston, Apr. 18, 1846, *Collected Works*, 1:378.

24   *"My childhood's home"*: Ibid.

25   *"biographers have supposed"*: Roy P. Basler, "Lincoln's Development as a Writer," *A Touchstone for Greatness: Essays, Addresses, and Occasional Pieces About Abraham Lincoln* (Westport, Conn.: Greenwood Press, 1973), 63–64.

25   *"failed poet"*: See James B. Merriwether and Michael Millgate, eds., *The Lion in the Garden: Interviews with William Faulkner 1926–1962* (New York: Random House, 1968), 217, 238.

25   *"to local affairs"*: "To the People of Sangamo County," Mar. 9, 1832, *Collected Works*, 1:5. One of Lincoln's New Salem friends, John McNamar, told Herndon, "I corrected at his request Some of the Grammatical Errors in his first address to the voters of Sangamon Co" (*Herndon's Informants*, 253).

26   *"Here's Mine"*: AL to the editor of the *Sangamo Journal*, June 13, 1836; *Collected Works*, 1:48.

26   *"force and elegance"*: Samuel Kirkham, *English Grammar in Familiar Lectures* (Cincinnati: E. Morgan & Co., 1838), 219. See also William Scott, *Lessons in Elocution* (many editions).

26   *prior to 1838*: For evidence that Lincoln was the author of some anonymous and pseudonymous newspaper pieces in this period, see "Lincoln—Author of the Letters by 'A Conservative,' " *Bulletin of the Abraham Lincoln Association* 50 (December 1937), 8–9; and Glenn H. Seymour, " 'Conservative'—Another Lincoln Pseudonym?" *Journal of the Illinois State Historical Society* XXIX:2 (July 1936), 135–50.

26   *feud with Cartwright:* Convincing evidence of Lincoln's authorship includes the independent testimony of two former New Salem residents, one of whom remembered the name of the long-forgotten Beardstown newspaper in which it appeared in 1834, and the other that it was published over the name of Samuel Hill. See "Abraham Lincoln Versus Peter Cartwright," in Douglas L. Wilson, *Lincoln Before Washington: New Perspectives on the Illinois Years* (Urbana: University of Illinois, 1997), 55–73.

27   *the* **Sangamo Journal:** See the testimony of James Matheny, who told Herndon, "He Lincoln used to write Editorials as far back as 1834—or 5 for Francis—the Sangamon Journal—took hundreds of such Editorials from Lincoln to the Journal office" (*Herndon's Informants*, 431).

27   *"Their's was the task"*: "Address Before the Young Men's Lyceum of Springfield, Illinois," Jan. 27, 1838, *Collected Works*, 1:108. Roy P. Basler finds "the essential germ of the 'Gettysburg Address' " in this sentence. See Basler, "Lincoln's Development as a Writer," 61.

27   *disappear after 1848*: The frequency of Lincoln's use of a given word can be readily ascertained by means of the Word Index feature of the Abraham Lincoln Association's posting of the *Collected Works* on the World Wide Web.

28   *"By the Sub-Treasury"*: "Speech on the Sub-Treasury," Dec. [26], 1839, *Collected Works*, 1:160.

29   *"high road to his reason"*: "Temperance Address," Feb. 22, 1842, *Collected Works*, 1:273.

29 *"The making of it"*: Ibid., 1:274.

29 *"while the other reads it"*: AL to Joshua F. Speed, Mar. 27, 1842, *Collected Works*, 1:282–83.

30 *"by hearing and sight"*: William H. Herndon to Jesse W. Weik, Oct. 21, 1885, Herndon-Weik Collection, Library of Congress; hereafter H-W.

30 *"of sounds to sense"*: Robert V. Bruce, *Lincoln and the Riddle of Death* (Fort Wayne, Ind.: Louis A. Warren Lincoln Library and Museum, 1981), 19.

30 *"I know that"*: *Collected Works*, 1:178.

31 *"fireworks as a tailpiece"*: Basler, "Lincoln's Development as a Writer," 57.

31 *"leave it shining on"*: "Temperance Address," *Collected Works*, 1:279.

31 *"So far as I"*: Joshua F. Speed to William H. Herndon, Dec. 6, 1866, *Herndon's Informants*, 499.

32 *"But it is attempted"*: Senate speech of Jan. 13, 1834, in Robert E. Meriwether, W. Edwin Hemphill, and Clyde N. Wilson, eds., *The Papers of John C. Calhoun* (1959–), 12:214.

32 *eventually perfected*: See Leonard Swett's account of Lincoln's shrewd yielding of points in a courtroom, as recorded in Henry C. Whitney to William H. Herndon, Aug. 29, 1887, *Herndon's Informants*, 635–36.

33 " 'There now' ": "Letter from the Lost Townships," Aug. 27, 1842, *Collected Works*, 1:293–94.

34 *his literary effort*: For a full account of Lincoln's dueling affair, see Douglas L. Wilson, *Honor's Voice: The Transformation of Abraham Lincoln* (New York: Alfred A. Knopf, 1998), 265–83.

35 *"utterly confounded"*: Abraham Lincoln, "Remarkable Case of Arrest for Murder," Apr. 15, 1846, *Speeches and Writings 1832–1858* (New York: Library of America, 1989), 135; hereafter *Speeches and Writings 1832–1858*. The Library of America volumes of Lincoln's writings were edited by Don E. Fehrenbacher.

35 *"When the doctor's"*: AL to Joshua F. Speed, June 19, 1841, ibid., 73.

36 *favorite American writer*: J. Q. Howard, *The Life of Abraham Lincoln: With Extracts from His Speeches* (Columbus: Follet, Foster and Company, 1860), 17.

36 *"resolved to accompany him"*: AL, "Remarkable Case of Arrest for Murder," 131.

37 *"than ever before"*: "Autobiography Written for Campaign," c. June 1860, *Speeches and Writings 1859–1865* (New York: Library of America, 1989), 167; hereafter *Speeches and Writings 1859–1865*.

37 *"aroused me again"*: AL to Jesse W. Fell, Enclosing Autobiography, Dec. 20, 1859, *Speeches and Writings 1859–1865*, 108.

37 *"to gather facts"*: For the Peoria speech, see *Speeches and Writings 1832–1858*, 307–48. For Lincoln speaking without notes, see Horace White, *Abraham Lincoln in 1854: An Address Delivered Before the Illinois State Historical Society, at Its 9th Annual Meeting at Springfield, Illinois, Jan. 30, 1908* (Illinois State Historical Society, 1908), 10. For Herndon's testimony, see William H. Herndon to J. S. Holland, Feb. 24, 1866, Holland Papers, New York Public Library.

38 *"jot or tittle of it"*: White, *Abraham Lincoln in 1854*, 10.

38 *"This declared indifference"*: *Speeches and Writings 1832–1858*, 315.

39 *"injustice and bad policy"*: Ibid., 18.

39 *"in the offspring"*: Ibid., 297.

40 *"rather a poor one"*: AL to F. C. Herbruger, Apr. 7, 1860, *Collected Works*, 4:40.

40 *"utter failure"*: William H. Herndon to Ward Hill Lamon, Mar. 6, 1870,

Lamon Papers, Huntington Library. The best treatment of the historical details of Lincoln's lecture is Wayne C. Temple, "Lincoln the Lecturer, Part I," *Lincoln Herald* 101:3 (Fall 1999), 94–110; "Part II," *Lincoln Herald* 101:4 (Winter 1999), 146–63. While the surviving manuscript, which exists in two parts, has led scholars such as the editors of *Collected Works* to believe there may have been two distinct versions, Temple shows conclusively that there was only one lecture, and that Lincoln gave it at least six times.

40 *"after he was dead"*: "Lecture on Discoveries and Inventions," Feb. 11, 1859, *Speeches and Writings 1859–1865*, 9. Henry C. Whitney, a fellow lawyer with Lincoln on the Eighth Circuit, claimed that Lincoln's inspiration for his lecture was Bancroft's oration "The Necessity, the Reality, and the Promise of the Progress of the Human Race," as printed in *Literary and Historical Miscellanies* (New York: Harper & Brothers, 1855). For Whitney's testimony, see *Herndon's Informants*, 630–31.

41 *"invention of the world"*: Transcription from the manuscript. For this text, see "Lecture on Discoveries and Inventions," 7.

Chapter Three: A Custom as Old as the Government

42 *"ignorant man's state papers"*: Quoted in Louis A. Warren, *Lincoln's Declaration: "A New Birth of Freedom"* (Fort Wayne, Ind.: Lincoln National Life Foundation, 1964), 48.

43 *"ever made in this city"*: Quoted in Harold Holzer, *Lincoln at Cooper Union: The Speech That Made Abraham Lincoln President* (New York: Simon & Schuster, 2004), 156.

43 *"impressive statement"*: Ibid., 158.

43 *"for your judgment"*: Ibid., 221.

43 *"So far as it"*: AL to Charles C. Nott, May 31, 1860, Roy P. Basler, et al., eds., *The Collected Works of Abraham Lincoln*, 9 vols. (New Brunswick: Rutgers University Press, 1953), 4:58.

44 *"Your proposed insertion"*: Ibid.

44 *"his own writing"*: Holzer, *Lincoln at Cooper Union*, 319n.

44 *suffered in silence*: Gillespie's account of his visit with Lincoln during this period is reported in Ida M. Tarbell, *The Life of Abraham Lincoln*, 2 vols. (New York: McClure, Phillips & Co., 1902), 1:405–7.

45 *"notes and memoranda"*: Robert Todd Lincoln to Isaac Markens, June 18, 1918, in Paul M. Angle, ed., *A Portrait of Abraham Lincoln in Letters by His Oldest Son* (Chicago: Chicago Historical Society, 1968), 62.

45 *"wrote out his speech"*: William H. Herndon, "Lincoln Individually" [August 1887], Herndon-Weik Collection, Library of Congress, microfilm edition, group 4, roll 11, exp. 3410.

45 *"put in writing"*: John G. Nicolay, "Some Incidents in Lincoln's Journey from Springfield to Washington," *An Oral History of Abraham Lincoln: John G. Nicolay's Interviews and Essays*, ed. Michael Burlingame (Carbondale and Edwardsville: Southern Illinois University Press, 1996), 107. This is described by Burlingame as an unpublished essay found in Nicolay's papers in the Library of Congress. For other testimony about Lincoln's practice of preparation by note taking, see Ward Hill Lamon, *The Life of Abraham Lincoln* (Boston: James R. Osgood and Company, 1872), 471; John E. Washington, *They Knew*

Lincoln (New York: E. P. Dutton & Co., 1942), 111–12; Noah Brooks, *Lincoln Observed: Civil War Dispatches of Noah Brooks*, ed. Michael Burlingame (Baltimore: Johns Hopkins University Press, 1998), 149; James F. Wilson, in Don E. Fehrenbacher and Virginia Fehrenbacher, eds., *Recollected Words of Abraham Lincoln* (Stanford: Stanford University Press, 1996), 500–1; Joseph H. Barrett, *Abraham Lincoln and His Presidency*, 2 vols. (Cincinnati: Robert Clarke Co., 1904), 2:372; William H. Herndon and Jesse W. Weik, *Herndon's Lincoln*, ed. Douglas L. Wilson and Rodney O. Davis (Urbana: University of Illinois Press, 2006), 243, 271.

45 *"copy of the Constitution"*: *Herndon's Lincoln*, 287. The sentence that follows this one in *Herndon's Lincoln* states that Lincoln later called for Webster's reply to Hayne, but this seems to be the work of Jesse W. Weik, who composed the text of *Herndon's Lincoln*. On two occasions when referring to this matter, Herndon did not say he provided Webster but rather indicated that Lincoln knew and admired Webster's reply, with the implication that he didn't need to consult it. See Herndon to Weik, Jan. 1, 1886, Herndon-Weik Collection, Library of Congress, and Herndon's Third Lecture on Lincoln, Ward Hill Lamon papers, Huntington Library. William Bailhache remembered this process as having begun earlier (see note below), but Henry Villard's report to the *New York Herald* seems to confirm Herndon's recollection. See his report of Jan. 29 in Henry Villard, *Lincoln on the Eve of '61: A Journalist's Story*, ed. Harold G. & Oswald Garrison Villard (New York: Alfred A. Knopf, 1941), 57–58.

45 *"communication and intrusion"*: *Herndon's Lincoln*, 287.

46 *"fragment of manuscript destroyed"*: Nicolay, "Some Incidents in Lincoln's Journey from Springfield to Washington," 107. Nicolay notes that the scrap referred to above is the only manuscript fragment from the First Inaugural known to have survived.

46 *"were entirely satisfactory"*: *Reminiscences of Abraham Lincoln by Distinguished Men of His Time*, ed. Allen Thorndike Rice (New York: North American Publishing Company, 1886), 224. Poore's account makes clear that he is here referring to the stage of the drafting that preceded setting the draft in type.

46 *"revise the proofs"*: Nicolay, "Some Incidents in Lincoln's Journey from Springfield to Washington," 108. Ida Tarbell quotes a statement from Bailhache to the effect that Lincoln delivered the manuscript to him and that he supervised the printing. Tarbell, *The Life of Abraham Lincoln*, 1:403–4. Bailhache's account differs in some details from Nicolay's.

46 *"First edition"*: AL, "First Inaugural Address, First Printed Draft," ALP (#7702). The documents in this collection are available on the Library of Congress Web site.

47 *relatively unequivocal*: All quotations in the following seven paragraphs are from "First Inaugural Address, First Printed Draft," ALP (#7702–9).

50 *"times demand a Jackson"*: Villard, *Lincoln on the Eve of '61*, 17. Note that Villard later (Dec. 7) changed his mind about Lincoln and Jackson: "Having closely observed him since the election, and well noted the impressions made upon him by the secession phases of the present imbroglio, I dare say that there are dormant qualities in 'Old Abe' which occasion will draw forth, develop and remind people to a certain degree of the characteristics of 'Old Hickory' " (36).

51 *"He frequently examines"*: *London Times*, Feb. 13, 1861.

51 *that was never given*: See *Collected Works*, 4:200–1, and "Fragments of Speech to Kentuckians," ALP (#6973–78).

52 **"Where hostility":** "First Inaugural Address, First Printed Draft, with Revisions in Lincoln's Hand," ALP (#7697).

53 **"the type distributed":** Nicolay, "Some Incidents in Lincoln's Journey from Springfield to Washington," *An Oral History of Abraham Lincoln,* 108.

54 **one of the subsequent drafts:** Although copies of only two separate printings have survived, a number of disparities present clear evidence of intervening printings that have not. Some examples are these:

> *a.* The two-paragraph passage "Some if not all the states . . . convey such a meaning" from the first printed draft, though not stricken, does not appear in the so-called second printed draft, the one that Lincoln carried with him to Washington.
>
> *b.* A handwritten change on the first printed draft, "of this character," shows up on the "second" printed draft as "of this sort."
>
> *c.* AL changed "national Union" to "national fabric" in the first printed draft, but this change does not appear in the "second" printed draft.

54 **"acts as well as in words":** AL, "Address at Cooper Institute," Feb. 27, 1860, *Collected Works,* 3:547.

55 **"In compliance with":** AL, "First Inaugural Address, Draft of Opening Paragraph," [January 1861], ALP (#7693).

56 **"assault" and "defense":** These stricken words were restored in a later draft and appeared in the final version.

57 **copies of his inaugural address:** Nicolay, "Some Incidents in Lincoln's Journey from Springfield to Washington," 108.

57 **advisers in the days ahead:** Only five copies of this printing are known. The Library of Congress has four copies in the Lincoln Papers: the one given to Seward, who numbered the lines for reference (#7715–21); a copy with most of Seward's suggestions added in red ink, presumably in the hand of Nicolay (#7722–28); a copy containing some revisions by AL (#7729–35); the final version, which was presumably AL's reading copy (#7738–44 plus five tabs). Orville H. Browning's copy is at the Huntington Library. A copy of the final text in John G. Nicolay's hand, said to be prepared for the press, is in the Houghton Library of Harvard University.

57 **"A look of stupefaction":** Nicolay, "Some Incidents in Lincoln's Journey from Springfield to Washington," 109–10.

58 **Carl Schurz:** Schurz wrote his wife on the evening of Feb. 10: "Suddenly bringing our conversation to a halt, he said: 'I will give you a mark of confidence which I have given to no other man.' Then he locked the door and read to me the draft of his inaugural address." Frederic Bancroft, ed. *Speeches, Correspondence and Political Papers of Carl Schurz* (New York: Putnam's, 1913), 1:179. I am grateful to Michael Burlingame for calling this to my attention.

58 **"even in the border states":** Orville H. Browning to AL, Feb. 17, 1861, ALP. Browning described his actions in an interview with John G. Nicolay in 1875. See Michael Burlingame, ed., *An Oral History of Abraham Lincoln: John G. Nicolay's Interviews and Essays* (Carbondale: Southern Illinois University Press, 1996), 5–6.

58 **"much more than this":** *London Times,* Feb. 26, 1861.

58 **"Must Be Checked":** See Robert S. Harper, *Lincoln and the Press* (New York: McGraw-Hill Book Company, 1951), 78. Michael Burlingame, who has been making a study of Lincoln's anonymous journalism, believes that these and several other hard-line editorials in the *Journal* may have been written by Lincoln.

59 *"irritating threat"*: Orville H. Browning to AL, Feb. 17, 1861, ALP.

59 *"will tell you this"*: William H. Seward to AL, Feb. 24, 1861, in John G. Nicolay and John Hay, *Abraham Lincoln: A History*, 10 vols. (New York: Century Co., 1890), 3:320.

60 *"soothe the public mind"*: Ibid., 3:319.

60 *"example in this crisis"*: Ibid., 3:320.

60 *"frenzied party"*: Ibid., 3:321.

60 *"write 'revolutionary' "*: For the list in its entirely, see William H. Seward, "Suggested Changes to Lincoln's First Inaugural Address," [Feb. 1861], ALP (#7710–14).

61 *March 4 inauguration*: AL, "First Inaugural Address, Final Version," [Mar. 1861], ALP (#7738–44).

61 *ignoring others*: AL, "First Inaugural Address, Second Printed Draft, with Changes in Lincoln's Hand," [Feb.–Mar. 1861], ALP (#7729–35).

61 *"abridged or modified"*: Nicolay and Hay, *Abraham Lincoln*, 3:321.

62 *"in the original draft"*: William H. Bailhache to his wife, Mar. 3, 1861, Lincoln Collection, Indiana University. This reference was kindly provided by Michael Burlingame and will appear in the documentation of his forthcoming biography of Lincoln.

62 *not suggested by Seward*: AL, "First Inaugural Address, Second Printed Draft, with Changes in Lincoln's Hand," ALP (#7734).

63 *"proposition of policy"*: Nicolay and Hay, *Abraham Lincoln*, 3:321.

63 *"a no-nonsense document"*: David Herbert Donald, *Lincoln* (New York: Simon & Schuster, 1995), 283.

63 *"But if the policy"*: AL, "First Inaugural Address, Second Printed Draft, with Line Numbers Added by William H. Seward," [Feb. 1861], ALP (#7720). This seven-page printed document (#7715–21) is the copy Seward worked from.

63 *"At the same time"*: See William H. Seward, "Suggested Changes to Lincoln's First Inaugural Address" [Feb. 1861], ALP (#7712). Lincoln inserted the phrase "to that extent" between the words "having" and "practically."

64 *"calm and cheerful confidence"*: Nicolay and Hay, *Abraham Lincoln*, 3:321.

64 *"Suggestions for a closing paragraph"*: [William H. Seward?], "Suggestions for a Closing Paragraph, First Inaugural Address," [Feb. 1861], ALP (#7737).

65 *"I close"*: William H. Seward, "Suggested Changes to Lincoln's First Inaugural Address" [Feb. 1861], ALP (#7712 verso).

66 *"can never be broken"*: Orville H. Browning to AL, Feb. 17, 1861, ALP.

66 *"all Republicans"*: This is the form in which Seward passed it on to Lincoln (see note above). What Jefferson actually said was, "We are all Republicans, we are all Federalists."

66 *"take the first trick"*: Nicolay and Hay, *Abraham Lincoln*, 3:371.

66 *"to his own use"*: Don E. Fehrenbacher, "The Words of Lincoln," *Lincoln in Text and Context* (Stanford: Stanford University Press, 1987), 285.

66 *"summit of his presidency"*: Ibid., 286.

67 *"world about to be lost"*: Ibid., 285–86.

67 *made familiar by Dickens*: I am grateful to Jeb Boasberg and Garry Wills for calling my attention to the connection between Seward's "better angel" and Charles Dickens's *Barnaby Rudge* and *Great Expectations*. I am most indebted in this regard to my Knox College colleague Jeffrey Douglas and his very illuminating unpublished paper on these and other literary antecedents of Seward's phrase, "The Better Angels of Dickens, Seward, and Lincoln."

67 **"I am loth"**: AL, "First Inaugural Address, Final Version" [Mar. 1861], ALP (#7744).

69 **Lucas E. Morel:** Lucas E. Morel, *Lincoln's Sacred Effort: Defining Religion's Role in American Self-Government* (Lanham: Lexington Books, 2000), 65.

69 **"clank of metal in it"**: *The Diary of George Templeton Strong*, ed. Allan Nevins (New York: Macmillan Company, 1962), Mar. 5, 1861, 106.

70 **"acquiescent and good-natured"**: Ibid., Nov. 11, 1860, 62.

70 **"It is unlike"**: Ibid., Mar. 5, 1861, 106.

Chapter Four: The Message of July 4, 1861

71 **"reliance on it was unqualified"**: Horace Greeley, "Greeley's Estimate of Lincoln: An Unpublished Address by Horace Greeley," *Century Illustrated Monthly Magazine*, 42 (July 1891), 376.

71 **"toward the seceded States"**: Cited by AL in "Reply to a Committee from the Virginia Convention," [Apr. 13, 1861], Roy P. Basler, et al., *The Collected Works of Abraham Lincoln*, 9 vols. (New Brunswick: Rutgers University Press, 1953), 4:329–30; hereafter *Collected Works*.

72 **"course I intend to pursue"**: Ibid., 4:330.

72 **"among the people anywhere"**: Ibid.

72 **"domestic or foreign"**: Quoted in AL to William H. Seward, Apr. 1, 1861, *Collected Works*, 4:316.

72 **"authority from [such] places"**: "Reply to a Committee from the Virginia Convention," *Collected Works*, 4:330.

73 **"the fall of Sumter"**: Theodore Calvin Pease and James G. Randall, eds., *The Diary of Orville Hickman Browning*, 2 vols. (Springfield: Illinois State Historical Library, 1925), 1:476; hereafter Browning Diary.

73 **"possible to survive them"**: John G. Nicolay memorandum, July 3, 1861, in Michael Burlingame, ed., *With Lincoln in the White House: Letters, Memoranda, and Other Writings of John G. Nicolay, 1860–1865* (Carbondale and Edwardsville: Southern Illinois University Press, 2000), 46.

74 **"he so easily might"**: Ralph Waldo Emerson, *Journals and Miscellaneous Notebooks*, ed. William H. Gilman, et al., 16 vols. (Cambridge: Harvard University Press, 1960–82), 15:520.

74 **"The conversation turning"**: Burlingame, *With Lincoln in the White House*, 41.

74 **"if they choose"**: Michael Burlingame and John R. Turner Ettlinger, eds., *Inside Lincoln's White House: The Complete Civil War Diary of John Hay* (Carbondale and Edwardsville: Southern Illinois University Press, 1997), 20.

75 **"hour & of the future"**: Burlingame, *Inside Lincoln's White House*, 20.

75 **manuscript of forty pages:** AL, "Message to Congress, July 4, 1861, Handwritten Draft" [May–June 1861], ALP (#10503–42).

76 **"I recommend"**: AL, "Draft Fragment, Message to Congress, July 4, 1861" [May? 1861], ALP (#13652).

76 **two other documents:** These are each incorporated into the handwritten draft by being pasted to one of the manuscript pages, #10526A, which is pasted onto the end of #10526, and an unnumbered slip is pasted onto the final page (#10542).

77 **drafting his "House Divided" speech:** See Herndon's description of this process in the previous chapter, page 45.

78 *"And this issue embraces"*: "Message to Congress, July 4, 1861, Handwritten Draft," ALP (#10514).

78 *"It forces us to ask"*: The text of this passage ends halfway down the page (#10515), which indicates that the page and its text were inserted after the surrounding pages were written but before the pages were numbered.

79 *"fortunes of the Civil War"*: Reinhold Niebuhr, "The Religion of Abraham Lincoln," *Christian Century* 82 (Feb. 10, 1965), 173.

79 *"or Expect to See"*: David Davis interview, Sept. 20, 1866, in Douglas L. Wilson and Rodney O. Davis, eds., *Herndon's Informants: Letters, Interviews, and Statements About Abraham Lincoln* (Urbana: University of Illinois Press, 1998), 348.

79 **unwilling to cooperate**: See the series of letters to AL from one of the editors of the *Chicago Press and Tribune*, Charles Ray (June 29, [July], July 27, 1858), in ALP.

79 *"not much of me"*: AL to Jesse W. Fell, Dec. 20, 1859, Abraham Lincoln, *Speeches and Writings 1859–1865* (New York: Library of America, 1989), 106.

79 *"In a purely military"*: "Message to Congress, July 4, 1861, Handwritten Draft," ALP (#10509). The wording here represents the text before revision.

82 *"could not be allowed"*: "Message to Congress in Special Session," July 4, 1861, *Collected Works*, 4:424.

82 **Ex Parte Merryman**: See Mark E. Neely Jr., *The Fate of Liberty: Abraham Lincoln and Civil Liberties* (New York: Oxford University Press, 1991), 10.

83 *"undermine the administration"*: Daniel Farber, *Lincoln's Constitution* (Chicago: University of Chicago Press, 2003), 199.

83 *"Nevertheless, the legality"*: "Message to Congress, July 4, 1861, Handwritten Draft," ALP (#10521). I quote here from the text of the handwritten draft in its earliest state, before any changes were made.

83 *"be violated"*: Ibid., #10522. This is what Lincoln first wrote in his handwritten draft. He subsequently made changes to this text on the same page. See Figs. 4-3, 4-4.

83 *"I should consider"*: Ibid., #10522–23.

85 *"Even in such"*: "Message to Congress in Special Session," *Collected Works*, 4:430.

86 *"limited extent, be violated"*: Ibid.

86 *"unusually labored"*: Neely, *The Fate of Liberty*, 13.

86 **clincher . . . remained intact**: See the successive versions in ALP. Note that in this passage only one word, a redundant one, was changed, and that was eliminated.

86 *"commas was excessive"*: J. G. Holland, *The Life of Abraham Lincoln* (Springfield, Mass.: Gurdon Bill, 1866), 322.

86 *"reduce the number"*: Cited in Allen C. Guelzo, "Holland's Informants: The Construction of Josiah Holland's 'Life of Abraham Lincoln,' " *Journal of the Abraham Lincoln Association* 23:1 (Winter 2002), 46.

90 *"just let it pass"*: Gibson William Harris, "My Recollections of Abraham Lincoln," *Woman's Home Companion*, Jan. 1904, 13.

90 *" 'What is the matter' "*: F. B. Carpenter, *Six Months at the White House with Abraham Lincoln: The Story of a Picture* (New York: Hurd and Houghton, 1866), 126–7.

91 **negro, or slavery question**: A photographic copy of this letter was sent to Lincoln in 1864 and is still in his papers. See Andrew Jackson to Andrew I. Crawford, May 1, 1833 (photographic copy), ALP.

91   *"understand the difference":* To give the flavor of the compositional process, the text cited in the discussion of "sugar-coated" that follows is that of the earliest draft, "Message to Congress, July 4, 1861, Handwritten Draft," ALP (#10529–36).

92   *"public morals":* Morals was later changed to "mind."

94   *"put the periods to suit":* Quoted in Guelzo, "Holland's Informants," 46.

94   *letter to Adams:* See William H. Seward to Charles F. Adams, May 21, 1861, ALP. The text of this letter, with AL's changes noted, is in *Collected Works,* 4:376–81.

95   *"treason in disguise":* AL, "Message to Congress, July 4, 1861, First Printed Draft," [May–June 1861], ALP (#10545–71).

95   *"treason in effect":* AL, "Message to Congress, July 4, 1861, Second Printed Draft, with Suggested Changes by William H. Seward," [June–July 1861], ALP (#10598–623).

95   *"injurious in effect":* Final version, as printed in *Appendix to the Congressional Globe,* July 4, 1861, 37th Cong. 1st Sess., 2.

96   *"These politicians":* "Message to Congress, July 4, 1861, Handwritten Draft," ALP (#10536).

96   *a very substantial addition:* Some of this discussion of the secession-rebellion issue, which may have originally been projected as a briefer one, is set down on originally unpaginated sheets and is inserted in the handwritten manuscript just prior to the last of the twenty-three numbered pages. But the discussion of these same issues is then continued so as to extend the length of the handwritten manuscript by six additional pages. See ibid., #10503–42.

98   *"This is essentially":* Ibid., ALP (#10540).

98   *"back to bullets":* Ibid., ALP (#10541–42).

98   *in a public letter:* See AL to James C. Conkling, Aug. 26, 1863, *Collected Works,* 6:410.

99   *"Lest there be":* "Message to Congress, July 4, 1861, Handwritten Draft," ALP (#10542).

100 *"confided to him":* "Message to Congress, July 4, 1861, First Printed Draft," ALP (#10571).

100 *"And having thus":* Ibid., ALP (#10571B).

102 *"or high officials":* John G. Nicolay to Therena Bates, July 3, 1861, in Burlingame, *With Lincoln in the White House,* 46.

102 *"grace and power":* John Lothrop Motley to his wife, June 23, 1861, *The Correspondence of John Lothrop Motley,* ed. George William Curtis, 3 vols. (New York: Harper and Brothers, 1900), 1:395. I am grateful to Michael Burlingame for furnishing this reference.

102 *"expectations of the Country":* Browning Diary, 475.

102 *"It is wholly free":* *A Philadelphia Perspective: The Diary of Sidney George Fisher Covering the Years 1834–1871,* ed. Nicholas B. Wainwright (Philadelphia: Historical Society of Pennsylvania, 1967), 396.

103 *"While many Presidents":* *Harper's Weekly* 5:238 (July 20, 1861), 450.

103 *"In the late Message":* *Douglass' Monthly* IV:III (Aug. 1861), 497.

104 *"commentary on fundamentals":* J. G. Randall, *Lincoln the President: Springfield to Gettysburg,* 2 vols. (New York: Dodd, Mead and Company, 1945), 1:381.

104 *"doubted were wrong":* Quoted in William E. Gienapp, *Abraham Lincoln and Civil War America* (New York: Oxford University Press, 2001), 85.

Chapter Five: Proclaiming Emancipation

105 **"our nation's history":** *Douglass' Monthly* V:VI (Mar. 1863), 804. Speaking at the Cooper Institute in New York City in Feb. 1863, Douglass opened a celebratory address by saying, "I congratulate you, upon what may be called the greatest event of our nation's history if not the greatest event of the century."

105 **"of my administration":** F. B. Carpenter, *Six Months at the White House with Abraham Lincoln: The Story of a Picture* (New York: Hurd and Houghton, 1866), 90.

105 **"reform in American history":** Don E. Fehrenbacher, "The Words of Lincoln," *Lincoln in Text and Context* (Stanford: Stanford University Press, 1987), 284.

106 **"And by virtue":** AL, "Emancipation Proclamation," Jan. 1, 1863, Roy P. Basler, et al., eds., *The Collected Works of Abraham Lincoln*, 9 vols. (New Brunswick: Rutgers University Press, 1953), 6:29–30; hereafter *Collected Works*.

106 **"bill of lading":** Richard Hofstadter, *The American Political Tradition and the Men Who Made It* (New York: Alfred A. Knopf, 1948), 131.

106 **"inclination to do so":** "First Inaugural Address—Final Text," *Collected Works*, 4:263.

107 **"the real question":** Don E. Fehrenbacher, "Only His Stepchildren," *Lincoln in Text and Context*, 108.

107 **Guelzo study:** Allen C. Guelzo, *Lincoln's Emancipation Proclamation: The End of Slavery in America* (New York: Simon & Schuster, 2004). I am grateful to the author and his editor for an opportunity to read this important work prior to publication.

108 **"constitution and the Union":** AL to Joshua F. Speed, Aug. 24, 1855, *Collected Works*, 2:320.

108 **"Slave Hound of Illinois":** Wendell Phillips to William H. Herndon, n.d., Douglas L. Wilson and Rodney O. Davis, eds., *Herndon's Informants: Letters, Interviews, and Statements About Abraham Lincoln* (Urbana: University of Illinois Press, 1998), 704.

108 **"the existing institution":** "Speech at Peoria, Illinois," Oct. 16, 1854, *Collected Works*, 2:255.

108 **implications for slavery and its reform:** This point is perceptively made in two recent and complementary commentaries on the Temperance speech, to both of which I am indebted: John Channing Briggs, *Lincoln's Speeches Reconsidered* (Baltimore: Johns Hopkins University Press, 2005), 58–81; and David Zarefsky, "Lecture 3: The Temperance Speech," *Abraham Lincoln in His Own Words*, tape recordings (Springfield, Va.: Teaching Company, 1999).

108 **"Another error":** AL, "Temperance Speech," *Collected Works*, 1:275.

109 **"surrender of this capitol":** AL to Orville H. Browning, Sept. 22, 1861, *Speeches and Writings 1859–1865* (New York: Library of America, 1989), 269.

110 **"upon hopeless lunacy":** Quoted in *Douglass' Monthly* V:VI (Jan. 1, 1863), 781.

110 **"Your race are suffering":** AL, "Address on Colonization to a Deputation of Negroes," Aug. 14, 1862, *Collected Works*, 5:371–72.

111 **presidential maneuverings:** See, for example, the assessment of Lyman Trumbull in Horace White, *The Life of Lyman Trumbull* (Boston: Houghton Mifflin Company, 1913), 428–30; and Charles Sumner to Lot M. Morrill, June 15, 1865, *The Selected Letters of Charles Sumner*, ed. Beverly Wilson Palmer, 2 vols. (Boston: Northeastern University Press, 1990), 2:306.

111   ***"make victory impossible":*** Fehrenbacher, "Only His Stepchildren," 108–9.

113   ***subject of these presidential writings:*** These stories are conveniently collected in Guelzo, *Lincoln's Emancipation Proclamation*, 126–31.

113   ***"notes upon them":*** John E. Washington, *They Knew Lincoln* (New York: E. P. Dutton & Co., 1942), 111.

114   ***"I further make known":*** AL, "Proclamation Revoking General David Hunter's General Order No. 11 on Military Emancipation of Slaves," May 19, 1862, ALP (#16046).

114   ***"Upon his arrival":*** David Homer Bates, *Lincoln in the Telegraph Office: Recollections of the United States Military Telegraph Corps During the Civil War*, ed. James A. Rawley (Lincoln: University of Nebraska Press, 1995 [1907]), 139. Bates made a point of getting Eckert, his superior, to write out this account, thus providing corroboration. Eckert remembers this as having occurred shortly after the "Seven Days" (June 26–July 2), which would put it in July, not June.

115   ***"carefully each sentence":*** Ibid., 140.

116   ***"end of the war":*** Ibid., 141.

116   ***"crowded summer of 1862":*** J. G. Randall, *Lincoln the President: Springfield to Gettysburg*, 2 vols. (New York: Dodd, Mead and Company, 1945), 2:151.

116   ***"would not fight":*** Theodore Calvin Pease and James G. Randall, eds., *The Diary of Orville Hickman Browning*, 2 vols. (Springfield: Illinois State Historical Library, 1925), July 25, 1862, 1:563; hereafter Browning Diary.

117   **working on text on boat:** See Gideon Welles, "History of Emancipation," *Selected Essays by Gideon Welles: Civil War and Reconstruction*, ed. Albert Mordell (New York: Twayne, 1959), 236.

117   ***"Our common country":*** AL, "Address to Border State Representatives," July 12, 1862, ALP (#17009).

117   ***"To Mr Seward":*** Gideon Welles, *Lincoln and Seward: Remarks Upon the Memorial Address of Chas. Francis Adams . . .* (New York: Sheldon & Company, 1874), 210. See also *The Diary of Gideon Welles*, ed. Howard K. Beale with the assistance of Alan W. Brownsword, 3 vols. (New York: W. W. Norton, 1960), 1:70–71; hereafter Welles Diary.

118   ***"deny him to everybody":*** Browning Diary, July 15, 1862, 559.

118   ***"To give governmental":*** AL, "Draft of Veto Message," July 17, 1862, ALP (#17158).

120   ***"by acting first":*** David Herbert Donald, *Lincoln* (New York: Simon & Schuster, 1995), 365.

120   ***"or lose the game":*** Carpenter, *Six Months*, 20–21.

120   ***"part of August 1862":*** Ibid., 21.

120   ***"In pursuance":*** AL, "Preliminary Draft of Emancipation Proclamation," [July 22, 1862], ALP (#17232).

121   ***"And I hereby make":*** Ibid. In changing "thenceforward to maintain" to "thenceforward to be maintained," AL neglected to add the inflection "ed" to the word "maintain."

122   ***document that was no longer extant:*** The paper on which this text and Lincoln's endorsement are written can be identified by the manufacturer's embossment, an image of the new dome of the Capitol that was completed in late 1863. Though no records been found showing when this stationery was first issued by the manufacturer, the Mt. Holly Paper Co. of Mt. Holly Springs, Pennsylvania, no document of this type (foolscap size with twenty-nine blue-green lines)

bearing this embossment has been located dated earlier than April 20, 1863. See also the note at page 330.

123   ***"And, as a fit"***: AL, "Preliminary Draft of Emancipation Proclamation," [July 22, 1862], ALP (#17232–33). Lincoln's endorsement is on the recto of #17233.

123   " *'[Secretary Seward] said'* ": Carpenter, *Six Months*, 21–22.

124   ***"waiting for a victory"***: Ibid., 22.

124   ***"history of Liberty"***: Ibid., 10–11.

124   ***"work out your idea"***: Ibid., 20.

124   ***limitations of Carpenter's account:*** Carpenter's book is padded with anecdotes gleaned from others, many of which have nothing to do with the Emancipation Proclamation or Carpenter's stay in the White House, but what he says pertaining to his own experience, and especially his many conversations with the president, are of great interest. Still, the usual caveats about reminiscence apply. The conversations reported with the president are recollections, not stenographic accounts. The words attributed to the president are Carpenter's approximations of what Lincoln said, and Lincoln himself, one should be aware, was recalling things that had happened a year and a half earlier.

125   ***"would also do that"***: AL to Horace Greeley, Aug. 22, 1862, *Collected Works*, 5:388–89.

125   ***"had been looking for"***: *New York Times*, "News from Washington," Aug. 24, 1862, 1. William Safire called attention to this notice in the useful "underbook" of his historical novel *Freedom* (Garden City: Doubleday & Co., 1987), 1066. See also Guelzo, *Lincoln's Emancipation Proclamation*, 136–7.

126   ***"darker than ever"***: Carpenter, *Six Months*, 22.

126   ***"the rebel States"***: AL, "Reply to Emancipation Memorial Presented by Chicago Christians of All Denominations," Sept. 13, 1862, *Collected Works*, 5:420.

126   ***"than his own side"***: *Reminiscences of Abraham Lincoln by Distinguished Men of His Time*, ed. Allen Thorndike Rice (New York: North American Publishing Company, 1886), 333.

126   ***"Is there a single"***: AL, "Reply to Emancipation Memorial Presented by Chicago Christians of All Denominations," *Collected Works*, 5:420.

127   ***"I will do"***: Ibid., 5:425.

127   ***Chase asked for confirmation:*** See David Donald, ed., *Inside Lincoln's Cabinet: The Civil War Diary of Salmon P. Chase* (New York: Longmans, Green and Co., 1954), 150; Welles Diary, 1:143; and Carpenter, *Six Months*, 90.

127   ***"progress of events"***: Carpenter, *Six Months*, 22.

127   ***"got it pretty much prepared"***: Guelzo, *Emancipation Proclamation*, 152, citing George Boutwell to Josiah G. Holland, June 10, 1865, in the Holland Papers, New York Public Library.

128   ***"the preliminary proclamation"***: Carpenter, *Six Months*, 23.

128   ***"send the proclamation after him"***: Don E. and Virginia Fehrenbacher, eds. *Recollected Words of Abraham Lincoln* (Stanford: Stanford University Press, 1996), 38.

128   ***"chief clerk of the State Department"***: Carpenter, *Six Months*, 86–87.

128   ***shown only on special occasions:*** I am grateful to Kathi Stanley, curator of manuscripts, and the official in charge of security, J. Van der Veer Judd, of the New York State Library, for permission to view this document in its protective case and to examine high-quality facsimiles of the document.

129 **refusing to see visitors:** See Donald, *Inside Lincoln's Cabinet*, 149, and Michael Burlingame and John R. Turner Ettlinger, eds., *Inside Lincoln's White House: The Complete Civil War Diary of John Hay* (Carbondale: Southern Illinois University Press, 1997), 40.

129 **"I, Abraham Lincoln":** "Preliminary Emancipation Proclamation," Sept. 22, 1862, *Collected Works*, 5:433–4.

130 **"including the loss of slaves":** Ibid., 5:436.

131 **"If a commanding":** AL to Orville H. Browning, Sept. 22, 1861, *Collected Works*, 4:531.

132 **" 'When I finished' ":** Carpenter, *Six Months*, 23–24

132 **"and the executive":** Manuscript of the Preliminary Emancipation Proclamation, Sept. 22, 1862, New York State Library.

132 **" 'fell short of actual freedom' ":** Randall, *Lincoln the President*, 2:162.

134 **"the words finally went in":** Carpenter, *Six Months*, 23–24. Carpenter's reconstruction has Lincoln reading from the amended text, with no mention of the stricken matter.

134 **"in a better condition":** Donald, *Inside Lincoln's Cabinet*, 150.

134 **"It is six days old":** AL to Hamlin, Sept. 28, 1862, *Collected Works*, 5:444.

135 **in the November elections:** Blair's letter to AL is quoted in the note to the text of the "Emancipation Proclamation—First Draft," July 22, 1862, *Collected Works*, 5:337n.

136 **"we shall save our country":** AL, "Annual Message to Congress," Dec. 1, 1862, *Collected Works*, 5:537.

136 **"Fellow-citizens":** Ibid.

137 **"without the United States":** Ibid., 5:530.

137 **"gradual abolishment of slavery":** AL, "Draft of Message to Congress," [Feb.–Mar. 1862], ALP (#14810). This is the document that was shown to Sumner. The text of the message as sent is in *Collected Works*, 5:144.

138 **politically charged word "abolition":** See Donald, *Lincoln*, 346.

138 **"but I think he will":** George Templeton Strong, *Diary of the Civil War 1860–1865*, ed. Allan Nevins (New York: Macmillan, 1962), 282.

138 **"sanguine on the subject":** Ibid., 284.

138 **"reviewing the president's penultimate draft":** See Guelzo, *Lincoln's Emancipation Proclamation*, 177–8.

138 **"this much to him":** Defrees to Nicolay, Dec. 17, 1862, ALP.

139 **"for or against us":** Welles, *Lincoln and Seward*, 210.

139 **"hands to the government":** Carpenter, *Six Months*, 22.

139 **"all sorts in said service":** AL, "Emancipation Proclamation," Jan. 1, 1863, *Collected Works*, 6:30.

139 **"all probability go under":** Carpenter, *Six Months*, 83–84.

140 **"all persons held as slaves":** AL, "Final Emancipation Proclamation—Final Draft [Lithograph Copy]," ALP (#20821).

141 **"hang the Proclamation on":** Guelzo, *Lincoln's Emancipation Proclamation*, 180–1.

141 **"dismember the Republic":** Salmon P. Chase, "Memorandum on Emancipation, [Dec. 31?, 1862], ALP (#20835).

141 **"favor of Almighty God":** For Chase's proposed sentence, see "Proposed Revision of Emancipation Proclamation," [Dec. 30–31, 1862], ALP (#208 30–31).

Chapter Six: Public Opinion

143 **"end of my bag":** Quoted in David Herbert Donald, *Lincoln* (New York: Simon & Schuster, 1995), 405.

143 **" 'Wa-al,' says Abe":** George Templeton Strong, *Diary of the Civil War 1860–1865*, ed. Allan Nevins (New York: Macmillan, 1962), Jan. 29, 1862, 204–5; hereafter Strong Diary.

144 **"deceived as we at Cincinnati":** See the choice account of the Cincinnati affair and its aftermath in William Lee Miller, *Lincoln's Virtues: An Ethical Biography* (New York: Alfred A. Knopf, 2002), 410–26. I am also indebted to Doris Kearns Goodwin for generously sharing her research material on this episode.

145 **"Public opinion . . . is everything":** Speech at Columbus, Ohio, Sept. 16, 1859, Roy P. Basler, et al., eds., *The Collected Works of Abraham Lincoln*, 9 vols. (New Brunswick: Rutgers University Press, 1953), 3:424; hereafter *Collected Works*. In fact, he had said essentially the same thing in his first debate with Douglas at Ottawa, Ill., in 1858. See *Collected Works*, 3:27.

145 **"practically just so much":** "Portion of Speech at Republican Banquet in Chicago, Illinois," Dec. 10, 1856, *Speeches and Writings 1832–1858* (New York: Library of America, 1989), 385–6.

145 **"With public sentiment":** AL, reply to Douglas at Ottawa, *Collected Works*, 3:27. For AL's notes using the antithesis in the first sentence, see "Fragment: Notes for Speeches," *Collected Works*, 2:552–3.

146 **"slavery perpetual and national":** *Collected Works*, 3:234.

146 **"debauching of public opinion":** Speech at Columbus, Ohio, Sept. 16, 1859, *Collected Works*, 3:423. AL used this term in speeches at Indianapolis, Indiana, and Janesville, Wisconsin.

146 **"debauching of the public mind":** *Collected Works*, 4:433.

146 **"tortoise with a rye straw":** "Temperance Address," Feb. 22, 1842, *Collected Works*, 1:273.

147 **"most democratic society in the world":** Phillip Shaw Paludan, *"The Better Angels of Our Nature": Lincoln, Propaganda and Public Opinion in the North During the Civil War* (Fort Wayne: Lincoln Museum, 1992), 9–10.

147 **"the principles of Aristotle":** Ronald C. White Jr., *The Eloquent President: A Portrait of Lincoln Through His Words* (New York: Random House, 2005), xxi.

147 **"we are pained and hostile":** Aristotle, *Rhetoric*, trans. W. Rhys Roberts, *The Complete Works of Aristotle: The Revised Oxford Translations*, ed. Jonathan Barnes (Princeton: Princeton University Press, 1984), 2155.

147 **"straightforward, honest old codger":** Strong Diary, Jan. 29, 1862, 204.

148 **"opinions are divided":** Aristotle, *Rhetoric*, 2155.

148 **"confidence of the hearer":** From the *Quincy Whig*, Jan. 1, 1841, quoted in Paul Simon, *Lincoln's Preparation for Greatness: The Illinois Legislative Years* (Urbana: University of Illinois Press, 1971), 231.

148 **"energy the country wants":** Strong Diary, Aug. 4, 1862, 244.

148 **"We require of you":** The entire "Prayer of Twenty Millions" is printed in Harlan Hoyt Horner, *Lincoln and Greeley* (Urbana: University of Illinois Press, 1953), 263–7; for the passage cited, see 263–4.

149 **"portion of the reflected glory":** Richard S. Harper, *Lincoln and the Press* (New York: McGraw-Hill Book Company, 1951), 176. Lincoln got wind of Greeley's agitation and tried, by sending him word of the forthcoming proclamation, to

placate him, but his message arrived too late. See Allen C. Guelzo's account in *Lincoln's Emancipation Proclamation* (New York: Simon & Schuster, 2004), 132–7.

149 **"*sincerity of the man*"**: Quoted in White, *The Eloquent President*, 48, citing the *New York Tribune*, Feb. 17 or 18, 1861.

149 **"*best way of accomplishing it*"**: "News from Washington," *New York Times*, Aug. 24, 1862, 1. This was also reported in similar language by Whitelaw Reid on the same day in the *Cincinnati Gazette*. See Whitelaw Reid, *A Radical View: The "Agate" Dispatches of Whitelaw Reid 1861–1865*, ed. James G. Smart (Memphis: Memphis State University Press, 1976), 215.

150 **Jefferson's letter to the newspaper:** See Henry Adams, *History of the United States of America During the Administrations of Thomas Jefferson* (New York: Library of America, 1986), 357.

150 **"*comment as might be expected*"**: Reid, *A Radical View*, 215.

150 **"*Dear Sir: I have*"**: *National Intelligencer*, Aug. 23, 1862; *Collected Works*, 5:388–9.

151 **"*I would save*"**: AL to Horace Greeley, Aug. 22, 1862. All citations follow the text of the manuscript. This manuscript is owned by the Wadsworth Athenaeum, Hartford, Conn. I am grateful to Librarian John Teahan for granting me access to the manuscript, and to Eugene R. Gaddis for helping me to make the most of it. I am also grateful to Adria Patterson for providing a high-quality scan of the document.

155 **"*will be past mending*"**: AL to August Belmont, July 31, 1862, *Collected Works*, 5:350.

155 **"*I can not retract it*"**: AL to John A. McLernand, Jan. 8, 1863, *Collected Works*, 5:48.

155 **"*The letter came*"**: *Reminiscences of Abraham Lincoln by Distinguished Men of His Time*, ed. Allen Thorndike Rice (New York: North American Publishing Company, 1886), 525–6n.

156 **"*all the slaves I would do it*"**: I have here removed the comma that was placed, probably inadvertently, after "do."

156 **early editors eliminated . . . emphasis:** Even though a facsimile of the manuscript of the letter was printed by James C. Welling in the *North American Review* in 1880, Nicolay and Hay removed all emphasis in their editions of the *Complete Works*.

156 **"*economy of expression*"**: Allen C. Guelzo, *Lincoln's Emancipation Proclamation: The End of Slavery in America* (New York: Simon & Schuster, 2004), 133.

156 **only 295 words:** This count includes the sentence that was not published, which contains seventeen words.

157 **"*save the Union with slavery*"**: *Harper's Weekly* 6:297 (Sept. 6, 1862), 562.

157 **"*unless slavery be destroyed*"**: Ibid.

157 **"*and intentionally so*"**: Fehrenbacher, "The Words of Lincoln," *Lincoln in Text and Context: Collected Essays* (Stanford: Stanford University Press, 1987), 284.

158 **"*means of saving the Union*"**: Ibid.

159 **" '*Now is the time*' "**: AL to August Belmont, July 31, 1862, *Collected Works*, 5:350.

159 **"*defined his policy*"**: "News from Washington," *New York Times*, Aug. 24, 1862, 1.

160 **"*fairly before the country*"**: Horace Greeley, "Greeley's Estimate of Lincoln: An Unpublished Address by Horace Greeley," *Century Illustrated Monthly Magazine* 42:3 (July 1891), 380.

160　**"people were with him":** Reported in a letter from *New York Tribune* correspondent Adam S. Hill to Sydney Howard Gay, Sept. 1, 1862, *Recollected Words of Abraham Lincoln,* ed. Don E. and Virginia Fehrenbacher (Stanford: Stanford University Press, 1996), 18.

160　**"than the nation can bear":** Thomas Jefferson to Walter Jones, Mar. 31, 1801, *The Writings of Thomas Jefferson,* ed. H. A. Washington, 9 vols. (Washington, D.C.: Taylor & Maury, 1853–54), 4:393.

160　**"educated up to it":** As told to John McClintock, in Fehrenbacher, *Recollected Words,* 314.

Chapter Seven: Rising with Each New Effort

162　**"finished proposition or statement":** John C. Nicolay, "Some Incidents in Lincoln's Journey from Springfield to Washington," *An Oral History of Abraham Lincoln: John G. Nicolay's Interviews and Essays,* ed. Michael Burlingame (Carbondale and Edwardsville: Southern Illinois University Press, 1996), 107. For more sources on Lincoln's practice of making notes on scraps of paper, see note on pages 303–4, "put in writing."

163　**" 'separate scraps of paper' ":** James F. Wilson, "Some Memories of Lincoln," *North American Review* 163 (Dec. 1896), 670.

164　**"cause célèbre of the Lincoln administration":** J. G. Randall, *Lincoln the President: Midstream* (New York: Dodd, Mead & Company, 1952), 212.

165　**"What will the country say?":** Noah Brooks, *Washington, D.C., in Lincoln's Time,* ed. Herbert Mitgang (Athens, Ga.: University of Georgia Press, 1989), 61.

165　**"in the spring of 1863":** James M. McPherson, *Battle Cry of Freedom: The Civil War Era* (New York: Oxford University Press, 1988), 645.

165　**"so deep and so widespread":** John G. Nicolay and John Hay, *Abraham Lincoln: A History,* 10 vols. (New York: Century Co., 1890), 7:349.

165　**"it establishes military despotism":** Quoted in Nicolay and Hay, *Abraham Lincoln,* 7:341–2.

166　**"put it in that drawer":** James F. Wilson, "Some Memories of Lincoln," 670.

166　**"is a good sign":** George Templeton Strong, *Diary of the Civil War 1860–1865,* ed. Allan Nevins (New York: Macmillan Company, 1962), Mar. 5, 1861, 106; hereafter Strong Diary.

166　**"left the consequences to God":** John G. Nicolay, "Lincoln's Literary Experiments," *The Century Magazine* 47:6 (Apr. 1894), 825.

167　**"to say nothing at all":** AL, "Remarks to Citizens of Gettysburg, Pennsylvania," Nov. 18, 1863, Roy P. Basler, et al., eds., *The Collected Works of Abraham Lincoln,* 9 vols. (New Brunswick: Rutgers University Press, 1953), 7:17; hereafter *Collected Works.*

167　**"color, life and energy":** Richard Carwardine, *Lincoln: A Life of Purpose and Power* (New York: Alfred A. Knopf, 2006), 264.

167　**"lest that one be violated":** *Collected Works,* 4:430.

168　**"measures for effecting that object":** AL to Erastus Corning, "Draft of Reply to Resolutions Concerning Military Arrests and Suspension of Habeas Corpus," [June 1863], ALP (#23995–24016). The text being followed here and in the ensuing discussion is that of the only known manuscript, which is also the text followed by the editors of the *Collected Works,* 6:260–9. The text that appeared in newspapers on June 15 contained only a few changes, and these are noted in *Collected Works*. The newspaper text presumably conforms to the text the president had printed and distributed to newspapers and some select friends, but no copy of this printing has yet been identified.

169 **only known manuscript:** AL to Erastus Corning, "Draft of Reply to Resolutions," ALP (#24001).

170 **more discreet observation:** Ibid. (#24002).

172 **writer decided to add:** Ibid. (#24009).

172 **the manuscript enables us to see:** Ibid.

174 **"means of persuasion he possesses":** Aristotle, *Rhetoric*, trans. W. Rhys Roberts, *The Complete Works of Aristotle: The Revised Oxford Translations*, ed. Jonathan Barnes (Princeton: Princeton University Press, 1984), 2155.

176 **"Among other things":** ALP (#24013)

176 **"under General Jackson":** Edward Everett to AL, June 16, 1863, ALP.

177 **"couldn't fight in a bad case":** Michael Burlingame, ed., *An Oral History of Abraham Lincoln: John G. Nicolay's Interviews and Essays* (Carbondale: Southern Illinois University Press, 1996), 39.

178 **"fought exceedingly well":** Mark E. Neely Jr., *The Fate of Liberty: Abraham Lincoln and Civil Liberties* (New York: Oxford University Press, 1991), 68.

178 **"will be a strong paper":** Quoted in *Collected Works*, 6:261n.

178 **"in the right spirit":** See the responses of E. D. Morgan (June 14, 1863), David P. Brown (June 15, 1863), John C. Ten Eyck (June 16, 1863), Hugh McCulloch (June 16, 1863), Edward Everett (June 16, 1863), George F. Train (June 16, 1863), Roscoe Conkling (June 16, 1863), and Daniel S. Dickinson (June 18, 1863), all in ALP.

178 **"10000 copies" of the letter:** Francis Lieber to AL, June 16, 1863, ALP.

178 **"were read by 10,000,000 people":** David Herbert Donald, *Lincoln* (New York: Simon & Schuster, 1995), 443–4.

179 **"to correct that impression":** Horace Maynard to AL, June 18, 1863, ALP.

179 **the subject of Military Arrests":** Hugh McCulloch to AL, June 16, 1863, ALP.

180 **"at the ludicrous conclusion":** Theodore Calvin Pease and James G. Randall, eds., *The Diary of Orville Hickman Browning*, 2 vols. (Springfield: Illinois State Historical Library, 1925), June 30, 1862, 1:555; hereafter Browning Diary. See Matthew Pinsker's excellent account of this incident in *Lincoln's Sanctuary: Abraham Lincoln and the Soldiers' Home* (New York: Oxford University Press, 2003), 34–35.

180 **read the First Inaugural to the elder Blair:** According to Norman B. Judd in an interview with John G. Nicolay, Feb. 28, 1876, in Burlingame, *Oral History of Abraham Lincoln*, 47.

181 **"I just let it pass":** Gibson William Harris, "My Recollections of Abraham Lincoln," *Woman's Home Companion*, Jan. 1904, 13. I am indebted to Michael Burlingame for calling my attention to this recollected remark.

181 **" 'judge of a thing by merely reading it' ":** William O. Stoddard, *Inside the White House in War Times: Memoirs and Reports of Lincoln's Secretary*, ed. Michael Burlingame (Lincoln and London: University of Nebraska Press, 2000), 130.

181 **"in the presence of his hearer":** Swett's story is rehearsed by one of his friends, Judge Peter Stenger Grosscup, in Ida Tarbell, *The Life of Abraham Lincoln* (New York: Lincoln Memorial Association, n.d. [1900]), 2:115.

181 **"Sit down":** Stoddard, *Inside the White House in War Times*, 130.

183   **"The unconditional Union men":** James C. Conkling to AL, Aug. 14, 1863, ALP.

183   **"probably the latter":** AL to James C. Conkling, Aug. 20, 1863, *Collected Works*, 6:399.

183   **"a rather good letter":** Nicolay and Hay, *Abraham Lincoln*, 7:385.

183   **draft of what would become the main body of the letter:** There is no conclusive evidence that the earliest draft was written before or after Aug. 20, when Lincoln received his invitation to Springfield. The operating assumptions here are that he was undoubtedly collecting ideas for defending the draft and the use of black soldiers before this time, and that his remark to Conkling about possibly sending a letter suggests that he already had produced this draft.

183   **"employing colored troops":** Frederick Douglass to George L. Stearns, Aug. 12, 1863, Historical Society of Pennsylvania.

183   **a manuscript that was originally eleven pages long:** Abraham Lincoln, "Draft Fragment Used in Letter to James C. Conkling," ALP (#25839–43).

184   **"sons of noblest sires":** Ibid. (#25839).

184   **"manhood of our race run out":** "Opinion on the Draft," *Collected Works*, 6:448. Read to the cabinet on Sept. 15, 1863, but never published, the manuscript is in ALP (#25922–32).

185   **"There are those":** AL, "Draft of Letter to be Read at Union Mass Meeting in Springfield," Aug. 26, 1863, ALP (#25846–53). The passages cited in the ensuing discussion are from this handwritten draft.

191   **"leave it in just as it is":** Stoddard, *Inside the White House in War Times*, 130.

191   **"I don't care":** Don E. Fehrenbacher and Virginia Fehrenbacher, eds., *Recollected Words of Abraham Lincoln* (Stanford: Stanford University Press, 1996), 137. I am grateful to Michael Burlingame for this reference.

191   **"from Maine to Minnesota":** Strong Diary, 355.

193   **"and to their fears":** Nicolay and Hay, *Abraham Lincoln*, 7:384, 385.

193   **"Read it very slowly":** AL to James C. Conkling, Aug. 27, 1863, *Collected Works*, 6:414.

193   **seventy-five thousand:** James C. Conkling to AL, Sept. 4, 1863, ALP.

193   **"a more instantaneous success":** Nicolay and Hay, *Abraham Lincoln*, 7:385n.

193   **"It cannot be answered":** Charles Sumner to AL, Sept. 7, 1863, ALP.

194   **"in the general applause":** *New York Times*, Sept. 7, 1863.

195   **"high ability and statesmanship":** *The Letters of President Lincoln on Questions of National Policy* (New York: H. H. Lloyd & Co., 1863; Boston: B. B. Russell, 1863).

195   **"wise forecast in the President":** Quoted in Roy P. Basler, *The Lincoln Legend: A Study in Changing Conceptions* (Boston: Houghton Mifflin Company, 1935), 79.

195   **"clear as it ought to be":** Ibid., 79.

195   **"We might congratulate":** Ibid., 79–80.

196   **"controlled the popular mind":** In Herbert Mitgang, *Abraham Lincoln: A Press Portrait* (Chicago: Quadrangle Books, 1971 [1956]), 376, 377. Called a "biographical appraisal," this was originally published in a religious journal, *Watchman and Reflector*, and reprinted in *Littel's Living Age*, Feb. 6, 1864.

196   **"the plainest plowman":** *New York Times*, Sept. 7, 1863.

197   **"Lincoln.—We must accept":** *Selections from Ralph Waldo Emerson*, ed. Stephen E. Whicher (Boston: Houghton Mifflin Company, 1960), 396–7.

Chapter Eight: The Gettysburg Address

198   *"class poet at Brown"*: Michael Burlingame, ed., *At Lincoln's Side: John Hay's Civil War Correspondence and Selected Writings* (Carbondale: Southern Illinois University Press, 2000), 237n.

199   *"have ended the war"*: AL to George G. Meade, Roy P. Basler, et al., eds., *The Collected Works of Abraham Lincoln*, 9 vols. (New Brunswick: Rutgers University Press, 1953), 6:327–8; hereafter *Collected Works*.

199   *"saving the life of a condemned soldier"*: Michael Burlingame, ed., *Inside Lincoln's White House: The Complete Civil War Diary of John Hay* (Carbondale: Southern Illinois University Press, 1997), 64; hereafter Hay Diary.

199   *"too terribly to shoot them"*: Ibid.

199   *"Gen. Lees invasion"*: Roy P. Basler, ed., *The Collected Works of Abraham Lincoln: Supplement 1832–1865* (Westport, Conn.: Greenwood Press, 1974), 194. For assistance in examining the original of this document and acquiring a high-quality scan of it, I am grateful to Holly Snyder and Ann Morgan Dodge of the John Hay Library of Brown University.

201   *"all at once"*: John Hay to John G. Nicolay, Aug. 7, 1863, in Burlingame, *At Lincoln's Side*, 49.

201   *"steady & equally firm"*: John Hay to John G. Nicolay, Sept. 11, 1863, in Burlingame, *At Lincoln's Side*, 54.

201   *other memoranda on reunion and the draft*: See AL, "Memorandum on Reunion," [1863?], ALP (#25844–5), and AL, "Opinion on the Draft," [Sept. 14, 1863], ALP (#25923–32). For edited texts of these documents, see *Collected Works*, 6:410–1, 444–9.

201   *"logicians of all schools"*: John Hay to Nicolay, Sept. 11, 1863, in Burlingame, *At Lincoln's Side*, 54.

201   *"remorseless revolutionary struggle"*: AL, "Annual Message to Congress," Dec. 3, 1861, *Collected Works*, 5:48–9.

202   *Confederate and Union losses at Gettysburg:* These figures are taken from James M. McPherson, *Battle Cry of Freedom: The Civil War Era* (New York: Oxford University Press, 1988), 664.

202   *"the ravages of war"*: Richard J. Carwardine, "Abraham Lincoln and the Fourth Estate: The White House and the Press During the American Civil War," *American Nineteenth Century History* 7:1 (forthcoming, 2006). I am grateful to Prof. Carwardine for an early look at his fine paper on Lincoln and the press.

202   *"practical equality of all men"*: AL, "Speech at a Republican Banquet," Dec. 10, 1856, *Collected Works*, 2:385. Believing that "was" is likely a misprint for "has," I have amended the text accordingly.

202   *"a self-evident lie"*: For a history of Lincoln's use of the Declaration in the 1850s, see Douglas L. Wilson, "Lincoln's Declaration," *Lincoln Before Washington: New Perspectives on the Illinois Years* (Urbana: University of Illinois Press, 1997), 166–81.

203   *" 'sacred right of self-government' "*: AL, "Speech at Peoria," Oct. 16, 1854, *Collected Works*, 2:275.

203   *"they cannot carry"*: AL, "Speech at Chicago," *Collected Works*, 2:499–500.

203   *"all men are created equal"*: Ibid., 2:501.

204   *Douglas makes Lincoln pay for an unguarded moment:* At their Galesburg

debate, for example, Douglas read the passages from Lincoln's Chicago speech quoted above (*Collected Works*, 3:213–4) and referred to that speech on numerous occasions throughout the 1858 senatorial campaign.

204 *AL forced to issue disclaimers:* These disclaimers continue to dog Lincoln's reputation down to the present. In the debates with Douglas, he had stubbornly insisted that the Negro, in being a man, was included in the Declaration's magic formula "all men are created equal" and therefore was endowed with the natural rights referred to therein, such as life, liberty, and the pursuit of happiness. Moreover, he refused to accept Douglas's position that Negroes were inferior to whites and incapable of self-government. But he did allow that "there is a physical difference between the white and black races which I believe will for ever forbid the two races living together on terms of social and political equality. And inasmuch as they cannot so live, while they do remain together there must be the position of superior and inferior, and I as much as any other man am in favor of having the superior position assigned to the white race." Debate at Charleston, Sept. 18, 1858, *Collected Works*, 3:145–6. For a similar disclaimer offered earlier, see the Ottawa debate, Aug. 21, 1858, *Collected Works*, 3:16, See also Wilson, "Lincoln's Declaration," 172–7.

204 *"re-appearing tyranny and oppression":* AL to Henry L. Pierce and others, April 6, 1859, *Collected Works*, 3:376.

205 *"I have often inquired":* AL, "Speech in Independence Hall," Feb. 22, 1861, *Collected Works*, 4:240.

205 *"than to surrender it":* Ibid.

205 *"authority of the people":* AL, "Message to Congress in Special Session," July 4, 1861, *Collected Works*, 4:438.

206 *"whose existence we contend":* Ibid.

206 *"practical equality of all men":* AL, "Speech at a Republican Banquet," Dec. 10, 1856, *Collected Works*, 2:385.

206 *"no written draft":* Martin P. Johnson, "Lincoln Greets the Turning Point of the Civil War, July 7, 1863," *Lincoln Herald* 106:3 (Fall 2004), 106. Johnson shows that the *New York Tribune* and *New York Times* texts that the *Collected Works* text is based on were not as full in their reporting as the one that appeared in the Washington newspapers. Johnson reprints the text printed by the *Washington Daily Morning Chronicle* for July 8, 1863, which, as he demonstrates, tends to show more about Lincoln's thinking about the war, the Declaration, the proposition that "all men are created equal," and the role of Providence.

206 *"all men were created equal":* Ibid., 104. The text cited here is that presented by Johnson from the *Washington Daily Morning Chronicle* for July 8, 1863. It differs from the text presented in the *Collected Works* in being somewhat fuller and more coherent. All subsequent references are to the *Chronicle* text, as given by Johnson.

207 *"on that very day":* Ibid., 104–5.

207 *"to turn tail and run":* Ibid., 105.

207 *"The prevailing ideas":* Quoted in John G. Nicolay and John Hay, *Abraham Lincoln: A History*, 9 vols. (New York: Century Co., 1890), 3:202–3. One should note that this account was later disputed by Stephens, who objected that the reporter's notes of this extemporaneous speech "were very imperfect, were hastily corrected by me; and were published without further revision and with

several glaring errors." *Recollections of Alexander H. Stephens*, ed. Myrta Lockett Avary (Baton Rouge: Louisiana State University Press, 1998 [1910]), 173. Nonetheless, Stephens did not deny or disassociate himself from the main implication conveyed here.

208 *"worthy of the occasion":* Johnson, "Lincoln Greets the Turning Point of the Civil War, July 7, 1863," 105.

208 *"what became of the original notes":* Robert Todd Lincoln to Belle F. Keyes, Dec. 16, 1885, quoted by William E. Barton, *Lincoln at Gettysburg: What He Intended to Say; What He Said; What He Was Reported to Have Said; What He Wished He Had Said* (New York: Peter Smith, 1950 [1931]), 108.

208 *"perform the consecrational service":* "Our Baltimore Letter" (dated Oct. 12), *The Philadelphia Inquirer*, Oct. 13, 1863. I am grateful to Gabor S. Boritt for sharing information about these newpaper reports. See also Joseph George, Jr., "The World Will Little Note? The Philadelphia Press and the Gettysburg Address," *The Pennsylvania Magazine of History & Biography*, 114:3 (July 1990), 385–98.

209 *burials at Soldiers' Home Cemetery:* Official government reports on the number of burials at the Soldiers' Home apparently vary, but one recent independent count of the records shows a total of 4,765 burials at the site by the end of 1863. For this information, I am grateful to Sophia Lynn and Erin Carlson of the National Trust's exemplary project to restore the Soldiers' Home.

209 *"he said, softly":* Quoted in Francis B. Carpenter, *Six Months at the White House* (New York: Hurd and Houghton, 1866), 223–4. The lines are from William Collins, "Ode, Written in the Beginning of the Year 1746."

209 *"The several States":* David Wills to AL, Nov. 2, 1863, ALP.

210 *"that of the memorial services":* Clark E. Carr, *Lincoln at Gettysburg: An Address* (Chicago: A. C. McClurg & Co., 1906), 22–3.

211 *Stanton had planned to go:* See Wayne MacVeagh, "Lincoln at Gettysburg," *Century Magazine* 79:1 (November 1909), 21.

211 *"to say some appropriate thing":* Quoted in David C. Mearns and Lloyd A. Dunlap, "Notes and Comments on the Preparation of the Address," *Long Remembered: Facsimiles of the Five Versions of the Gettysburg Address in the Handwriting of Abraham Lincoln* (Washington: The Library of Congress, 1963), [3].

211 *"written, 'but not finished' ":* Noah Brooks, *Washington, D.C. in Lincoln's Time*, ed. Herbert Mitgang (Athens: University of Georgia Press, 1989 [1895]), 253. This book was originally published in 1895 as *Washington in Lincoln's Time*. Brooks told this story many times, usually in conjunction with a story about Lincoln's having received an advance copy of Edward Everett's address. As this copy could not have been received by AL until a day or two before his departure for Gettysburg (Everett only sent it to the printer on Nov. 14), the likelihood is that Brooks had more than one conversation with AL on the subject, one of which must have been just before he left for Gettysburg. His claim in some versions that the president mentioned receiving Everett's address on a visit to a photographer's studio is apparently not compatible with known chronology.

    The point critics such as David C. Mearns refuse to acknowledge is that the relative accuracy and pertinence of what Brooks remembered Lincoln's saying about his speech does not depend on the accuracy of his recollected chronology. Mearns, for example, argues that getting the date of a conversation with the president wrong "puts the kibosh on Brooks' fantasy." Mearns is thus willing to dismiss everything Brooks reports, even though the errors in this case are among the commonest and the most familiar kinds of mistakes that memory is subject to and hardly deserve the name of "fantasy." Notwithstanding that Mearns is an admirable scholar, how such commonplace errors of memory can negate the truth or validity of everything else a witness has to say is difficult to understand. David C. Mearns, "Unknown at This Address," *Lincoln and the Gettysburg Address: Commemorative Papers*, ed. Allan Nevins (Urbana: University of Illinois Press, 1964), 123.

211 *"come and tell me"*: AL to John Defrees, Nov. 12, 1863, *Collected Works*, 7:12. Defrees sent this note to be sold at a sanitary fair and explained that he complied with Lincoln's instruction, as a result of which "the young man was liberated on the President's order."

211 *"the famous Gettysburg speech"*: The story of Defrees calling on the president and being shown the speech was related by Defrees's son-in-law, J. O. Smith, in a highly embroidered form, including the claim that Lincoln locked the door, handed Defrees the speech, and told him to "make any changes your judgment dictates." The son-in-law's version may be doubted as to details, but the existence of the Nov. 12 note proves that Defrees had a reason to visit the president a few days before he went to Gettysburg, and Defrees was a person whose opinion on such a matter might have been sought. This anecdote is reported, apparently from a newspaper clipping, in Louis A. Warren, *Lincoln's Declaration: "A New Birth of Freedom"* (Fort Wayne, Ind.: Lincoln National Life Foundation, 1964), 54.

211 *"Just before the dedication"*: Ward Hill Lamon Collection, "Drafts and Anecdotes," folder 8, Huntington Library, San Marino, California. I am grateful to John Rhodehamel, curator of American historical manuscripts, for assistance in accessing this document. This is the earliest version of Lamon's account and is cited as the one closest to the actual events described. Printed versions of this account seem to have appeared in the *Philadelphia Times*, Oct. 4, 1887, and the *Washington Critic*, Feb. 18, 1888. See also Ward Hill Lamon, *Recollections of Abraham Lincoln, 1847–1865*, ed. Dorothy Lamon Teillard (Washington, D.C., 1911), 172–9.

212 *"about half of a speech"*: *Long Remembered*, [3], citing an interview with Speed printed in the *Illinois Daily State Journal*, Nov. 17, 1879, reprinted from the *Daily Louisville Commercial*. The text of the interview actually reads, "The day before he left Washington," but this leaves the doubtful implication that Lincoln did not begin work on his speech until Nov. 17.

212 *secretary believed speech partially written in Washington*: See John G. Nicolay, "Lincoln's Gettysburg Address," *Century Magazine* 47 (Feb. 1894), 601.

213 *"presented by the president to John G. Nicolay"*: For reasons to doubt that this presentation was ever made or that Nicolay even laid claim to it as his personal property, see Martin P. Johnson, "Who Stole the Gettysburg Address?" *Journal of the Abraham Lincoln Association* 24:2 (summer 2003), 1–19.

213 *second page of Nicolay copy a "half-sheet"*: This is evident in examining the document. The Hay copy, to be discussed below, is written on an intact bifold of this same foolscap-size paper. I am grateful to John R. Sellers of the Manuscript Division, Library of Congress, for assistance in accessing the Nicolay and Hay copies of the Gettysburg Address. I am also grateful to Sylvia Rodgers Albro and Maria Nugent of the library's Conservation Division for their valuable assistance in examining the priceless manuscripts in their custody.

213 *Nicolay's testimony on the writing of the Nicolay copy:* John G. Nicolay, "Lincoln's Gettysburg Address," 601. It is usually pointed out that these two leaves show clear signs of having been folded together, suggesting that they were folded and carried as a single document.

216 *What AL said on platform very different from Nicolay copy:* The editors of the *Collected Works* find Nicolay's account "incomplete and vague" (7:18n). For a telling critique of Nicolay's claims, see Garry Wills, *Lincoln at Gettysburg: The Words That Remade America* (New York: Simon & Schuster, 1992), 193–5.

216 *"two or three times":* Noah Brooks, "Personal Reminiscences of Lincoln," *Scribner's Monthly* 15:4 (Feb. 1878), 565.

217 *notion that the address was dashed off quickly:* For example, his host, David Wills, Wayne MacVeagh, and Edward McPherson. See *Long Remembered,* [6].

217 *Wills, subsequently testified:* See Wills's statement, ibid., [6].

217 *"that was the address":* Quoted ibid., [7], citing Andrew G. Curtin to John G. Nicolay, Apr. 7, 1892, Nicolay Papers, Library of Congress. The quotation in *Long Remembered* does not include the sentence that makes clear that the notes Curtin saw Lincoln copying came from the yellow envelope, perhaps because it is not entirely clear: "For I do not believe now that there was anything material from the copy which he made of the notes in the yellow envelope." This letter is in the subject files of the Nicolay Papers, Library of Congress, in a folder labeled "A. Lincoln. 19 Nov. 1863. Gettysburg Address. Notes. (not used in 'Personal Traits')." For assistance in locating this elusive document, I am grateful to John R. Sellers and Jeffrey Flannery of the Manuscript Division.

217 *a speech Seward had given:* See MacVeagh, "Lincoln at Gettysburg," 22.

217 *had come prepared:* See David Wills to Seward, Nov. 14, 1863, in the Gideon Welles Papers, Library of Congress, cited in *Long Remembered,* n. 8.

217 *Seward's remarks:* Seward's speech was printed in the pamphlet Edward Everett saw through the press in January 1864: *Address of Hon. Edward Everett, at the Consecration of the National Cemetery at Gettysburg, 19th November, 1863: With the Dedicatory Speech of President Lincoln, and the Other Exercises of the Occasion, Accompanied by an Account of the Origin of the Undertaking . . . and by a Map of the Battle-Field and a Plan of the Cemetery* (Boston: Little, Brown, 1864), 20–21.

218 *"practically will be, immortal":* Ibid., 21.

218 *"that I did not do it":* Curtin to Nicolay, Apr. 7, 1892, quoted in *Long Remember,* [7].

218 *"But when, at Gettysburg":* Nicolay, "Lincoln's Gettysburg Address," 601–2.

219 *Nicolay ignoring testimony:* See the folders containing Nicolay's research materials in the Nicolay Papers, LC, Box 9.

219 *"procession began at ten":* Nicolay, "Lincoln's Gettysburg Address," 601.

219 *Lincoln had already toured the grounds: Washington Chronicle,* Nov. 21, 1863. Seward is quoted as saying, "I visited the ground around the Seminary this morning, and Mr. Lincoln joined in." Michael Burlingame suggests that Hay may have been the author of this account.

219 *"He requested me":* Quoted in Orton H. Carmichael, *Lincoln's Gettysburg Address* (New York: Abingdon Press, 1917), 88. *Long Remembered,* [7], quotes this passage, but not the sentence that follows it.

219 *"at the Eagle Hotel":* Quoted in Carmichael, *Lincoln's Gettysburg Address,* 88.

220 *"Four score and seven": Chicago Tribune,* Nov. 21, 1863.

221 **"The number of men":** Quoted in Barton, *Lincoln at Gettysburg*, 87.

221 **"partly from Lincoln's manuscript":** *Collected Works*, 7:19n. This follows Barton, who wrote that Gilbert's report "was made up hastily, partly from his own notes and partly from Lincoln's manuscript" (*Lincoln at Gettysburg*, 85). In addition to Gilbert's own testimony (see below), another reporter, John Russell Young, testified that he saw Gilbert consulting Lincoln's manuscript. See John Russell Young, *Men and Memories: Personal Reminiscences*, ed. May D. Russell Young, 2 vols. (New York: F. Tennyson Neely, 1901), 1:70.

221 **"shorthand notes was necessary":** Quoted in Barton, *Lincoln at Gettysburg*, 192, citing remarks "at the National Shorthand Reporter's Association in August 1917."

222 **Charles Hale:** *Address of His Excellency John A. Andrew, to the Two Branches of the Legislature of Massachusetts, January 8, 1864,* Senate Document No. 1 (Boston: Wright & Potter, State Printers, 1864), lxxii. This text is different from the one that actually appeared in the *Boston Daily Advertiser* on Nov. 20, 1863, the text that is mistakenly printed as Hale's in J. G. Randall, *Lincoln the President: Springfield to Gettysburg,* 2 vols. (New York: Dodd, Mead & Co., 1945), facing 2:312. The *Advertiser* used the first AP transmission in its Nov. 20 edition, probably because it was available and Hale's was not. Hale was delayed in returning to Boston, but he was almost certainly the author of the report of the Gettysburg ceremony the *Advertiser* ran on Nov. 23 that commented that the president's remarks "suffered somewhat at the hands of the telegraphers."

222 **"actually said at Gettysburg":** Barton, *Lincoln at Gettysburg*, 81. The note accompanying Hale's transcription says that the president's speech "has not generally been printed rightly, having been marred from errors in telegraphing." See *Address of His Excellency John A. Andrew* for the remark about the accuracy of the president's address (xxxv) and for the text of Hale's transcription (lxxii).

222 **Gilbert text:** This text is a corrected version of the Associated Press text given in *Collected Works*, 7:19–21. Papers in which the corrections appear include the *American and Commercial Advertiser* (Baltimore, Md.), Nov. 20; *National Intelligencer* (Washington, D.C.), Nov. 21; *Cincinnati Daily Commercial,* Nov. 23; *Adams Sentinel* (Gettysburg, Pa.), Nov. 24; *Citizen & Telegraph* (Cumberland, Md.), Nov. 26. All of these texts contain minor variations, presumably introduced by either editors or telegraphers.

224 **"as the Gettysburg address":** Noah Brooks, "Personal Reminiscences of Lincoln," *Scribner's Monthly* 15:4 (Feb. 1878), 567.

225 **"a great many times":** Ibid., 565.

225 **"connected with the project":** David Wills to AL, Nov. 23, 1863, ALP.

225 **may have authorized sending his delivery copy to Wills:** The best answer to the question of what became of Lincoln's delivery text has come from Garry Wills, who suggested that Lincoln sent it to David Wills, who then sent it to Edward Everett for use in a pamphlet containing the Gettysburg speeches (*Lincoln at Gettysburg*, 195–8). But in sending the president a copy of this pamphlet, Everett asked for "the manuscript of your dedicatory Remarks, if you happen to have preserved them." Why, if Everett had recently received from David Wills a copy of Lincoln's delivery manuscript, would he be in doubt as to whether the president had preserved it, much less ask him to send it to him? Only, it would seem, if he had not recognized the manuscript Wills sent him as the president's

own copy. Joseph L. Gilbert did say of the delivery manuscript that he saw and copied from immediately after the speech, "The letter sheets from which he read were from Judge Wills' office" (Barton, *Lincoln at Gettysburg*, 192). This could indicate that they carried a letterhead that gave Everett the impression that he had been sent a copy. A difficulty with this theory is that the text of Lincoln's address that Everett prints in his pamphlet, which Garry Wills calls the "Little, Brown text," contains two of the telltale errors that appeared in the first AP dispatch, suggesting that even if Everett received Lincoln's delivery manuscript, he edited it from the uncorrected AP version. Everett, as Wills points out, was wary of newspaper accounts, but he may have been aware that the AP reporter had copied Lincoln's manuscript and mistakenly believed the uncorrected AP text to be superior to the one he had in hand. Confirmation of Wills's very promising proposal thus awaits more conclusive evidence.

225   ***This would explain why:*** It may also explain the strange alteration at the bottom of the first page, which could have been done in the mistaken belief that some such connector would make the text of the first page match that of the second.

225   ***"has become the standard text":*** Nicolay's account (see "Lincoln's Gettysburg Address," 605) must be read circumspectly, as it deliberately ignores other accounts and is carefully geared toward affirming his own claims about the composition and delivery of the address, but it is valuable nonetheless for spotlighting the revision process.

226   ***testimony that AL's speech was warmly received:*** See Barton, *Lincoln at Gettysburg*, 165, 168, 170, 181, 188, 194.

226   ***"long-continued applause":*** See *Collected Works*, 7.21.

226   ***that the crowd was undemonstrative and surprised by the speech's brevity:*** Barton, *Lincoln at Gettysburg*, records many instances of eyewitnesses who referred specifically to this phenomenon (163, 176, 179, 181–2, 184, 188–9, 193, 198, 202).

226   ***"his speech was finished":*** Quoted from a letter in private hands in Wayne C. Temple, *Abraham Lincoln from Skeptic to Prophet* (Mahomet, Ill.: Mayhaven Publishing, 1995), 254.

226   ***"manifestations of feeling":*** Gilbert's testimony is quoted in Barton, *Lincoln at Gettysburg*, 192. Barton quotes a substantial number of eyewitnesses who say they heard (or remember) no interrupting applause (163, 173, 179, 187, 188, 191, 192, 193, 200, 202).

226   ***"he answered":*** John Russell Young, *Men and Memories: Personal Reminiscences*, ed. May D. Russell Young, 2 vols. (New York: F. Tennyson Neely, 1901), 69.

227   ***"have made a speech":*** Clark E. Carr, *Lincoln at Gettysburg: An Address* (Chicago: A. C. McClurg & Co., 1906), 58–59. Barton singled Carr out as the one "whose testimony I rank the highest of all among those with whom I have conversed on the subject." Barton, *Lincoln at Gettysburg*, 148.

227   ***"people would think":*** Lamon mss. See Lamon's testimony on pages 211–12 and the accompanying note on page 322. There is little doubt that Lamon was here attempting, long after the event, to attract attention by relating something about the famous Gettysburg Address that no one else knew, and while there is good reason to think the anecdote is much embroidered, there is no reason to believe, as some have charged, that he made up this incident out of whole cloth. As chief marshal and master of ceremonies (responsibilities Lincoln urged him

to assume), Lamon certainly talked to Lincoln before and after the event, and if the response of the audience was awkward and lukewarm, Lamon was, in fact, one of the few people in the president's circle with whom he might share his disappointment.

227   ***"cheering streets":*** Hay Diary, 113.

227   ***"what they heard":*** Nicolay, "Lincoln's Gettysburg Address," 602.

228   ***"he had succeeded":*** Barton, *Lincoln at Gettysburg*, 90.

228   ***"written, but unfinished":*** This assumes that what Brooks relates belongs to a conversation that occurred after Lincoln had received Everett's speech, which could not have reached him until shortly before he went to Gettysburg. It is also possible that it belongs to an earlier conversation when Brooks accompanied the president to a photographer's studio. See note on pages 321–22.

228   ***" 'short, short, short' ":*** Brooks, *Washington, D.C., in Lincoln's Time*, 253.

228   ***"time to make it short":*** This is from Blaise Pascal's *Provincial Letters*, No. 16.

228   ***"while to make it short":*** Henry David Thoreau to H.G.O. Blake, Nov. 16, 1857, *The Correspondence of Henry David Thoreau*, eds. Walter Harding and Carl Bode (New York: New York University Press, 1958), 498.

229   ***"I am ready now":*** Josephus Daniels, *The Wilson Era: Years of War and After, 1917–1923* (Westport, Conn.: Greenwood Press, 1974 [1946]), 624. I am grateful to Steven L. Carson for calling this quotation to my attention.

229   ***"President of the United States":*** Quoted in Robert S. Harper, *Lincoln and the Press* (New York: McGraw-Hill, 1951), 187.

229   ***"did in two minutes":*** Edward Everett to AL, Nov. 20, 1863, ALP. Quoted in *Collected Works*, 7:25n.

229   ***not even mentioning it . . . in his diary:*** Everett's diary entries for Nov. 19 are reproduced in *Edward Everett at Gettysburg: A Massachusetts Historical Society Picture Book* (Boston: Massachusetts Historical Society, 1963), page unnumbered. Lamon claims that both Seward and Everett confessed their disappointment with Lincoln's speech immediately afterward, but this account suggests an atmosphere of intimacy that is hard to reconcile with the activity on the crowded platform. See the Huntington Library manuscript cited above. See also Lamon, *Recollections of Abraham Lincoln*, 172–9.

230   ***"not entirely a failure":*** AL to Edward Everett, Nov. 20, 1863, *Collected Works*, 7:24.

230   ***"prized more highly":*** Quoted in Barton, *Lincoln at Gettysburg*, 105.

230   ***"every word and comma":*** Quoted in Louis A. Warren, *Lincoln's Declaration: "A New Birth of Freedom"* (Fort Wayne, Ind.: Lincoln National Life Foundation, 1964), 143.

230   ***"as was ever spoken":*** *Harper's Weekly* 7:362 (Dec. 5, 1863), 770.

231   ***"changing the government":*** Richard Carwardine, *Lincoln: A Life of Purpose and Power* (New York: Alfred A. Knopf, 2006), 48.

231   ***"angels of our nature":*** Phillip Shaw Paludan, *"The Better Angels of Our Nature": Lincoln, Propaganda and Public Opinion in the North During the Civil War* (Fort Wayne: Lincoln Museum, 1992), 1.

231   ***likened his presidency to a card game:*** For example, he once wrote: "I shall not surrender this game leaving any available card unplayed." AL to Reverdy Johnson, July 26, 1862, *Collected Works*, 5:343.

231   ***"any other occasion":*** Johnson, "Lincoln Greets the Turning Point," 107.

232   ***AL's treatment of past and present:*** Garry Wills lists this trope as one that Lin-

coln's speech at Gettysburg shares with those that were standard in ancient Greek prose and classical funeral orations. See *Lincoln at Gettysburg*, 57.

233 **"needed no argument":** *Reminiscences of Abraham Lincoln by Distinguished Men of His Time*, ed. Allen Thorndike Rice (New York: North American Publishing Company, 1886), 194.

233 **equality and self-government were linked:** See Phillip S. Paludan, "Lincoln's Pre-War Constitutional Vision," *Journal of the Abraham Lincoln Association* 15:2 (Summer 1994), 1–21. I am much indebted to this study for its insights.

233 **"that only is self government":** AL, "Speech at Peoria," *Collected Works*, 2:266.

234 **interrelation of equality, freedom and self-government:** See Paludan, "Lincoln's Pre-War Constitutional Vision," passim.

234 **no other word:** Reported in Warren, *Lincoln's Declaration*, 106.

234 **"and then we see":** Walter Lippmann, *Public Opinion* (1922), quoted in Paludan, "*The Better Angels of Our Nature*", 3.

235 **"He makes history":** Wills, *Lincoln at Gettysburg*, 174.

236 **"in manner or style":** Joshua F. Speed, *Reminiscences of Abraham Lincoln and Notes of a Visit to California: Two Lectures* (Louisville: John P. Morton, 1884), 34.

236 **"that makes a poem":** Ralph Waldo Emerson, "The Poet," *Essays and Lectures* (New York: Library of America, 1983), 450.

236 **"Four score and seven years ago":** *Collected Works*, 7:23

Chapter Nine: A Truth That Needed to Be Told

238 **reply to a political attack:** AL to John Hill, Sept. 1860, Roy P. Basler, et al., eds., *The Collected Works of Abraham Lincoln*, 9 vols. (New Brunswick: Rutgers University Press, 1953), 4:104–8.

239 **"Breck":** AL, "Meeting and Dialogue of Douglas and Breckinridge," Sept. 29, 1860, ALP.

239 **agreed to cancel:** See E. N. Powell to William H. Herndon, Feb. 10, 1866, Douglas L. Wilson and Rodney O. Davis, eds., *Herndon's Informants: Letters, Interviews, and Statements About Abraham Lincoln* (Urbana: University of Illinois Press, 1998), 199–201. There is a related story that persisted among Lincoln's friends that Lincoln and Douglas made a truce after their joint appearance in Peoria on Oct. 16, 1854, agreeing to make no more speeches. Since the record shows that both continued to speak, the "truce" story is probably an outgrowth of the canceled debate at Lacon the next day. See the several accounts indexed under "Peoria Truce" in *Herndon's Informants*, and Paul M. Angle, "The Peoria Truce," *Journal of the Illinois State Historical Society* 21 (1929), 500–5.

239 **"It is now less":** AL, "Draft of Article on the Canal-Scrip Fraud," [Oct. 1860], ALP.

241 **"personal & pecuniary sacrifice":** Charles Gibson to AL, July 11, 1864, ALP. The text contains a few minor changes by Hay.

242 **"According to the request":** John Hay to James C. Welling, July 25, 1864, ALP.

242 **"to hear a story":** Noah Brooks, "Personal Recollections of Lincoln," in Michael Burlingame, ed., *Lincoln Observed: Civil War Dispatched of Noah Brooks* (Baltimore: Johns Hopkins University Press, 1998), 221–2; originally printed in *Harper's New Monthly Magazine* (July 1865).

242 **"On thursday":** AL, "Story Written for Noah Brooks," [Dec. 6, 1864], *Collected Works*, 8:154–5.

244 *"see it in print right away":* Noah Brooks, "Personal Reminiscences of Lincoln," *Scribner's Monthly* 15:4 (Feb. 1878), 566. This article contains a retelling of the story of "The President's last, shortest, and best speech" and a facsimile of the original document.

244 *"The change of opinion":* George Templeton Strong, *Diary of the Civil War 1860–1865,* ed. Allan Nevins (New York: Macmillan, 1962) 408; hereafter Strong Diary.

245 *"What a marvelous change":* Strong Diary, 408.

245 *"He wrote the Greeley letter":* *Harper's Weekly,* Mar. 5, 1864. I am grateful to Doris Kearns Goodwin for bringing this editorial to my attention.

246 *"Mr. Hodges of Kentucky":* "Lincoln to Hodges," *New York Tribune,* Apr. 29, 1864.

246 *"He said when":* Theodore Calvin Pease and James G. Randall, eds., *The Diary of Orville Hickman Browning,* 2 vols. (Springfield: Illinois State Historical Library, 1925), 1:665; hereafter Browning Diary.

246 *met with the Kentuckians on March 26:* Earl Schenck Miers, ed., *Lincoln Day by Day: A Chronology 1809–1865,* 3 vols. (Washington: Lincoln Sesquicentennial Commission, 1960), 3:249.

246 *for a political assignment:* AL to Barrett, *Collected Works,* 7:279.

246 *"date of April 4, 1864":* Joseph H. Barrett, *Abraham Lincoln and His Presidency,* 2 vols. (Cincinnati: Robert Clarke Co., 1904), 2:372.

247 *"I am naturally":* AL to Albert G. Hodges, ALP. This is Lincoln's retained draft.

249 *"sin against the clearest light":* "Lincoln to Hodges," *New York Tribune,* Apr. 29, 1864, transcribed from a clipping in ALP endorsed by AL: "Horace Greeley on Hodges letter."

250 *"arrest the decree":* AL's wife and his law partner agreed that this was a favorite saying of Lincoln's. See Mary Todd Lincoln, interview with William H. Herndon, Sept. 1866, *Herndon's Informants,* 360.

250 *Herndon to characterize him as "passive":* William H. Herndon to Ward Hill Lamon, Mar. 3, 1870, Ward Hill Lamon Papers, Huntington Library.

250 *fair copy of Hodges letter:* This manuscript is in Lincoln's personal papers apparently because AL gave his secretary Edward Neill, an older man whose judgment he trusted, the option of sending either the original or the copy he was asked to make. Probably because of the changes to the last sentence, Neill sent the copy. See Edward Neill, "Reminiscences of the Last Year of President Lincoln's Life," *Abraham Lincoln and His Mailbag: Two Documents by Edward D. Neill, One of Lincoln's Secretaries,* ed. Theodore C. Blegen (St. Paul: Minnesota Historical Society, 1964), 30.

250 *"justice and goodness of God":* We should note that there is an intervening step in the revising process not mentioned here, which is the substitution of the word "applaud" for "question," and the consequent necessity for changing "or" to "and."

250 *"not by luck, but by law":* Ralph Waldo Emerson, "Power," *The Collected Works of Ralph Waldo Emerson,* vol. VI, *The Conduct of Life,* ed. Barbara L. Packer, Joseph Slater, and Douglas Emory Wilson (Cambridge: Belknap Press, 2003), 28.

251 *"universal chain of causation":* William H. Herndon to Ward Hill Lamon, Mar. 3, 1870, Lamon Papers, Huntington Library.

251   **"Rough-hew them how we will":** *Hamlet* 5.2.10. See William H. Herndon to Jesse W. Weik, Feb. 25, 1887, Herndon-Weik Collection, Library of Congress; hereafter H-W.

252   **"a good deal about 1864":** Mary Todd Lincoln, interview with William H. Herndon [Sept. 1866], *Herndon's Informants*, 360.

252   **"I said to him substantially":** Orville H. Browning, interview with John G. Nicolay, June 17, 1875, in Michael Burlingame, ed., *An Oral History of Abraham Lincoln: John G. Nicolay's Interviews and Essays* (Carbondale: Southern Illinois University Press, 1996), 5.

252   **"see a ray of hope":** Browning Diary, Dec. 18, 1862, 600.

252   **not until the Hodges letter:** This statement does not include presidential proclamations, which were often drafted by others. For example, the "Proclamation Appointing a National Fast Day" of Mar. 30, 1863, speaks of "divine law" and "punishments and chastisements" inflicted upon the nation for its sins, but it seems clearly the work of another hand.

252   **"than to resist":** *New York Tribune*, Apr. 29, 1864.

253   **"slave children in this country":** "Concord Massachusetts Children to Abraham Lincoln," Apr. 1864, ALP.

253   **"He wills to do it":** AL to Mary Mann, Apr. 5, 1864, *Collected Works*, 7:287.

253   **"When the war began":** "Address at Sanitary Fair, Baltimore, Maryland," *Collected Works*, 7:301.

253   **"All knew that":** "Second Inaugural Address," *Collected Works*, 8:332–3.

254   **"The will of God":** Transcribed from the manuscript in the John Hay Library, Brown University. See *Collected Works*, 5:403–4.

255   **problems with the date of the "Meditation on the Divine Will":** John Hay, who owned the document in later years, first made it public in a lecture he delivered in the early 1870s (see Burlingame, *At Lincoln's Side*, 113–31). Hay said in the lecture that it was written "in a time of profound national gloom," and he implied that it was a product of "the deeply solemn musings, which carried him down to the very bed-rock of things, [in which] he passed a large portion of his time during the Summer of 1862." These profound "musings," Hay says, "produced the act which is more his own than any other of his life—the Proclamation of Emancipation" (127). The biography of Lincoln that Hay wrote with John G. Nicolay, published almost twenty years later, reports that the document was written "in September, 1862, while his mind was burdened with the weightiest question of his life" (*Abraham Lincoln: A History*, 6:341). When the two men brought out their edition of Lincoln's *Complete Works* in 1894, the document they now called the "Meditation on the Divine Will" was dated "September [30?], 1862" (2:243). The editors of the *Collected Works* (1953) argued that "if [Nicolay and Hay's attribution] means anything, September 30 is too late," since the Preliminary Emancipation Proclamation had been issued on September 22. They suggested that the document was possibly written "as early as September 2," the date of the Bates remark quoted in the text below.

The upshot of all this is that Nicolay and Hay did not know exactly when the "Meditation" was composed, speculating that it must have come out of the anguished days of 1862. But Nicolay and Hay were almost certainly mistaken about this date. What caused them to focus finally on late September 1862 appears to have been an anonymous handwritten account of Lincoln's meeting with the Quaker activist Mrs. Eliza P. Gurney, a meeting they believed to have taken place about this time ("Reply to Eliza P. Gurney," *Collected Works,* 5:478). They apparently knew little about the meeting (it had actually taken place late in October), but they had a copy of a letter Lincoln had written to Mrs. Gurney on September 4, 1864, in which he recalled a "very impressive meeting occasion when yourself and friends visited me on a Sabbath forenoon two years ago" (*Collected Works,* 7:535). The twenty-eighth was the last Sabbath in September. The handwritten account of the meeting, which is in an unknown hand, purports to quote from Mrs. Gurney's brief sermon to Lincoln, but more important from the president's own reply, suspiciously echoing some famous passages from Lincoln's later writings.

No source is given or has subsequently been found for this handwritten account, which deserves to be treated with skepticism. The careful scholar Don E. Fehrenbacher, presumably because he could not verify the source, did not include it either in his *Recollected Words of Abraham Lincoln* (1996) or in the Library of America edition of Lincoln's *Speeches and Writings* (1989). In addition to calling the war a "fiery trial," using a phrase that would appear two months later in the Annual Message to Congress, the anonymous account has the president offer a version of one of the central points of the Second Inaugural: "If I had been allowed my way this war would have been ended before this, but we find it still continues; and we must believe that He permits it for some wise purpose of his own, mysterious and unknown to us; and though with our limited understandings we may not be able to comprehend it, yet we cannot but believe, that He who made the world still governs it" (*Collected Works,* 5:478). Taking these words to be authentic clues to the inception of the "Meditation on the Divine Will," Nicolay and Hay dated the document, albeit approximately, to follow by a few days what they took to be the likeliest Sabbath in September. The editors of *Collected Works* saw the actual unlikelihood of this date, but their suggestion, which followed Lincoln's "two years ago" more strictly, may have simply compounded the error.

One other circumstance that needs further investigation is the evidence of the paper on which the "Meditation" is written. The foolscap-size sheet carries the embossment of the Mt. Holly Springs Paper Company, clearly depicting the U.S. Capitol building with its majestic new dome. The dome was not completed until the end of 1863, but its design was public knowledge, and paper bearing this embossment was available at least as early as April 1863, which is the earliest example I have been able to find. Whether this paper was even available in September 1862 is yet to be established. For more on the possible significance of this paper, see the note on pages 311–12.

256   *"almost ready to hang himself"*: Quoted in Don E. and Virginia Fehrenbacher, eds. *Recollected Words of Abraham Lincoln* (Stanford: Stanford University Press, 1996), 28.

256   *"this unnecessary duty"*: Matthew Pinsker, *Lincoln's Sanctuary: Abraham Lincoln and the Soldiers' Home* (New York: Oxford University Press, 2003), 153.

256   *"You boys remind me"*: Ibid., 153.

257   *"The conversation next turned"*: George Borrett, "An Englishman in Washington in 1864," *Magazine of History with Notes and Queries* 38, extra no. 149 (1929), 14. In the place cited, "reason's" is incorrectly printed as "treason's." This article is an excerpt from Borrett's book *Letters from Canada and the United States* (London, 1865).

257 *"whatever* isn't *must be wrong"*: Ibid., 15.

258 *"My . . . friend"*: AL to Eliza P. Gurney, Sept. 4, 1864, ALP.

260 *"Your people"*: Ibid.

260 *"to the Divine Will"*: Eliza P. Gurney to AL, Aug. 18, 1863, ALP.

261 *"has ruled otherwise"*: AL to Eliza P. Gurney, Sept. 4, 1864. ALP.

261 *"ends He ordains"*: Ibid.

261 *"with a job to do"*: Joshua Wolf Shenk, *Lincoln's Melancholy: How Depression Challenged a President and Fueled His Greatness* (Boston: Houghton Mifflin Company, 2005), 191–2.

261 *"that regard while here"*: John G. Nicolay to William H. Herndon, May 27, 1865, *Herndon's Informants*, 6.

262 *"developing emancipation policy"*: Richard Carwardine, *Lincoln: A Life of Purpose and Power* (New York: Alfred A. Knopf, 2006), 228.

262 *AL cultivating religious leaders:* Ibid., 274ff.

263 *"I was sitting"*: Francis B. Carpenter, *Six Months at the White House* (New York: Hurd and Houghton, 1866), 234.

264 *AL's handwritten manuscript of the Second Inaugural:* AL, Second Inaugural Address [Mar. 4, 1865], ALP (#43613–17).

264 *a grand total of 701:* The count depends on whether hyphenated words are counted as one word or two; here they have been counted as two. For the details on the change to the ending, see below.

264 *"seven o'clock p.m."*: *National Republican*, Mar. 2, 1865, quoted in Doris Kearns Goodwin, *Team of Rivals: The Political Genius of Abraham Lincoln* (New York: Simon & Schuster, 2005), 697.

264 *Second Inaugural first appeared in print:*

> In preparation for the 100th anniversary of the Second Inaugural in 1965, David C. Mearns and Lloyd A. Dunlap, both experienced Lincoln scholars working at the Library of Congress, uncovered clear evidence that Lincoln had caused his speech to be printed in advance and that newspapers had been provided copies of this printed text. They found in Nicolay's papers a request from a Washington newspaper editor, Thomas B. Florence, who wrote on White House stationery: "I called to enquire how the Constitutional Union can obtain for publication copies of the Inaugural of the President of the U.S. to be delivered to-morrow. Be good enough to include that paper with those who may be favored by the distribution if any such purpose is contemplated." (David C. Mearns and Lloyd A. Dunlap, Library of Congress Press Release, February 8, 1965, p. 3). The next day, only a few hours after its delivery at the Capitol, the text of Lincoln's address appeared in the *Constitutional Union* with the note: "We are deeply indebted to Hon. J. C. Nicolay, the polite Secretary of the President, for his gentlemanly courtesy in promptly furnishing us with early copies of the Inaugural Address" (*ibid.*). Mearns and Dunlap noted that the text printed in this newspaper perfectly matched that of an "extremely rare" three-page leaflet titled *Inaugural Address. March 4, 1865.* (Douglas L. Wilson, "A Note on the Text of Lincoln's Second Inaugural," *Documentary Editing* 24:2 [June 2002], 38.)

For a more detailed account of the story of the press handout (Fig. 9-8) and how its text relates to the manuscript and delivery texts, see the article cited above. For locating the press release, I am greatly indebted to the detective work of Jeffrey Flannery of the Library of Congress Manuscript Division. For assistance in locating and examining the Library of Congress's two copies of the rare press handout leaflet and for other valuable assistance, I am grateful to Clark Evans of the Rare Book and Special Collections Division.

264 **he decided to fashion his delivery text from the uncorrected proof sheets:** This process and the evidence for it are detailed in Wilson, "A Note on the Text of Lincoln's Second Inaugural," 37–41.

268 **"to say about the war":** Garry Wills, "Lincoln's Greatest Speech?" *Atlantic Monthly* 284:3 (Sept. 1999), 63.

269 **"Now, at the expiration":** This quotation and those that follow are from the text of Lincoln's delivery copy (Fig. 9-9). A gift to the Library of Congress of John Hay's family in 1916, it was not kept with the other Lincoln papers and was therefore not microfilmed with them. It is now housed with the manuscript of the Second Inaugural in the vault of the Conservation Division and can be viewed on the Library's American Memory Web site for "Presidential Inaugurations," as the final image under the heading "Inaugural Address, March 4, 1865, in Lincoln's hand."

272 **"If God now wills":** AL to Albert G. Hodges, Apr. 4, 1864, *Collected Works*, 7:282.

273 **Frederick Douglass, who could quote it from memory:** For example, Douglass quoted this passage in a manuscript referred to below, "Abraham Lincoln, a Speech" (see page 277), in which the text is sufficiently different from Lincoln's as to indicate that Douglass was not copying from a printed source.

274 **pasted a slip over the last two lines:** This slip, which Lincoln's editors have failed to note, is still attached to the manuscript. I am grateful to Maria Nugent and Sylvia Rodgers Albro of the Library of Congress Conservation Division for assistance in examining the manuscript and for sharing a photocopy taken under conditions that revealed the original text under the slip (see Figs. 9-7, 9-11).

276 **"intense study and admiration":** Mark Noll, *America's God: From Jonathan Edwards to Abraham Lincoln* (New York: Oxford University Press, 2002), 426.

276 **"fateful events impending on it":** Wills, "Lincoln's Greatest Speech?" 70.

276 **asking if he had received it:** AL to Albert G. Hodges, Apr. 22, 1864, *Collected Works*, 7:308.

276 **"Every one likes a compliment":** AL to Thurlow Weed, Mar. 15, 1865, *Collected Works*, 8:356. It takes nothing away from Lincoln's superlative speech to note that it contains an implicit message for his critics, whose most persistent complaint was that the agonizing duration of the war was attributable to his own ineptitude and inefficiency. It seems possible that Lincoln's last sentence to Weed, whose letter did not actually mention the inaugural address, makes a sly allusion to this.

277 **"that was a sacred effort":** Frederick Douglass, *Life and Times of Frederick Douglass*, in *Autobiographies* (New York: Library of America, 1994), 804.

277 **"an unspeakable calamity":** Frederick Douglass, "Abraham Lincoln, a Speech" [1865], manuscript, Frederick Douglass Papers, Library of Congress Web site. I am indebted to Michael Burlingame for drawing my attention to the fact that this and many of Douglass's other manuscripts can viewed on this Web site. For more on Douglass's lesser-known tributes to Lincoln, see Michael Burlingame, " 'Emphatically the Black Man's President': New Light on Frederick Douglass

and Abraham Lincoln," *Lincoln Ledger: A Publication of the Lincoln Fellowship of Wisconsin* 4:1 (Feb. 1996), 4.

277 **"The last days"**: Douglass, "Abraham Lincoln, a Speech."

Epilogue: A Notable Elevation of Thought

279 **"any recorded occasion"**: "Abraham Lincoln: Remarks at the Funeral Services Held in Concord, April 19, 1865," *Miscellanies*, vol. 11 of *The Complete Works of Ralph Waldo Emerson* (Boston: Houghton Mifflin Company, 1906), 333–4.

280 **"Mr. Clay's eloquence"**: AL, "Eulogy on Henry Clay," July 6, 1852, *Collected Works*, 2:126.

280 **"in spite of yourself"**: Noah Brooks, "Personal Reminiscences of Lincoln," *Scribner's Monthly* 15:4 (Feb. 1878), 562.

281 **"with a rhetorical flourish"**: James M. McPherson, *Abraham Lincoln and the Second American Revolution* (New York: Oxford University Press, 1990), 93–112.

281 **"What do you think"**: Charles Francis Adams Jr. to his father, Mar. 7, 1865, *A Cycle of Adams Letters*, ed. Worthington Chauncey Ford, 2 vols. (Boston: Houghton Mifflin Company, 1920), 2:257–8.

282 **" 'American attitude' "**: Whitelaw Reid, *A Radical View: The "Agate" Dispatches of Whitelaw Reid 1861–1865*, ed. James G. Smart (Memphis: Memphis State University Press, 1976), 188–9. It should be noted that the principal thing Reid is referring to as "most American" is the report on foreign affairs that concentrates on Western Hemisphere countries and almost ignores the great powers of Europe.

282 **viewed the Second Inaugural with grave misgivings:** Sumner wrote to Francis Leiber on Mar. 13, 1865: "The Presdt's speech, & other things augur confusion & uncertainty in the future—with hot controversy. Alas! Alas!" *The Selected Letters of Charles Sumner*, ed. Beverly Wilson Palmer, 2 vols. (Boston: Northeastern University Press, 1990), 2:275.

282 **"takes him by the hand"**: Sumner to Sen. Lot M. Morrill, June 15, 1865, ibid., 2:306.

283 **"have made that address"**: John M. Taylor, *William Henry Seward: Lincoln's Right Hand* (New York: HarperCollins, 1991), 224.

283 **"I wish here"**: Joshua F. Speed, *Reminiscences of Abraham Lincoln and Notes of a Visit to California: Two Lectures* (Louisville: John P. Morton, 1884), 34–35.

283 **"it went from him, poetry"**: Ralph Waldo Emerson, "The American Scholar," *Essays and Lectures* (New York: Library of America, 1983), 56.

284 **"embodied in words"**: Swett's story is retold by one of his friends, Judge Peter Stenger Grosscup, in Ida Tarbell, *The Life of Abraham Lincoln* (New York: Lincoln Memorial Association, n.d. [1900]), 2:115.

284 **"most truly alive"**: George Santayana, "The Moral Background," *The Genteel Tradition: Nine Essays*, ed. Douglas L. Wilson (Cambridge: Harvard University Press, 1967), 79.

Appendix: Lincoln's Postdelivery Revisions of the Gettysburg Address

285 **"the revision before me"**: Martin P. Johnson, "Who Stole the Gettysburg Address?" *Journal of the Abraham Lincoln Association* 24:2 (Summer 2003), 8.

285 **"holograph versions of the Address"**: Johnson, "Who Stole the Gettysburg Address?" 9.

285 *"five copies Lincoln made"*: Caption for facsimile of the Hay copy in *Long Remembered: Facsimiles of the Five Versions of the Gettysburg Address in the Handwriting of Abraham Lincoln* (Washington: Library of Congress, 1963).

285 *a gift to Hay from the president*: For reasons to doubt that this presentation was ever made, see Martin P. Johnson, "Who Stole the Gettysburg Address?" 8–11.

286 *"a step in the revision process"*: Robert T. Lincoln to Isaac Markens, Dec. 8, 1915, in Paul M. Angle, ed., *A Portrait of Abraham Lincoln in Letters by His Oldest Son* (Chicago: Chicago Historical Society, 1968), 21.

286 *"before one was adopted"*: Ibid., 20.

286 *"return to Washington"*: Johnson, "Who Stole the Gettysburg Address?" 10.

287 *referred to as "half-sheets"*: See, for example, Nicolay's references to leaves of manuscript of this size in his description of the contents of the "Carpet-Bag Papers." John G. Nicolay, March 14, 1874, "Carpet Bag Papers," ALP.

288 *"has become the standard text"*: Nicolay's account must be read circumspectly, as it is carefully geared toward affirming his own claims about the composition and delivery of the address, but it is valuable nonetheless for spotlighting the revision process. See "Lincoln's Gettysburg Address," 605.

289 *Everett copy text . . . introduces . . . new commas:* Some of the new commas, such as those after "field" and "lives," persist in subsequent versions, but those after the following do not: "consecrated it," "remember," "for us," "fought here," and "government."

291 *Bancroft copy cancels many of the Everett commas:* See previous note.

291 *handwritten drafts . . . delivery text:* These six texts in chronological order are Nicolay, Gilbert/Hale, Hay, Everett, Bancroft, Bliss.

293 *take better advantage of the resonance that the word "here":* As indicated earlier (page 213), the second page of the Nicolay copy seems not to have been written specifically to follow the text of the first page, but rather was part of a two-page pencil draft, of which the first page is missing. It remains a possibility that the penciled revision at the bottom of the first page is either not actually by Lincoln or that it represents a hurried and imperfect version of the revised sentence being concluded on another page. In either case, the importance of "here" still holds.

Index

A NOTE ABOUT THE AUTHOR

DOUGLAS L. WILSON is codirector of the Lincoln Studies Center at Knox College and the author of *Honor's Voice: The Transformation of Abraham Lincoln*, which was awarded the Lincoln Prize for 1999. He lives in Galesburg, Illinois.

A NOTE ON THE TYPE

THIS BOOK was set in Janson, a typeface long thought to have been made by the Dutchman Anton Janson, who was a practicing typefounder in Leipzig during the years 1668–87. However, it has been conclusively demonstrated that these types are actually the work of Nicholas Kis (1650–1702), a Hungarian, who most probably learned his trade from the master Dutch typefounder Dirk Voskens. The type is an excellent example of the influential and sturdy Dutch types that prevailed in England up to the time William Caslon (1692–1766) developed his own incomparable designs from them.

Composed by North Market Street Graphics,
Lancaster, Pennsylvania
Printed and bound by Berryville Graphics,
Berryville, Virginia
Designed by Virginia Tan